Beowulf and Beyond

STUDIES IN ENGLISH MEDIEVAL LANGUAGE AND LITERATURE

Edited by Jacek Fisiak

Advisory Board:
John Anderson (Methoni, Greece), Norman Blake (Sheffield),
Ulrich Busse (Halle), Olga Fischer (Amsterdam),
Richard Hogg (Manchester), Dieter Kastovsky (Vienna),
Marcin Krygier (Poznań), Roger Lass (Cape Town),
Peter Lucas (Cambridge), Donka Minkova (Los Angeles),
Ruta Nagucka (Cracow), Akio Oizumi (Kyoto),
Katherine O'Brien O'Keeffe (Notre Dame, USA),
Matti Rissanen (Helsinki), Hans Sauer (Munich),
Liliana Sikorska (Poznań), Jeremy Smith (Glasgow)

Vol. 18

PETER LANG
Frankfurt am Main · Berlin · Bern · Bruxelles · New York · Oxford · Wien

Hans Sauer/Renate Bauer (eds.)

Beowulf and Beyond

PETER LANG
Europäischer Verlag der Wissenschaften

Bibliographic Information published by the Deutsche Nationalbibliothek
The Deutsche Nationalbibliothek lists this publication in the Deutsche Nationalbibliografie; detailed bibliographic data is available in the internet at <http://www.d-nb.de>.

ISSN 1436-7521
ISBN 3-631-55925-9
US-ISBN 0-8204-8751-1

© Peter Lang GmbH
Europäischer Verlag der Wissenschaften
Frankfurt am Main 2007
All rights reserved.

All parts of this publication are protected by copyright. Any utilisation outside the strict limits of the copyright law, without the permission of the publisher, is forbidden and liable to prosecution. This applies in particular to reproductions, translations, microfilming, and storage and processing in electronic retrieval systems.

Printed in Germany 1 2 3 4 5 6 7

www.peterlang.de

Contents

Abbreviations..vii

Introduction
    Hans Sauer (Munich, Germany)..xv

Beowulf in Arabia: Teaching heroic poetry in a post-heroic age
    Manfred Malzahn, Muhammad Abu al-Fadl Badran
    (Al-Ain, United Arab Emirates)...1

Translating Doomsday: *De die iudicii* and its Old English translation
(*Judgement Day II*)
    Patrizia Lendinara (Palermo, Italy)..17

Old English runic inscriptions: Textual criticism and historical grammar
    Alfred Bammesberger (Eichstätt, Germany)..............................69

The Narragansett runic inscription, Rhode Island
    Ian Kirby (Lausanne, Switzerland)..89

Old English preverbal elements with adverbial counterparts
    Michiko Ogura (Chiba, Japan)..101

Old English words for people in the *Épinal-Erfurt glossary*
    Hans Sauer (Munich, Germany)..119

The assize of bread (1256)
    Claire Fennell (Trieste, Italy)...183

Revising the Wyclif Bible
    Conrad Lindberg (Linköping, Sweden)....................................197

Chaucer's Latinity
    Michael W. Twomey (Ithaca/NY, USA)....................................205

Chaucer's *Troilus* in a new comparative context
    Saburo Oka (Tokyo, Japan)..223

Between penance and purgatory: Margery Kempe's *Pélerinage de la vie humaine* and the idea of salvaging journeys
    Liliana Sikorska (Poznan, Poland)..235

Malory's critique of violence before and just after the oath of the Round Table
    Carol Kaske (Ithaca/NY, USA)..259

Observations on the loss of final plosive consonants in late Middle English rhyme-words
    Saara Nevanlinna (Helsinki, Finland)..271

Hyphens and hyper-hyphens in Middle English (corpus-based)
    Manfred Markus (Innsbruck, Austria)..293

Medieval English and German: A guide to modern similarities and dissimilarities
    Horst Weinstock (Aachen, Germany)..309

Notes on contributors..329

Abbreviations

a) General abbreviations

acc.	accusative
adj.	adjective
AmE	American English
AN	Anglo-Norman
arch.	archaic
Aux	auxiliary verb
Bk.	book
BL	British Library
CCCC	Corpus Christi College Cambridge
dat.	dative
dm	determinatum
dt	determinant (determiner)
EETS	Early English Text Society
EM	East Midlands
EME	early Middle English
f.	feminine
G	German
gen.	genitive
Gk	Greek
Gmc	Germanic
IE	Indo-European
imp.	imperative
imperf.	imperfect
ind.	indicative
inf.	infinitive
Lat	Latin
lit.	literally
m.	masculine
ME	Middle English
MS/MSS	manuscript/manuscripts
N	noun
n.	neuter
NME	northern Middle English
nom.	nominative
OE	Old English
OF	Old French
OHG	Old High German

OI	Old Irish
OLG	Old Low German
P	free-morph prefix or adverb
p.	page
part.	participle
partic.	particle or adverbial element
pass.	passive
PDE	Present-day English (~ Modern English)
pl.	plural
Prep	preposition
Prep + N	prepositional phrase
pres.	present
pret.	preterite
S	subject
sg.	singular
stz.	stanza
subj.	subjunctive
subst.	substantive
trans.	translator/translation
V	verb
WGmc	West Germanic
WM	West Midlands
WRY	West Riding of Yorkshire

b) Authors and texts

Ad^1	British Library, London, MS Additional 5140		
ÆCHom	Peter Clemoes (ed.)		
		1997	Ælfric's Catholic homilies: The first series. (EETS s.s. 17.) London: Oxford University Press.
	Malcolm Godden (ed.)		
		1979	Ælfric's Catholic homilies: The second series. (EETS s.s. 5.) London: Oxford University Press.
ÆGram	Julius Zupitza (ed.)		
		1880	Ælfrics Grammatik und Glossar. Berlin: Weidmann.
		2001	(3rd edition.) With a preface by Helmut Gneuss.

Abbreviations

ASPR	The Anglo-Saxon Poetic Records: A Collective Edition. New York: Columbia University Press.

    vol. 1: George Philip Krapp (ed.)
        1931   *The Junius manuscript.*
    vol. 2: George Philipp Krapp (ed.)
        1932   *The Vercelli book.*
    vol. 3: George Philipp Krapp -- Elliott van Kirk Dobbie (eds.)
        1936   *The Exeter book.*
    vol. 4: Elliott van Kirk Dobbie (ed.)
        1953   *Beowulf and Judith.*
    vol. 5: George Phillip Krapp (ed.)
        1932   *The Paris Psalter and the Meters of Boethius.*
    vol. 6: Elliott van Kirk Dobbie (ed.)
        1942   *The Anglo-Saxon minor poems.*

AV	*Authorised Version*, or King James Bible (1611)
BlHom	Richard Morris (ed.)
	1874 *The Blickling homilies.* (EETS o.s. 58, 63, 73.) London: Oxford University Press.
Chron	Charles Plummer (ed.)
	1892-99 *Two of the Saxon chronicles parallel.* 2 vols. Oxford: Clarendon.
CT	Chaucer's *Canterbury tales*
Ddi	*De die iudicii*
El	Huntington Library, San Marino, MS Ellesmere 26 C 9
ELV	Early and later version (of the Wyclif Bible)
Ép	Bibliothéque municipale, Épinal, MS 72 (2)
ÉpErf	the *Épinal-Erfurt glossary*
Erf	Wissenschaftliche Allgemeinbibliothek, Erfurt, Codex Amplonianus F. 42
EV	Early version (of the Wyclif Bible)
Hg	National Library of Wales, Aberystwyth, MS Hengwrt 154 (Peniarth 392D)
JDay II	*Judgement Day II* (cf. ASPR 6)
Li	*Lindisfarne Gospels*, ed. Skeat (see below *Ru 2*)
LV	Later version (of the Wyclif Bible)

Or	Janet Bately (ed.)	
	1980	*The Old English Orosius.* (EETS s.s. 6.) London: Oxford University Press.
Riverside	Larry D. Benson (ed.)	
	1987	*The Riverside Chaucer.* (3rd edition.) Boston: Houghton Mifflin.
Ru 1	Rushworth 1 (i.e. Mt.; Mk. 1-2,15; Jn. 18,1-3), ed. Skeat (see *Ru 2*)	
Ru 2	Rushworth 2 (except Mt.; Mk. 1-2,15, Jn. 18,1-3), ed. Skeat Walter W. Skeat (ed.)	
	1871-87	*The Holy Gospels in Anglo-Saxon, Northumbrian, and Old Mercian Versions.* Cambridge: Cambridge University Press.
VercHom	Donald G. Scragg (ed.)	
	1992	*The Vercelli Homilies and related texts.* (EETS o.s. 300.) Oxford: Oxford University Press.
WSCp	West Saxon Gospels (MS CCCC 140), ed. Liuzza R.M. Liuzza (ed.)	
	1994-2000	*The Old English Version of the Gospels.* 2 vols. (EETS o.s. 304 & 314.) Oxford: Oxford University Press.

c) Books of the bible and apocrypha

Apoc.	Apocalypsis
Bar.	Baruch
D.A.	Deeds of the Apostles
Dan.	Daniel
Deut.	Deuteronomy
Ecclus.	Ecclesiasticus = Jesus Sirach
1, 2 Esd.	Esdras
Est.	Ester
Ezek.	Ezekiel
Gen.	Genesis
Is.	Isajah
Jer.	Jeremiah
Jgs.	Judges

Jn.	John
Kgs.	Kings
Lev.	Leviticus
Lk.	Luke
1,2 Macc.	Maccabees
Mk.	Mark
Mt.	Matthew
Num.	Numbers
Prov.	Proverbs
Pss.	Psalms
Rom.	St. Paul's letter to the Romans
Tob.	Tobit
Wisd.	Wisdom
Zeph.	Zephaniah

d) Dictionaries and reference works

AND	William Rothwell *et al.* (eds.)	
	1992	*Anglo-Norman dictionary*, London: Modern Humanities Research Association.
BEASE	Michael Lapidge *et al.* (eds.)	
	1999	*The Blackwell encyclopedia of Anglo-Saxon England*. Oxford: Blackwell.
BT	Joseph Bosworth -- T.Northcote Toller	
	1882-1898	*An Anglo-Saxon dictionary*. Oxford: Oxford University Press.
BTS	T. Northcote Toller	
	1908-1921	*An Anglo-Saxon dictionary: Supplement*. Oxford: Oxford University Press.
ClH	John R. Clark Hall	
	1960	*A concise Anglo-Saxon dictionary*. (4th edition with a supplement by Herbert D. Meritt.) Cambridge: Cambridge University Press.
CHEL	Richard M. Hogg (gen. ed.)	
	1992-2001	*The Cambridge history of the English language*. Cambridge: Cambridge University Press.

	vol. 1: Richard M. Hogg (ed.)
	1992 *The beginnings to 1066.*
	vol. 2: Norman Blake (ed.)
	1992 *1066-1476.*
	vol. 3: Roger Lass (ed.)
	1998 *1476-1776.*
	vol. 4: Suzanne Romaine (ed.)
	1998 *1776 to present day.*
	vol. 5: R.W. Burchfield (ed.)
	1994 *English in Britain and overseas.*
	vol. 6: John Algeo (ed.)
	2001 *English in North America.*
DMLBS	R.E. Latham -- D.R. Howlett
	1975-97 *Dictionary of medieval Latin from British sources.* Vol 1: A-L. Oxford: Oxford University Press, for the British Academy.
DOE	Angus Cameron *et al.*
	2003 *The dictionary of Old English.* Fascicles A-F on CD-ROM, version 1.0. Toronto: Pontifical Institute of Medieval Studies.
DOEC	Antonette di Paolo Healey (ed.)
	2004 *The dictionary of Old English corpus in electronic form,* Toronto, <http://ets.umdl.umich.ed/o/oec>.
EWDS	Friedrich Kluge
	1995 *Etymologisches Wörterbuch der deutschen Sprache.* (23. Aufl. bearbeitet von Elmar Seebold *et al.*) Berlin: de Gruyter.
IMEPC	2004 *The Innsbruck Middle English prose corpus on CD-Rom* (2nd edition.) Innsbruck: University of Innsbruck, English Department.
IMEV	Carleton Brown -- Rossell Hope Robbins (eds.)
	1943 *The index of Middle English verse.* New York: Columbia University Press.

LALME	Angus McIntosh et al.	
	1986	*A Linguistic Atlas of Late Medieval English*. 4 vols. Aberdeen: Aberdeen University Press.
Lewis&Short	Charlton D. Lewis	
	1879	*A Latin dictionary*. Oxford: Oxford University Press.
LexMA	R.-H. Bautier et al. (eds.)	
	1977-1999	*Lexikon des Mittelalters*. 9 vols. (& register). Munich: Artemis, Stuttgart: Metzler.
MED	H. Kurath et al. (eds.)	
	1952-2001	*Middle English dictionary*. 17 vols. Ann Arbor, Michigan: Michigan University Press.
ManualME	J. Burke Severs -- A.E. Hartung -- P.G. Beidler (gen. eds.)	
	1967-	*A manual of the writings in Middle English 1050-1500*. 11 vols. (The Connecticut Academy of Arts and Sciences.) Hamden: Archon Books.
ODEE	C.T. Onions	
	1966	*The Oxford dictionary of English etymology*. Oxford: Oxford University Press.
OED	J.A.H. Murray et al. (ed.)	
	1884-1928	*The Oxford English dictionary*.
	1989	(2nd edition.) Prepared by J.A. Simpson, E.S.C. Weiner. 20 vols. Oxford: Oxford University Press.
STC	Alfred W. Pollard -- Gilbert R. Redgrave (eds.)	
	1976-1986	*A short-title catalogue of books printed in England, Scotland, and Ireland and of English books printed abroad 1475-1640*. (2nd edition.) 2 vols. London: Bibliographical Society.
ThLL	1900-	*Thesaurus Linguae Latinae*. Leipzig: Teubner.

Introduction

Hans Sauer (Munich, Germany)

IAUPE, the International Association of University Professors of English, was founded in 1950/51 and has held triennial conferences since 1950. Since 1977, a Medieval Symposium has been held immediately before (or sometimes after) the main IAUPE conference, usually in a city not far from the venue of the main conference. The venues and the organisers of the ten IAUPE Medieval Symposia so far have been:[1]

1977	Cracow	Przemyslaw J. Mroczkowski
1980	York	Jacques Berthoud & Derek Pearsall
1983	Aachen	Wolf-Dietrich Bald & Horst Weinstock
1986	Newcastle	Richard N. Bailey
1989	Zurich	Andreas Fischer & Udo Fries
1992	Ottawa	Douglas Wurtele
1995	Roskilde	Bent Preisler
1998	Sheffield	Norman Blake
2001	Munich	Hans Sauer
2004	Vancouver	Stephen Partridge

So far, proceedings have only been edited for the 1983 Aachen symposium.[2] The present volume contains a selection of papers from the Medieval Symposium held at the University of Munich in 2001 (25-28 July, to accompany the main conference in Bamberg) as well as from the Medieval Symposium held in Vancouver in 2004 (St. John's College, 6-7 August); they are supplemented by some papers from the Middle English Section (section 6) of the main 2004 IAUPE conference, also held in Vancouver (University of British Columbia, 8-14 August).[3]

The speakers at the Munich Medieval Symposium were: Alfred Bammesberger, Andrew Breeze, George Clark, Ian Kirby, Patrizia Lendinara, Conrad Lindberg, Manfred Malzahn, Manfred Markus, Saara Nevanlinna, Michiko Ogura, Saburo Oka, Hans Sauer, A.C. Spearing, Horst Weinstock. The speakers at the Vancouver Medieval Symposium were: Andrew Breeze, George Clark, Monika Fludernik, Carol Kaske, Ian Kirby, Conrad Lindberg, Hans Sauer, Michael W. Twomey, Horst Weinstock, Gernot Wieland. The speakers at the Middle English section of the Vancouver IAUPE conference were Claire Fennell, Sangsup Lee, Manfred Markus, Michiko Ogura, Liliana Sikorska, Michael W. Twomey.

The papers collected in this volume are mainly concerned with aspects of Old and Middle English language, literature, and culture. They are arranged in rough chronological order, first those dealing with Old English, then those dealing with Middle English; the more literary papers preceding the linguistic papers. Some of the best-known literary authors and texts are represented (*Beowulf*, Margery Kempe, and Malory with one paper each, Chaucer with two papers), but also runic inscriptions (two papers) and a legal document (*The assize of bread* of 1256).

There is also no strict separation between linguistics, literature, and culture: Alfred Bammesberger's analysis of some of the runes on the Ruthwell Cross has also necessarily to take the poem *Dream of the rood* into account; Saara Nevanlinna uses late Middle English rhymes and rhyme words for a linguistic analysis. Nor is there a strict division between past and present, between research and teaching: While most of the papers deal with the literary or linguistic interpretation of their material, two are more concerned with how to teach the medieval texts to university students in our time: Manfred Malzahn and Muhammad Abu al-Fadl Badran show that *Beowulf* can be made interesting to Arab students of English; Carol Kaske asks which moral lessons the warlike and continuously fighting Arthurian society depicted in Malory's *Morte Darthur* and related texts can teach to students in the USA. I give a brief overview of the contributions:

(1) **Manfred Malzahn & Muhammad Abu al-Fadl Badran** ("*Beowulf* in Arabia: Teaching heroic poetry in a post-heroic age") deal with a pedagogical and cultural question: They show that *Beowulf* can today be successfully taught to Arab students, especially in the United Arab Emirates (UAE), because in these countries a traditional heroic society with many parallels to the one depicted in *Beowulf* persisted well into the 20th century.

(2) **Patrizia Lendinara** ("Translating Doomsday: *De die iudicii* and its Old English translation, *Judgement Day II*") takes a close look at the Old English poem *Judgement Day II*, and compares it in great detail with its Latin source, the poem *De die iudicii*. *Judgement Day II* is interesting for a number of reasons: Whereas most Old English poems (including *Beowulf*) are difficult to date (though some may be early) and are presumed to be ultimately of Anglian origin, *Judgement Day II* is generally regarded as a late Old English poem (10th century) and of West-Saxon origin. Moreover, it is one of the few Old English poems where a Latin source is extant, namely the anonymous (Pseudo-Bedan?) *De die iudicii*. Lendinara also attempts to re-evaluate *Judgement Day II*: Whereas this poem has sometimes been viewed as a slavish translation, she sees it on the whole as a successful rendering, a literal translation that nevertheless "finds room for imaginative variations".

(3) The meaning of some of the Old English runic inscriptions is discussed by **Alfred Bammesberger** ("Old English runic inscriptions: Textual criticism and historical grammar"); in particular, he analyses the inscription on the Harford Farm Brooch (7th century; "A wish for the person who wore or carried the brooch"), the Brandon Antler Runic Inscription ("Grew on a wild animal"), the Overchurch Stone ("For the people we erected this monument: Pray for Æthelmund"), and the much-discussed Ruthwell Cross Inscription. Bammesberger supports recent attempts to look at the latter (the *Ruthwell crucifixion poem*) as a poem in its own right rather than just a short version of the poem *Dream of the rood* transmitted in the Vercelli Book.

(4) Different kinds of runes are dealt with by **Ian Kirby** ("The Narragansett Runic Inscription, Rhode Island"). These are connected with the question of whether Norsemen (Vikings) sailed to North America and if so, how far they got. Whereas it now seems to be clear that they certainly reached Newfoundland in the 11th century, it is unclear whether their explorations led them any further. Runic inscriptions found further to the south have often been regarded as later forgeries, e.g. the Kensington inscription. Kirby, however, argues that it is possible that the Narragansett Runic inscription found in Rhode Island, although difficult to decipher and to interpret, may be genuine and may be a further testimony to Norse explorations in America.

(5) **Michiko Ogura** ("Old English preverbal elements with adverbial counterparts") assembles the Old English verbs of motion (e.g. *gan, gangan, cuman, feran, astigan* etc.) and their Latin counterparts (*ire, abire, exire, introire, transire, uenire, ascendere, descendere* etc.), and investigates under which conditions particles (adverbial elements) are prefixed to the verbs (e.g. *ingan, utgan*) and under which conditions particles are placed after the verb (*gan in, gan ut*). On the whole, the historical development has been away from pre-position (*ingan*) to post-position (*go in*), i.e. phrasal verbs and prepositional verbs.

(6) The Épinal-Erfurt glossary (archetype ca. 680-690) is the oldest English text of any length that we have. Among other things it provides information on early English word-formation. **Hans Sauer** ("Old English names for people in the Épinal-Erfurt glossary") tries to define the word-field 'people', and he counts more than 60 Latin and more than 60 Old English words referring to 'people' in *ÉpErf*. He analyses their etymology, their word-formation patterns (mainly compounding, prefixation, suffixation, and derivation with a change of the stem vowel), as well as their semantic structure (agent, experiencer and patient nouns); he also pays attention to the relation between the Latin lemmata and their Old English renderings and to the question of Old English loan formations modelled on Latin words.

(7) *The assize of bread* (1256) is a statute issued under Henry III (1216-72). It attempts to regulate the size and weight of the loaves of bread and what they cost; the reconstruction of size and price involves a certain amount of mathematics for us. *The assize of bread* exists in several manuscripts: some contain a Latin version, some a French one, and some an English one. **Claire Fennell** describes this text and edits the versions from four manuscripts:
J = Oxford, Jesus College, MS 29 (II) (Latin)
P = Peterborough, MS 1 (Latin)
S = London & Oslo, The Schøyen Collection, MS 563 (Latin and French)
R = Oxford, Bodleian Library, Rawlinson, MS B 520 (Middle English).

(8) The Wyclif Bible (2nd half of the 14th century) exists in two versions, the earlier is more literal, the revised later version is more idiomatic. **Conrad Lindberg**, who has devoted much of his life's work to a new edition of the Wyclif Bible, edits a kind of conflated version of Baruch 3 in his paper "Revising the Wyclif Bible" in order to show the revision procedure and the different stages in the development of the text.

(9) One of the less well studied aspects of Chaucers poetry, namely his use of Latin words, phrases and sentences, is investigated by **Michael W. Twomey** ("Chaucer's Latinity"). Twomey distinguishes between intra-textual Latinisms, i.e. those spoken by the narrators and the characters (e.g. the Prioress's *Amor vincit omnia* and the boy's *Alma redemptoris mater*, or the Summoner's *questio quid iuris*), and extra-textual Latinisms, e.g. textual markers such as explicits and incipits between sections of works, furthermore marginal glosses – whereas the former (intra-textual) are usually Chaucer's, some of the latter (extra-textual) may have been inserted by later scribes. Twomey concludes that Chaucer used quotations and formulae from Latin but, unlike his contemporary Gower, did not attempt to create his own Latin phrases and sentences. Twomey furthermore discusses the Latin pronunciation which Chaucer might have used.

(10) **Saburo Oka** ("Chaucer's *Troilus* in a new comparative context") interprets Chaucer's description of the appearance and character of Troilus. First, he compares it with earlier versions of the Troy story where Troilus appears (e.g. Dictys Cretensis, Benoît de Sainte-Maure, Guido delle Colonne, Joseph of Exeter); then, he looks at some passages in Chaucer's *Troilus and Criseyde* which are central for the description of Troilus.

(11) The genre of the *Book of Margery Kempe* is difficult to pinpoint. It combines the elements of a mystical treatise, of an autobiography (the first, or at least the first extended one in English), and of a travel account. Margery Kempe's (c. 1373-c. 1439) character and motivation have also caused a lot of debate. **Liliana Sikorska** ("Between penance and purgatory: Margery Kempe's

'Pélerinage de la vie humaine' and the idea of salvaging journeys") interprets Margery Kempe's role as that of a 'fool of Christ', who endures dislike and slander for the love of God.

(12) **Carol Kaske** deals with Sir Thomas Malory's (c. 1410-c. 1471) great collection of Arthurian stories (*Le Morte Darthur*) and their frequent depiction of violence. She argues that Malory sometimes criticises this violence, e.g. in *The tales of Balin*. This criticism can appear in different forms: for example, sometimes fighters who kill their opponents are rebuked, and sometimes restraint in knights is praised. Kaske also looks at the numerous scenes where knights rehorse fallen comrades by unhorsing an enemy, and she proposes that "Malory is trying to portray battle as a matter of helping your friends more than hurting your foes" in these scenes.

(13) **Saara Nevanlinna** ("Observations on the loss of final plosive consonants in late Middle English rhyme-words") uses the Helsinki Corpus in order to find out more details about the deletion of final plosives in Middle English poetry (c. 1350-1500), mainly in rhyming pairs such as ... *wirschip/*... *Egipt*, or ... *óf/*... *sóft*, where apparently the final *-t* was dropped in the pronunciation of *Egip(t)* and *sof(t)*. She stresses that this must have been an oral phenomenon (poetry was usually recited) and she establishes different types and contexts of deletion or assimilation. She also stresses the regional aspect and concludes that the deletion of final plosives occurred most frequently in areas that had earlier been under Scandinavian influence, i.e. mainly the northern and eastern areas.

(14) Hyphens have not been studied much either synchronically or diachronically. **Manfred Markus** ("Hyphens and hyper-hyphens in Middle English [corpus-based]") tries to fill this gap in our knowledge – at least partly. He distinguishes between link hyphens (used within words), and break hyphens (used for breaking the line), and he arrives at a number of interesting conclusions, e.g. that until c. 1400, prefixes were often hyphenated, whereas after 1400, compounds were often hyphenated, or, that the native prefix *a-* and the prefix *de-* (borrowed from French) were often hyphenated in Middle English, whereas others were almost never hyphenated.

(15) English and German are both West-Germanic languages and thus closely related; but subsequently, they developed quite a number of differences, in their vocabulary as well as in their phonological, morphological and syntactic structure. **Horst Weinstock** ("Medieval English and German: A guide to Modern similarities and dissimilarities") looks at some of these differences, from the pronunciation of the letters of the alphabet (German /a:, be:, tse:/ etc. but English /ei, bi:, si:/ etc.), to syntax: Whereas German still has variant patterns of

word-order (SVO, but also SOV, OVS etc.), English almost exclusively employs the pattern SVO.

This volume thus shows at least some of the many aspects of Medieval English language, literature, and culture as well as of the history of English, and it also exhibits some of the various possible approaches to these areas.

My thanks are due to my co-editor **Renate Bauer**, who formatted this volume and produced the electronic version for the publisher. Both of us have to thank Jacek Fisiak for his constant encouragement, our contributors for their patience while this volume was in the making, and Susan Bollinger, Eva Gachstetter, Julia Hartmann, Ursula Lenker and Judith Rodrigues for checking the final version of the manuscript.

Notes

[1] The next main conference will be in Lund, 6-10 August 2007; the 2007 Medieval Symposium will be in Ystad (3-4 August 2007), see <iaupe.academic@englund.lu.se>. In order to reconstruct the dates and venues of the earlier Medieval Symposia, I had to ask several colleagues; my thanks are especially due to Andreas Fischer, Ian Kirby and Horst Weinstock.

[2] Wolf-Dietrich Bald -- Horst Weinstock (ed.). 1984. *Medieval Studies Conference Aachen 1983: Language and Literature.* (Bamberger Beiträge zur Englischen Sprachwissenschaft 15.) Frankfurt am Main: Lang.

[3] A selection of the papers given at the Bamberg IAUPE Conference (2001) has just been prublished: Herbert Grabes -- W. Viereck (ed.). 2006. *The wider scope of English.* (Bamberger Beiträge zur Englischen Sprachwissenschaft 51.) Frankfurt am Main: Lang.

Beowulf in Arabia: Teaching heroic poetry in a post-heroic age

Manfred Malzahn, Muhammad Abu al-Fadl Badran (Al-Ain, United Arab Emirates)

1. Purpose and scope of this paper

Within the framework of the present collection, it seems no more than fair to admit right at the outset of this contribution that it cannot lay claim to any original discoveries in either Anglo-Saxon or Classical Arabic scholarship. It is rather intended to demonstrate the fact that the two literatures concerned can be studied and taught comparatively, and to underpin the contention that works such as *Beowulf* should be seen as having their rightful place in English curricula especially in Arab countries, where the discussion of Old English literature can be integrated very well into a contemporary cultural debate.

2. OE literature in a United Arab Emirates (UAE) context

For anyone who teaches English literary texts in an entirely different setting from that in which they originated, questions of canon will of course have an added poignancy. Today, Old English writings occupy at best a marginal position within the framework of English studies in anglophone countries. Even in England itself, many curriculum planners would agree with the verdict that "a nodding acquaintance with the language and literature of the Anglo-Saxons is all that it is reasonable to demand" (Bateson -- Meserole 1976: 14). One might thus be tempted to bypass it completely wherever the temporal distance between author and reader is matched by spatial, linguistic, and cultural removes that would seem to make understanding, let alone enjoyment, highly unlikely indeed.

The United Arab Emirates can certainly be counted as one of those locations that fit the above description. Of the students majoring in English here, only few bring with them a command of the language that makes them see the prospect of reading literature in English as holding a promise of pleasure rather than of pain. For most of them, Britain is an island of which they have no first-hand experience, and often no more than some vague and general ideas. As in many other regions, the image of anglophone culture is nowadays clearly dominated by the overwhelming presence of the USA, particularly on various kinds of screens. In spite of Britain's past role as a colonial power on the Arabian peninsula, its inhabitants have become more and more inclined to regard the United States of America, for better or worse, as the representative norm not only of the English-speaking world, but of the entire occident.

If a fairly undifferentiated perception of Western culture is common among UAE students, then the young female English majors who outnumber their male counterparts at a ratio of about 18 to 1, and who lead their lives within relatively narrow geographical and social boundaries, can hardly be expected to represent too much of an exception. Among them as among other members of their society, the West tends to be perceived as appealing and appalling at the same time. From a typical Arab viewpoint, the allure of the commercial and cultural artifacts that epitomise the Western way of life masks a lack of what Arab-Islamic culture preserves: namely, traditional values and forms of social organisation based primarily on the bonds of kinship, and on the notion of the family or clan as the all-important social unit.

To students with such expectations in mind, the encounter with the world of *Beowulf* at the outset of their obligatory historical survey course can come as an eye-opener. The version of the text used will obviously be a modern translation, but this is really all it takes to facilitate the engagement with a tale that is bound to strike UAE students as surprisingly familiar, because of the very recent past of their own country as well as because of their indigenous literary heritage. Neither heroic ideals and lifestyles, nor the heroic poetry that describes them, are as remote to young Arabs at the beginning of the 21st century as they are to their English contemporaries, in whose eyes medieval epic heroes would likely belong to the virtual world of fantasy role-playing, an "ephemeral art" which is mainly "sheer entertainment", with only the feeblest connection to practical modern reality (Schick 1991: 15).

In the United Arab Emirates, on the other hand, the post-heroic age has only just arrived. From the very top right down to the bottom of the social pyramid, relationships between a sheikh and his followers can still be said to resemble those between Hrothgar and his retainers more than those between any elected president and his voters in the western world. Clan loyalties and boundaries are well-marked, and blood-money, locally known as *diya*, is paid to the victims of accidental and deliberate killings, in the manner of the Anglo-Saxon *wergild*. Gift-giving is still important in expressing and cementing personal relations between rulers and ruled, even if it may often be symbolic rather than substantial: public holidays, for instance, are decreed at short notice, rather than fixed in advance and hence taken as a matter of employees' rights. In exchange for material and ritual tokens of goodwill, the populace in turn publicly show corresponding signs of gratitude and of loyalty to the leadership on every suitable occasion.

But while the political organisation of the state thus still bears many of the ancient hallmarks, much else has changed so radically that the air-conditioned country in which the present-day generation of students dwells, looks almost totally alien to the environment that their grandfathers and grandmothers knew, while their fathers and mothers lived to see the whirlwind transition from near-medieval to futuristic. The following extract from the 40th-anniversary brochure of Oasis Hospital in Al-Ain, at about 300,000 inhabitants the second largest city in the Emirate of Abu Dhabi and likewise the seat of UAE University with its about 17,000 students, may serve in lieu of a lengthy documentation:

> In 1960, the population of Al-Ain and its related villages was approximately 2000. Population growth was totally stagnant. The infant mortality rate was estimated at 50%, and the maternal mortality rate was around 35%. ... The 'home remedies' practiced by the people seemed to have done more damage than good. But the doctors were obviously a great help, and the local population was thrilled to have live, happy, bouncing babies, and to have mothers who would care for the family a day after delivery. It was also a joy for the hospital staff, to see the people's excitement– often expressed by shooting holes into the roof of the hospital. The practice at the time was to fire seven rifle shots for the birth of a boy, and three for a girl. Thus the staff always knew how many babies were born and their sexes, by simply counting the rifle shots. (Anonymus 2000: 4)

Such was the custom only four decades ago: today, men in the UAE are no longer in the habit of carrying guns around, and they do not even wear the *khanjar*, the ornamental dagger which still adorns some of their Omani neighbours. To see fully armed tribal warriors, one would have to venture as far as Yemen. The memory of a heroic past, however, is kept alive not only in the official image of its history which the country proudly preserves and promotes, but also in the popular imagination.

By way of evidence, we would once again like to cite just one significant example: namely, the legends surrounding a burial site just outside Dubai. The copse marking the site is now enclosed by a roundabout, one of whose exits leads onto the broad and brightly lit Al-Ain motorway. A newspaper report published in March 2001 quotes the great-great-grandson of Saeed Bu Khadra, after whom the spot was named, telling the story of his ancestor who died there in a battle against an invading tribe around the year 1900. According to the descendant Ali Bu Khadra, Saeed Bu Khadra had continued to fight even after one of his legs was severed from his body. Today, the location is credited with miraculous happenings, which Ali Bu Khadra was ostensibly doing his best to discredit in front of the interviewer.[1] The article closes, however, with the following:

> Yet strangely, when asked if he would pose for a photograph in the shaded glade, Bu Khadra resisted, giving no clear reason for his reticence. Visibly uncomfortable at the thought, he shivered: 'I just wouldn't want to go in there...' (Langley -- Idris 2001: 3)

What transpires here is the survival of archaic patterns of thought and behaviour beneath a relatively thin layer of modernity, and this is more or less typical not only of the Arabian peninsula, but of large parts of the Arab world. In today's UAE, the nomadic freedom of the *bedu* lifestyle belongs to the recent past, but nevertheless to the past, and the life-experience of the present generation is that of a largely regulated and sedentary existence among an abundance of modern conveniences. At the same time, however, families try to maintain traditional forms of social organisation, and to keep close control especially over their female members. For young males, the scope for thrill-seeking is thus severely limited on two fronts. The result is one which a criminologist might well identify as anomy, with reckless driving or drug-taking supplanting the martial raids or amorous visits celebrated in that ancient poetry which most of the young would still be familiar with.

A high degree of acquaintance with classic poems can indeed be found not only in the Gulf countries, but throughout the Arab world. In a study of an Egyptian village, for example, Dwight Fletcher Reynolds notes that quoting from time-honoured texts is part of a widespread communicational pattern there, with social status to be gained from or manifested in "the deployment of memorized classical Arabic poetry" (Reynolds 1995: 33). However, the question regarding the relevance or the precise role of heroic poetry in contemporary Arab society is a potential bone of contention. A recent survey by John Renard contrasts the perpetuation of "a rather distant and idealistic" heroism in some modern Arabic literature with the contemporary criticism voiced by other authors such as Nizar Qabbani from Syria:

> In my land,
> In the land of the simple,
> Where we slowly chew on our unending songs –
> A form of consumption destroying the east –
> Our east is chewing on its history.
> Its lethargic dreams,
> Its empty legends (Renard 1999: 10)

3. Heroic parallels and peculiarities

Whether it perceives ancient texts as supplying an inspirational counter-image to actual reality, or rather as affording an easy escape route into fantasy and hence an easy excuse for reality's deficiencies, the reception of early heroic poetry in Arabic cannot but highlight the fact that its poetic heroes are made such by non-heroes who receive, remember, and reiterate their epic narratives. Unlike in *Beowulf* with its third-person narration, the poet in Classical Arabic texts tends to be the singer of his own deeds, *scop* and skirmisher blended into one figure reminiscent of the Celtic Ossian, or indeed of the Germanic Odin, the god of poetry and "actor of diverse roles" who speaks in the *Hávamál* (Edwards -- Pálsson 1998: 12).

Because of the method of narration, the voice of the heroic-poetic speaker in early Arabic poetry often carries a greater immediacy than that of the *Beowulf* poet, who talks of past events which he did not personally witness. The boasting of Beowulf is commented on by the narrator and other characters; the boasting of the heroes in the *Mu'allaqat*, the classic ten long poems of the pre-Islamic period, is bound to reverberate without either mediation or retort. The egocentric or narcissistic nature of the poetic statement shows clearly enough in the opening motif, the lament for the departure of the beloved as her tribe or clan break up their camp, leaving only fading traces in the sand behind them. As in Renaissance sonnets, the speaker is prone to profess himself not only deserted, but cruelly wronged, like Imru'ul-Qais, who addresses his lady with the following words: "When you shed tears, those were only your arrows, / plunged into the depth of a slain heart."[2]

This is clearly not a sentiment that Beowulf or the *Beowulf* poet would express or share, but the *Mu'allaqat* do thematise, as palpably as does the Beowulf tale, the contrast and possible contradiction between individual-heroic desires and aspirations on the one hand, and social-communal obligations and restraints on the other. When Imru'ul-Qais speaks the famous words "Today I'll have wine, tomorrow I'll have revenge", he signals a turn from the extravagant and hedonistic life of a Prince Hal to the single-minded pursuit of retribution for the killing of his father: this makes him the true leader of his tribe, through a metamorphosis not unlike that of the "sluggard" and "feeble princeling" Beowulf into giant-crusher and monster-slayer (Crossley-Holland 1999: 72-3).

Another type of hero in ancient Arabic poetry may even openly turn against his community: the prime example here is Antara Ibn Shaddad. As the illegitimate child of a high-born leader of the Banu Abs tribe and a black slave woman, Antara rebels against his unfree status by demonstrating excellence in the aristocratic pursuits of martial arts and poetry. When Antara's heroic prowess is needed to help fend off an attack on his people, this opens the road to reconciliation with his tribe, recognition by his father, and union with his beloved, his cousin Abla whose praise he sings in his verse. The image of the hero as a lover stands in a marked contrast to the *Beowulf* poem, where the main character seems to have no special interest in women. In the case of Antara, images of the warlike and the amorous qualities of a champion are fused in lines such as the following:

> When the battle began I would fain kiss the swords,
> For their gleam looked like that of your smiling teeth.

With regard to feats of superhuman physical strength, on the other hand, the speaker of these verses does resemble "the megalomaniac hero who can swim for eight days and eight nights over the Baltic Sea in full armor slaying whales all the way". Cedric H. Whitman (1982: 20) thus sums up the character of Beowulf, by way of contrast with the all-embracing humanity which he perceives in the heroes of the Greeks. If, for the sake of the present argument, we accept the view of Beowulf as cutting an essentially catalectic figure, and hence the view of the Anglo-Saxon heroic ideal as restrictive, we would have to ask whether Antara comes any closer to that all-round perfection which makes Whitman and others see the Greek heroic notion as a link between the human and the divine. Whitman (1982: 20) formulates what he calls the heroic paradox as follows:

> The hero is ourself, expanded for our inspection and understanding ... and pushed to logical – or illogical – extremes. And, as the Greek tradition presents him to us, we see him motivated by two simultaneous, opposite needs: the need for absolute status, and the need for human context, commitment; or, as the Greeks would put it, the urge toward divinity, and the necessity of remaining mortal.

In spite of his double identity as warrior and lover, and thus of his apparently richer humanity, the application of the above-mentioned formula to the case of Antara would encounter major obstacles in the form of many grave weaknesses. He is shown as having a lack of self-control that results in drunkenness, rape, and even gratuitous killing. Antara thus stands as the very opposite to the Stoic ideal of keeping the passions at bay; he indulges even the noblest of his emotions to an extent at which they have unethical consequences, as for instance the execution of many hundreds of prisoners, ordered by Antara because he is "unrestrained in grief" for a dead friend or a dead son (Lyons 1995: 95). A parallel to this incident can indeed be found in *Beowulf,* but given only in the form of a warning to the hero, with the bad king Heremod named as perpetrator:

> In mad rage he murdered his table-companions,
> his most loyal followers; it came about
> that the great prince cut himself off
> from all earthly pleasures, though God had endowed him
> with strength and power above all other men,
> and had sustained him. For all that his heart
> was filled with savage blood-lust. He never gave
> gifts to the Danes, to gain glory. He lived joyless,
> agony racked him; he was long an affliction
> to his people. Be warned, Beowulf,
> learn the nature of nobility. (Crossley -- Holland 1999: 57)

It would appear that Antara learns the treacherous nature of nobility when he loses his restraint,[3] and that his union of the lover's and the fighter's passion yet leaves him a less accomplished human being than Beowulf. After all, as Hrothgar remarks to Beowulf at the outset of his mission, the young Geat embodies the unlikely union of youth and wisdom. To find exemplary wisdom in dealings with women in the Old English epic, however, one would have to go to a minor character: namely, the dauntless Offa who tames and reforms the evil queen Thryth by means which are so mysteriously unspecified that they might once again recall the divine Odin and his spells, culminating in an infallible, but ultimately secret recipe for patriarchal bliss. As is hinted earlier in *Hávamál*, such happiness is beyond the ken and hence beyond the scope of mere mortals, who err when they think themselves the masters of their households and their possessions:

> The man's a born fool
> who boasts he can rule
> either women or wealth:
> his pride is so dense,
> it defies commonsense,
> and inflates his wild fancies. (Edwards -- Pálsson 1998: 57)

But not even Odin gets it right all the time,[4] and the many shortcomings of the immortals in the polytheistic universes of the Hellenic and the Germanic peoples stand in a marked contrast to stories which show a belief in the perfectibility or near-perfectibility of men. Like the greatest of the Greek heroes, Beowulf is made to look morally superior to some of those whom he would have worshipped, and of whom the extant version of his story is conspicuously silent. The Christianisation of Beowulf's tale has a parallel in the Islamisation of hero figures such as Antara, but while the coexistence of pagan and Christian elements in *Beowulf* has given rise to widely divergent theories about the composition and the original audience, the editorial process is slightly more obvious in Antara's case. Here, existing texts contain explicit references to the fact that he was not a Muslim, but likewise reassure the reader that he would certainly have been one if he had not been born before the revelation of Islam.

In both cultural traditions, literary texts document the need or the desire to adopt or adapt a pagan heroic ideal in the transition to a new monotheistic religion with a different ethic. In the case of *Beowulf*, the adaptation appears most clearly in the association of Grendel and his mother, through their being simultaneously "under God's curse and the instrument of God's justice", not only with the race of Cain but also with the arch-ambivalent Satan (Fajardo-Acosta 1989: 69).[5] The hero's foes are thus the enemies of God and Man; this identification, however, cannot change the fundamental tone of the tale, which not only J.R.R. Tolkien quite rightly calls elegiac. Man's struggle may be heroic and bring temporary victory over the forces of doom, but even as we celebrate such short-lived triumphs, "we approach slowly and reluctantly the inevitable victory of death" (Tolkien 1963: 84).

The Arabic as well as the Anglo-Saxon hero distinguishes himself by the unflinching acceptance of his ultimate fate. "Death is a well I must drink from", says Antara; but although he has no hesitation to risk his life in combat, he does not hold life's pleasures in disregard either. As Muraqqash Al-Akbar puts it: "We sell our life cheap in battle, but we don't trifle with it in time of peace." Anglo-Saxon heroes would appear inclined to agree that a man's time is well spent not only on the battlefield, but likewise on occasions of ceremonial splendour and conviviality. Beowulf himself reports the goings-on in Heorot with admiration:

> Then there was revelry; never in my life,
> under heaven's vault, have I seen men
> happier in the mead-hall. (Crossley -- Holland 1999: 67)

However, while telling the story of his victory over Grendel and complimenting his audience on their festive spirit, the hero suddenly switches to dark forebodings of discord and bloodshed between rival parties of revellers. The moment at which he relishes and, as today's talk-show hosts would say, shares the memories of past triumph with others, is thus fraught with foreknowledge of coming evil, and Beowulf, though called "unfated", cannot help bearing the burden of the one who sees ahead, instead of merely living out the moment in the blissful hæcceity of the young. The last words of the dying Abu Firas al-Hamdani can serve as a fit comment on this predicament:

> When you call me and I can't reply, say:
> 'The best of young men, Abu Firas, never had youth.'

It is worth noting that in Beowulf's prophecy, it is an old man who incites a young warrior to break the peace of the festivities. The burden of the past is thus borne by the young, and the defeat of evil never complete: consequently, feasting and fighting follow each other in the endless cycle of heroic life, where periods of peace and happiness must be bought by heroic action. This suggests that the ideal leader would possess a dual nature, showing the same degree of excellence both in the field and in the hall. In *Beowulf*, it is possible to see the different virtues as divided between different characters, such as the "wise, generous, and legislative" Hrothgar, and the "fierce, terrifying, and hugely strong" Beowulf (Hill 1995: 75). It has likewise been claimed, however, that Beowulf himself has a dual nature, and that the darker of his two sides is a downright monstrous one. Fidel Fajardo-Acosta (1989: 3) asserts the following:

> The monsters are embodiments of the temptations with which Beowulf is confronted – to all of which he succumbs – and also mirror-images of Beowulf, of what he slowly becomes as he moves up the ladder of heroic achievement.

For those who are reluctant to see a hero-monster or monster-hero in Beowulf, Classical Arabic poetry has some more clearly marked specimens to offer. Above all, there is Shanfara of Azd:[6]

> In the cold night so bitter that men will burn
> Their most precious bow and arrow to warm them,
> I wandered alone through the rainy dark,
> No fellows but fog, horror, hunger and danger;
> I slew fathers of children and grooms of brides,
> And as I had left, returned before daybreak.
> In the morning, I sat safely back at Qumaisa,
> Leaving two pale-faced crowds to ask,
> 'In truth, we did hear the dogs howl last night:
> Is a wolf passing by, we said, or hyenas?'
> 'No, it was muffled growling; they sleep now;
> They were surely disturbed by some errant bird.'
> 'If a jinn was here, he did much evil work;
> If a man–but this cruelty was not human.'

4. Conclusions and perspectives

At this point, it should be evident that a critical reading of heroic poetry in the 21st century calls for a critical examination of heroic concepts and their possible place in a civic society. What Old English and Arabic texts offer us is a window into the lives and thoughts of "face-to-face, non-centralized people" (Hill 1995: 150), whose social organisation is designed to give any two members of a tribe "some reason why the two should not attempt to kill each other" (Diamond 1998: 272), while making it rather more difficult to find such reasons for any two members of different tribes. Tribal identity and allegiance is as central a motif in ancient Arab poems as it is in Anglo-Saxon ones. When the egocentric 'I' is displaced by a phylocentric 'We', the boasting becomes communal, but the underlying ethic remains the same, as in the following example by Amr Ibn Kulthum of the Taghlib:[7]

> The earth, all its people, belong to us;
> And when we seize, we seize with might.
> The firm dry land we flood with our men;
> The back of the sea is filled with our ships.

Comparable passages can easily be found in Anglo-Saxon texts, and a comparative discussion may serve as an apt reminder of the fatal tendency of human beings to see the world's inhabitants as divided, whether it be along tribal, racial, religious or other lines, into two groups thought of as 'we' and 'they', while regarding the first of those as naturally favoured. Classical Arabic and Old English literature show extreme forms of behaviour resulting from such thought, as well as narrative or poetic attempts to rationalise the claim to a privileged status for a particular 'we-ness' in view of the fact that it must seem no more than one among many 'they-nesses' to others. Especially in *Beowulf*, we find hints at a possible squaring of the circle through a moral dimension: the vindication of the just through association with others who are just, in a manner that shows virtue to be consistent with self-interest. This is the gist of Robert Frank's theory of moral sentiments, as summed up in the following:

> The virtuous are virtuous for no other reason than that it enables them to join forces with others who are virtuous, to mutual benefit. And once cooperators segregate themselves off from the rest of a society a wholly new force of evolution can come into play: one that pits groups against each other, rather than individuals. (Ridley 1997: 147)

One problem is, of course, that in order to achieve cooperation among groups, the process must be repeated on the collective level. The other is that, in order to tell both the cooperative or virtuous individuals and the cooperative or virtuous groups from the unjust or selfish, virtues must not only be claimed, but unequivocally seen as being practised by the claimants. An extended walk through the streets of Belfast or Al-Quds[8] would certainly provide more evidence of mutually exclusive claims to righteousness than of any collective moral superiority. However, no group – whether it claims to defend the true faith against infidels, or the civilised world against terrorism – should be exempted from the need to vindicate its self-definition as 'good' through measuring its own actions by the most rigorous moral standards. The critical evaluation of the values proclaimed or embodied in heroic poetry can provide a useful means of testing moral principles and their practical application, for in heroic tales, justice is always a subject, whether given implicitly or explicitly, as here by Labid Ibn Rabiah:

> When our glorious tribe gathers, it never lacks
> One who dares to act high as honour demands,
> Nor a judge with wisdom to weigh each clan's claims,
> And stay calm in the clamour till all are content.

Apart from thus encouraging ventures onto the ground of moral philosophy and practical ethics or gender issues,[9] the teaching of *Beowulf* in Arabia can finally help to foster a debate that treats evil not only as a metaphysical datum, but more importantly, as a type of behaviour whose every instance asks for an individual explanation. In the case of Grendel and his mother, their fiendish nature furnishes only one half of the reason, and it is surely no less important to note that the crimes begin when the monsters have to suffer the inadvertent addition of insult to injury, in form of a daily reminder of the abjectness of their condition:

> Then the brutish demon who lived in darkness
> impatiently endured a time of frustration:
> day after day he heard the din of merry-making
> inside the hall, and the sound of the harp
> and the bard's clear song. (Crossley -- Holland 1999: 4-5)

Not only for the citizens of oil-rich Gulf states, would it make sense to try an alternative way of thinking of Grendel and his mother, as representing those underprivileged who live within earshot of the wealthy. In our global village, this definition would include urban slum-dwellers and starving peasants virtually anywhere. If we think of the story of Beowulf in terms of social psychology, we can read it as a nightmare in which the ugly forms of the have-nots surface from the stinking swamps to which they have been relegated, to haunt those who would love to have their enjoyment untainted by such unsightly spectacles. We feel that such a reading may set off a train of thought which it is perhaps as useful to pursue in Derby as in Dubai, and in Cambridge as in Cairo.

Notes

[1] Such miracles are popularly credited to the *awliya 'Allah* or 'Friends of God'; the singular term for a saintly miracle-worker or religious hero is *wehli*.

[2] Here as well as in the following, English versions of Arabic texts are offered by the authors of this paper, unless marked otherwise. The aim is not philological accuracy, but a rendering that approximates the poetic power of the original.

[3] The figure of Alexander the Great, whose royal blood infused with alcohol boiled hot enough to cause the murder of his friend Cleitus, furnishes another parallel in the occidental tradition.

[4] He confesses, for instance, his improper timing of social calls, and reports an instance of unrequited love or lust that brought him "nothing but shame" (Edwards -- Pálsson 1998: 62).

[5] The line that Fajardo-Acosta cites in support of his reading, "Grendel gongan, Godes yrre baer", seems to be in itself ambivalent (cf. Fajardo -- Acosta 1989: 69).

[6] This version follows the German translation by Reuss (1853).

[7] This version follows the German translation by Landau (1968).

[8] The Arabic name for the city which is otherwise known as Jerusalem.

[9] For suggestions concerning a feminist approach to literary heroism, we would recommend Daly (1993).

References

Anonymus (ed.)
    2000   *In touch with you... for 40 years*. Al-Ain: Oasis Hospital.

Bateson, F.W. -- Harrison T. Meserole
    1976   *A guide to English and American literature*. (3rd edition.) London: Longman.

Crossley-Holland, Kevin (trans.)
    1999   *Beowulf*. (Oxford World's Classics.) Oxford: Oxford University Press.

Daly, Pierrette
    1993   *Heroic tropes: Gender and intertext*. Detroit: Wayne State University Press.

Diamond, Jared
    1998   *Guns, germs and steel: A short history of everybody for the last 13,000 years*. London: Vintage.

Edwards, Paul -- Hermann Pálsson (trans.)
    1998   *The words of Odin: Hávamál*. Edinburgh: Lockharton Press.

Fajardo-Acosta, Fidel
    1989   *The condemnation of heroism in the tragedy of Beowulf: A study in the characterization of the epic*. (Studies in Epic and Romance Literature 2.) Lewiston: Edwin Mellen Pess.

Hill, John M.
    1995   *The cultural world in Beowulf*. Toronto: University of Toronto Press.

Landau, Jacob
    1968   *Arabische Literaturgeschichte*. Stuttgart: Kroener.

Langley, Joanna -- Abdullah Idris
2001   "Remains of a hero under gaff trees", *Gulf news* 27 May: 3.

Lyons, M.C.
1995   *The Arabian epic: Heroic and oral story-telling*. Vol. I: *Introduction*. (University of Cambridge Oriental Publications 49.) Cambridge: Cambridge University Press.

Nicholson, Lewis E. (ed.)
1963   *An anthology of Beowulf criticism*. Notre Dame: University of Notre Dame Press.

Renard, John
1999   *Islam and the heroic image: Themes in literature and the visual arts*. Macon: Mercer University Press.

Reuss, Ed.
1853   "Schanfara: Übersetzt von Prof. Ed. Reuss", *Zeitschrift der Deutschen Morgenländischen Gesellschaft* 7: 97-100.

Reynolds, Dwight Fletcher
1995   *Heroic poets, poetic heroes: The ethnography of performance in an Arabic oral epic tradition*. Ithaca: Cornell University Press.

Ridley, Matt
1997   *The origins of virtue*. Harmondsworth: Penguin.

Schick, Lawrence
1991   *Heroic worlds: A history and guide to role-playing games*. Buffalo: Prometheus Books.

Tolkien, J.R.R.
1936   "*Beowulf*: The Monsters and the Critics", *Proceedings of the British Academy* 22: 245-95.
1963   Reprinted in: Nicholson (ed.), 51-103.

Whitman, Cedric H.
1982 *The heroic paradox: Essays on Homer, Sophocles, and Aristophanes.* Ithaca: Cornell University Press.

Translating Doomsday: *De die iudicii* and its Old English translation (*Judgement Day II*)

Patrizia Lendinara (Palermo, Italy)

1. *De die iudicii (Ddi)*

The Latin poem beginning with the words "Inter florigeras fecundi cespitis herbas" is currently known as *De die iudicii* (*Ddi*); this title is not authorial, but was drawn by the poem's modern editors from line 8.[1] The poem enjoyed a large circulation both in England[2] and on the Continent (cf. Lendinara 2001b), and such a wide diffusion weighs negatively on the possibility to ascertain the name of the author and the country of origin of the poem.[3] The success of *Ddi* in England is witnessed also by an Old English translation, which is datable to the second half of the tenth century (*Judgement Day II*).[4] This vernacular version is likewise anonymous; it is more than three hundred lines long and is uniquely preserved in MS Cambridge, Corpus Christi College 201, at pp. 161-167. This manuscript was copied by several hands in the last part of the eleventh century (Gneuss 2001: nos. 65, 65.6) and contains a number of late Anglo-Saxon poems, as well as homilies, juridical and ecclesiastical material, a translation of the *Pater Noster* (the so called *LPr II*) and of the *Gloria* (*Glor I*).[5]

After a short *Natureingang*, *Ddi* introduces the "iudiciique diem" (l. 8) and, in the following sections, lingers on the theme of the imminent end of the world and the subsequent Day of Judgment. The poem offers models of conduct and stresses the need of penitence – which is indeed the main theme of *Ddi*. A few signs of the impending Doom are mentioned (l. 50-56 and 72-77), followed by a description of the Last Judgment itself (l. 57-71 and 78-86), the terror of Hell (l. 93-123), and the happiness of Heaven awaiting the blessed (l. 124-154). Though not entirely devoted to Judgement Day, as announced in the prologue, the poem has a balanced structure: the initial description of a windy grove is echoed by the flowery description of Heaven, and the list of the torments of Hell is matched by that of the joys of Heaven. The warning to repent while one has still got time is repeated twice in lines 43ff. and 87ff.[6]

As far as style is concerned, *Ddi* is characterized by a remarkable accumulation of words, a stylistic feature cherished by Dracontius and Venantius Fortunatus (cf. Clerici 1973). The poem borrows *iuncturae* and entire lines from Vergil and Venantius Fortunatus and displays a sufficient prosodic competence.[7] Notwithstanding the lack of originality – the poem is a cento of common themes and images – it enjoyed a considerable fortune, which is witnessed also by the translation into Old English.

2. *Ddi* and *JDay II*

The Old English poem has been defined as "a close expanded translation" of the Latin original (Greenfield -- Calder 1986: 238). This short and effective definition needs some adjustment, and a careful analysis of *JDay II* will enable us to assess not only the procedure of this translation, but also to reach a better understanding of the translation techniques in use in Anglo-Saxon England.

The rendering of the first lines is quite free (*Ddi* l. 1-12 = *JDay II* l. 1-25), and greatly expands on the Latin source. In the following lines the translation strives to provide a literal rendering of the Latin antecedent. The opening lines of the Old English poem, although quite imaginative, contain themes and formulas which occur elsewhere in vernacular poetry, such as the *hwæt*-formula, and the insistence on the seclusion of the narrating voice (for *ic ana*, cf. *The Wife's Lament* l. 35 and *The Wanderer* l. 8). The leafy grove described in the opening passage – at variance with the gloomy scene of the Latin version – suggests a sense of security and protection (for a similar use of *bearu*, cf. *Phoen* l. 71, 80, 122, and *Gen* l. 902). The translation adds the detail of the water running across the garden where the first scene is set (cf. *Phoen* l. 62-63).[8]

The first penitential note occurs at the beginning of the poem, when the focus shifts from the problems of an unnamed individual, brooding on his troubles, to a general homiletic address concerning the future afterlife of the sinful (*synfulra gehwam* l. 18a). *Ddi* employs the familiar penitential imagery and so does the Old English translation; the distressed man beats his breast, cries and prostrates himself in the dust. The theme of the Old English poem is made clear in line 56, where it is said that man should look for *seo soðe hreow* 'the true repentance', a phrase which repeats but, at the same time, transforms the Latin antecedent, which instead reads *confessio vera* (l. 28).[9] The poem outlines the stages of penance, from the injunction to confess the individual's sins to a general address to all mankind (the first shift from personal to homiletic occurs in *Ddi* l. 9-10 = *JDay II* l. 17-20).[10] Weeping for one's guilt is one of the ways by which to reach true repentance and the recourse to penitential tears (foreshadowed by the very first image of the flowing water) will be mentioned again later. Crying will also betray the fear of each man when he stands waiting for judgement before God's throne; however, weeping is, above all, the means by which man may cleanse his soul from sins. The passage on the purifying function of tears prepares for the image of the divine Physician healing the wounds of sin (*Ddi* l. 22-46 = *JDay II* l. 43-91), which introduces the exemplum of the penitent thief, Dismas (*Ddi* l. 27-32 = *JDay II* l. 53-64). The need for repentance is stressed and the audience is reminded that, on Judgement Day, every deed performed in life will be revealed.

The poem describes a few eschatological events, such as the *parousia*, the resurrection of mankind, the end of the world and the Last Judgement. The *Ddi* betrays knowledge of the Sibylline acrostic in its insistence on the role of Christ as judge,[11] the account of his arrival and the signs preceding it, which are accumulated rather than listed in a few central lines of the poem (*Ddi* l. 50-57 = *JDay II* l. 97-114a, and lines *Ddi* l. 72-76 = *JDay II* l. 145-154). The description of the Last Judgement (*Ddi* l. 60-86 = *JDay II* l. 119-175) is followed by a brief allusion to the soul and body theme (*Ddi* l. 87-91 = *JDay II* l. 176-184). Hell, with all sorts of terrors and fire everywhere, is beyond description, but the poet tries his best for many lines (*Ddi* l. 92-122 = *JDay II* l. 185-246). On Doomsday, all the wicked pleasures of this world, which the damned used to be devoted to in life, will vanish one by one. The transitory nature of this world is stressed and the poet bitterly comments that the damned will discover the truth all too late.

The poem reverts to the happy destiny of the blessed (*Ddi* l. 124-125 = *JDay II* l. 247-250). The description of Heaven with the joy of the blessed (*Ddi* l. 128-152 = *JDay II* l. 254-301) contrasts with the picture of Hell and is concluded by the beatific vision of Mary, who leads the white-clad band through the kingdom of God. The poem ends with a homiletic exclamation commenting on the fact that no hardship of this life is too hard to bear, as it earns us the bliss of Heaven (*Ddi* l. 153-154 = *JDay II* l. 303-306).

3. The translation technique

As far as the rendition of Latin poetry into Old English is concerned, it is generally argued that it follows a rigid and mechanic technique of "two-for-one", insofar as two Old English lines translate one Latin hexameter. In fact, this is not the rule and the Old English version of the *Ddi* features several variants which are worth investigating. Moreover, being one of the few translations of a known Latin source into the vernacular, its analysis will yield more general and relevant data. If we compare the *Ddi* (which, excluding the address to Acca, is 154 lines long), to the Old English poem in CCCC 201 (306 lines in all), it is evident that the method of translating each hexameter with two alliterative lines is followed half of the time, that is precisely in ninety-seven instances.[12]

There are also instances when a hexameter is translated with one line of Old English (ratio 1:1). This is the case with seventeen lines of *Ddi*: for example, "Et reserate nefas Christo cum voce gementi" (l. 18) is translated with "and geopeniað man ecum drihtne" (l. 37). This kind of translation is the same as the one used for the Latin proverbs in MSS London, BL, Cotton Faustina A. x and Royal 2. B. v. (ASPR 6, 108). Also, two lines of the *De actibus apostolorum* by Aratus (I, 226-227) are translated by two alliterative lines in Byrhtferth's *Enchiridion*.[13] In other instances, a hexameter is matched by three or four lines of Old English, but there are also examples of a ratio 1:1 and ½ or 1:2 and ½. It is as if the translator was trying his hand at always new solutions, and also within the most common scheme of 1:2 a number of variants are possible.

The procedure followed in the "two-for-one" translation of the *JDay II* needs a careful examination. Indeed, the commonplace rule that the translator of this poem, as well as the authors of other translations from Latin poetry into Old English, would fit a hexameter into a pair of first half-lines, filling out the second halves with alliterating synonyms, is not consistently followed. The addition of a word or phrase is needed either to round off the line or to meet the alliteration's requirements. These half-line fillers usually – but not always – occupy the b-lines. There are also instances where the words which translate the Latin text are concentrated in the b-line, e.g., in "þonne stedelease steorran hreosað" (l. 107), where the b-line faithfully translates the Latin *astra cadunt* (l. 54), and *stedelease* of the a-line alliterates with *steorran*.

The use of a high number of fillers is evident also in the Old English riddles which were translated, *in toto* or in part, from a Latin *enigma* (cf. Whitman 1973: 81-86); the same technique was used when the *Metres of Boethius* were changed from prose to poetry. The a-line fillers of *JDay II* are mainly additions, consisting, for example, of the subject and verb which were implicit in the source; rarely are they mere fillers.[14] By contrast, the b-line additions are, in several instances, mere fillers, which vary or repeat a concept already expressed, and do not contribute anything to the meaning of the translated material. They provide further details of destination, space, time, colour, and effect.[15] The Latin "cum voce gementi" (*Ddi* l. 18) is not translated in the corresponding Old English line (*JDay* II l. 37), and to fill the second half-line the adjective *ece* 'eternal' is added. The same kind of translation technique is applied a few lines ahead, when "Pectoris et linguae, carnis vel crimina saeva" (*Ddi* l. 21) is translated as "breostes and tungan, and flæsces swa some" (*JDay II* l. 42). The first half-line of the Old English is a literal translation of the first part of the Latin hexameter, while the translator, once again struggling with the second part of the Latin hexameter, chose not to translate *crimina saeva* and to add *swa some* 'at the same time' instead. The latter phrase does not contribute anything as far as the meaning is concerned, but fills out the b-line.

Several additions have a Scriptural background, such as *þæt þu beo hrædra* 'be ready' (*JDay II* l. 75; cf. Mk. 8.32), and *weana to leane* 'as a rewards for sins' (*JDay II* l. 184; cf. Rom 6.23). Entirely orthodox, the Old English poem highlights the importance of God, by changing the phrase *gaudia sanctorum* into *mærðe drihtnes / and þara haligra* (*JDay II* l. 21b-22a); a number of fillers, for example, *æt lifes frean* (*JDay II* l. 81b) or *drihtne to willan* (*JDay II* l. 85b) are meant to stress the role of God in the absolution of sins.

4. Holonomastic lines

It is interesting to see how the holonomastic lines of the Latin version, which were not easy to fit into the metrical patterns of Old English poetry, were recast. Holonomastic lines consisted entirely of either nouns or adjectives and were a stylistic feature cherished by Venantius Fortunatus, whose works are among the sources of the *Ddi* (cf. Lendinara 2001b: 320-323). The holonomastic lines are concentrated in the central parts of the poem (*Ddi* l. 115, 118-120, 130-137, 140), and the Old English translation seems to experiment with always new and different solutions.

Faced with these thirteen compressed holonomastic lines, the Anglo-Saxon translator generally resorts to the familiar solution of the "two-for-one" translation,[16] although trying out different degrees of freedom in the rendering of the elements of each holonomastic line. The craftsmanship in handling these lines demonstrates his talent in a wide range of styles. For example, *Ddi* (l. 118) "Ebrietas, epulae, risus, petulantia, iocus" ('Drunkenness, banquets, laughter, wantonness, play') is translated as "þonne druncennes gedwineð mid wistum, / and hleahter and plega hleapað ætsomne" (*JDay II* l. 234-235). Both lines are provided with a verb, the former with *gedwinan* 'disappear' and the latter with *hleapan* 'leap'. In the two-fold restructuring of the hexameter, with *druncennes* 'drunkenness' and *wist* 'feasting' in one line and *hleahter* 'laughter' and *plega* 'play' in the other, the fourth word of the Latin version, *petulantia*, is irremediably lost. In the other instances, too, the translation is unable to reproduce the overall sequence of the nouns in the Latin original, and often, at least one of them is omitted. In lines 240-241 three synonyms, *somnus, torpor* and *desidia*, are reduced to one. In line 265 the Latin pair *nix* and *grando* (*Ddi* l. 133) is felicitously translated as "hagulscuras hearde mid snawe".

A different solution was tried out before, where one Latin verse is reworked into four lines of Old English, which are, nonetheless, insufficient to provide a complete translation of the Latin ("Dira cupido, tenax luxus, scelerata libido", *Ddi* l. 119):

and wrænnes eac gewiteð heonone,
and fæsthafolnes feor gewiteð,
uncyst onweg and ælc gælsa
scyldig scyndan on sceade þonne. (*JDay II* l. 236-239)

In the Old English version, the three Latin adjectives, *dirus, tenax* and *sceleratus*, are not translated. The numerous verbs employed in the translation succeed in creating an impressive progression in which the earthly lusts glide away, one by one. This image was already anticipated by *gedwinað heonone* in l. 232b and by *gewitað mid ealle* in l. 233b, followed by *gedwineð* and *hleapað* (*JDay II* l. 234 and 235), and, further down, by *gewiteð heonone, feor gewiteð* and *scyndan* (*JDay II* l. 236, 237, and 239, respectively). All these Old English verbs are verbs of motion combined with an adverb of motion (see also *onweg* in *JDay II* l. 238), which replace the static *cessabunt* of the Latin version (*Ddi* l. 117). The translation "and hleahter and plega hleapað ætsomne" (*JDay II* l. 235) is remarkably felicitous.

When dealing with another holonomastic line ("Taedia, tristititiae, curae, tormenta, ruinae", *Ddi* l. 132, that is 'weariness, sadness, anxieties, torments, disasters'), the Anglo-Saxon translator is, once again, compelled to move away from its model by the different practice of vernacular versification and translates: "Nis þær unrotnes ne þær æmelnys,/ ne hryre ne caru ne hreoh tintrega" (*JDay II* l. 261-262). The translation cannot follow the asyndetic series of nouns and hence reshapes them into either word-doublets or three-word combinations, as well as altering the order in which the five dreads are listed. To meet the metrical and alliterative requirements of Old English verse, the adjective *hreoh* is added in order to alliterate with *hryre* of the first half-line. The use of the anaphoric *ne* is typical of Old English poetry where it occurs quite frequently, both in positive and negative descriptions, such as those of Heaven and Hell (cf. Tristram 1978: 102-113).

5. Omissions and additions

The translation is faithful to the original and preserves as much as possible of the Latin text. Even when a number of adjectives and adverbs of the Latin original are apparently omitted, they are in fact replaced, at short distance, by an Old English equivalent. For example, four occurrences of the adjective *cunctus* are omitted in the Old English version, but OE *eall* figures among the most frequent additions; the same can be said of the Latin adverb *nunc*. It is not possible to establish the principles guiding the omission of passages of the Latin version: among the largest omissions are *commissa meorum* (*Ddi* l. 6), *cum voce gementi*

(*Ddi* l. 18, reproduced later in *JDay II* l. 35 as *dreccað mid wope*), *vel crimina saeva* (*Ddi* l. 21), and the pair *ab arce polorum* (*Ddi* l. 48) and *in sede polorum* (*Ddi* l. 141). Holonomastic lines undergo a great reshuffling as we have seen. As to the rest, there are a few simplifications, such as *fetor praeingenti* [...] *putredine* (*Ddi* l. 103) rendered with *unstenc* 'stench' (*JDay II* l. 208), or *nix* and *grando* (*Ddi* l. 133), which are condensed into a remarkable compound, *hagulscur* 'hailshower' (*JDay II* l. 265).

As is customary in the Old English translations from Latin, the major changes are aimed at amplification, expanding on the Latin phrases and applying, in some instances, the technique of variation. If one compares the Old English poem with the Latin one, the introduction of lines, phrases, and words with no counterpart in the original is evident. This is not simply a device to cope with the structural difference between Germanic and Latin metrics, but, at least as far as *JDay II* is concerned, the additions originate from a desire to expand on the source with a swarm of vivid details, comments, personal asides, and addresses to the audience. Many of the additions are indeed connective comments. There are entire lines without a counterpart in the Latin version: lines 3, 4, 16, 98 (an explanation), 106, 110, 151 (an enlarged repetition of "impletur", *Ddi* l. 72), 153, 165 (an explanation), 182 (a digression), 193, 244, 246, 279 (which adds the subject), 293 (a variation), and 302. Some of the new lines are mere repetitions; other lines restate the idea in a different syntactic form.

The most common single fillers are Old English adjectives and adverbs. Quite regular is the addition of adverbs of place and time: *æghwær* (l. 228), *aweg* (l. 223), *embutan* (l. 114), *forð* (l. 306), *her* (l. 45, 84, 95, 157, 179, 301), *hider* (l. 111), *in* (l. 63), *inne* (l. 38, 205), *nu* (l. 82, 178, 243), *sona* (l. 36, 108), *swa lange* (l. 66), *swa some* (l. 42), *þa* (l. 10), *þær* (l. 5, 38, 162, 164, 174, 194, 196, 209, 220, 223, 226, 228, 230, 256, 257, 259, 261, 261, 263, 265, 266, 268, 274, 284, 287, 289, 290), *þær inne* (l. 198), *þider* (l. 129), *þonne* (l. 111, 117, 135, 158, 234, 252), *ufon* (l. 111).[17] Both poems underscore, at every step, the difference between life and afterlife, Heaven and Hell. Emphasis is also put on the difference between the time for forgiveness and the time for either suffering or joy. The contrast between this world and the next is intensified by the use of locative and temporal adverbs, which, abundant though they may be in the *Ddi* (*ibi*, *ubi*, *illic*, *tum*, *tunc*), are exponentially multiplied in the Old English translation. The other Old English adverbs, mainly added for alliteration's sake, have little semantic content: *ætsomne* (l. 143, 172), *eac* (l. 5, 17, 104, 145, 230, 236), *fægere* (l. 277), *færinga* (l. 119), *forhte* (l. 161), *freolice* (l. 277), *glædlice* (l. 273), *horxlice* (l. 168), *hwæne* (l. 141), *miclum* (l. 103), *recene* (l. 48), *samod* (l. 268), *symle* (l. 289), *swiðe* (l. 29, 49), *swiðlice* (l. 160), and *wel* (l. 27, 250, 276).[18]

There are several Old English adjectives without a counterpart in the Latin version: *ænlic* (l. 282), *ana* (l. 46, 72), *atol* (l. 218), *biter* (l. 242), *breme* (l. 297), *ece* (l. 37, 76, 269, 272, 299), *eall* (l. 9, 26, 32, 99, 103, 104, 115, 128, 137, 141, 145, 146, 149, 163, 172, 175, 213, 233, 292, 297),[19] *earm* (l. 9, 43, 65, 213), *færlic* (l. 259), *fela* (l. 159), *gearu* (l. 68), *glæd* (l. 179), *halig* (l. 285), *hean* (l. 39), *heanlic* (l. 258), *heard* (l. 265), *hreoh* (l. 262), *hreowlic* (l. 75), *laðlic* (l. 260, 263), *lytel* (l. 219), *mihtig* (l. 19), *read* (l. 288), *reðe* (l. 166), *rice* (l. 300), *scearplic* (l. 53), *scene* (l. 296), *synnig* (l. 67), *sweart* (l. 199), *swiðlic* (l. 227), *torn* (l. 79), *unbleoh* (l. 304), *ungeryd* (l. 102, referred to the tossing sea), *uplic* (l. 146), *wac* (l. 51), *wælgrim* (l. 211, referred to the worms of Hell), *wælhreow* (l. 228), *werig* (l. 245), and a pres. part. *weallend* (l. 200).

Of the additional Old English adjectives, many convey a negative connotation: for example, *biter* 'dire', *earm* 'wretched' (with this meaning in l. 43 and 240), *hean* 'abject', *heanlic* 'abject', *laðlic* 'loathsome', *synnig* 'sinful', *torn* 'distressing', *swiðlic* 'excessive'. There are also a few adjectives with a positive connotation – though the lexical variety is limited: *ece* 'eternal', *ænlic* 'incomparable', and *halig* 'holy'. The adjectives occurring in the frame of larger fillers also have either a negative connotation, such as *atol* (l. 218), *biter* (l. 173), *digol* (l. 20, see also l. 40), *deorc* (l. 106), *dimhiw* (l. 106), *dimm* (l. 14), *earh* (l. 125), *hearm* (l. 137), *heortleas* (l. 125), *lað* (l. 244), *laðlic* (l. 206, 210), *mihtleas* (l. 126), *read* (l. 150, 153), *reaðe* (for *reðe* 'fierce' l. 153), *stedeleas* (l. 107, referring to the stars falling from the firmament), *sweart* (l. 106), or a positive one. The latter generally refer to the divinity, *ælmihtig* (l. 287), *bliðe* (l. 279), *ece* (l. 115), *freolic* (l. 298), *mihtig* (l. 19), *rice* (l. 74), *micel* (l. 129), *healic* (l. 281), *scyppend* (l. 73), *waldend* (l. 52). Many adjectives are in the comparative or superlative, *mære* (l. 55), *beorhtost* (l. 291), *leofest* (l. 244), *gesæligost* (l. 248), *mæst* (l. 125, 253), and *selast* (l. 295).

Several additions in the Old English version of the poem form the first or second member of a word pair; they are nouns or verbs or, in a few instances, adjectives: for example, Lat *mordebunt* is rendered as *ceorfað and slitað* (l. 169b), Lat *fletus* as *wop and wanung* (l. 202), and Lat *impius* as *scyldig and manful* (l. 57b). Half-line fillers supply the indirect object: for example, *þissere worulde* (l. 178), *ænegum on eorðan* (l. 188) and other complements, such as the genitive of specification: *ænigre wihte* (l. 203). The additions fill metrical and alliterative patterns, but, at the same time, add details lacking in the source: for example, *of hleorum* (l. 28), *mid lustum* (l. 70), *on mode* (l. 92), *manes* (l. 139b), *on worulde* (l. 141b), *on grunde* (l. 189), *on sceade* (l. 239), *þeostrum* (l. 254). Among the new spatial indications are *on eorðan* (l. 14b, 16b, 31b, 87b, 98b), *on heofonan rice* (l. 22b), *on gebedstowe* (l. 30b), *on grunde* (l. 189b). The addition of *on ecnesse* (l. 304b) contributes a specification of time.

An evident effort to bind the sentences of the Anglo-Saxon poem brings about the accumulation of OE conjunctions: *ac* (l. 61, 71), *and* (l. 7, 9, 18, 22, 25, 31, 36, 76, 91, 158, 167, 179, 180, 192, 206 [twice], 229, 229, 235, 235, 236, 237, 238, 247, 248, 250, 252, 269, 269, 270, 271, 275, 275, 276, 277), *oþþe* (l. 138, 139, 156, 258), *ne* (l. 221, 222, 259, 259, 261, 262, 262, 262, 263, 263, 264, 264, 265, 266, 266, 266, 267, 267, 267), and *swylce* (l. 271).[20]

6. Word pairs

Among the fillers of *JDay II*, there is a large number of word pairs, that is two nearly synonymous words linked by a conjunction (cf. Malkiel 1959). Word pairs, which are typical of all Germanic traditions,[21] are a recurrent feature of the Old English translations from Latin – and *JDay II* is no exception. Several word pairs replace a single word: OE *synna and gylta* (l. 56b) for Lat *peccata*; OE *scyldig and manful* (l. 57b) for Lat *impius*; OE *beþunga and plaster* (l. 80b) for Lat *fomenta*; OE *henða and gyltas* (l. 88b) for Lat *crimina*; OE *dreosað and hreosað* (l. 100a) for Lat *ruent*; OE *ceorfað and slitað* (l. 169b) for Lat *mordebunt*; OE *wop and wanung* (l. 202a) for Lat *fletus*; OE *(bið) breged and swenced* (l. 214b) for Lat *torquetur*. In some word pairs, or rather word-doublings, it is the first member that repeats the Latin, for example in OE *wop and wanung* (l. 202a), which translates the single *fletus*. In other instances the first member is independent from the Latin text, for example, OE *wagedon and swegdon* (l. 7b) for Lat *resonantis*, OE *bugað and myltað* (l. 101b) for Lat *liquescent*, and OE *wean and þrosme* (l. 200b) for Lat *caligine*. There are also several instances where the entire word pair is an addition by the Anglo-Saxon translator, such as *swegdon and urnon* (l. 3b), *weoxon and blowon* (l. 5b), *todæleð and todemeð* (l. 20a), *heaf and wopas* (l. 90b), *sweart and gesworcen* (l. 105a), *deorc and dimhiw (and dwolma sweart)* (l. 106), *mihte and þrymme* (l. 116b), *heortleas and earh* (l. 125b), *amasod and amarod* (l. 126a), *read and reaðe, ræsct and efesteð* (l. 153); finally Lat *salsis* [...] *guttis* (l. 17) are translated with *mid wope and sealtum dropum* (l. 35b-36a). It is remarkable how literally *earm and eadig* (l. 163) render the Latin *miser et dives* (l. 81), whereas OE *lig and cyle* (l. 206) switch the asyndetic *frigora, flammae* (l. 102).

Most of the word pairs are exclusive of *JDay II* and are to be reckoned among the peculiar features of this translation; only a few have a limited number of occurrences elsewhere, mainly in the homilies. The pair *heaf and wopas* (l. 90) occurs in the form *wop and hof* both in poetry (*Genesis* 1. 924, *Guthlac* 1. 1047) and prose (*BlHom* no. 7, p. 85, 28 and no. 11, p. 115, 15), while the phrase *in heaf ond in wop* occurs only once in the Preface to the translation of Gregory's *Dialogi*.[22]

7. Incorrect renderings and variant readings

There are a few instances where the translation is quite awkward, if not plainly wrong. The Latin line "Membra solo sternam, meritosque ciebo dolores" (*Ddi* l. 15) is translated too slavishly as "and minne lichaman lecge on eorðan / and geernade sar ealle ic gecige" (*JDay II* l. 31-32). The same is the case with *bonum cunctis Deus* [...] *ministrant* translated as "ece drihten / him ealra goda gehwylc [...] ðenað" (*JDay II* l. 272b-273), owing to a mistake or a voluntary change. Similarly – but more felicitously – *laetitiae facies* [...] *nulla* is transformed into "ansyn [...] ænigre blisse" (*JDay II* l. 225). A consecutive Latin clause, introduced by *quin*, is transformed into a final Old English clause introduced by *þæt* (*JDay II* l. 40). The translation of *insuper* with "ufenan eall ðis" (*JDay II* l. 145, 213, 272) is quite clumsy. The rendering of *inamabile* with *langan* (*JDay II* l. 13) is debatable, although the latter could possibly be emended into *laðan*; Lat *errantes* is taken to mean 'guilty' and therefore translated as *synnge* (*JDay II* l. 230).

There are instances where the Latin text was misunderstood, as if the copy on which the translation was based was in a bad condition or hastily read. Some errors seem to be the product of an oral performance of the Latin poem: "qui solet" (*Ddi* l. 24) was mistaken for *qui solus* and translated "se ana mæg" (*JDay II* l. 46); Lat *solio fulget* was read as *sol fulget* (see "sicut sol" of Mt. 13.43 and Apoc. I.16) and translated as *sigelbeorht* 'as bright as the sun' (cf. *JDay II* l. 117).[23] By the same token Lat *turmis* 'throng, swarm' was mistaken for Lat *turris* 'tower' and translated *hleo* 'defence' (*JDay II* l. 127); the meaning of Lat *scelerum* (gen. pl. 'mischiefs') was misunderstood and rendered with *synnful* 'guilty' (*JDay II* l. 154); Lat *parvo tempore* was translated with OE *frecnan tid*, owing to a misreading of *parvo* as *pavido* (*JDay II* l. 215); Lat *laetatur* was rendered with OE *bliðe* possibly because of a misreading of the verbal form as *laetus* or *laetatus* (*JDay II* l. 251); Lat *pia* was mistaken for *pura* and translated as *clæne* (*JDay II* l. 294); *benedicta* ("per benedicta regna" *Ddi* l. 149) was taken for an apposition to *Maria* and translated *gebletsodost (ealra)* (*JDay II* l. 297). The translation of "flebilis hora" (*Ddi* l. 87) is "(hwæt miht þu on þa tid) þearfe gewepan" 'cry in distress' (*JDay II* l. 177), which is possibly based on a variant reading *flebis*. However, the Old English rendering may also have originated from a misreading.

There are a number of errors which undoubtedly stem from corruptions of the text underlying the Old English translation. In line 32 of *Ddi* there occurs *apertas* 'open' which, if written *ap'tas*, could easily be taken for *aptas* 'proper' as the OE translation *ænlican* 'incomparable, unique' suggests. *Ddi* changed the Biblical phrase *linum fumigans* (Is. 42.3, a prophecy applied to Christ in Mt.

12.20) into *lini tepidos*, which the Old English translator in turn rendered with *waces *fle(a)xes* 'of soft linen'. When copying down *JDay II*, the CCCC 201 scribe unravelled the metaphor, producing a vivid though mistaken image, *waces flæsces* 'of the week flesh', which cannot be maintained because of impossible accord with *wlacan smocan* (*JDay II* l. 51). In the sentence "Ne mæg þær æni man bearnum gewyrhtum" (*JDay II* l. 170) *bearnum* is clearly an error for *be agnum (gewyrhtum)* (= Lat *meritis*). Lat *flentibus* is rendered with OE *wera* (*JDay II* l. 222), but in the original Old English version there probably was *wependra*. The original translation of Lat *signa minantia mortem* was "deaðbeacnigende tacn", and the last word, omitted in CCCC 201, has been restored by the editors (*JDay II* l. 112). The manuscript's *fule stowa* has been emended by some of the editors to "fulle stowa" (*JDay II* l. 189) on the basis of the Latin text which has *loca plena ignibus*, and that might indeed be the original reading.

The Old English poem reproduces the variant readings of a manuscript or a group of manuscripts of the English Benedictine Reform: "quassatos animos" (*Ddi* l. 25, instead of *calamos*) is rendered with "wanhydige mod" (*JDay II* l. 50), with substitution of the plural with a singular (as it happens throughout the poem); Lat *dabat* (instead of the future *dabit*) is translated with *gesceop*, a preterite (*JDay II* l. 53); Lat *mercedem (reddere)* (instead of *rationem reddere*): *deman* (*JDay II* l. 95); Lat *timidus* (instead of *tumidus*): *afæred* (*JDay II* l. 163); Lat *virorum* (instead of *vivorum*): *manna* (*JDay II* l. 186); Lat *durus* (instead of *dirus*): *stearcheard* (*JDay II* l. 201); Lat *felix o nimium* (instead of *felix omnium*): *ofersælig* (*JDay II* l. 247); Lat *laetatus* (instead of *laetatur*): *bliðe* (*JDay II* l. 251); Lat *fulmina* (instead of *flumina*): *liget* (*JDay II* l. 263); Lat *regnant* (instead of *regnum*): *ricxað* (*JDay II* l. 268); finally, *þæt analyfed is nu* (*JDay II* l. 243) is not the translation of *illicitat* ('allures' of line 121) but of the adjective *illicita* 'forbidden' which occurs in some manuscripts of the *Ddi*. As to the variant readings *turma / turba* of *Ddi* l. 86, the translation *heap* (*JDay II* l. 175) suggests that the manuscript which was used by the transaltor had *turma* (as in l. 283; but at l. 288, *heap* renders 'triumphis'). The pret.ind. *beseah* (*JDay II* l. 242) might well translate the two attested variants *merget* and *mergit*. Moreover, the translation of lines 86-87 fits perfectly the reading *vindice iudice* of line 44 of the *Ddi*, as attested by CCCC 139, where this variant reading is written in the left margin of the folio.

Finally, lines 121-123 of the Latin poem need a reshuffling: although it is not witnessed by any manuscript, the original order must have consisted of lines 123-121-122, as it was reproduced as such by the Old English poem.

8. The grammatical treatment of the original

A series of changes and additions were made necessary by the differences in the morphology of Latin and Old English, such as the introduction of the OE prepositions *be* (l. 122, 170), *for* (l. 34, 195, 196), *mid* (l. 29, 49, 58, 61, 75, 78, 79, 161, 180, 214),[24] *on* + dat. (l. 6, 31, 179, 217, 230), *þurh* (l. 8), *wið* + acc. (l. 224). The Old English text is marked by the presence of demonstrative pronouns used as articles: *se* nom. sg. m. (l. 53, 86, 102, 123, 155, 192, 192, 240, 260), *seo* nom. sg. f. (l. 56, 108, 137, 138, 294), *þæt* nom. sg. n. (l. 92, 166, 213), *þæt* acc. sg. n. (l. 17, 76, 245), *þone* acc. sg. m. (l. 15, 51, 116), *þa* acc. sg. f. (l. 13), *þæs* gen. sg. m. (l. 14, 180, 195, 255, 297), *þam* dat. sg. m. (l. 44, 74, 282, 303), *þære* dat. sg. f. (l. 136, 299), *þa* nom. pl. (l. 7, 99, 196, 209, 245, 287), *þa* acc. pl. (l. 63, 167, 224, 296), *þara* gen. pl. (l. 22, 93, 204, 222), *þæra* gen. pl. (l. 283, 290), and *þas* acc. sg. f. (l. 215).

Several additions stem from the effort to clarify the Latin text by repeatedly specifying the subject. Hence the recurrent Old English pronouns: *ic* (l. 1, 10, 24, 25, 26, 32, 33, 65, 75), *þu* (l. 66, 66, 67, 68, 78, 80, 82, 123, 176, 177, 178, 181), *he* (l. 45, 59, 61, 157), *hit* (l. 40, 217), *se* (l. 247), *we* (l. 119), and noun phrases: "þæt man lange hæl" (l. 144), "His sunu bliðe, sigores brytta" (l. 279). The main verb is provided in many occasions: *bið* (l. 226, 228, 247, 259, 263, 266), *is* (l. 92), *nis* (l. 261), *sy* (l. 157), *synt* (l. 191), as well as *wyle* (l. 52), *byrnað and yrnað* (l. 231), *gedwineð* (l. 234), *hleapað* (l. 235), *gewiteð* (l. 236, 237), *scyndan* (l. 239), *flyhð* (l. 240), *gelimpeð* (l. 257), *hwyrfð* (l. 290). In some instances both OE subject and verb are added: *heo let* (l. 296), *ic ondræde me* (l. 15, 17), *ic gemunde* (l. 21). Sometimes the addition concerns the direct object: *eow* (l. 26), *wiht* (l. 34), *hy* (l. 211), and the indirect object *drihtene* (l. 59), *þe* (l. 65, 178), *anra gehwam* (l. 280). The proliferation of possessive adjectives is meant to identify the person referred to: *min* (l. 9, 16, 30, 31), *his* (l. 20, 49, 60, 62, 252), *heora* (l. 160, 168, 212), the same can be said of *agen* (l. 170), and *sylf* (l. 18, 122, 182).

As far as the verbs are concerned, the translator had to face abrupt changes of both person (from the first to the third) and tense (from the past tense to the present and future), which, however, were all successfully coped with. There are several differences which stem from the different verbal system of the two languages.[25] Usually, the Latin future is rendered with the OE present; Latin simple future passive is translated with the present of *beon* + pass. part.: for example, *cogentur adesse*: *bið aboden* (*JDay II* l. 129); *implebitur*: *beoð gefylde* (*JDay II* l. 209); *videbitur*: *bið gemet* (*JDay II* l. 225). The future passive, such as in *homines cogentur (adesse)* is rendered with *Adames cnosl (bið) aboden* (*JDay*

II 1. 128-129), and the subj. passive *reddantur luci* with *sy abæred* (*JDay II* 1. 40-41).

Also, the future perfect of Lat *venerit* is rendered with the OE present, *demeð* (*JDay II* 1. 71). Latin future is also translated with a periphrasis employing modal verbs: *praestabit*: *mæge fremman* (*JDay II* 1. 224); *effugiet*: *mæg forbugon* (*JDay II* 1. 250); *tenebit*: *mot habban* (*JDay II* 1. 252-253). Modal verbs are also used in periphrasis with decorative function: pres. ind. *confidit* is translated with *mæg gedyrstig wesan* (*JDay II* 1. 170-171); pres. ind. *valet* with *mæg beon* (*JDay II* 1. 187); *flebis* with *miht gewepan* (*JDay II* 1. 177). Latin pres. ind. is rendered with *wile* + inf.: *vindicat*: *wrecan wile* (*JDay II* 1. 89), and when passive, it is once translated with *mæg* + inf., *censetur*: *mæg beon* (*JDay II* 1. 301). The OE verb *sceal*, as elsewhere, expresses both future and obligation (*JDay II* 1. 72). Once, the Latin pres. subj. *valeat* is translated with an OE pres. ind. *forstent* (*JDay II* 1. 55).

Active forms are translated as passive ones: for example, the Latin future *patebunt* is rendered with *beoð gesweotolude* (*JDay II* 1. 135), and *timebunt* with *beoð afæred* (*JDay II* 1. 163). The same happens with the impersonal future *licebit scire*: *bið alyfed* (*JDay II* 1. 143-144), the pres. ind. *diffundit*: *bið gefylled* (*JDay II* 1. 151), and the past perfect subj. *meruisset (poenas)*: *wurde cwylmed* (*JDay II* 1. 217). Vice versa, once, the perfect pass. *fuerunt parata* is changed into active pret. *drihten geteode* (*JDay II* 1. 183).

The rendering of Latin participial phrases with an OE clause is a common practice in the translations from classical languages. In *JDay II*, pres. participles are replaced by finite verbs and verb phrases: *ramis resonantis* with *þa wudubeamas swegdon* (*JDay II* 1. 7); *commemorans* with *(ic) gemunde* (*JDay II* 1. 12); *memorans* with *ic gemunde* (*JDay II* 1. 24); *sedens* with *swegles brytta sitt* (*JDay II* 1. 117); *oculos* [...] *flentes* with *eagan wepað* (*JDay II* 1. 194); *stridentes* [...] *dentes* with *teþ* [...] *gryrrað* (*JDay II* 1. 196); *tradens* with *his sunu* [...] *sylð* (*JDay II* 1. 279-280); *splendentia* with *þær* [...] *scinað* (*JDay II* 1. 289).[26] In a few instances, the pres. part. is translated with an adjective *calentes*: *hate* (*JDay II* 1. 28), *praesens*: *gehende* (*JDay II* 1. 171), *horrens*: *angryslic* (*JDay II* 1. 226), *praesens*: *andweard* (*JDay II* 1. 274). Vice versa, *sub murmure* become *murcnigende* (*JDay II* 1. 25), *salubre*: *halwende* (*JDay II* 1. 84), *vindex*: *wrecenda* (*JDay II* 1. 155), and *noxia*: *deriende* (*JDay II* 1. 232). Passive participles are replaced by sentences with finite and infinite verbs: for example, *turbatus* is rendered with "and min earme mod eal wæs gedrefed" (*JDay II* 1. 9); *discretis* with *frea* [...] *todæleð* (*JDay II* 1. 19-20); *stipata* with *stillað* [...] *werod* (*JDay II* 1. 114-115); *comitata* [...] *agmina* with *werod ymtrymmað* (*JDay II* 1. 128); *ablutus* with *he* [...] *sy* [...] *afeormod* (*JDay II* 1. 157); *coniunctus Christo* with *his þeodne geþeon* (*JDay II* 1. 252); *iunctos* with *hy beoð geþeode*

(*JDay II* l. 284). Vice versa, once, *mixta* is translated with *gemenged* (*JDay II* l. 191). The gerundive *metuendus* is correctly rendered with the adjective *egeslic* (*JDay II* l. 94), and the gerund *flendi* with an OE noun, *wop* (*JDay II* l. 83).

Lat *suadeo* + subj. is rendered with a *þæt* clause with subj.: *suadeo praevenias*: *Ic lære þæt þu beo* [...] *forfoh* (*JDay II* l. 75-76), *rogo* + imp. is rendered with a *þæt* clause with subj. *rogo* [...] *aperite*: *bidde þæt* [...] *ontynan* (l. 26-27); *precor* + imp. is translated with a *þæt* clause with either subj. or ind.: *precor* [...] *non parcite*: *Ic bidde* [...] *þæt* [...] *ne wandian* (*JDay II* l. 33-34) *dreccað* (*JDay II* l. 35) *ofergeotaþ* (*JDay II* l. 36) *geopeniað* (*JDay II* l. 37); *sis memor*: *Ic bidde* [...] *þæt þu gemune* (*JDay II* l. 123). Several infinitive constructions are translated as finite *þæt* clauses: *est* [...] *salus* [...] *reserare*: *is* [...] *hæl* [...] *he* [...] *gecyðe* (*JDay II* l. 43-45); *tardas* [...] *pandere*: *latast* [...] *þæt* [...] (*JDay II* l. 66); *pænituisse iuvat tibi* [...] *flere salubre est*: *is halwende þæt man* [...] *wepe* (*JDay II* l. 84); *and dædbote do* (*JDay II* l. 85); *verebar scire*: *þæt* [...] *sceamode* [...] *þæt he* [...] *ypte* (*JDay II* l. 141-142); on the other hand, *gaudes servire* is rendered with a couple of correlated sentences *þu þeowast* [...] *and* [...] *leofast* (*JDay II* l. 178-179).

The constant switch of personal and impersonal in the Latin poem is not always reproduced in the Old English. Impersonal phrases are translated as personal: *nec lateat quicquam*: *owiht* [...] *ne belife* (*JDay II* l. 38); *fletibus assiduis*: *þu scealt greotan* (*JDay II* l. 82-83); *liceat*: *þu mote* (*JDay II* l. 303). On the other hand, personal utterances are rendered as impersonal in at least three occasions: *pænituisse iuvat tibi*: *is halwende þæt man* [...] (*JDay II* l. 84); *sis memor*: *Ic bidde, man, þæt þu* [...] (*JDay II* l. 123); *quod* [...] *aliquem* [...] *scire verebar*: *eal þæt* [...] *sceamode* [...] *þæt he* [...] *ypte* (*JDay II* l. 142). In two occasions, the subject changes: the Lat passive *miseri* [...] *volvuntur* is rendered with *þis atul gewrixl earmsceapene men* [...] *wendað* (*JDay II* l. 197-198), and Lat *fetor* [...] *complet* [...] *nares* with a longer clause *hy mid nosan ne magon naht geswæccan* (*JDay II* l. 207).

Genitive constructions are recurrent in Old English translations. *JDay II* is no exception to this and introduces several instances of noun + gen. partitive (pl. or sg.): *genus humanum*: *manna cynn* (*JDay II* l. 19); *spes certa*: *selest hihta* (*JDay II* l. 44); *lacrimis* [...] *profusis*: *teara gyte* (*JDay II* l. 79); *Deus aetherius*: *heofenes god* (*JDay II* l. 88); *coetibus angelicis*: *engla werod* (*JDay II* l. 115); *cælestibus* [...] *turmis*: *of swegles hleo* (*JDay II* l. 127); *angelica* [...] *agmina*: *engla werod* (*JDay II* l. 128); *cunctorum* [...] *virorum*: *manna gehwylces* (*JDay II* l. 186); *picea caligine*: *pices* [...] *þrosme* (*JDay II* l. 200); *fetor praeingenti*: *unstences ormætnesse* (*JDay II* l. 208); *angelicas* [...] *turmas*: *engla werode* (*JDay II* l. 282); *sanctas* [...] *cohortes*: *haligra heapum* (*JDay II* l. 283); *roseis* [...] *triumphis*: *rosena* [...] *heapas* (*JDay II* l. 288); *candida* [...] *agmina*: *þæra hwittra* [...] *mædenheap* (*JDay II* l. 290); *aetherium* [...] *senatum*: *rædwitan rodera* (*JDay II* l. 300). In one instance, the first noun is in the instrumental case: *celsithronus* [...] *iudex*: *heahþrymme cyningc* (*JDay II* l. 95). All in all, the partitive genitives proliferate: *synfulra gehwam* (*JDay II* l. 18, for *reis*), *on heofonan rice* (*JDay II* l. 22), *anra gehwylcum* (*JDay II* l. 96), *goda gehwylc* (*JDay II* l. 273), *anra gehwam* (*JDay II* l. 280); *populi* is translated as *folca unrim* (*JDay II* l. 159).

Adj. + subst. is thrice translated with a compound: *florigeras* [...] *herbas* is rendered with *wynnwyrta* (*JDay II* l. 5); *solio* [...] *alto*: *heahsetle* (*JDay II* l. 118); *cælestia regna*: *heofonrice* (*JDay II* l. 253). Partitive genitives are also translated with a compound: *cordis in antro*: *on heortscræfe* (*JDay II* l. 39), or with a word pair: *spes* [...] *quietis*: *ne hopa ne swige* (*JDay II* l. 221); *poenarum* [...] *clades*: *cwyldas and witu* (*JDay II* l. 249b-250a); *solo* [...] *fidei sermone*: *mid lyt wordum ac geleaffullum* (*JDay II* l. 61); and *scelerum* [...] *piaclis*: *leahtrum* [...] *mid synnum* (*JDay II* l. 77b-78a).

The change of Lat pl. nouns or adjectives into the OE sg. has a stylistic function and it deliberately aims at avoiding abstract images. Such a shift occurs so often as to become one of the most relevant features of the entire translation.[27] The abstract images are transformed into simpler terms, *allisos* is rendered with *aglidene mod* (*JDay II* l. 47); *Titan*: *sunne* (*JDay II* l. 108); *in ortu*: *on morgen* (*JDay II* l. 108); *arcana*: *digle geþancas* (*JDay II* l. 136); *ultricibus*: *ættrenum* (*JDay II* . 146); *ditione*: *lage* (*JDay II* l. 164); *loca* [...] *gehennae*: *on helle* (*JDay II* l. 190); *frigora*: *gicela* (*JDay II* l. 192); *ferventibus* [...] *flammis*: *þrosma lig* (*JDay II* l. 192); *dolor*: *sari mod* (*JDay II* l. 227); *delectatio carnis* [...] *cæca scelerum mergit vertigine mentem*: *þæt werige mod wendað þa gyltas* (*JDay II* l. 245); *virgineo flore*: *blostmum (behagen)* (*JDay II* l. 291);[28] *senatum*: *rædwitan* 'counsellors' (*JDay II* l. 300).

A series of passages which might be hard to grasp, are either clarified, such as *qui* translated with *se sceaþa* (*JDay II* l. 57); or implemented, as *gessit* rendered with *manes gefremede* (*JDay II* l. 139); or simplified as *Iudiciique diem* translated as *dom* (*JDay II* l. 15); *usque crucem*: *on rode* (*JDay II* l. 57); *iudex* [...] *venerit*: *demeð god* (*JDay II* l. 71); and *mortis in articulo*: *deaðe gehende* (*JDay II* l. 59). Further simplifications include *sceleratis* [...] *actis*: *undædum* (*JDay II* l. 58), *verba precantia*: *bena* (*JDay II* l. 60), and *est* [...] *data gratia flendi*: *tima sy* (*JDay II* l. 83). The references to the final Judgement are carefully reworked into a coherent description: *mercedem reddere* becomes *deman* (*JDay II* l. 95), *gestus*: *dæd* (*JDay II* l. 122), and *tribunal*: *domsetl drihtnes* (*JDay II* l. 124).[29]

Another process of simplification, which is perhaps intended to provide more clarity, is that by which the Latin verbs *censeri* (*Ddi* l. 301), *manere* (*Ddi* l.

93), *praestare* (*Ddi* l. 223), *stare* (*Ddi* l. 162), and *valere* (*Ddi* l. 55, 187) are rendered with OE *beon*. Similarly, OE *ænlic* renders a series of Latin words with a wide range of meanings: *fecundus* (l. 6), *aptus* (for *apertus*) (l. 63), *almus* (l. 292); in l. 282 it is also referred to the angels' throngs; *eall* renders both *omnis* (l. 143) and *cunctis* (l. 135 [twice], 273, 274), *synn* translates *scelus* (l. 12), *peccatum* (l. 56, 79), and *piaclum* (l. 78). The same words are repeated over and over, such as *afæran* (*JDay II* l. 126 and 163, in both cases as a free rendering), *feormian* (*JDay II* l. 78) and *afeormian* (*JDay II* l. 157), *ansyn* (*JDay II* l. 120 – a variation –, 204, 225), *astyrian* (*JDay II* l. 114, 180), *atol* (*JDay II* l. 198, 218), *laðlic* (*JDay II* l. 206, 210, 260, 263), and *dæd* and its compounds (*JDay II* l. 16, 58, 93, 96, 122).

9. The vocabulary of *JDay II*

The Old English poem contains a large number of *hapax legomena*: *abæran* (l. 41), *amarian* (l. 126), *beweorþian* (l. 118), *braslian* (l. 152), *brynig* (l. 212), *dægcuð* (l. 40), *deaðbeacnigende* (l. 112), *dimhiw* (l. 106), *drut* (l. 292), *eahgemearc* (l. 149), *eoredheap* (l. 113), *flecgan* (l. 110, if not emended into *fleogan*), *frowe* (l. 293), *geþuxian* (l. 105), *gryrran* (l. 196), *heofonsetl* (l. 278), *heortleas* (l. 125), *heortscræf* (l. 39), *mædenheap* (l. 290), *ofersælig* (l. 247), *scad* (l. 73), *stearcheard* (l. 201), *stiþmægen* (l. 114), *synscyldig* (l. 169), *uncræftig* (l. 240), *unstenc* (l. 208), *wæterburne* (l. 3), *wynwyrt* (l. 5).[30] The verb *geswæccan* (l. 207) is employed in the transitive form (for the intransitive use of this verb, see *Vitellius, Royal*, and *Arundel Psalter*, Pss. 113.14 and *ÆGram*, p. 221, 5).

A few lexemes of the poem belong to the poetic lexicon, where they have a limited number of occurrences, such as *behlænan* (l. 115 and *Seasons* l. 112, *Jul* l. 577, and *Christ* l. 870), *breostgehygd* (l. 60, 173 and *Gen* l. 1289, 2318, *And* l. 997, *Christ* l. 262, *Prec* l. 22, and *Beo* l. 2819), *hagulscur* (l. 265 and *Men* l. 35, *And* l. 1257), *heahþrym* (l. 95 and *Guth* l. 1324), and *sigelbeorht* (l. 117 and *Men* l. 89, 203). In many instances, these lexical choices betray the effort to create *ad hoc* compounds, capable to render the Latin counterpart, such as *heortscræf* 'hearth' (literally 'cave of the hearth', *JDay II* l. 39) translating the Latin *cordis in antro* (l. 19). Some compounds, though based on traditional models, are the Anglo-Saxon translator's own coinage: for example, *wæterburne* is modelled on other *wæter*-compounds such as *wæterædre* 'source' or *wætergefeall* 'waterfall'.

However, the contrary is much more frequently true, that is, the Old English poem employs words which otherwise occur prevalently or exclusively in prose. There are several words in *JDay II* which are never used elsewhere in poetry.[31] Some of them have only a limited number of occurrences in the Old English corpus,[32] such as *æmelnes, -nys* (l. 229, 261), *ærdæd* (l. 93, 96), *afeormian* (l. 157), *amasian* (l. 126, the word also occurs once in a gloss to Canticle 5, 16, in the same MS of the *Lambeth Psalter*), *beþung* (l. 80), *brysan* (l. 49, the only other occurrence in a gloss to the *Liber scintillarum* 20, 20), *cwelre* (l. 204), *emnes* (l. 151), *fæsthafolnes* (l. 237), *fleax* (l. 51), *foresteal* (l. 147), *gebrasl* (l. 260 and *VercHom* no. 21, p. 359, 191), *gedwæscan* (l. 52), *gedwinan* (l. 232, 234), *gehæge* (l. 4), *gehreran* (l. 8), *gemang* (preposition, l. 282, 303), *gesyman* (l. 58), *gewepan* (l. 177), *gicel* (l. 192), *gnagan* (l. 212), *ligspiwel* (l. 210 and a gloss to Prudentius I, 207), *mihtleas* (l. 126), *murcnian* (l. 25), *ofergeotan* (l. 36), *ormætnes* (l. 208), *plaster* (l. 80), *rædwita* (l. 300 and a gloss to a Calendar Prognostic for New Year's Day, p. 297, 31), *ræscettan* (l. 153, 166), *sargung* (l. 246 and a gloss to the *Liber scintillarum* 6, 27), *slincan* (l. 241), *smoca* (l. 51), *stedeleas* (l. 107), *todeman* (l. 20 and a gloss to the *Lambeth Psalter*, Pss. 81.1), *towearde* (adverb, l. 134), *tuxl* (l. 212), *þrece* (l. 192 and a gloss to *Lambeth Psalter*, Pss. 118.28), *þunerrad* (l. 264), *ufenan / ufenon* (preposition, l. 145, 213, 272), *unbleoh* (l. 304 and in the prose part of the *Paris Psalter* 15.6), *undæd* (l. 58), *ungeryde* (l. 102 and in the *Visio Leofrici* 45), *unhyrlic* (l. 11 and *Alexander's Letter to Aristotle* 30), *wlacu* (l. 51), and *wylspring* (l. 27). The Middle English continuations of *sluma* (which occurs only at l. 241 and in *Guth* l. 243) make its classification as a poetic word highly improbable.

In *JDay II*, there occur prose words with a larger diffusion in Old English, such as *æmtig* (l. 149), *astifian* (l. 174), *biterlice* (l. 167), *cweartern* (l. 217), *dædbot* (l. 85), *færlic* (l. 259), *fefer* (l. 259), *fers* (l. 11), *gælnes* (l. 179), *geclypian* (l. 138), *gehende* (l. 59, 171), *geþwærnes* (l. 271), *gyte* (l. 79), *lagu* (l. 164), *oga* (l. 172), *pic* (l. 200), *scearplic* (l. 53), *sticel* (l. 180), *swegan* (l. 3, 7), *unalyfed* (l. 243), *underfon* (l. 121), *wanung* (l. 202), and *ymtrymman* (l. 128).[33]

This striking presence of many prose words may be due to the fact that *JDay II* is much younger than most of the surviving Old English poetry (which is, however, often preserved in late manuscripts).[34] In the literary production of the late Anglo-Saxon period the distinction between prose and poetry is blurred as far as content and style, as well as language are concerned. The use in poetry of words typical of prose is one of the features of late poems,[35] but, even so, in its high number of prose words *JDay II* is exceptional and may be compared only to *An Exhortation to Christian Living*.

Much poetry of the late tenth and early eleventh century draws on Latin and vernacular sources. In fact, another version of *JDay II* is represented by a section of a homily in Oxford, Bodleian Library, Hatton 113, ff. 66-73.[36] The manuscript contains twenty-seven homilies in Latin and Old English. The homily in question is generally known as Napier no. 29. It is an anonymous piece on Judgement Day and includes a passage overlapping with lines 92-285 of *JDay II* (the section based on the poem begins in line 10 of fol. 68^r, with no indication of source). Napier no. 29 does not provide a parallel for several words and short phrases of the poem, and lines 166-175, 213-218, 232-243 and 271b-284 of *JDay II* have no counterpart in the homily. The presence in Napier no. 29 of such an overlap with *JDay II* may be compared to the overlap between *Exhort* and two anonymous homilies, namely *VercHom* no. 21 and Napier no. 20 (Whitbread 1963: 347-364). Napier no. 29 provides evidence that there was either a prose version of *Ddi* in circulation or that a vernacular prose version and the extant verse version, namely *JDay II*, were a double product, the prose having precedence (Stanley 1971: 389-390). Since the extant prose version is less extensive than the poem it is likely that the compiler of the homily used only part of the prose text that underlies or went with *JDay II*.[37] The copy of this original prose version used by the homilist was less corrupted than that used by the author of *JDay II*, and in some instances Napier no. 29 may indeed be used to emend *JDay II*. According to Eric Stanley an Old English prose translation *Ddi* pre-dates the poetic one[38] and both extant vernacular works (that is *JDay II* and Napier no. 29) had a lost prose version in Old English as their source. However, as Roberta Frank (1994: 106) warily remarks, the question of priority between the poem and the homily is still unanswered.

Dialectal difference may have played a role in the word choices of the poem, because *JDay II* was probably first composed in West Saxon (Menner 1947: 583-597; Wenisch 1979: 328). Therefore, it did not undergo the process of adaptation from Anglian which characterizes almost the entire Old English poetic corpus. The content of the poem should also be taken into account, because words such as *plaster* 'plaster' (l. 80), *fleax* 'flax' (l. 51) or *fers* 'verse' (l. 11), which have no counterpart in Old English poetry, were introduced to translate the words of the Latin poem verbatim.

Finally, the vocabulary of *JDay II* is characterized by idiosyncratic choices, for example, a penchant for adjectives with the *-ig* suffix,[39] such as *ælmihtig* (l. 69, 287), *æmtig* (l. 149), *ænig* (l. 170), *brynig* (l. 212), *dreorig* (l. 35), *eadig* (l. 163, 305), *gedyrstig* (l. 171), *gesælig* (l. 247, 248), *halig* (l. 22, 283, 285), *mihtig* (l. 19), *ofersælig* (l. 247), *sarig* (l. 227), *scyldig* (l. 57, 239), *synnig* (l. 67, 160, 230), *synscyldig* (l. 169), *uncræftig* (l. 240), *wanhydig* (l. 50), *weleg* (l. 164), and *werig* (l. 245).[40]

10. The features of the translation

A comparison between *De die iudicii* and *Judgement Day II* can shed light on the techniques of translation in Anglo-Saxon England, but, at the same time, it reveals the translator's idiosyncrasies and his personal interpretation of the Latin poem.

There are lines where the translation is deliberately literal and almost overlaps with the Latin original. One can compare *Ddi* l. 39 and *JDay II* lines 77-78a, as well as l. 40 and lines 78b-79; l. 41 and 80-81a; l. 50 and 97; l. 61 and 121-122b; l. 89 and 180: l. 92 and 185-186a; l. 97 and 196; l. 126 and 251. But even in the lines where the translation is apparently closer, the Latin and the Old English version are hardly ever identical.

Remarkable is the balanced and regular translation of some lines, such as l. 100 of *Ddi* = l. 201-202a of *JDay II*; l. 109 = l. 219-220a, which is particularly felicitous; l. 113 = 225; l. 116 = l. 230-231a; l. 117 = l. 232-232a; l. 120 = l. 240-241a; l. 127 = l. 252-253a; l. 128 = l. 254-255; l. 138 = l. 272-273; l. 139 = l. 274-275. There are examples of quite mechanic translations at short distance: *JDay II*, lines 136, 137, 138, 140, 142, and 144 (each with a b-line filler). From line 290 onwards the translation is very free.

At times the Old English translation is independent from the Latin source: l. 63 of *Ddi* = l. 125-126 of *JDay II*, l. 67 = 131-134, l. 73 = 147-148, l. 76 = 154. The same can be said of l. 190 of the *JDay II* (replacing *gehennae* of the original), l. 216 (translating *sibimet*), l. 218 (rendering *perpetuas* [...] *poenas*), l. 244 is very felicitous in Old English, but independent of the original. Entirely free but effective is the translation of l. 55 (= l. 109-110), but so different to allow the supposition that it might have been drawn from a different source. Totally autonomous but felicitous is the translation of *solo* [...] *fidei sermone* with *mid lyt wordum ac geleafullum* (l. 61). Quite successful is the translation of *bis* with *ofer ænne siþ* (l. 89), of *minantia mortem* with *deaðbeacnigende* (l. 112), and of *potestas* with *stiþmægen* (l. 114).

A few simple sentences of *Ddi* receive an over-elaborate translation, for example, l. 66 (= l. 129). The same is true with lines 107-108 (= l. 215-218). In some instances one word of the source is translated with an entire line of Old English: one Latin adjective, *apostolicus* (*Inter apostolicas animis laetantibus arces Ddi* l. 145) is expanded into a whole Old English line, *þær þa ærendracan synd ælmihtiges godes* (*JDay II* l. 287). Also *turbatus* (l. 9), and *genitrix* (l. 293) are expanded into an entire clause; the same happens with *sis memor* [...] *pavor* (l. 123); *tortorum* is rendered with *þara cwelra þe cwylmað ða earman* (*JDay II* l. 204), and *illicita* with *þæt unalyfed is nu* (*JDay II* l. 243).

The translation is at times redundant: details and specifications are added by means of different strategies: *sub tegmine* is translated as *mid helme bepeht* (*JDay II* l. 2), *ramis*: *wudubeamas* (*JDay II* l. 7); *mortis* [...] *tempus*: *tid þæs dimman cyme deaðes* (*JDay II* l. 13-14); *signum*: *forebeacn* (*JDay II* l. 97); *medelae*: *lifes lǣcedomes* (*JDay II* l. 81); *memento*: *gemyne* [...] *on mode* (*JDay II* l. 92); *montes*: *beorga hliðu* (*JDay II* l. 101); *mentes*: *manna mod* (*JDay II* l. 103); *caelum*: *upheofon* (*JDay II* l. 104); *manus*: *mannes hand* (*JDay II* l. 139); *scelerum*: *synscyldigra* (*JDay II* l. 169); *dentes*: *teþ* [...] *manna* (*JDay II* l. 196); *flentibus*: *wependra worn* (*JDay II* l. 222); *stridor*: *gristbitung* (l. 227); *flammae*: *liges gebrasl* (*JDay II* l. 259); *mors*: *deaðes gryre* (*JDay II* l. 266, rhyming with *lyre*, "ne lyre ne deaðes gryre"); *altithrona*: *heofonsetle hean* (*JDay II* l. 278). Similarly, *ulli* is translated with *ænigum men* (l. 89); *aliquem*: *ænigum men* (*JDay II* l. 142); and *nullus*: *æni man* (*JDay II* l. 170). Some adjectives used as nouns are replaced by OE adj. + subst.: *miseros* is rendered by *earman saula* (*JDay II* l. 167); *miseri*: *earmsceapene men* (*JDay II* l. 197); *malignis*: *awyrgendum gastum* (*JDay II* l. 184). Both for metrical reasons and the natural tendency of Old English poetry to slow down the pace of narration, *cecini* is translated with *onhefde mid sange* (*JDay II* l. 11); *precor*: *ic bidde* [...] *benum* (*JDay II* l. 33); *sanare*: *gode gehǣlan* (*JDay II* l. 47); *solvere*: *recen onbindan* (*JDay II* l. 48); *reddere rationem*: *gyldan scad wordum* (*JDay II* l. 73); *penituisse*: *dǣdbote do* (*JDay II* l. 85); *praecurrunt*: *feran onginnað* (*JDay II* l. 97); *gessit*: *manes gefremede* (*JDay II* l. 139); *stupet*: *stǣnt astifad* (*JDay II* l. 174); *gaudes*: *glǣd leofast* (*JDay II* l. 179); *edicere*: *spellum areccan* (*JDay II* l. 187); *gaudere*: *brucan bliðnesse* (*JDay II* l. 306).

There is a recherché use of parallelism, e.g. between the two fillers *for ǣrdǣdum* (*JDay II* l. 93) and *be ǣrdǣdum* (*JDay II* l. 96).[41] The translation introduces a parallel between the anguish of the nature, *wolcn wǣs gehrered* (*JDay II* l. 8) and the state of mind of the guilty man, *mod* [...] *wǣs gedrefed* (*JDay II* l. 9), with a repetition in l. 25: "mode gedrefed". With an envelope pattern, *winda gryre* (*JDay II* l. 8a) is echoed by *deaðes gryre* (*JDay II* l. 266, where *gryre* is unparalleled in the Latin text). A number of parallels may stem from lack of ingenuity, and the recourse to stereotyped phrases, which are common late Old English poetry, brings along the homologation of unrelated Latin phrases, such as *eall engla werod* (*JDay II* l. 115a and 128a) translating both *coetibus angelicis* and *angelica* [...] *agmina* respectively. The same happens with *hu micel is þæt wite* (*JDay II* l. 92), translating *quanta* [...] *tormenta*, and *hu micel bið se broga* (*JDay II* l. 123), translating *pavor*, as well as with *ne bið þǣr ansyn* (*JDay II* l. 203 and 225) translating both *non* [...] *facies ibi cernitur ulla* and *facies* [...] *nulla videbitur illic*.

The poem makes consistent use of a number of different stylistic figures such as plain repetition, which has an unquestionable structural function.[42] There are six cases of *figura etymologica*, *mearn / murcnigende* (*JDay II* l. 24-25), *tima / tid* (*JDay II* l. 83), *geþancas / geþohte* (*JDay II* l. 136-137), *leohtes / leoht* (*JDay II* l. 219), *lof / leoflic* (*JDay II* l. 271), *unalyfed / leofest* (*JDay II* l. 244-245), and six of paronomasia: *rican / riht* (*JDay II* l. 74), *sweart / gesworcen* (*JDay II* l. 105), *amasod / amarod* (*JDay II* l. 126), *mannes / manes* (*JDay II* l. 139), *leofest / life* (*JDay II* l. 244), *lof / lif / leoflic* (*JDay II* l. 271). They are all quite effective.

Echoic repetition is a stylistic feature of Old English poetry, but the repetition of the same words and phrases, to the detriment of variation, such as occurs in *JDay II*, is typical of the late poetic compositions.[43] There is a core of words that recur repeatedly, such as the adjectives *eall*, *ece*, and *earm*.[44] Greenfield (1966: 149-151) has remarked that *eall* is a key word in the second half of the *Wanderer*, lending "its collective semantic weight to the observations reported". When compared to the remaining corpus of Old English poetry, *JDay II* is characterized by repetitions of all sorts[45] while it avoids both variation and synonymy. A remarkable exception is represented by the epithets for God and Christ, which present a number of variations. *Christus* is translated by *drihten* (l. 37), *nerigend* (l. 64), *þeoden* (l. 252), and, when unparalleled in the Latin version, he is referred to as *waldend Crist* (l. 52), *Crist* (l. 54), as well as two widespread epithets, *swegles brytta* (l. 117) and *sigores brytta* (l. 279); *se godes sunu* (l. 86) is also used. *Deus* is translated by *drihten* (l. 272), and *god* (l. 88, 292). *Drihten* (l. 21, 59, 85, 122, 124, 183) is also used independently of the Latin, as well as *fæder* (l. 275), *frea* (l. 19, 74), *lifes frea* (l. 81), *god* (l. 287), *scyppend god* (l. 73), *wealdend engla* (l. 50), and the traditional epithet *heofonrices weard* (l. 70).

Apart from the restrictions imposed by the faithfulness to the original, *JDay II* has a place within the tradition of Old English poetry. It shares its incipit, *hwæt*, with several other Old English poems such as *Beowulf*, *Exodus*, *Andreas*, and the *Dream of the Rood*. There are a few concessions to widespread poetic clichés, such as *eorðan ymbhwyrft* (l. 72) translating *orbis*; *homines* is translated by *Adames cnosl eorðbuendra* (l. 130); and *pectus: breostgehygd* (l. 60, 173). Finally, the phrase *wanhydige mod* (l. 50) also occurs in *The Wanderer* (l. 67).

11. *JDay II* and the Old English prose versions

The technique of translating from Latin into the vernacular which was in use in Anglo-Saxon England – if there ever was one which was somehow codified and generalized –, has never been examined in detail.[46] Yet, a number of studies have been devoted to single works or authors.[47] Although it is common knowledge that bilingualism, such as that existing in Anglo-Saxon England, fosters the practice of translation, the number of translations from Latin poetry into Old English is small, and in general, the works which were translated were not so much by Classical or late antique poets, as by Insular writers,[48] such as riddles nos. XXXIII (*De lorica*)[49] and C (*De creatura*) by Aldhelm.[50] The first part of the *Phoenix*[51] (up to l. 296) is translated from the *De ave phoenice*, once attributed to Lactantius.[52] The translation of the *De die iudicii* may be compared to the three poems mentioned above, but also to other apparently quite different compositions, that is, prose versions of Latin works.

The prose versions of the Latin texts provide interesting parallels for some of the translation procedures of *JDay II*. There are three examples of prose versions from Anglo-Saxon England: that of the third book of the *Bella Parisiacae urbis* by Abbo of Saint-Germain-des-Prés (cf. Lendinara 1999: 73-89), the *Expositio hymnorum* in London, BL, Cotton Julius A. vi and Cotton Vespasian D. xii (a prose paraphrase of 95 hymns accompanied by a continuous gloss), and the prose recast of 24 monastic canticles in the latter manuscript, where each paraphrase follows the hymn or canticle it belongs to. All three prose versions are accompanied by Old English interlinear glosses.[53]

Analysis of these prose versions yields very similar results to those reached by analysis of syntactical glosses.[54] There are several common features: in the prose versions the vocative, preceded by *o*, always opens the phrase. Otherwise it was the verb to open the sentence, displaced only by conjunctions or adverbs like *haud*, *minime* or *ne*, and followed, in that order, by the subject, the direct object, the indirect object and the other complements. The genitive case always follows its referent. The adjective precedes the substantive it refers to, but this rule does not apply to the possessive adjective, which is often put after the noun.

In the translation of l. 33 of *Ddi*: "Cur, rogo, mens, tardas medico te pandere totam?" which is rendered with "Ic acsige þe, la, earme geþanc / hwi latast þu swa lange, þæt þu ðe læce ne cyþst" (*JDay II* l.65-66) there are a number of additions: the subject *ic* and the interjection *la* are added to point out that the Latin *mens* is a vocative, a grammatical case which is not formally distinguished from the nom. in Old English. *þe* (acc. of *þu*) was also added to specify that the question is addressed to the mind (*geþanc*), which is further connotated by the adjective *earm*, alliterating with *acsige* of the first half-line.

The addition of pronouns (either as subject or complement) and of *la* (or *eala*) has a counterpart in interlinear glosses,[55] where such additions are dictated by pedagogic aims and not by stylistic preoccupations. In the latter of the two

Old English lines discussed above, *cur* is translated by *hwi* and *tardas* by *latast*; the verb is followed by the subject, *þu* and by the filler *swa lange* 'for such a long time' which completes the a-line, providing another allitterant (l). The Latin infinitive, *te pandere* is rendered with a *þæt*-clause with explicit subject, *þu*. Similar choices are evident in the translation of l. 124 of *Ddi* ("Felix o nimium, semperque in saecula felix"), which reads:

Eala, se bið gesælig and ofersælig
and on worulda woruld wihta geseligost (*JDay II*, ll. 247-248)

The two long lines render faithfully and symmetrically the first and the second part of the Latin hexameter respectively. In l. 247 *eala* translates the Latin exclamation *o*; once again subject (*se*) and verb (*bið*) are provided. The translation of the adverb *nimium* with the adjective *ofersælig* is felicitous, since this adjective repeats but, at the same time, varies the former *gesælig*, corresponding to the Latin *felix*. The phrase *semper in saecula* is translated, as is common practice in both Old English poetry and prose, with *worulda woruld*, which elsewhere renders the Latin *in saecula saeculorum*. The redundancy of the line, which is modelled, as far as the first part is concerned, on Vergil and other poets, is not shunned by the translator. By contrast he has emphasized it by using a compound, the second member of which is *sælig*; the same adjective (*gesælig*) is used, once more, in the superlative, at the end of line 248.

12. A successful translation

The importance of the translation of the *Ddi* lies in the fact that it represents one of the few instances in which it is possible to compare an Old English poetic text with its Latin source. If one takes into account the entire translation of the poem, the assessment can only be positive. Its redundancy is dictated by the unavoidable devices employed to match the Germanic long line to the Latin original. The translation is literal but finds room for imaginative variations. The diction and style of the poem are occasionally marred by infelicities and awkwardness, but these are compensated by felicitous choices of words and phrases. The translation is, at times, very successful. For example, the rendering of "Et solo meruit fidei sermone salutem" (*Ddi* l. 31) with "He mid lyt wordum ac geleaffullum / his hæle begeat and help recene" (*JDay II* l. 61-62) is excellent, and so is that of "lucis ubi miseris nulla scintilla relucet" (*Ddi* l. 109) with "þær leohtes ne leoht lytel sperca / earmum ænig" (*JDay II* l. 219-220a).

The translation is accurate, but not slavish: the indebtedness to the Latin source is not avoided by the translator, but the manner in which the source is employed affords ample evidence that he was a lettered man well steeped in Anglo-Saxon poetic technique and conventions. It is this technique that conditions and determines both the grammatical and the literary adaptation of the Latin source. *JDay II* was evidently written with a certain target in mind, as its location within CCCC 201 proves. The penitential and educational potentiality of the *Ddi* was understood and it fostered a brilliant recast which was meant to be enjoyed as well as studied and meditated.

Notes

[1] The most recent edition of the poem, henceforth *Ddi*, is that by Fraipont (1955: 439-444).

[2] A number of manuscripts of the *Ddi* were written in England: CCCC 139, ff. 57^r-58^v (s. XII^{med}, Durham), Cambridge, Trinity College O. 2. 31, ff. 41^r-43^v and 45^r (s. X/XI, Christ Church, Canterbury), Cambridge, University Library, Gg. 5. 35, ff. 416^r-418^v (s. XI^{med}, St Augustine, Canterbury), London, BL, Additional 11034, f. 2 (X, ?England), London, BL, Cotton Domitian i, ff. 51^r-54^v (s. X^2-X^{med}, St Augustine, Canterbury), Paris, Bibliothèque Nationale, lat. 8092, ff. 42^v-45^r (s. $XI^{2/4}$, England), Salisbury, Cathedral Library, 168, ff. 85^v-87^r (s. XI^{ex}, Salisbury), Worcester, Cathedral Library F. 57, ff. 70^r-70^v (s. XIII, Worcester), and York, Chapter Library XVI Q. 14, ff. 48^v-49^r (s. XII/XIII, ?England).

[3] The attribution of the poem to Bede is still a matter of scholarly debate; in the past the *Ddi* has been attributed, among others, to Alcuin: see Whitbread (1944: 198-199).

[4] The first editors of *JDay II* coined a neologism and gave the poem the title of *Be domes dæge*, see Lumby (1876) and Löhe (1907). The most recent edition of the Old English poem is that by Caie (2000). The edition of Dobbie (cf. ASPR 6, 58-67) is still useful. All quotations are from this edition, as well as references to line numbers.

[5] All short titles of OE texts are given according to the *DOEC*.

[6] In l. 156 a personal epilogue begins where the narrator of *Ddi* takes leave from Acca and his brethrens in Hexham, saying that the poem was written at the request of this bishop. These lines are attested only in a few manuscripts; they may well have been added to the poem at a later date and were not translated into Old English.

[7] See Whitbread (1944: 198-206 and 1966: 635-656).

[8] Huppé (1959: 80-94), Hoffman (1968: 170-178) and Caie (2000: 58-64), suggest an allegorical interpretation for the garden image, see also Whitbread (1966: 645-646).

[9] The penitential theme is accentuated, for example, in *JDay II* l. 86-89; cf. *Ddi* l. 44-45.

[10] In these first lines the translation tries to ease the transition by introducing a correlation between the penitent and mankind ("ic eac [...] ondræde me / and synfulra gehwam" lines 17-18), after several additions have made clear the first-person speaker ("Ic ondræde me" l. 15, "for mandædum minum" l. 16). Elsewhere the shift from personal to general and homiletic is only in the Old English text: one can compare "Paenituisse iuvat tibi" (l. 43) with "nu is halwende þæt man her wepe / and dædbote do" (l. 84-85a).

[11] Knowledge of the acrostic is suggested, not only by the title given to the poem in several manuscripts, but also by lines 9, 36, 38, 44, 49, 61, and 84, cf. Lendinara (2003: 100-101).

[12] These data are conveniently summarized in Appendix I and II.

[13] Baker -- Lapidge (1995), cf. Whitbread (1948: 476), and the comment by Stubbs (1874: xx).

[14] There are 17 a-verse fillers: see l. 12a, 14a, 15a, 21a, 52a, 54a, 70a, 74a, 107a, 119a, 129a, 188a, 191a, 218a, 238a, 240a, 294a.

[15] There are 83 b-verse fillers: see l. 1b, 2b, 8b, 5b, 20b, 22b, 24b, 25b, 28b, 30b, 33b, 40b, 55b, 58b, 60b, 62b, 73b, 74b, 81b, 82b, 85b, 87b, 90b, 93b, 94b, 96b, 105b, 112b, 113b, 115b, 116b, 117b, 118b, 120b, 122b, 136b, 137b, 138b, 139b, 141b, 144b, 147b, 149b, 150b, 156b, 158b, 161b, 164b, 173b, 174b, 175b, 176b, 178b, 184b, 186b, 195b, 202b, 203b,. 204b, 206b, 210b, 222b, 224b, 228b, 231b, 233b, 235b, 236b, 237b, 239b, 241b, 248b, 253b, 254b, 257b, 264b (? if not a mistaken translation of *procellae*), 275b, 281b, 284b, 291b 295b, 298b, 304b.

[16] This is how l. 115, 118, 120, 130, 131, 132, 134, 135, and 137 of the Latin were translated. Line 136 of *Ddi* was not translated and was probably missing either in the Latin source or in the translation owing to an eye-skip.

[17] This list includes only the additions which are not part of half-line fillers, of lines without a counterpart in the Latin or of lines with a free translation.

[18] Some may be intensifying. The following adverbs occur in half-line fillers or lines with a free translation: *æfre* (l. 257), *ætsomne* (l. 165, 235, 275), *eac* (l. 15, 21), *elles* (l. 202), *emnes* (l. 151), *feor* (l. 237), *heonone* (l. 236), *næfre* (l. 254), *nu* (l. 33), *on hinder* (l. 241),

onweg (l. 238), *recene* (l. 28, 62), *swiðe* (l. 24, 105, 246), *þa* (l. 33), *þænne* (l. 129, 244), *þær* (l. 191, 218), *þearle* (l. 158), *þonne* (l. 107, 239), and *wihte* (l. 222).

[19] The adjective *eall* occurs 35 times (24 times without a counterpart in the Latin); *ece* occurs 10 times (7 times without a counterpart in the Latin); *earm* occurs 13 times (9 of which without a counterpart in the Latin); in some occurrences this adjective is used as a noun.

[20] The connectives of word pairs (cf. section 6 of this paper), as well as those occurring in the larger fillers, are not listed.

[21] A number of these doublets are common in several Indo-European traditions, cf. Krause (1922) and, as far as other Germanic languages are concerned, Bremmer Jr. (1983). On Old English word pairs cf. Kail (1889), Koskenniemi (1968), and Guerrieri (1982).

[22] The word pairs which occur elsewhere are *ypte oððe cyôde* (l. 143), *earm and eadig* (l. 163), *wop and wanung* (l. 202), *ege and fyrhtu* (l. 226), *hleahter and plega* (l. 235) – which occurs once in the *Liber scintillarum* 55, 22 – *sorh ne sar* (l. 256), *hunger oþþe þurst* (l. 258), *wuldor and wurðmynt* (l. 270), and *lof and life* (l. 271).

[23] It was Whitbread (1966: 640) who pointed out this kind of mistake.

[24] The conjunction *mid* is also used to bind asyndetic sequences of words (l. 234, 241, 265, 268).

[25] Latin passive ind. pres. was translated with the OE present of *beon* + passive participle: *obducitur: bið gesworcen* (l. 104-105), *rapimur: beoð brohte* (l. 119), *impletur: bið gefylled* (l. 145), *cernitur: bið gesewen* (l. 203), *sentitur: bið gemeted* (l. 205), *torquetur: bið breged* (l. 213-214).

[26] An active pres. participle is rendered with a passive relative sentence: *pendens* [...] *latro* with "sescaþa [...] þe mid Criste wæs cwyldmed" (*JDay II* l. 53-54).

[27] See *gaudia: mærðe* (l. 21), *rea: synful* (l. 29), *pectora: breost* (l. 29), *pugnis: fyste* (l. 29), *membra: lichaman* (l. 31), *lacrimis: wope* (l. 45), *allisos: aglidene mod* (l. 47), *quassatos: wanhydige* (l. 50), *animos: mod* (l. 50), *tepidos: wlacan* (l. 51), *fumos: smocan* (l. 51), *undis: wætere* (l. 52), *exempla: bysne* (l. 53), *certa: gearugne* (l. 91), *tempora: timan* (l. 91), *tormenta: wite* (l. 92), *mentes: mod* (l. 103), *turris: hleo* (l. 127), *ultricibus: ættrenum* (l. 146), *flammis: lige* (l. 146), *pectora: breost* (l. 160), *pugnis: mid fyste* (l. 161), *dicta: spræce* (l. 185), *ignibus: fyres* (l. 189), *flammis: lig* (l. 192), *facies: ansyn* (l. 203), *frigora: cyle* (l. 206), *flammae: lig* (l. 206), *curis: care* (l. 214), *solatia: frofor* (l. 223), *tristitiae: unrotnes* (l. 228), *tedia: adl* (l. 229), *flammis: on lige* (l. 230), *caelestia*

regna: *heofonrice* (l. 253), *febres*: *fefur* (l. 259), *morbi*: *adl* (l. 259), *clades*: *cwyld* (l. 259), *flammae*: *liges gebrasl* (l. 260), *frigora*: *cyle* (l. 260), *tristitiae*: *unrotnes* (l. 261), *taedia*: *æmelnys* (l. 261), *ruinae*: *hryre* (l. 262), *curae*: *caru* (l. 262), *tormenta*: *tintrega* (l. 262), *fulmina*: *liget* (l. 263), *perpetuis*: *ece* (l. 280), *donis*: *mede* (l. 280), *turmas*: *werode* (l. 282), *agmina*: *mædenheap* (l. 290), *patres*: *fæder* (l. 298), *natos*: *sunu* (l. 298), *cohortes*: *werode* (l. 303). The opposite occurs only six times: *sermone*: *wordum* (l. 61), *pauper*: *þearfan* (l. 162), *potens*. *þeodcyningas* (l. 162), *grando*: *hagulscuras* (l. 265), *flore*: *blostmum* (l. 291).

[28] At the same time, Latin *candida agmina* is rendered with "þæra hwittra [...] mædenheap" (*JDay II* l. 290) owing to the influence of *virgineo flore*.

[29] The word *iudex* is translated with *dema* at lines 76 and 171, with a specification, "eces deman", at l. 76, otherwise, it is rendered with *god* (*JDay II* l. 18, 71), *cyningc* (*JDay II* l. 95), and "se godes sunu" (*JDay II* l. 86).

[30] The homily Napier no. 29 features a further occurrence of *amarian*, *braslian*, *dæþbeacnigende* (written as two words), *dimhiw*, *geþuxian* (*geþuhsian*), *heortleas*, *ofersælig*, *prece*, and *unstenc*.

[31] These words are in part listed by Stanley (1971).

[32] The homily Napier no. 29 features a further occurrence of *amasian*, *æmelnes*, *ærdæd*, *afeormian*, *biterlice*, *færlic*, *gebrasl*, *gewepan*, *gycel*, *gnagan*, *ligspiwel*, *mihtleas*, *ormætness*, *towearde*, *prece*, and *ungeryde*.

[33] Another group of prose words in *JDay II* occur at least once in other poems: *ærendraca* (l. 287 and *Creed* l. 12), *angryslic* (l. 226 and *PPs* CIL.33, 3), *arfæstnes* (l. 220, 269 and *KtHy* l. 24), *cwylman* (l. 54, 204, 217 and *El* l. 688), *drunceness* (l. 234 and *Exhort* l. 44), *dwolma* (l. 106 and *Met* 5, 43), *forgifnes* (in the meaning "forgiveness", l. 68, 91 and *Christ* l. 427), *forsweorcan* (l. 108, 199 and *Beo* l. 1767), *fyrenian* (ms. *fyrgende*) (l. 215 and *Soul I* l. 103, *Sat* l. 619, *Rid* 20, 34), *gebedstow* (l. 30 and *Jul* l. 376), *gegladian* (l. 221 and *Seasons* l. 191), *gristbitung* (l. 227 and *Sat* l. 333), *halwende* (l. 84 and *PPs* CXVIII.103, 3), *hopa* (l. 221 and *Exhort* 10, *Inc* l. 253), *horh* (l. 77, 157 and *El* l. 297), *horxlice* (l. 168 and *Soul* 2 l. 109), *hreowlic* (l. 75 and *PPs* CVIII.9, 2), *micelnys* (l. 186 and *PPs* LXVI.1, 4), *nosu* (l. 207 and *PPs* CXIII.14, 1, CXXXII.17, 3), *ræpling* (l. 48, and *Rid* 52, 1; it has only another occurrence in the *Stowe Psalter* Ps LXVIII.34), *swiðlic* (l. 182, 227 and *Christ* l. 954, *Jul* l. 55, *Jud* l. 240), *upcund* (l. 307 and *Christ* l. 268 and *OrW* l. 34), and *wrænnes* (l. 236 and *Met* 25, 41).

[34] The phrase *lifes frea* (l. 81), instead of the more common compound *liffrea*, is also found in *Creed* l. 5 and *Seasons* l. 3.

[35] Literature of the late Anglo-Saxon period is marked by bilingualism, and, as far as poetry is concerned, by the decay of metrics, the use of rhyme, the introduction of new stylistic features instead of those typical of the previous productions (such as variation), and the use of prose words. As far as the content is concerned, late Old English poetry is characterized by the frequency of eschatological motifs as well as homiletic, penitential and didactic themes (cf. Lendinara 2001a).

[36] Napier (1967: 136, 27-140, 2). The manuscript is a companion volume to Hatton 114 and Oxford, Bodleian Library, Junius 121 (cf. Gneuss 2001: nos. 637, 638 and 644).

[37] The former view that the prose passage of the homily Napier no. 29 is "eine sehr verderbte widergabe" of the poem (Napier [1967]: viii) has been questioned both by Stanley (1971: 389-390), and Frank (1994: 106-107).

[38] Stanley (1971: 389) quoted by Caie (2000: 23).

[39] On this suffix see Ahlsson (1991: 80-85).

[40] Frequent are also the adjectives ending in *–lic*: *ænlic* (l. 6, 63, 282, 292), *angryslic* (l. 226), *earmlic* (l. 188), *egeslic* (l. 102 and the adverb *egeslice* l. 94), *færlic* (l. 259), *freolic* (l. 298), *gelic* (l. 174), *healic* (l. 281), *heanlic* (l. 258), *heofenlic* (l. 255, 281), *hreowlic* (l. 75), *laðlic* (l. 206, 210, 260), *leoflic* (l. 271), *scearplic* (l. 53), *swiðlic* (l. 182, 227), *unhyrlic* (l. 11), *uplic, upplic* (l. 46, 113, 146, 299) and the *-lice* adverbs: *biterlice* (l. 167), *freolice* (l. 277), *gelice* (l. 144), *glædlice* (l. 273), *horxlice* (l. 168), and *swiðlice* (l. 160).

[41] See also "eal swa ic secge" (*JDay II* l. 4) and "eall swylce þu cwæde" (*JDay II* l. 12), "ic gemunde" (*JDay II* l. 21 and 24), *swegdon* is said of the water and the trees (*JDay II* l. 3 and 7).

[42] Several Old English poems feature the repetition of key words or phrases. Beaty (1934) has studied instances of identical words or root-syllables, which are repeated with a different meaning, connotation or association. For the structural function of repetition in Anglo-Saxon poetry, cf. Huppé (1943), Greenfield (1954), Hieatt (1971), Kintgen (1974), and Gardner (1975: 18-32).

[43] See, for example, *Mald*: *sendon* l. 29 and *sendan* l. 32, *Seasons*: *lar* and *læran* at l. 2, 3, 8, 9 and 11, *Creed*: *giftum* and *handgyft*, *earðbuendum* and *foldbuendum*, *engla* and *englas*; *uplic* is repeated thrice (l. 11, 32, and 37).

[44] On the semantic value of the adjective *earm*, see Coppola (1988-1989).

[45] Several repetitions should be added to those already noted above: *gyldan / agyldan* (l. 73-74), *lifes / lifes* (l. 81), *sweart / sweart* (l. 105-106), *wæron / wæron* (l. 133-134), *eall / eall* (l. 145-146), *earm / earm* (l. 163-164), *gewiteð / gewiteð* (l. 236-237), *nawih / wihte* (l. 202-203), *gesælig / ofersælig* (l. 247), *worulda / woruld* (l. 198, 248), *fæder / fæder* (l. 297-298), see also "ne se mona næfð nanre mihte wiht" (l. 109).

[46] See the remarks by Bodden (1987: 24-39). As far as the whole Germanic tradition is concerned, see Luiselli Fadda (1991) and the essays in the volume published by Contamine in 1989. As to the Old English tradition, the book by Gonser (1909) is still valuable.

[47] Several examinations have been devoted to the translation techniques of Alfred and Ælfric, including studies of the prefaces to their works, which both reflect on the value and the aims of translation, see Minkoff (1976), St-Jacques (1983), and Marsden (1991), see also the two volumes published by Szarmach in 1978 and 1986.

[48] Two prose works by Alcuin were translated into Old English: the *Liber de virtutibus et vitiis* and the *Interrogationes Sigewulfi in Genesin*.

[49] A translation into Northumbrian dialect is preserved in Leiden, Bibliotheek der Rijksuniversiteit, Vossianus lat. 4° 106, see Smith [1990] and, for the edited text, ASPR (6, 109), for the West Saxon version, see ASPR (3, 198).

[50] ASPR (3, 200-203), cf. O'Brien O'Keeffe (1980) and (1985).

[51] See Blake (1990: 24-35). According to the estimate of Emerson (1926), the translator used only 107 lines of the Latin poem, which correspond to 380 lines of the OE *Phoenix*, the entire poem is 677 lines long.

[52] The text of the *De ave phoenice* (which is 170 lines long) is printed in Blake (1990: 88-92).

[53] See, respectively, Zupitza (1887), Gneuss (1968: 91-101, 135-155, 194-206), and Korhammer (1976: 128-138).

[54] Syntactic patterns analogous to those of prose versions are shown by syntactical glosses, see Robinson (1973) and O'Neill (1992).

[55] For similar instances, see the Old English glosses to Ælfric's *Colloquy* (ed. Garmonsway 1978) and to the third book of the *Bella Parisiacae urbis*.

References

Ahlsson, Lars-Erik
    1991   "Untersuchungen zum suffigierten Adjektiv im Altniederdeutschen und Altfriesischen unter Berücksichtigung des Altenglischen", *Niederdeutsches Wort* 31: 77-122.

Baker, Peter -- Michael Lapidge (eds.)
    1995   *Byrhtferth's Enchiridion*. (EETS s.s. 15.) Oxford: Oxford University Press.

Beaty, John O.
    1934   "The echo-word in *Beowulf* with a note on the *Finnsburg Fragment*", *PMLA* 49: 365-73.

Blake, Norman F. (ed.)
    1964   *The Phoenix*. Manchester: Manchester University Press.
    1990   Revised edition. Exeter: University of Exeter Press.

Bodden, Mary Catherine
    1987   "Anglo-Saxon self-consciousness in language", *English studies* 68: 24-39.

Bremmer Jr., Rolf H.
    1983   "Old English *feoh* and *feorh*, Old Norse *fé* ok *fjǫr*, ergo: Old Frisian *fiā* and *ferech* 'money and life'", *Us Wurk* 32: 55-62.

Caie, Graham D. (ed.)
    2000   *The Old English poem* Judgement Day II: *A critical edition with editions of* De die iudicii *and the Hatton 113 Homily* Be domes dæge. (Anglo-Saxon Texts 2.) Cambridge: Brewer.

Clerici, Ergisto
    1973   "Due poeti: Emilio Blossio Draconzio e Venanzio Fortunato", *Rendiconti dell'Istituto Lombardo, Cl. di lettere e scienze morali e storiche* 107: 108-50.

Contamine, Geneviève (ed.)
    1989   *Traduction et traducteurs au moyen âge: Actes du colloque international du CNRS organisé à Paris, Institut de Recherche et d'Histoire des Textes, les 26-28 mai 1986.* Paris: CNRS.

Coppola, Maria Augusta
    1988-1989   "... gebleod wundrum, eadgum ond earmum ungelice. La parusia nel *Cristo III*", *Romanobarbarica* 10: 31-63.

Emerson, Oliver F.
    1926   "Originality in Old English Poetry", *Review of English studies* 2: 18-31.

Fraipont, John (ed.)
    1955   *Bedae venerabilis liber hymnorum, rhythmi, variae preces. Bedae opera* IV. (Corpus Christianorum, Ser. lat. 122.) Turnhout: Brepols.

Frank, Roberta
    1994   "Poetic words in Late Old English prose", in: Godden -- Gray -- Hoad (eds.), 87-107.

Gardner, John
    1975   *The construction of christian poetry in Old English.* Carbondale-Edwardsville: Southern Illinois University Press.

Garmonsway, George N. (ed.)
    1939   *Ælfric's Colloquy.* (Methuen's Old English Library). London: Methuen.

1978 Revised edition. Exeter: University of Exeter Press.

Gneuss, Helmut
1968 *Hymnar und Hymnen im englischen Mittelalter.* (Buchreihe der Anglia 12.) Tübingen, Winter.

2001 *Handlist of Anglo-Saxon manuscripts.* Tempe: Center for Medieval and Renaissance Studies.

Godden, Malcolm -- Douglas Gray -- Terry Hoad (eds.)
1994 *From Anglo-Saxon to Early Middle English: Studies presented to E. G. Stanley.* Oxford: Clarendon.

Gonser, Paul (ed.)
1909 *Das angelsächsische Prosa-Leben des Heiligen Guthlac.* (Anglistische Forschungen 27.) Heidelberg: Winter
1966 Reprinted edition. Amsterdam: Swets-Zeitlinger.

Greenfield, Stanley B.
1954 "Attitudes and values in *The seafarer*", *Studies in philology* 51: 15-20.

1996 "The Old English Elegies", in: Stanley (ed.), 149-51.

Greenfield, Stanley B. -- Daniel G. Calder
1986 *A new critical history of Old English literature.* New York: New York University Press.

Guerrieri, Anna Maria
1982 "La congiunzione *ond* nel *Beowulf*: problemi di dizione, di sintassi e di stile", *AION, fil. germ.* 25: 7-55.

Hieatt, Constance B.
1971 "Dream frame and verbal echo in the *Dream of the rood*", *Neuphilologische Mitteilungen* 72: 251-63.

Hoffman, Richard L.
1968 "Structure and symbolism in the *Judgement Day II*", *Neophilologus* 52: 170-78.

Huppé, Bernard F.
1943 "*The Wanderer*: Themes and structure", *Journal of English and Germanic philology* 42: 516-38.

1959 *Doctrine and poetry: Augustine's influence on Old English poetry*. New York: State University of New York.

Kail, J.
1889 "Über die Parallelstellen in der ags Poesie", *Anglia* 12: 17-47.

Kintgen, Eugene R.
1974 "Echoic repetition in Old English poetry, especially the *Dream of the rood*", *Neuphilologische Miteilungen* 75: 202-23.

Korhammer, Michael
1976 *Die monastischen Cantica im Mittelalter und ihre altenglischen Interlinearversionen: Studien und Textausgabe*. (TUEPh 6.) Munich: Fink.

Koskenniemi, Inna
1968 *Repetitive word pairs in Old and Early Middle English prose*. (Annales Universitatis Turkuensis, ser. B, 107.) Turku: Turun Yliopisto.

Krause, Wolfgang
1922 "Die Wortstellung in den zweigliedrigen Wortverbindungen, untersucht für das Altindische, Awestische, Litauische und Altnordische", *Zeitschrift für vergleichende Sprachforschung* 50: 74-129.

Lendinara, Patrizia
1986 "The third book of the *Bella parisiacae urbis* by Abbo of Saint-Germain-des-Prés and its Old English gloss", *Anglo-Saxon England* 15: 73-89
1999 Revised reprint, in: Lendinara 1999, 157-75.

1999 *Anglo-Saxon glosses and glossaries*. (Variorum Collected Studies Series CS622.) Aldershot: Ashgate.

2001a "La poesia anglosassone alla fine del X secolo e oltre", *AION, sez. studi tedeschi, fil. germ.* n. s. 11: 7-46.

2001b "Alcuino e il *De die iudicii*", *Pan* 18-19 (= *Miscellanea di studi in memoria di Cataldo Roccaro*): 303-24.

2003 "The *Versus sibyllae de die iudicii* in England", in: Powell -- Scragg (eds.): 85-101.

Löhe, Hans
1907 *Be domes dæge*. (Bonner Beiträge 22.) Bonn: Hanstein.

Lumby, J. Rawson (ed.)
1876 *Be domes dæge: De die iudicii*. (EETS o.s. 65.) London: Trübner.

Luiselli Fadda, Anna Maria
1991 "La traduzione nel Medioevo germanico: condizioni culturali e linguistiche e procedimenti operativi", *Romanobarbarica* 11: 257-90.

Malkiel, Yakov
1959 "Studies in irreversible binomials", *Lingua* 8: 113-60.

Marsden, Richard
1991 "Ælfric as translator: The Old English prose 'Genesis'", *Anglia* 109: 319-56.

Menner, Robert J.
1947 "The vocabulary of the Old English poems on Judgement Day", *PMLA* 62: 583-97.

Minkoff, Harvey
1976 "Some stylistic consequences of Ælfric's theory of translation", *Studies in philology* 73: 29-41.

Napier, Arthur (ed.)
1883 *Wulfstan: Sammlung der ihm zugeschriebenen Homilien nebst Untersuchungen über ihre Echtheit.* Berlin: Weidmann
1967 Reprinted edition with an app. by Klaus Ostheeren. Dublin: Weidmann.

O'Brien O'Keeffe, Katherine
1980 "Exeter riddle 40: The art of an Old English translator", *Proceedings of the patristics, medieval, and Renaissance conference* 5: 107-17.

1985 "The text of Aldhelm's 'Enigma' no. C in Oxford, Bodleian Library, Rawlinson C. 697 and Exeter riddle 40", *Anglo-Saxon England* 14: 61-73.

O'Neill, Patrick P.
1992 "Syntactical glosses in the Lambeth Psalter and the reading of the Old English interlinear translation as sentences", *Speculum* 46: 250-56.

Powell, Kathryn -- Donald Scragg (eds.)
2003 *Apocryphal texts and traditions in Anglo-Saxon England.* (Publications of the Manchester Centre for Anglo-Saxon Studies 2.) Cambridge: Brewer.

Robinson, Fred C.
1973 "Syntactical glosses in Latin manuscripts of Anglo-Saxon provenance", *Speculum* 48: 443-75.

Smith, Albert H. (ed.)
1933 *Three Northumbrian poems.* London: Methuen.
1978 Revised edition. Exeter: University of Exeter Press.
1990 Reprinted edition.

Stanley, Eric G. (ed.)
1966 *Continuations and beginnings.* London: Nelson.
1971 "Studies in the prosaic vocabulary of Old English verse", *Neuphilologische Mitteilungen* 72: 385-418.

St-Jacques, Raymond
1983 "*Hwilum word be worde, hwilum andgit of andgiete?* Bede's 'Ecclesiastical history' and its Old English translator", *Florilegium* 5: 85-104.

Stubbs, William (ed.)
1874 *Memorials of Saint Dunstan Archbishop of Canterbury.* (Rolls Series 63.) London: Longman.

Szarmach, Paul E. (ed.)
1978 *The Old English homily and its background.* Albany: University of New York Press.

1986	*Studies in earlier Old English prose.* Albany: University of New York Press.

Tristram, Hildegard L. C.
1978   "Stock descriptions of heaven and hell in Old English poetry", *Neuphilologische Mitteilungen* 79: 102-13.

Wenisch, Franz
1979   *Spezifisch anglisches Wortgut in den nordhumbrischen Interlinearglossierungen des Lukasevangeliums.* (Anglistische Forschungen 132.) Heidelberg: Winter.

Whitbread, Leslie
1944   "A study of Bede's 'Versus de die iudicii'", *Philological quarterly* 23: 193-221.

1948   "Byrhtferth's hexameters", *Notes & queries* 193: 476.

1963   "Wulfstan' homilies XXIX, XXX and some related texts", *Anglia* 81: 347-64.

1966   "The Old English poem *Judgement day II* and its Latin source", *Philological quarterly* 45: 635-56.

Whitman, Frank H.
1973   "A major compositional technique in Old English verse", *English language notes* 11: 81-86.

Zupitza, Julius
1887   "Altenglische Glossen zu Abbos Clericorum Decus", *Zeitschrift für deutsches Altertum und deutsche Literatur* 31: 1-27.

Appendix I

In Appendix I, fillers (+a) are distinguished from the additions (+*a*) which were compelled by the different linguistic systems, for example, the articoloids or the auxiliary verb for the passive forms. Half-line fillers are not preceded by +. An asterisk marks the single half-lines of the *JDay II*.

Ddi	JD II	*a*-verse	*b*-verse	ratio
v. 3	v. 1	+2a+ *sæt* (= *sedi* v. 4)	2a	1:2
	v. 2	+1a	2a (variation)	
+	v. 3	descriptive addition (including a word pair)		0:1
+	v. 4	3a	personal aside	0:1
v. 1	v. 5	+2a	3a (a word pair)	1:2
	v. 6	+*1a*+1a	+1a	
v. 2	v. 7	+1a+*1a*	+2a (second member of a word pair)	1:2
	v. 8	+*1a*	3a (aside comment)	
v. 4	v. 9	free transl. of *turbatus*		1:1
v. 5	v. 10	+2a+ *færinga* (= *subito* v. 4)	2a+ *unrot* (=*maestus* v. 3) (forming a word pair)	1:2
	v. 11		+2a	
+	v. 12a	personal remark		0:½
v. 6	v. 12b			1:½
v. 7	v. 13		+*1a*	1:2
	v. 14	3a	+2a	
+	v. 15a	connective addition		0:½
v. 8	v. 15b		+*1a*	1: ½
+	v. 16	explanatory addition		0:1
v. 9	v. 17	+*1a*+2a	+2a	1:2
	v. 18	+2a	+2a	
v. 10	v. 19	+3a		1:2
	v. 20	+2a (second member of a word pair)	4a	
+	v. 21a	addition (anticipation of v. 24a)		0:½

v. 11	v. 21b		+1a	1:2 and ½
	v. 22	+1a+*1a*	3a	
	v. 23		+2a (first member of a word pair)	
v. 12	v. 24	+1a+*1a*	4a (anticipation of v. 25a)	1:2
	v. 25	+2a	2a	
v. 13	v. 26	+2a	+1a	1:3
	v. 27	+2a (*þæt* clause)	+1a	
	v. 28	+2a	3a (variation)	
v. 14	v. 29		+1a+*1a*	1:2
	v. 30	+2a	2a	
v. 15	v. 31	+2a	+*1a*	1:2
	v. 32		+2a	
v. 16	v. 33	+1a	3a	1:2
	v. 34	+2a (*þæt* clause)	+1a+*1a*	
v. 17	v. 35		3a (incl. *mid wope* = *cum voce gementi* v. 18)	1:2
	v. 36	+1a	+1a	
v. 18	v. 37		+1a	1:1
v. 19	v. 38	+1a	+2a	1:2
	v. 39		+1a	
v. 20	v. 40	+1a+*1a*	4a (explanatory addition)	1:2
	v. 41		+1a (variation)	
v. 21	v. 42		+2a	1:1
v. 22	v. 43		+1a	1:2
	v. 44	+*1a*		
v. 23	v. 45	+3a (*þæt* clause)		1:1 and ½
	v. 46a			
v. 24	v. 46b		+1a	1:2 and ½
	v. 47	+1a	+1a	
	v. 48		+1a	

v. 25	v. 49	+1a+*1a*+1a	+1a	1:2
	v. 50		2a (subject)	
v. 26	v. 51	+*1a*	+1a	1:2
	v. 52	3a (including a further transl. of *vult* v. 25)		
v. 27	v. 53	+*2a*	+1a	1:2
	v. 54	4a (relative clause)		
v. 28	v. 55	+*1a*	4a (variation)	1:2
	v. 56	+*1a*	+2a (second member of a word pair)	
v. 29	v. 57	+1a	+2a (second member of a word pair)	1:2
	v. 58	+*1a*	2a	
v. 30	v. 59	+2a+*1a*		1:2
	v. 60	+1a	1a	
v. 31	v. 61	+1a+*1a*	+1a	1:2
	v. 62	+1a	3a	
v. 32	v. 63	+1a	+*1a*	1:2
	v. 64			
v. 33	v. 65	+3a	+1a	1:2
	v. 66	+3a	+3a (*þæt* clause)	
v. 34	v. 67	+1a	+1a	1:2
	v. 68	+1a	+1a	
v. 35	v. 69			1:2
	v. 70a	2a (variation)	+2a	
v. 36	v. 71	+1a		1:1 and ½
	v. 72a	+1a		
v. 37	v. 72b		+1a	1:2 and ½
	v. 73	+1a	3a	
	v. 74	4a (variation of v. 73b)	2a (variation of v. 73a)	
v. 38	v. 75	+5a (*þæt* clause)	+*1a*+1a	1:2
	v. 76	+1a+*1a*	+1a	
v. 39	v. 77			1:1 and ½
	v. 78a	+*1a*		

v. 40	v. 78b		+1a	1:1 and ½
	v. 79	+1a	+1a	
v. 41	v. 80	+2a	+2a (second member of a word pair)	1:2
	v. 81	+1a	3a	
v. 42	v. 82	+2a+1a	2a (variation)	1:2
	v. 83	+1a	+2a (second member of a word pair)	
v. 43	v. 84		+3a (*bæt* clause)	1:2
	v. 85	+1a	3a	
v. 44	v. 86	+1a+1a	free transl. of *te vindice*	1:2
	v. 87	? free transl. of *te iudice*	4a	
v. 45	v. 88		+2a (second member of a word pair)	1:2
	v. 89	free transl. of *bis vindicat*	+1a	
v. 46	v. 90	+1a	3a (a word pair)	1:2
	v. 91	+1a		
v. 47	v. 92	+2a	+1a+1a+1a	1:2
	v. 93	+1a+1a	2a	
v. 48	v. 94		3a (variation)	1:1 and ½
	v. 95a	+1a		
v. 49	v. 95b		+1a	1:1 and ½
	v. 96	+1a	2a	
v. 50	v. 97		+1a	1:1
+	v. 98	explanatory addition		0:1
v. 51	v. 99	+1a	+*2a*	1:3
	v. 100*	+2a (second member of a word pair)		
	v. 101	+1a	+2a (second member of a word pair)	
v. 52	v. 102	+*1a*	+1a	1:2
	v. 103	+2a	+1a	

v. 53	v. 104*	+1a+*1a*+1a		1:3
	v. 105	+2a (second member of a word pair)	2a (variation)	
	v. 106	variation (including a three words cluster)		
v. 54	v. 107	2a		1:2
	v. 108	+*1a*	+1a	
v. 55	v. 109	free transl.		1:1
+	v. 110	addition (*þæt* clause)		0:1
v. 56	v. 111	+2a	+1a	1:2
	v. 112		3a	
v. 57	v. 113		1a (variation)	1:1 and ½
	v. 114a			
v. 58	v. 114b		+1a	1:2 and ½
	v. 115	+1a	2a (variation)	
	v. 116	+*1a*	3a (a word pair)	
v. 59	v. 117	+1a	2a (explicit subject)	1:2
	v. 118		2a	
v. 60	v. 119	+1a+*1a*+1a		1:2
	v. 120		3a (variation)	
v. 61	v. 121*			1:2
	v. 122	+1a	3a	
v. 62	v. 123	free transl. of *sis memor*	free transl. of *pavor* (*þæt* clause)	1:2
	v. 124		+1a	
v. 63	v. 125	free transl. (including a word pair)		1:2
	v. 126	free transl. (including a word pair)		
vv. 64-65	v. 127		+1a	2:2
	v. 128	+1a		
+	v. 129a	4a (addition)		0: ½
v. 66	v. 129b		+1a	1:1 and ½
	v. 130	redundant transl. of *omnes homines*		

v. 67	v. 131	free and redundant transl.		1:4
	v. 132	free and redundant transl.		
	v. 133	free and redundant transl.		
	v. 134	free and redundant transl.		
v. 68	v. 135	+1a+*1a*		1:2
	v. 136	+1a	3a	
v. 69	v. 137	+1a+*1a*	2a	1:4
	v. 138	+1a+*1a*	3a	
	v. 139	+2a	+1a	
	v. 140		3a	
v. 70	v. 141	+2a	3a	1:2
	v. 142	+3a (*þæt* clause)	3a (a word pair)	
v. 71	v. 143	+*1a*	+1a	1:2
	v. 144		4a (explicit subject)	
v. 72	v. 145	+1a+*1a*	+1a+*1a*	1:2
	v. 146	+2a		
v. 73	v. 147	+*1a*	5a (commenting remark)	1:2
	v. 148	free transl. of *ruptis habenis*		
v. 74	v. 149	free transl. of *inane*	1a	1:1 and ½
	v. 150a	3a		
+	v. 150b		enlarged repetition of v. 146b	0:½
+	v. 151	enlarged repetition of v. 145b		0:1
v. 75	v. 152		+2a (second member of a word pair)	1:2
	v. 153	3a (a word pair)	3a (variation: a word pair)	
v. 76	v. 154	free transl.		1:1
v. 77	v. 155	+*1a*		1:2
	v. 156	+1a	2a (variation)	

v. 78	v. 157	+2a	+1a	1:2
	v. 158	+2a	2a (variation)	
v. 79	v. 159	+1a	+1a	1:3
	v. 160	+1a	+1a	
	v. 161	+1a+*1a*	2a	
v. 80	v. 162	+1a		1:1
v. 81	v. 163		+1a+*1a*	1:3
	v. 164	+2a	4a (variation)	
	v. 165	explanatory addition and variation		
v. 82	v. 166	+1a+*1a*	+1a	1:2
	v. 167	+1a	+*1a*+1a	
v. 83	v. 168	+1a	+1a	1:2
	v. 169		+2a (second member of a word pair)	
v. 84	v. 170	+*1a*+1a+*1a*	+*1a*+1a	1:2
	v. 171	+1a		
v. 85	v. 172	+1a	+1a	1:2
	v. 173		4a	
v. 86	v. 174	+2a	2a (a simile)	1:2
	v. 175	+1a	3a (variation)	
v. 87	v. 176	+2a	3a (repetition of v. 176a)	1:2
	v. 177	+2a+*1a*	+1a	
v. 88	v. 178	+4a	2a	1:2
	v. 179	+3a	+1a	
v. 89	v. 180	+1a+*1a*	+*1a*	1:1
v. 90	v. 181	+1a		1:2
	v. 182	repetition of v. 181		
v. 91	v. 183		+1a	1:2
	v. 184	+1a (variation)	3a	
v. 92	v. 185			1:2
	v. 186		2a	
v. 93	v. 187	+1a	+1a	1:2
	v. 188	3a		
v. 94	v. 189		+2a	1:2
	v. 190	free transl. of *gehennae*		

Translating Doomsday   61

v. 95	v. 191	4a		1:3
	v. 192	+*1a*	+1a+*1a*	
	v. 193	variation		
v. 96	v. 194	+1a		1:1 and ½
	v. 195a	+*2a*		
+	v. 195b		5a (aside)	0:½
v. 97	v. 196	+*2a*	+2a	1:1
v. 98	v. 197		+1a	1:2
	v. 198	+*1a*	+2a	
v. 99	v. 199		+1a	1:2
	v. 200	+2a	+2a (first member of a word pair)	
v. 100	v. 201			1:2
	v. 202	+2a (second member of a word pair)	2a	
v. 101	v. 203	+*1a*	2a	1:2
	v. 204	+*1a*	4a (relative clause)	
v. 102	v. 205	+*1a*+1a		1:1 and ½
	v. 206a	+1a		
v. 103	v. 206b		3a (anticipation of *fetor*)	1:2 and ½
	v. 207	+4a	+1a	
	v. 208	+1a (second transl. of *fetor*)		
v. 104	v. 209	+1a+*2a*		1:2
	v. 210		2a	
v. 105	v. 211	+2a		1:2
	v. 212	+1a+*1a*+1a (variation)		
v. 106	v. 213	+1a+*1a*	+*2a*+1a	1:2
	v. 214	+*1a*	+2a (second member of a word pair)	
v. 107	v. 215	+*1a*	+*1a*	1:2
	v. 216	free transl. of *sibimet*		

	v. 217	+2a+*1a*	+*1a*	
v. 108	v. 218	+1a+*1a*+2a (relative clause)		1:2
v. 109	v. 219	+*1a*	+1a	1:1 and ½
	v. 220a			
v. 110	v. 220b		+1a	1:1
	v. 221a		+1a	
v. 111 (*flentibus arridet*)	v. 221b	+1a		½:1 and ½
	v. 222	+1a+*1a*	2a	
v. 111 (*Fugiunt...*)	v. 223a	+1a		½:½
v. 112	v. 223b		+*1a*+1a	1:1 and ½
	v. 224	+1a+*2a* (relative clause)	3a (variation)	
v. 113	v. 225	+*2a*		1:1
v. 114	v. 226	+2a		1:2
	v. 227	+1a	+1a	
v. 115	v. 228	+2a	2a	1:2
	v. 229	+1a	+1a	
v. 116	v. 230	+2a	+*1a*	1:2
v. 117	v. 231		3a (a word pair)	1:2
	v. 232		+1a	
	v. 233		3a (variation)	
v. 118	v. 234	+1a	+2a	1:2
	v. 235	+2a	2a (variation)	
v. 119	v. 236	+2a	2a (variation)	1:4
	v. 237	+1a	2a (repetition)	
	v. 238	2a	+2a	
	v. 239	+1a	3a	
v. 120	v. 240	4a		1:2
	v. 241	+1a	3a (variation)	

Translating Doomsday 63

v. 123	v. 242		+1a	1:1
	v. 243a			and ½
v. 121	v. 243b		+3a	1:½
+	v. 244	further remark without a counterpart in the Latin		0:1
v. 122	v. 245	+*1a*+1a	+*1a*	1:1
+	v. 246	additional remark (including a word pair)		0:1
v. 124	v. 247	+2a	+1a (*ofersælig* = *nimium*)	1:2
	v. 248	+1a+*1a*	2a	
v. 125	v. 249	+*1a*+1a		1:2
	v. 250	+2a	+1a	
v. 126	v. 251			1:1
v. 127	v. 252	+1a	+2a	1:1
	v. 253a	+1a		and ½
+	v. 253b		4a (exclamatory aside)	0:½
v. 128	v. 254		2a	1:2
	v. 255	+*1a*		
v. 129	v. 256	+1a		1:1
v. 130 (*non labor ullus*)	v. 257	+1a	2a	½:1
v. 130 (*Non ... somnus*)	v. 258	+1a	+1a	½:1
v. 131	v. 259	+3a	+2a	1:2
	v. 260	+2a	+*1a*+1a	
v. 132	v. 261	+2a	+2a	1:2
	v. 262	+2a	+2a	
v. 133	v. 263	+3a	+2a	1:3
	v. 264	+1a	3a (? a wrong transl. of *procellae*)	
	v. 265	+2a	+2a	

v. 134	v. 266	+4a	+2a	1:2
	v. 267	+2a	+2a	
v. 135	v. 268	+2a	+1a	1:2
	v. 269	+1a	+2a	
v. 136	-	the Latin verse is not translated		1:0
v. 137	v. 270*	+1a		1:2
	v. 271	+2a+ *lif* (= *vita* v. 136)		
v. 138	v. 272	+*1a*	+1a	1:2
	v. 273	+2a	+1a	
v. 139	v. 274	+1a		1:2
	v. 275	+2a	2a	
v. 140	v. 276*	+2a		1:2
	v. 277	+1a	+2a	
v. 141	v. 278			1:1
v. 142	v. 279	3a (explicit subject)	2a (variation)	1:2 and ½
	v. 280	+2a		
	v. 281a			
+	v. 281b		4a (exclamatory aside)	0:½
v. 143	v. 282	+*1a*+1a		1:2
	v. 283	+*1a*	+2a (second member of a word pair)	
v. 144	v. 284	+2a+*1a*	3a	1:2
	v. 285	+1a	+1a	
v. 145	v. 286			1:2
	v. 287	expanded transl. of *apostolicas*		
v. 146	v. 288		+1a	1:2
	v. 289*	+2a		
v. 147	v. 290	+1a+*1a*	+1a	1:2
	v. 291	+1a	2a (variation)	
v. 148	v. 292	+1a	+1a	1:4
	v. 293	expanded transl. of *genitrix*		
	v. 294	3a (variation)	+*1a*	
	v. 295	+2a	2a	
v. 149	v. 296	+2a+*1a*+1a		1:2
	v. 297	+1a	+*1a*+1a	

v. 150	v. 298		2a	1:1
v. 151	v. 299	+*1a*+1a		1:2
	v. 300	+1a	+1a (variation)	
v. 152	v. 301	+*1a*	+1a	1:1
+	v. 302	addition		0:1
v. 153	v. 303	+*1a*+1a	+*1a*	1:2
	v. 304	+1a	2a	
v. 154	v. 305	+1a		1:2
	v. 306	+1a	+*1a*+1a	

Appendix II

Additions
ratio 0:½: vv. 12a; 15a; 21a; 129a; 149b; 195b; 253b; 281b.
ratio 0:1: vv. 3; 4; 16; 98; 110; 151; 244; 246; 302.

Omissions
ratio 1:0: v. 136 is omitted in the OE translation.

Translation
ratio 1:½ : v. **6**: 12b; v. **8**: 15b; **121**: 243b.
ratio ½:½: v. **111** (2nd part): 223a.
ratio 1:1: v. **4**: 9; v. **18**: 37; v. **21**: 42; v. **50**: 97; v. **55**: 109; v. **76**: 154; v. **80**: 162; v. **89**: 180; v. **97**: 196; v. **110**: 220b-221a; v. **113**: 225; v. **122**: 245; v. **126**: 251; v. **129**: 256; v. **141**: 278; v. **150**: 298; v. **152**: 301.
ratio 2:2: vv. **64-65**: 127-128.
ratio ½:1: v. **130** (2nd part): 257; v. **130** (1st part): 258.
ratio ½:1 and ½: v. **111** (1st part): vv. 221b-222.
ratio 1:1 and ½: v. **23**: 45-46a; v. **36**: 71-72a; v. **39**: 77-78a; v. **40**: 78b-79; v. **48**: 94-95a; v. **49**: 95b-96; v. **57**: 113-114a; v. **66**: 129b-130; v. **74**: 149-150a; v. **96**: 194-195a; v. **102**: 205-206a; v. **109**: 219-220a; v. **112**: 223b-224; v. **123**: 242-243a; v. **127**: 252-253a.
ratio 1:2: v. **1**: 5-6; v. **2**: 7-8; v. **3**: 1-2; v. **5**: 10-11; v. **7**:13-14; v. **9**: 17-18; v. **10**: 19-20; v. **12**: 24-25; v. **14**: 29-30; v. **15**: 31-32; v. **16**: 33-34; v. **17**: 35-36; v. **19**: 38-39; v. **20**: 40-41; v. **22**: 43-44; v. **25**: 49-50; v. **26**: 51-52; v. **27**: 53-54; v. **28**: 55-56; v. **29**: 57-58; v. **30**: 59-60; v. **31**: 61-62; v. **32**: 63-64; v. **33**: 65-66; v. **34**: 67-68; v. **35**: 69-70; v. **38**: 75-76; v. **41**: 80-81; v. **42**: 82-83; v. **43**: 84-85; v. **44**:

86-87; v. **45**: 88-89; v. **46**: 90-91; v. **47**: 92-93; v. **52**: 102-103; v. **54**: 107-108; v. **56**: 111-112; v. **59**: 117-118; v. **60**: 119-120; v. **61**: 121-122; v. **62**: 123-124; v. **63**: 125-126; v. **68**: 135-136; v. **70**: 141-142; v. **71**: 143-144; v. **72**: 145-146; v. **73**: 147-148; v. **75**: 152-153; v. **77**: 155-156; v. **78**: 157-158; v. **82**: 166-167; v. **83**: 168-169; v. **84**: 170-171; v. **85**: 172-173; v. **86**: 174-175; v. **87**: 176-177; v. **88**: 178-179; v. **90**: 181-182; v. **91**: 183-184; v. **92**: 185-186; v. **93**: 187-188; v. **94**: 189-190; v. **98**: 197-198; v. **99**: 199-200; v. **100**: 201-202; v. **101**: 203-204; v. **104**: 209-210; v. **105**: 211-212; v. **106**: 213-214; v. **107**: 215-216; v. **108**: 217-218; v. **114**: 226-227; v. **115**: 228-229; v. **116**: 230-231; v. **117**: 232-233; v. **118**: 234-235; v. **120**: 240-241; v. **124**: 247-248; v. **125**: 249-250; v. **128**: 254-255; v. **131**: 259-260; v. **132**: 261-262; v. **134**: 266-267; v. **135**: 268-269; v. **137**: 270-271; v. **138**: 272-273; v. **139**: 274-275; v. **140**: 276-277; v. **143**: 282-283; v. **144**: 284-285; v. **145**: 286-287; **146**: 288-289; v. **147**: 290-291; v. **149**: 296-297; v. **151**: 299-300; v. **153**: 303-304; v. **154**: 305-306.

ratio 1: 2 and ½ : v. **11**: 21b-23; v. **24**: 46b-48; v. **37**: 72b-74; v. **58**: 114b-116; v. **103**: 206b-208; v. **142**: 279-281a.

ratio 1:3: v. **13**: 26-28; v. **51**: 99-101; v. **53**: 104-106; v. **79**: 159-161; v. **81**: 163-165; v. **95**: 191-193; v. **133**: 263-265.

ratio 1:4: v. **67**: 131-134; **69**: 137-140; v. **119**: 236-239; v. **148**: 292-295.

Summary

Additions

Lat: OE		Lat lines	OE lines
ratio 0:1	(x 9)	0	9
ratio 0:½	(x 8)	0	4
	Sub-total	0	13

Omissions

Lat: OE		Lat lines	OE lines
ratio 1:0		1	0
	Sub-total	1	0

Translation

Lat: OE		Lat lines	OE lines
ratio 1:½	(x 3)	3	1 and ½
ratio ½:½	(x 1)	½	½
ratio 1:1	(x 17)	17	17
ratio 2:2	(x 1)	2	2
ratio ½:1	(x 2)	1	2
ratio ½:1 and ½	(x 1)	½	1 and ½
ratio 1:1 and ½	(x 15)	15	22 and ½
ratio 1:2	(x 97)	97	194
ratio 1:2 and ½	(x 6)	6	15
ratio 1:3	(x 7)	7	21
ratio 1:4	(x 4)	4	16
	Sub-total	152	293
	Total lines	154	306

Old English runic inscriptions: Textual criticism and historical grammar

Alfred Bammesberger (Eichstätt, Germany)

The editorial problems[1] presented by runic epigraphical material are in some ways similar to those presented by texts preserved in manuscripts employing the Latin script,[2] but in some ways they are notably different.[3] Whereas modern technology allows us to read certain faded and almost erased passages from manuscripts, epigraphical material has often suffered damage beyond repair. If a stone monument has been impaired by the inclemency of the weather or by human barbarism we have in most cases little hope of restoring the pristine shape of an inscription. But taking into account details of comparative linguistics and the history of the language may be of help in interpreting fragmentary inscriptions.

The following lines will deal with philological problems presented by four selected Old English runic inscriptions. Two of these inscriptions were found recently, the remaining two have been known from the beginning of serious runic studies. The emphasis in my account will lie on questions of historical grammar.

1. The *Harford Farm Brooch*

The *Harford Farm Brooch* was published by John Hines in 1991, who introduced his account as follows: "A seventh-century runic inscription has been found on an Anglo-Saxon brooch excavated from a cemetery site at Harford Farm, Caistor-by-Norwich, Norfolk" (Hines 1991: 6). A somewhat more detailed account of the inscription is available in Parsons's monograph (Parsons 1999: 53-4); figure 1 is taken from Parsons (1999: 54).

The inscription is partly legible without any trouble, but some runes are less clear.
The inscription can be transcribed as follows:

l	u	d	a	:	g	i	b	œ	t	æ	s	i	g	i	l	æ
1	2	3	4		5	6	7	8	9	10	11	12	13	14	15	16

At least part of the text seems to make sense immediately. If we take the points following the runes for **luda** (1-4) as a word divider, then it is likely that **luda** represents a name, which is actually what all specialists who dealt with the inscription find acceptable. The remaining sequence readily splits up as **gibœtæ sigilæ**, and the second of these words is likely to refer somehow to the brooch, so that what precedes may be considered as a finite verbal form belonging to the verb OE *ge-bētan* 'to improve, repair, make amends'.

Hines thinks the inscription means 'manifestly': 'Luda repaired the brooch'. He appends the following note:

> *Luda* is a recorded Old English masculine personal name, and *gibœtæ* is the predictable form in a runic inscription of this date of the 3rd person singular preterite of the verb recorded in later Old English as *gebētan* 'to repair'. The form *sigilæ* is just slightly unusual in its ending *-æ*, which as an accusative singular inflection is that of a strong feminine noun, but a strong feminine *sigel* is recorded in Toller's *Supplement* to Bosworth and Toller's *An Anglo-Saxon Dictionary* beside the more familiar neuters *sigel* and *sigle*. (Hines 1991: 7)

The interpretation outlined so far is certainly possible. Some misgivings remain, however. The preterite of *gibǣtan* is to be expected in Old English as *gibǣttæ* in the seventh century, the period to which the brooch has usually been assigned. It is perhaps conceivable that the geminate *-tt-* was simplified in the runic inscription, but the preterite of *gebētan* is regularly *gebētte* in Old English. We may therefore wonder whether **gibœtæ** should morphologically be accounted for in a different way.

The ending *-æ* functioned in Old English as the marker for singular of the present subjunctive (see now my 2003 paper), a form that at a later stage appeared regularly as *-e*.[4] It is therefore readily possible to interpret **gibœtæ** as third person singular of the present subjunctive of **gibœtan**. The form can be assumed to mean 'may (he) improve, may (he) get better', possibly also 'may he repair'.

We now turn to the following word, which according to Hines is mostly found as a neuter. The ending *-æ* can represent the dative, and the dative had also taken over the function of the instrumental. If we allow **sigil** to mean 'brooch', then a dative instrumental **sigilæ** can readily mean 'by means of the brooch'.

In the final analysis, I suggest that the whole inscription should be interpreted as a wish for the person who wore or carried the brooch. Theoretically the precise syntactic analysis of the inscription allows two possibilities: **luda** can be the nominative, then we would translate 'may Luda make amends by means of the brooch'. Alternatively **luda** could be a vocative, but then the finite verb would be expected as a second person imperative. Since

gibœtæ cannot be analysed as an imperative, this alternative is unconvincing. Even if uncertainties remain with regard to the interpretation of the complete inscription, I think that **gibœtæ** should definitely be parsed as a third person singular of the present subjunctive.

2. The *Brandon Antler* runic inscription

The so-called *Brandon Antler* was published by David Parsons in 1991, but had already been referred to in a slightly earlier publication by R.I. Page (1991: 39): "The runes run along the length of the artefact, with some twelve letters visible and traces of others." Parsons offered a detailed description of the piece together with a drawing of it and a special drawing and transliteration of the runes. The inscription[5] consists of fifteen runic units, which will be numbered consecutively. Runes 1-12 can be identified without major difficulty. Only runes 13 and 14 are unclear, therefore question marks will be put in their places. Rune 15 is a ligature, of which we can readily identify an **a** and an **n**. The inscription may be transliterated as follows (see also Mitchell 1994; Flowers 1999: 6):

w	o	h	s	w	i	l	d	u	m	d	e	?	?	a͡n
1	2	3	4	5	6	7	8	9	10	11	12	13	14	15

Parsons interpreted runes 1-4 as OE *wōhs* 'grew' (preterite of *weaxan* 'grow') and 5-10 as *wildum* 'wild' (dative singular of the adjective *wilde*), which is likely to be correct. The remaining five runic units pose some problems, however, although runes 11 and 12 are likely to be read as **d** and **e**. It would certainly seem plausible to read runes 13 and 14 as **o** and **r** respectively, since what is visible in the drawing may well represent traces of these letters. Parsons (1991: 10) concluded: "The text is clearly: *wōhs wildum dēoran* 'grew on a wild animal'."

But the form *dēoran* is unexpected in the paradigm of the *a*-stem *dēor* (neuter) 'animal', as Parsons noted. The assumption of "a weak masculine *dēora* (otherwise found only as a possible personal name element in place names) beside the familiar strong neuter *dēor*" (Parsons 1991: 10) cannot really be supported by further evidence and is therefore very doubtful indeed. Theoretically, one could perhaps assume that *deoran* as dative plural (with *-um* appearing as *-an*) would be in congruence with a dative plural *wildum*, but the resulting translation 'grew on wild animals' does not make sense in the given context, since the tine certainly grew on one animal. The reading *wildum deoran* does not lead to a viable analysis of the text.

In the year following Parsons's edition, the Belgian runologist René Derolez published a brief note on the *Brandon Antler* inscription, in which he gave the following interpretation:

> *wōhs wildum dēor an* (or *on*, if that reading is possible), with the preposition in postposition. The grammar would be different than in David Parsons' suggestion in *Nytt om Runer* 6 (1991), pp. 9-10: *wōhs wildum dēoran*, with an anomalous inflection of *deor*. The translation, however, would be the same: 'grew on a wild animal'. (Derolez 1992: 8)

Derolez's analysis has been accepted by Page (1999: 170).

Derolez's approach seems correct, but the analysis of the unit given as rune 15 allows some further discussion. If runes 13 and 14 are indeed to be read as **o** and **r**, then the resulting form *deor* (nominative or accusative) is not congruent with the dative *wildum*. We expect a dative *deore*. One could suggest that *-e* was left out before the vocalic initial of the following word. But this is possibly too facile.

If we take into consideration that **wohs** (= OE *wōx*) represents the historically correct preterite of a strong verb of class VI with the vowel *ō*, which was then replaced by the diphthong *ēo* taken over from class VII (see Campbell 1959: 318), we may assume that the inscription belongs to an early stage of Old English. Since Mitchell (1994) dates the inscription to "late 7th to early 9th century", we may assume that the distinction of the final vowels *-æ* and *-i*, which later fell together under *-e*, was still preserved (Campbell 1959: 153). For an early period of Old English the dative singular of *dēor* could be postulated as *dēoræ* (Campbell 1959: 224).

The final phoneme *-æ* of *dēoræ* may perhaps be contained in the ligatured rune 15. Rune 15 has so far been interpreted as a ligature of **a** + **n**, which is plausible. But if the ligature was originally intended to represent **æ** + **a** + **n**, it would probably not have had a different shape. One may even surmise that **o** as the second member of the sequence would not have caused a modification in the shape of the ligature either, so that Derolez's reading of the postposition as *on* seems acceptable: The preposition appears as *on* in the majority of its occurrences, but *an* is also found.

The sequence of runes on the *Brandon Antler* can therefore be transliterated as either *wōhs wildum dēoræ an* or *wōhs wildum dēoræ on*. The text meaning 'grew on a wild animal' suggests "a link with Anglo-Saxon riddle tradition" (Parsons 1991: 11).

3. The *Overchurch Stone*

The so-called *Overchurch Stone* was found in 1887 when a small church at Upton (Wirral) was dismantled. Formerly the stone was in the Grosvenor Museum in Chester, now it is on permanent loan to the Williamson Art Gallery, Birkenhead, near Liverpool. The runic text in two lines can be transcribed as follows:[6]

f	o	l	c	æ	a	r	æ	r	d	o	n	b	e	c
1	2	3	4	5	6	7	8	9	10	11	12	13	14	15

b	i	d	d	a	þ	f	o	t	e	æ	þ	e	l	m	u	n
16	17	18	19	20	21	22	23	24	25	26	27	28	29	30	31	32

Although the inscription is not complete, certain elements can be distinguished without major difficulty. The sequence **ærærdon** (runes 6-12) is likely to represent the preterite of *arœran* 'raise', and **biddaþ** (runes 16-21) can be interpreted as the imperative of *biddan* 'pray'. It may be assumed that two runes were lost preceding **biddaþ**, and **gebiddaþ** will certainly fill the space. The last three runes **bec** (runes 13-15) of line one may represent the beginning of the word **becun** 'sign'. Furthermore, it is probable that **fote** (runes 22-25) is miswritten for **fore**. The preposition is likely to have been followed by a name, and the incomplete sequence **æþelmun** (runes 26-32) may be assumed to stand for the name **æþelmundæ**. The second line can therefore be translated as 'pray for Æthelmund', which is what may be expected in this context.

Problematic is the first line. The usual assumption is that the line means 'the people erected this monument' (Elliott 1959: 71; 1989: 95). The translation is meaningful, but the initial five runes are not compatible with it. The subject of a clause with this meaning could only be expected as **folc**, since the neuter *folc* would remain unchanged in the plural. It is unlikely that **æ** was inserted by accident, therefore we have to inquire whether a form **folcæ** can reasonably be interpreted in the given context. Grammatically, **folcæ** is the regularly shaped dative singular of **folc**, and we have to examine whether a dative singular 'for the people' makes sense in the given context.

If we assume that **folcæ** is the dative object and **becun** the accusative object of **rærdon**, then the clause would be without an expressed subject. This is by no means unheard of in Old English. The beginning of Cædmon's Hymn *Nu scylun hergian* (Smith 1933: 38) is rendered in the Latin version as 'nunc laudare debemus', which shows that a plural form like *scylun* could be analysed by speakers of Old English as first person plural even if no personal pronoun was added.[7] If we assume that in a similar way **aræerdon** means 'we erected', then the inscription can be interpreted in a meaningful way: Æthelmund was evidently an important and wealthy person, and his heirs set up a monument in his honour. On the monument they inscribed a text which means: 'For the people (i.e. so that the people can see it) we erected this monument: Pray for Æthelmund.'

4. The *Ruthwell Cross* inscription

Howlett (1993: 71) characterised the *Ruthwell Cross* (Dumfriesshire, Scotland) and its inscriptions as follows:

> The Ruthwell Cross, one of the most glorious relics of Anglo-Saxon culture, exhibits an extensive program of sculpture, the longest extant series of Anglo-Latin inscriptions, the longest Old English runic inscription, and the most beautiful poem in the Old Northumbrian dialect.

Although the interpretation of the runic inscription on the *Ruthwell Cross* has always benefitted from the Vercelli Book version of the poem entitled *The dream of the rood*, there are certainly also some respects in which the parallelism was detrimental. With some 260 runes still clear on the cross the runic inscription is certainly "the most sustained piece of runic carving in Anglo-Saxon England, and so gives us the clearest opportunity for seeing English runes in action in formal expression" (Page 1973: 151; 1999: 148).[8]

Only in the seventies and eighties of the twentieth century did a completely new approach to the *Ruthwell Cross* inscription develop. The main innovation was provided by David Howlett's 1978 paper. This short paper represents the first serious attempt to reconstruct the text of what has since been called the *Ruthwell Crucifixion poem* as a poem in its own right. Previously, the Ruthwell text had been viewed as a minor version of the Vercelli Book *Dream of the rood*. The interpretation of the *Ruthwell Crucifixion poem* was further advanced in a long paper by Ó Carragáin (1987-8).[9]

I wish to deal mainly with four separate textual problems: The first word **]geredæ** on the east panel is only partly preserved, so that the restoration of the original reading presents problems (4.1.). In the cases of **fusæ** (4.2.) and **strelum** (4.3.), the grammatical analysis of well preserved forms is at issue. And finally the form **gastæ**, which Howlett (1978) posits, is no longer legible at all; we can therefore only examine whether the reconstruction is linguistically tenable (4.4.). Finally, a speculation concerning the inscription on the top of the cross is submitted (4.5.).

4.1. -geredæ

The first word on the east panel can be read as **geredæ** nowadays; the preceding part of the word was destroyed when the Cross was toppled down. There is an early drawing (see Page 1959a) which allows us to read the word as **+ondgeredæ**, although the identification of the first rune remains doubtful, because in early drawings the runes for o, a, and æ were not consistently distinguished. But the reconstruction **+ondgeredæ**, accepted also by Howlett (1978), is probably correct.

The point I want to make is not affected by this question, however. I am mainly concerned with Howlett's *Anglia* paper, in which he offers a totally new interpretation of this form: "one might translate *ondgeredæ hinæ god almeʒttig* not 'God almighty stripped himself', nor even 'God almighty girded himself', but 'God almighty prepared himself for conflict' or 'girded himself as an adversary'" (Howlett 1998: 235). Since *ond-* and its far more frequent form *on-* in verbal compounds regularly have the meaning of 'off, away', I would certainly maintain that **ondgeredæ** must mean 'he stripped himself', namely Christ took off his clothes, and of course in iconography he normally wears just a loincloth.[10]

4.2. fusæ

The runic inscription on the west face of the *Ruthwell Cross* clearly corresponds to the following lines in the *Dream of the rood*:

    Crist wæs on rode.
 Hwæðere þær fuse feorran cwoman
to þam æðelinge. Ic þæt eall beheold. (*Dream of the rood*, 56b-58)

Although not all runes can be read nowadays and the lower part of the inscription is completely destroyed, a considerable number of individual runes can be deciphered without major trouble. If we split up the sequence of runes into sixteen words we can distinguish three main clauses in five half-lines:[11]

    krist wæs on rodi;
 hweþræ þer fusæ fearran kwomu
æþþilæ til anum; ic þæt al biheald;

Page (1973: 151; 1999: 148) translated the runic sequence as follows: "'Christ was on the cross. Yet to this solitary one there came men from afar, eager and noble. I beheld it all.'"

There is no doubt that the translation of the first and the third clause is correct. With regard to the second clause some uncertainty remains, however. Part of the problem lies in the fact that the Vercelli Book version diverges to a certain extent from the epigraphical one. Since the *Dream* version can be translated as 'however there came from afar eager ones to the noble one' it has often been assumed that **til anum** means something like 'to the solitary one' and refers to Christ. It is somewhat strange that **æþþilæ** on the *Ruthwell Cross*, most likely to be an adjective used as the subject of its clause and meaning 'noble ones', should appear as *æðelinge*, evidently dative singular of *æðeling* 'noble one', in the Vercelli Book version.

In a detailed study Rissanen (1967) showed that **til anum** cannot refer to Christ. That **anum** should in any way indicate 'solitariness' seems quite unlikely because neither the epigraphical document nor the manuscript tradition mentions Christ's loneliness. But the strongest indication that **til anum** cannot mean 'to this solitary one' is provided by the fact that a construction in this sense cannot be evidenced from our Old English documentation. If anything like 'noble ones came to him, namely Christ' had been intended, we would certainly expect the anaphoric pronoun *him to have been used.

With regard to **til anum** Rissanen is likely to have found the right solution. Rissanen also raises the question who **fusæ** and **æþþilæ** in the clause **hweþræ þer fusæ fearran kwomu æþþilæ til anum** may refer to. A definitive answer does not seem possible, and Rissanen (1967: 287) concludes: "... it is evident, in any case, that **fusæ** and **æþþilæ** refer to two or more persons".

As far as I can see, **fusæ** and **æþþilæ** have always been interpreted as grammatically identical, namely as forms for the nominative plural of the strong adjective. For **æþþilæ** this interpretation is evidently correct. For **fusæ** an alternative can be suggested, however. Since adverbs derived from adjectival stems regularly end in *-e* in Old English and this ending points back to earlier *-æ* we may well ask whether **fusæ** represents an adverb. Corresponding adverbs in **-æ** occur as **hweþræ** 'however' and **saræ** 'sorely, painfully' in the *Ruthwell Cross* inscription. The rendering 'noble persons came eagerly together' avoids the otherwise most difficult question what precisely the meaning of an adjective **fusæ** would be in the given context, since 'eager nobles' or the like does not seem meaningful.[12]

4.3. miþ strelum giwundad

The left margin of the west face of the *Ruthwell Cross* contains in eight rows of mostly two runes a sequence that can be split up into three words: **miþ strelum giwundad**. These three words scan metrically as a half-line and call to mind line 62b of the *Dream of the rood*:

Forleton me þa hilderincas
standan steame bedrifenne; eall ic wæs mid strælum forwundod
(*Dream of the rood*, 61b-62)

Whereas in the Vercelli Book *wæs mid strælum forwundod* clearly functions as the predicate of the Cross speaking to the first person narrator in his dream, it is likely that **miþ strelum giwundad** on the *Ruthwell Cross* refers to Christ. The half-line is mostly translated as 'wounded by arrows', but Swanton (1970: 122) added the following remark: "Alternatively *stræl* might refer to the soldier's spear which pierced the side of Christ (19-20, 48-9) were it not for the plural form of the noun supported by the sense of *eall*." Ó Carragáin (1987-8) also considers a translation 'wounded by the lance', which seems reasonable.

The main question to be dealt with here is the precise analysis of **strelum**. With regard to Swanton's comment it may be pointed out that the adverbial *eall* 'completely' does not tell us anything at all about the number of *strælum* because we can say 'I was completely wounded by an arrow' or 'by arrows'. But the main problem is the analysis of **strelum**, which definitely is not a singular form. It should be mentioned, however, that words for weapons in particular do occur in non-singular form although clearly a singular is meant. This applies to forms like *mecum, sweordum, hiltum*, which mean 'by the sword'. The reason for this at first sight surprising usage of a form in -*um* certainly is that we are here concerned with fossilised dual forms, so that *mecum* originally meant 'by means of the two edges of the sword'. Therefore, we should not hesitate to interpret **strelum** as meaning 'by the lance', which is of course perfectly meaningful theologically, because Christ's body was opened by one wound inflicted by a soldier, and from this wound his blood gushed forth; later theologians considered Christ's wound as the source for the church. Rendering **strelum** by 'arrows' in the plural would destroy the whole theological context of the poem.[13]

4.4. gastæ

The left border of the east panel is incomplete towards the bottom. Howlett (1978) gave a probable reconstruction of what the original reading may have been. The last half-line is reconstructed as follows: **siþþan He His gastæ sendæ**.[14] There is hardly any doubt that originally the inscription was similar to what Howlett reconstructed, but one detail definitely requires a correction.

With regard to the form **gastæ** Howlett refers to *Bede's death song*, in which this form certainly occurs (Smith 1933: 42). But in the sequence *huaet his gastae ... doemid uueorthae* the form *gastae* is no doubt a dative of the singular, as is regularly to be expected in this syntactic context. A dative singular would make no sense whatsoever in the reconstructed passage of the *Ruthwell Crucifixion poem*. Since the half-line should mean 'after he sent forth his spirit', the form for 'spirit' must be in the accusative; we therefore need **gast**. Furthermore the simplex verb *sendan* would probably not mean 'send forth', therefore a prefix is likely to have occurred. I suggest that Howlett's reconstruction should be corrected as follows: **siþþan he his gast ondsendæ**,[15] but the precise shape of the verbal prefix can hardly be determined.

4.5.][.]æ f a u œ þ o [

By way of conclusion to an inconclusive paper, I wish to add a short remark on the panel on top of the cross. This panel now depicts a bird perched on a branch bearing fruit. What is left of the runic inscription has been given by Page (1999: 146) as follows: **][.]æ f a u œ þ o [** "standing amidst other, unidentifiable, runes". With regard to explaining this inscription Page icily comments: "Attempts at interpreting this sequence have shown more ingenuity than judgement." The assessment is fully justified.

Since all previous suggestions are certainly not convincing, I wish to point out that this could be simply a representation of the futhark, with the new Old English runes inserted between the regular futhark signs: **f - u - þ - o** would represent the regular sequence of the runic "alphabet" in Anglo-Saxon times, whereas **æ - a - œ** would draw attention to the innovations that occurred in prehistoric Old English times. But this is of course also only a speculation.

Notes

[1] This revised text of my paper read at the Munich 2001 Medieval Symposium incorporates suggestions made in the discussion following its presentation. Basically, the text of

the oral delivery has been preserved, but footnotes referring to further investigations and providing bibliographical details have been added.

[2] On editing manuscript material see above all Gneuss (1998) with many references to further literature on the question.

[3] Runes are transliterated in **boldface**. Some preliminary indications towards an edition of the Old English runic material are given in Bammesberger (1994).

[4] The Germanic subjunctive goes back to the optative of Indo-European. In thematic presents the optative was characterized by IE *-o-i-* preceding the person markers, IE *-oi-* yielded *-ai-* in Germanic (cf. Go. *bairai* 'he may carry'), and final *-ai* led to *-æ* in early Old English, which was weakened to *-e*. On the history of the subjunctive paradigm see Brunner (1965: 277), Campbell (1959: 298), and Bammesberger (1984: 70).

[5] Figure 2 gives illustrative material made available by Robert Carr, Archaeological Service, Conservation Team, Environment & Transport department, Suffolk County Council, Archaeological Unit, Shire Hall, Bury St Edmunds, Suffolk.

[6] Figure 3 gives a drawing of the inscription. A photograph provided by the museum is available in Bammesberger (1991, plate 2).

[7] The beginning of *Cædmon's hymn* can be analysed in different ways however; see above all Ball (1985: 40).

[8] A very detailed account of the runes is available in Page (1959a).

[9] For readily accessible editions of both the *Ruthwell crucifixion poem* and *The Dream of the rood* see ASPR 2, Dickins -- Ross (1934), Bütow (1935), Swanton (1970), Schwab (1978), and Kelly -- Quinn (1999).

[10] I argue this point at greater length in Bammesberger (2002a).

[11] The semicolon is used to mark off three syntactic units.

[12] A somewhat more detailed account of this problem will be found in Bammesberger (2003a).

[13] Ultimately in most cases of this type we are probably concerned with dual forms. Klaeber (1950: 151) briefly comments on these forms, which he terms 'generic plural'. I have collected some relevant material in my 2001 paper.

[14] Howlett (1978) uses capitals in **He** and **His**, but since the runic script would not distinguish capitals from lower case letters, no distinction is made in the following discussion.

[15] I deal with this part of the inscription in more detail in my paper Bammesberger (2002a).

References

Baker, Peter S. -- Nicholas Howe (eds.)
    1998   *Words and works: Studies in medieval English language and literature in honour of Fred C. Robinson.* (Toronto Old English Series 10.) Toronto: University of Toronto Press.

Ball, C. J. E.
    1985   "Homonymy and polysemy in Old English: A problem for lexicographers", in: Bammesberger (ed.), 39-46.

Bammesberger, Alfred
    1984   *A sketch of diachronic English morphology.* Regensburg: Pustet.

    1994   "Editing Old English runic inscriptions", G. Blaicher -- B. Glaser (eds.), *Anglistentag 1993 Eichstätt*, Tübingen: Niemeyer, 503-15.

    2001   "Altenglisch *æt hēafdum* und der elliptische Dual", in: Fritz -- Zeilfelder (eds.), 25-34.

    2002a   "A doubtful reconstruction in the Old English *Ruthwell Crucifixion poem*", *Studia Neophilologica* 74: 143-45.

2002b	"The *Brandon Antler* runic inscription", *Neophilologus* 86: 129-31.
2003a	"Das erste Wort der altenglischen Runeninschrift auf dem *Ruthwellkreuz*", *Anglia* 121: 265-73.
2003b	"The Harford Farm Brooch runic inscription", *Neophilologus* 87: 133-35.
2003c	"Zu **fusæ** in der Runeninschrift auf dem Ruthwell-Kreuz", in: Heizmann -- van Nahl (eds.), 28-34.

Bammesberger, Alfred (ed.)
    1985   *Problems of Old English lexicography: Studies in memory of Angus Cameron*. Regensburg: Pustet.

    1991   *Old English runes and their continental background*. Heidelberg: Winter.

Brunner, Karl
    1965   *Altenglische Grammatik nach der Angelsächsischen Grammatik von Eduard Sievers*. (3rd edition.) Tübingen: Niemeyer.

Bütow, Hans
    1935   *Das altenglische 'Traumgesicht vom Kreuz', Textkritisches, Literaturgeschichtliches, Kunstgeschichtliches*. Heidelberg: Winter.

Campbell, A[listair]
    1959   *Old English grammar*. Oxford: Clarendon.

Cassidy, Brendan (ed.)
    1993   *The Ruthwell cross: Papers from the colloquium sponsored by the Index of Christian Art, Princeton University, 8 December 1989*. Princeton: Princeton University Press.

Derolez, René
    1992   "Comment on the deer's antler from Brandon, Suffolk", *Nytt om Runer* 7: 8.

Dickins, Bruce -- Alan S. C. Ross (eds.)
    1934   *The Dream of the rood.* London: Methuen.

Elliott, R. W. V.
    1959   *Runes: An introduction.* Manchester: Manchester University Press.
    1989   2nd edition.

Flowers, Stephen
    1999   *A concise edition of the Old English runic inscriptions.* Smithville, Texas: Rûna-Raven Press.

Fritz, Matthias -- Susanne Zeilfelder (eds.)
    2001   *Novalis Indogermanica: Festschrift für Günter Neumann zum 80. Geburtstag.* Graz: Leykam.

Gneuss, Helmut
    1998   "Old English texts and modern readers: Notes on editing and textual criticism", in: Baker -- Howe (eds.), 127-41.

Heizmann, Wilhelm -- Astrid van Nahl (eds.)
    2003   *Runica – Germanica – Mediaevalia.* Berlin: de Gruyter.

Hines, John
    1991   "A new runic inscription from Norfolk", *Nytt om Runer* 6: 6-7.

Howlett, David
    1978   "A reconstruction of the Ruthwell Crucifixion Poem", *Studia neophilologica* 50: 54-58.
    1992   "Inscriptions and design of the Ruthwell Cross", in: Cassidy (ed.), 71-93.
    1998   "English *ondgierwan, ongierwan, ungierwan*", *Anglia* 116: 223-26.

Kelly, Richard J. -- Ciarán L. Quinn (eds.)
1999   *Stone, skin, and silver: A translation of the Dream of the rood.* Middleton: Litho.

Klaeber, Frederick
1950   *Beowulf and The fight at Finnsburg.* (3rd edition.) Boston: D.C. Heath.

Mitchell, M.
1994   *Corpus of English runes.* Basle: [no publisher given].

Ó Carragáin, Éamonn
1987-1988   "The Ruthwell Crucifixion Poem in its iconographic and liturgical contexts", *Peritia* 6-7: 1-71.

Page, Raymond I.
1959a   "An early drawing of the Ruthwell Cross", *Medieval archaeology* 3: 285-88.

1959b   *The inscriptions of the Anglo-Saxon rune-stones.* Unpublished Ph.D. dissertation, University of Nottingham.

1973   *An introduction to English runes.* London: Methuen.

1991   "Anglo-Saxon runic studies: The way ahead?", in: Bammesberger (ed.), 15-39.

1999   *An introduction to English runes.* (2nd edition.) Woodbridge: Boydell.

Parsons, David
1991   "New runic finds from Brandon, Suffolk", *Nytt om Runer* 6: 8-11.

1999   *Recasting the runes: The reform of the Anglo-Saxon futhorc.* (Runrön. Runologiska bidrag utgivna av Institutionen för nordiska språk vid Uppsala universitet 14.) Uppsala: Institutionen för nordiska språk.

Rissanen, Matti
    1967   "Two notes on Old English poetic texts", *Neuphilologische Mitteilungen* 68: 276-88.

Schwab, Ute
    1978   "Das Traumsgesicht vom Kreuzesbaum: Ein ikonologischer Interpretationsansatz zu dem ags. *Dream of the rood*', in: Schwab -- Stutz (eds.), 131-92.

Schwab, Ute -- Elfriede Stutz (eds.)
    1978   *Philologische Studien, Gedenkschrift für Richard Kienast*. Heidelberg: Winter.

Smith, A. H. (ed.)
    1933   *Three Northumbrian poems*. London: Methuen.

Swanton, Michael (ed.)
    1970   *The Dream of the rood*. Manchester: Manchester University Press.

Old English runic inscriptions 85

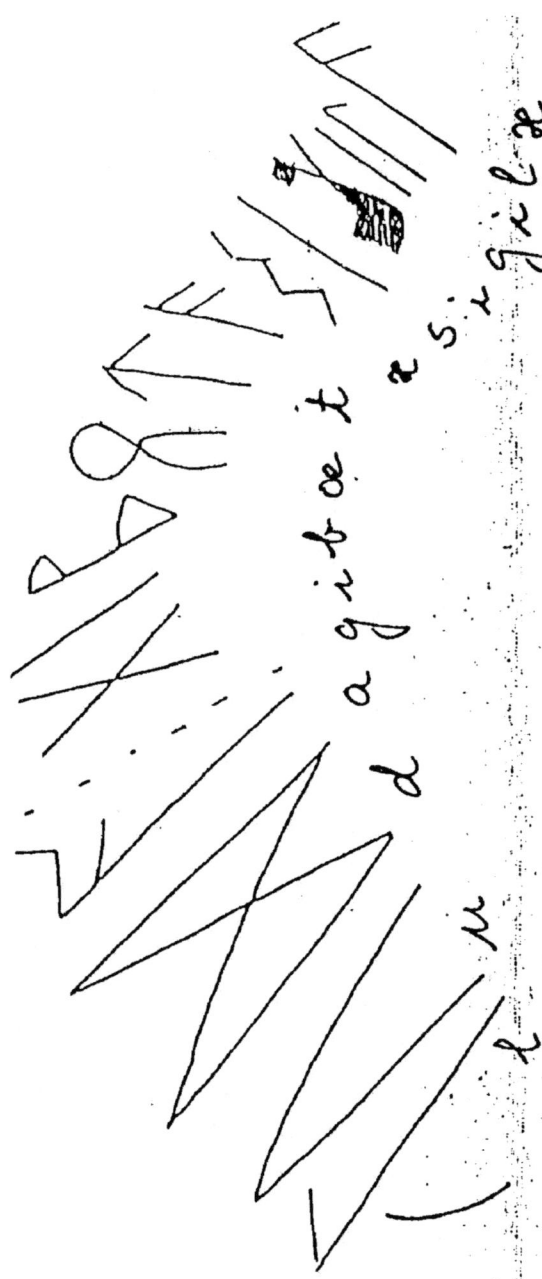

Figure 1: The *Harford Farm Brooch* inscription

86 Alfred Bammesberger

Figure 2: The *Brandon Antler*

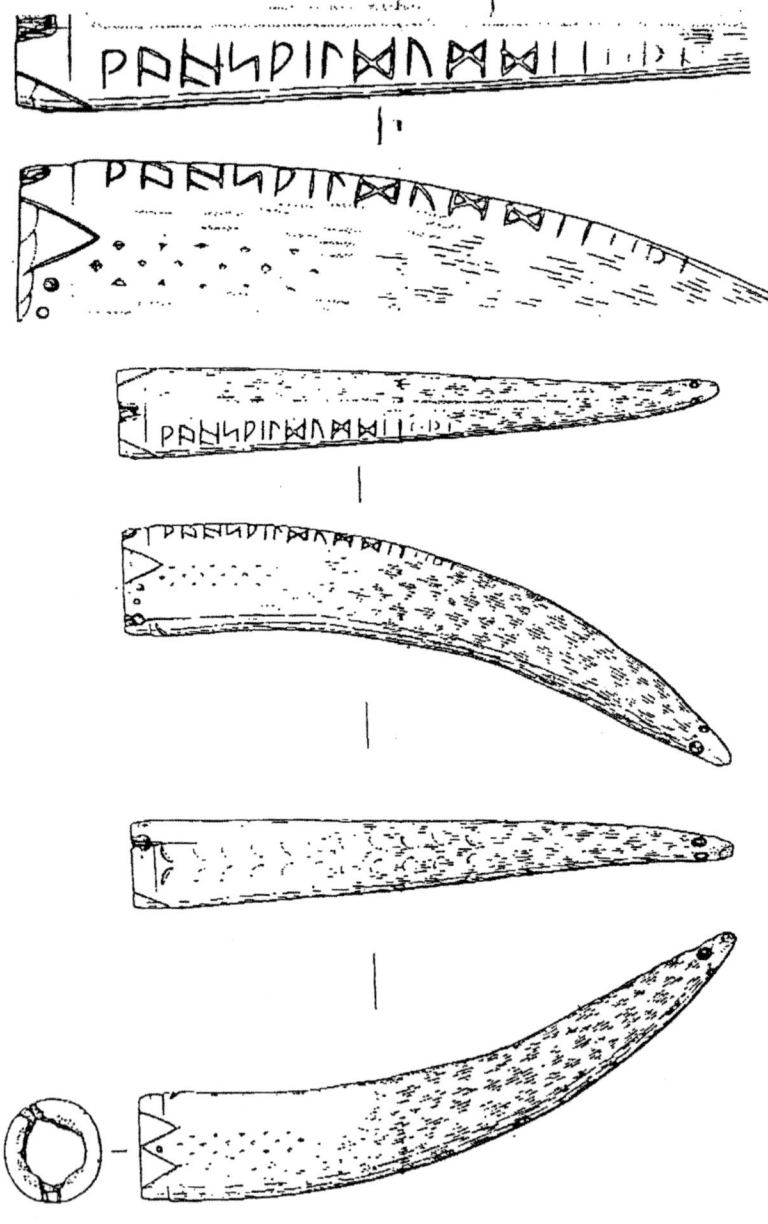

Old English runic inscriptions 87

Figure 3: The *Overchurch Stone* inscription

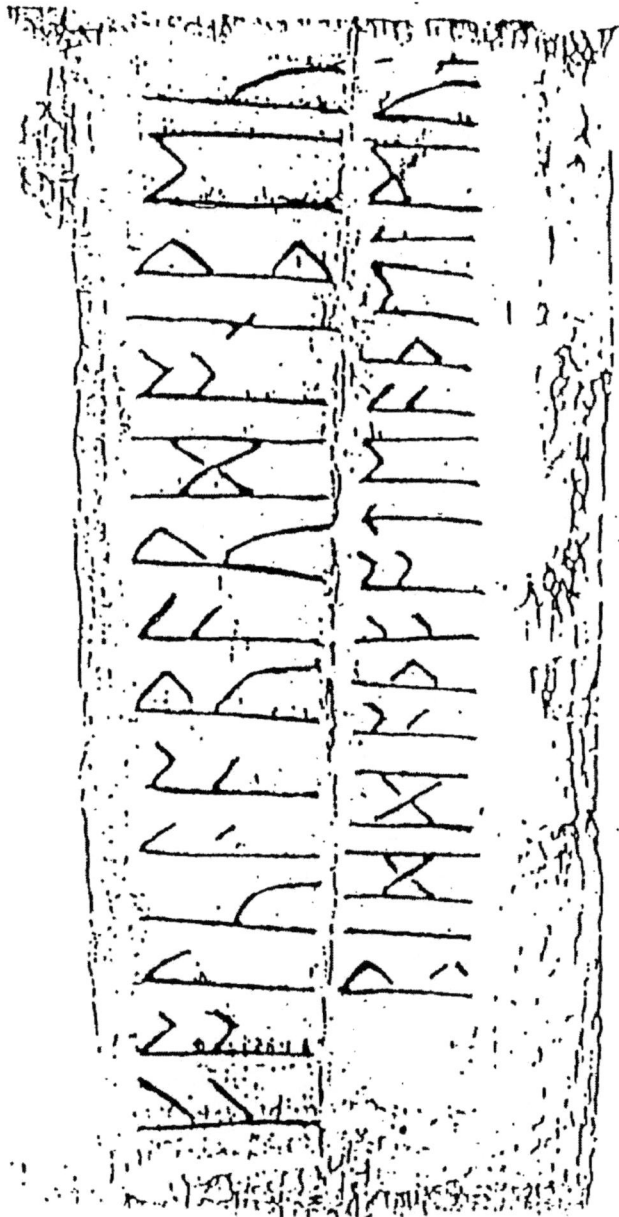

The Narragansett runic inscription, Rhode Island[1]

Ian Kirby (Lausanne, Switzerland)

Half a century ago it was the common view, held even by some scholars in the field of Scandinavian studies, that Norsemen got no further west than Greenland, and this in spite of the accounts in the Norse sagas of the Greenlanders and of Erik the Red. This view ceased to be widely held in the nineteen-sixties as a result of the identification of the L'Anse aux Meadows site close to the north-western tip of Newfoundland as a Norse settlement, or way station, inhabited briefly early in the 11th century. But it seems to me that another kind of invisible barrier has subsequently come into being, this time an east-west line just to the south of L'Anse aux Meadows: for it appears to be the common view among Scandinavian scholars today that the Norse explorations did not extend significantly southwards from this site. Even the discovery in the New England state of Maine of a late 11th-century Norwegian penny has not modified this view, for the common scholarly opinion is that the coin came into the possession of the Native Americans much further north and made its way more than a thousand miles southwards to Penobscot Bay via their coastal trade routes – a valid explanation, certainly, but not, of course, the only possible one. In this paper I shall examine another potential source of evidence that the Norsemen did in fact extend their exploration of the North American continent much further south than Newfoundland.

Runic inscriptions in North America have been a scholarly problem for more than a century, though there is no *a priori* reason to rule out the possibility that a genuine medieval one might some day be identified. After all: the L'Anse aux Meadows discovery demonstrated beyond reasonable doubt the presence of Norsemen in Newfoundland; wherever the Norsemen went, from northern Greenland to Piraeus and Istanbul, they carved runes; we must therefore allow that they could have done so in North America. This possibility was admitted by the archeologists who worked on the Newfoundland site, and who looked unsuccessfully for an inscription in the neighbourhood of L'Anse aux Meadows.

As is well known, the nature of the problem is not that there are no runic or might-be-runic inscriptions in North America, but that there are rather too many of them. The best known is the Kensington inscription, which has been almost unanimously rejected by runologists as a late 19th-century fake; but this is only one of fifty or so inscriptions which have at one time or another been considered genuine by some investigators. In the early nineteen-sixties the German scholar Hertha Marquardt published a substantial list containing most of these, and concluded that not one of them was a genuine medieval runic inscription: they were either plough marks, the result of natural weathering, man-made but not runic symbols, or runic but modern. Her views have been generally accepted by runologists, though in at least one case, that of the Bourne stone on Cape Cod, some uncertainty may remain. Since then, we have had the discovery of the Spirit Pond stones, now in the Augusta, Maine, museum, which can most certainly be regarded as fakes: the ultra-violet fluorescence test demonstrates this beyond reasonable doubt, and confirms the views of runologists. However, there is one inscription, which came to scholarly attention in 1985, which is not so readily dismissed: the Narragansett inscription.

This inscription is found on a rock currently situated at a point between high and low tide on the west side of Narragansett Bay, in the community of North Kingstown, Rhode Island State. It is a few hundred yards from the Potowomut river mouth, which separates North Kingstown from the township of Warwick. The inscription is covered by the tide for about nine hours in every twelve. It is one of a fair number of inscriptions in the Bay area, some of which have been claimed to be runic; but to the best of my knowledge it is the only one that is.

The rock is a relatively hard quartzite. It is of uneven shape, the maximum measurements being about 2.4 m long, 1.6 m wide at the seaward side but tapering land-wards, and 65 cm above the sand. It would appear that not much of the rock is hidden under the sand. The relatively flat side on which the inscription is carved faces skywards. It is partly covered by green weed and small white barnacles, which latter tend to cluster in the inscription cuts and thus help to render it visible.

The inscription is close to the seaward, wider side of the rock, and is read from the landward side; it may well have been cut by someone sitting close to the landward edge, if the rock was in its current position when the inscription was carved. It is carefully cut with hammer and chisel-type implements, though it seems likely that the surface disturbance in front of the first symbol was caused by an initial attempt which caused the surface to shear off, and the same thing may have happened at the end of the first line. The first four symbols of the first line are very distinct, as are the two of the second line; the fifth and sixth are uncertain, while the seventh vertical does not show clear traces of human intervention, and may be no more than a natural line. The symbols are some 5 to 6 cm in height, and are quite smooth.

The inscription first came to the notice of scholars in 1985. It was reported by a clam-digger, locally known as a *quahogger*, whose attention was drawn to it in December 1984 by the white barnacles in the cuts. It was then examined by local members of the New England Antiquities Research

Association (NEARA), and several articles and comments on it have subsequently been written.

In 1993, I was informed about the inscription by the State Archeologist of Massachusetts, the late Mr James Whittall, and made a brief and superficial initial examination of it in difficult circumstances – the tide was out at the beginning and end of each day, and weather conditions were poor. But enough was visible to make it clear that this is quite definitely a runic inscription: not plough marks, not natural weathering, not in a non-runic script. The problem, however, is (and for the moment remains) the date it was cut: on first inspection it seemed that it could have been done any time between about AD 600 and 1984.

In August 1999, in virtually perfect climatic conditions, I returned to Narragansett Bay together with Dr Peter Pieper, a forensic scientist from the University of Düsseldorf, who had worked with me on an earlier investigation. He made a detailed scientific documentation of the inscription, while I concerned myself more particularly with the historical information which might be gleaned about it from different sources.

First, however, a provisional analysis of the individual symbols of the inscription, since it does not yield an obvious meaning (see figure 1). The first symbol is clearly runic; in most runic alphabets it corresponds to the letter *s*. Other possibilities include *j*, and *a* (on the Istaby stone from southern Sweden, see Moltke 1985: 145). The second symbol is uncertain. One possibility is that it represents a later *h*-rune, but in this the *x*-shape arms are not normally as long. Another is that it is a bind-rune, representing *ig* or *gi*, or *an* or *na*; but I have not seen an instance of the former elsewhere, and only one of the second (on the Føvling stone in Jutland, see Moltke 1985: 409). The third symbol seems to represent the runic *r*. Although the runic form does not usually have the angled lines meet the vertical in the middle, there are numerous instances where they do, including, for example, the Kingiktorsoak stone from northern Greenland. The fourth symbol is runic and appears in the older Germanic alphabet and some others: it normally stands for *o*. The fifth symbol is uncertain, partly because it was not possible to determine whether or not there is an angled cut to the right of the vertical, as the spacing between the runes might seem to indicate. If there was, it may be the final *R*-rune, or the later *m*-rune; if not, we may have the later *k* in reverse. The sixth symbol is very uncertain. The vertical is clear; the cut rising diagonally from the bottom is very probable; if this is a complete rune we may have an upside-down *l*. On the other hand, these two lines might be part of another rune, perhaps a *d*, not completed because of shearing off.

The first symbol of the second line is a major problem. Without the nick on the higher right-hand stave the symbol is a normal older runic *g*; but close examination suggests that the nick was cut at the same time as the rest of the inscription. This gives us a symbol which is otherwise solidly attested only in North America, and only on the Kensington Stone, usually regarded as a late-19th-century forgery, and the Spirit Pond stones, which as indicated earlier we regard as 20th-century forgeries: in all cases it is used to represent *a*. The second symbol is runic, almost always *a*. So one problem with the previous identification is that we seemingly have two different symbols representing the same sound or closely similar ones. The final dot is usually a word division, indicating that the inscription was to be continued. There is, however, no sign of a continuation.

The interpretation of this inscription is thus, for the moment, highly uncertain. The symbols do not seem to fit exactly with any of the known runic alphabets. Though there is a high degree of correspondence with the early Germanic and the transitional Norse futhark of the 7th and 8th centuries, not to mention the Anglo-Saxon one, no obvious meaning results in any case. One approach might be to take the first three symbols of the first line as indicating the Norse word *sigr* 'victory'; even more speculatively, the first five symbols might represent *sigrom* 'we conquer'. But this does not cover the whole of the first line, and can at the very most be the best available guess – assuming, of course, that this is an ancient rather than modern inscription. As to the second line, *ga* (if indeed that is what it is) is reminiscent of the mysterious bind-runes on a Danish spear-shaft (Kragehul) and an English bracteate (Undley: see Moltke 1985: 101, 104f), and the Norse verb in this form has the meaning 'pay attention (to)'; but the problem of the nick, or hook, remains.

In view of all this uncertainty, it was necessary to consider other kinds of information which might lead to an answer to the question whether the inscription is ancient or modern. The first that I shall examine is historical.

Two kinds of information can be adduced under this heading: that resulting from conversations with present and past residents of the immediate neighbourhood, and that available from historical records of various kinds. As already mentioned, the rock is at the present time on the beach between high and low tide: it is completely exposed at low tide, completely covered at high tide. But this has not always been the case. In conversation with Mr James McMahon, owner of the immediately adjacent property for the 30 years between 1947/48 and 1978, we learned that he had known of the inscription since before he acquired the land, and that, when he first saw it, it was not covered by the tide nor, in consequence, by the barnacles etc. which are there today; he and his children had often sat by the rock and wondered what the inscription meant.

That it was not covered by the tide at that time was confirmed by Mr David Brusby, owner of the Mobil station a few miles from the rock. Furthermore, about a hundred metres from the rock, at the same relative position between high and low tide, there is a partly-calcified tree stump. It would thus seem that the beach was much more substantial in the earlier part of the 20th century, and that it was severely damaged by the devastating hurricanes of 1954 and, perhaps, 1938. It follows from this that water erosion and smoothing of the inscription has only been operating for some fifty years, not for centuries.

I was also able to obtain, from books and records in the North Kingstown Public Library, further information about the early history of this spot and its immediate neighbourhood, known as Pojac Point. It was apparently deeded by the local Native American sachem Coquinoquant on June 11, 1659 to a company associated with the English Major Atherton; and in the following centuries it has been owned by different persons, all except the most recent being of English, or at any rate British, stock, to judge by their names. In 1686, it came into the hands of a family named Green; and it remained in their possession until 1848, when it was given to the Welling family as part of a dowry – Mr Bert Welling, greatgrandson of the first Welling owner, still lives in a house near Pojac Point proper, and gave us this information. In 1947, the piece of land closest to the rock was sold to Mr McMahon, who in turn sold it in 1978 to the present owner and builder of the house on it, Mr John Di Giulio. Our thanks are due to these gentlemen for sharing their knowledge with us, and to Mr Di Giulio for allowing us access to the beach through his property.

The rock is about 100 yards northwards from another, much larger, parcel of land giving on to the Bay which has a somewhat different history. The site was acquired in or about 1872 by John Carter Brown, best known perhaps through his association with Brown University at Providence, who in that year constructed the first of several buildings now on the site. In 1907 it became a hospital for tubercular and/or crippled children; and since 1957 it has been a Catholic nursing home for aged Americans of Italian origin. There would seem to be no reason to assume that any of the persons associated with this property would have had either the knowledge or the inclination to have produced the inscription.

It seems then that the inhabitants of the immediate area up to about a century ago were either of Native American or British origin; and it would appear safe to assume that none of them were responsible for the cutting of the inscription. Indeed, with the exception of Mr Di Giulio and Mr McMahon and their families, the inscription was apparently unknown to any of the residents in the area until very recently: Mr Brusby, for example, only got to know of it a few years before our visit, probably as a result of the investigation by the

NEARA people. This may seem surprising: but the beach is remote and adjacent to private land, and only normally visited by persons such as quahoggers who make their way along the Bay. Furthermore, there is now little beach space: and bathing is not attractive since the water contains tiny mites which bite, as we discovered to our very painful cost. The quahoggers, and the nuns from the Catholic home, go into the water fully dressed!

What of the 20th century? From the census information available in the North Kingstown Public Library it would seem that by the beginning of the century Scandinavians and Germans had begun to move into the district in some numbers; and the Scandinavians were overwhelmingly Swedish. Furthermore, Mr Brusby told me that his grandfather employed a stonemason of Swedish origin in or about 1880 to build a stone wall in the adjacent community of Warwick, some three miles from the rock. And the records show that at least two families of Swedish origin have lived on the Point from the 1940s onwards, and in one of these cases to the present day. To summarise the information we obtained on this: a G. Elmer Lindberg is first mentioned as being in the area in 1926, as having owned land on the Pojac Point road, and as having built a house there around 1956; he died soon after, but his widow was still living there in 1964. However, this family is no longer traceable. On the other hand: a certain Gustav Viktor Carlson was in the area in the early 1940s, did a number of different jobs, married, and settled down close to the entrance to the Catholic rest home. I telephoned his daughter, who told me that she and her mother had not known of the inscription until very recently, her father had never mentioned it, and they thought it unlikely in the highest degree that it had been made by him, a statement echoed by Mr Welling. From all of this it can be seen that, while there have in the 20th century been people living in the Pojac Point area who could have had the knowledge and ability to carve the inscription, we have no solid evidence that any one of them did so.

However, the position of the rock makes it necessary to consider a second possibility; that the inscription was carved, not by someone living in the immediate vicinity, but by someone who came along the beach, or by boat from an adjacent area. From the historical perspective, one might certainly build up a case for the possibility that the above-mentioned stonemason or one of his fellow-countrymen made his way along the beach from Warwick to Pojac Point and cut the inscription, which he could have done in, say, two or three hours. On the beach Dr Pieper found a metal railway spike which is the kind of implement which might have been used for the purpose; alternatively, a stonemason could have had suitable tools with him. The existence of the hooked symbol suggests the possibility that the cutter knew of the Kensington controversy, though this would push the date of cutting well into the first decade of the 20th century. Be that as it may: the most probable conclusion from this is that if the inscription should prove to be modern it was carved by a person of Swedish origin some time from around 1880 to the 1940s.

The final possibility, and by no means the weakest, is that the inscription was carved by someone who had come from a greater distance one or many centuries ago, had sailed into Narragansett Bay and stopped at Pojac Point for a shorter or longer time, leaving only the inscription as evidence of his passage. But we have no further evidence for this possibility.

Thus much for the historical evidence. I turn next to the scientific evidence of different kinds which Dr Pieper examined, and which I shall summarise for the purposes of the present paper. The first relates to the degree of weathering of the inscription. Several factors have to be taken into account here. As mentioned, the Narragansett inscription is very smooth: it shows no signs of recent cutting. However, some of the runes are still fairly deep; and at this stage in our investigation we cannot be sure whether this is because they were cut early in the 20th century or very much earlier. Other rock inscriptions in the Narragansett Bay area still clearly show dates in the 19th century; and some of the carvings on the Dighton Rock, which is a softer rock than Narragansett, were first seen as long ago as 1680 but are still clearly visible. Dighton Rock, on the east side of the Taunton river some thirty miles north-eastwards from North Kingstown, seems to have a similar history to the Narragansett rock, though it was between high and low tide when Delabarre wrote about it in 1928, and has been in an on-site museum since 1973.

Secondly, Dr Pieper used a hand-held ultra-violet lamp in an examination of the Narragansett and other rock inscriptions in the Bay area, to see which inscriptions showed fluorescence and which did not. Particularly fruitful was the examination of the Dighton Rock, which has a large number of inscriptions dating from before 1680 until well into the 20th century. It transpired that, in general terms, inscriptions of 20th-century date showed a degree of fluorescence on the inscription cuts, while pre-20th century inscriptions did not. On the Narragansett rock, which we examined at night, there was a degree of generalised fluorescence, which we think is likely to have been caused by the cleaning of the inscription in 1985 by the first investigators. But there was no separate evidence of fluorescence on the inscription cuts. This test, therefore, though unfortunately not definitive for the dating of the Narragansett inscription, would seem to suggest that the inscription was not made after the early decades of the 20th century.[2]

Finally, for the present, on the beach near the Narragansett rock Dr Pieper found a piece of iron slag. From the North Kingstown records it transpires that in the 18th century there was a forge in the near vicinity of Pojac

Point where wrought iron was made out of bog iron. But it is well known that there was a smithy at the Norse settlement at L'Anse aux Meadows where bog iron was smelted: and it thus seemed appropriate to take a piece of this slag and have it tested by the C14-AMS processes. I submitted it to Professor Bonani of the ETH Zurich for this purpose. Unfortunately, his report was that there was so little carbon in the sample that no date could be given. At the time of writing it is our hope that it may prove possible to date the slag by other methods. Of course, the probability is that the slag is 18th century: but we do not propose to leave any stone unturned.

What highly provisional conclusions may be drawn from the investigation to date concerning the interpretation and the date of the Narragansett inscription? No normal reading of the inscription according to the Germanic, early Norse or Anglo-Saxon futharks gives a clearly discernible meaning: the *sigrom ga* suggestion is no more than that, and begs a number of questions, notably the significance of the Kensingtonian-style hooked *a*.

However, reading it as a Kensingtonian-type inscription is highly problematic as well. Of the six certain letters, only the *s* and *r* (and of course the hooked *a*) correspond closely to Kensington: Narragansett's *o* and *a* are not found in Kensington, and the second letter of the first line is the later *h*-rune in Kensington, and its form corresponds there to the norm. The Narragansett runes are all cut in straight lines: many of Kensington's are rounded. Also, the word-division in Kensington is a colon-type, not a single central dot as in Narragansett. There is no reason, apart from the hooked *a*, to surmise that Narragansett is dependent on Kensington; and certainly no reason to suppose that the carver of Narragansett ever saw Kensington, or a reproduction of it. At most he may have got his information second or third hand.[3]

I have tested the Narragansett runes against certain hidden systems known to have been in use in Scandinavia, without coming to any conclusion. They do not, for instance, seem to relate to the *orklaski* type, where to obtain the name one must substitute the immediately preceding rune in the shorter futhark (Moltke 1985: 132). The names of the runic letters do not seem to be significant. On the other hand, Dr Pieper noticed that the symbols, if interpreted suitably, can be re-ordered to form the initials and surname of G. V. Carlson, which may or may not be a coincidence. And when I presented a similar paper to a runologists' conference last year, my attention was drawn to a certain Professor Dag Sandström who could have carved the symbols as a hoax in the early 20th century. But this presents problems too. For me at least, the question is still wide open.

As to the date of the inscription: neither the scientific nor the historical tests have enabled us, so far, to say whether the cutting was done in the medieval period or early in the 20th century. A case can be made out for the latter possibility, but not a strong one. What can be said about the possibility that it is medieval? Here again, the evidence is circumstantial. That the Norsemen could have come this far southwards does not in itself seem to be a major problem. We know that they got to Newfoundland; we know that a Norse coin was found in Maine, and one possible explanation of this is that it came thus far south with them. We know that bog iron was smelted at L'Anse aux Meadows; it is an interesting coincidence that in the vicinity of both Bourne and Pojac Point there is also bog iron. All these places are close to, or on, the sea shore.

To this may be added the following points. Like many genuine runic inscriptions, Narragansett is not easily interpreted; it could not therefore have been made primarily for financial profit, as the Spirit Pond stones most probably were. It is remote from the normal land routes, and remained unknown until very recently: if a modern carver did it for fame, he has had to wait a long time for recognition. The purpose of such a carving, if modern, thus remains very obscure. The best guesses are that it is somehow connected with the Kensington controversy, and that its lettering largely coincides with the name of a Swede who lived on Pojac Point; but as we have seen we have limited evidence for these guesses, and some information which argues against them.

All in all, I am of the opinion that unless and until further scientific or historical evidence comes to light, and until the above-mentioned objections are disposed of, the Narragansett inscription needs to be regarded as potentially a most important piece of evidence in regard to Norse explorations in America.

Notes

[1] This paper is an interim report on work in progress.

[2] It may be added that we subsequently tested the Bourne stone on Cape Cod, which we studied in 1993, in the same way, and the inscriptions on it showed no sign whatever of fluorescence. Since this stone has been in the Aptucxet Trading Post museum since the 1930s, we can confidently affirm that whatever the inscriptions are, they are not from the 20th-century, and most probably not from the late 19th-century either. But this is another story.

[3] If the Narragansett runes are to be compared with any other inscriptions in North America, three come to mind: the Bourne stone on Cape Cod, and the Heavener and Poteau inscriptions, all of which are short and in the same general style. Unlike Kensington and the Spirit Pond stones, but like Narragansett, they have no obvious meaning; two of the Bourne symbols, and the Heavener/Poteau runes, are also largely in

accord with the older Germanic futhark, and the letters they have in common with Narragansett are similar to that inscription - in particular, they all have the *o*-rune. This may, of course, be coincidence.

References

Delabarre, E. B.
1928 *Dighton Rock: A study of the written rocks of New England.* New York: Walter Neale.

Marquardt, Hertha
1961 *Die Runeninschriften der Britischen Inseln.* Göttingen: Vandenhoeck und Ruprecht.

Moltke, Erik
1985 *Runes and their origin: Denmark and elsewhere.* Peter G. Foote (trans.). Copenhagen: Nationalmuseets Forlag.

The Narragansett runic inscription 99

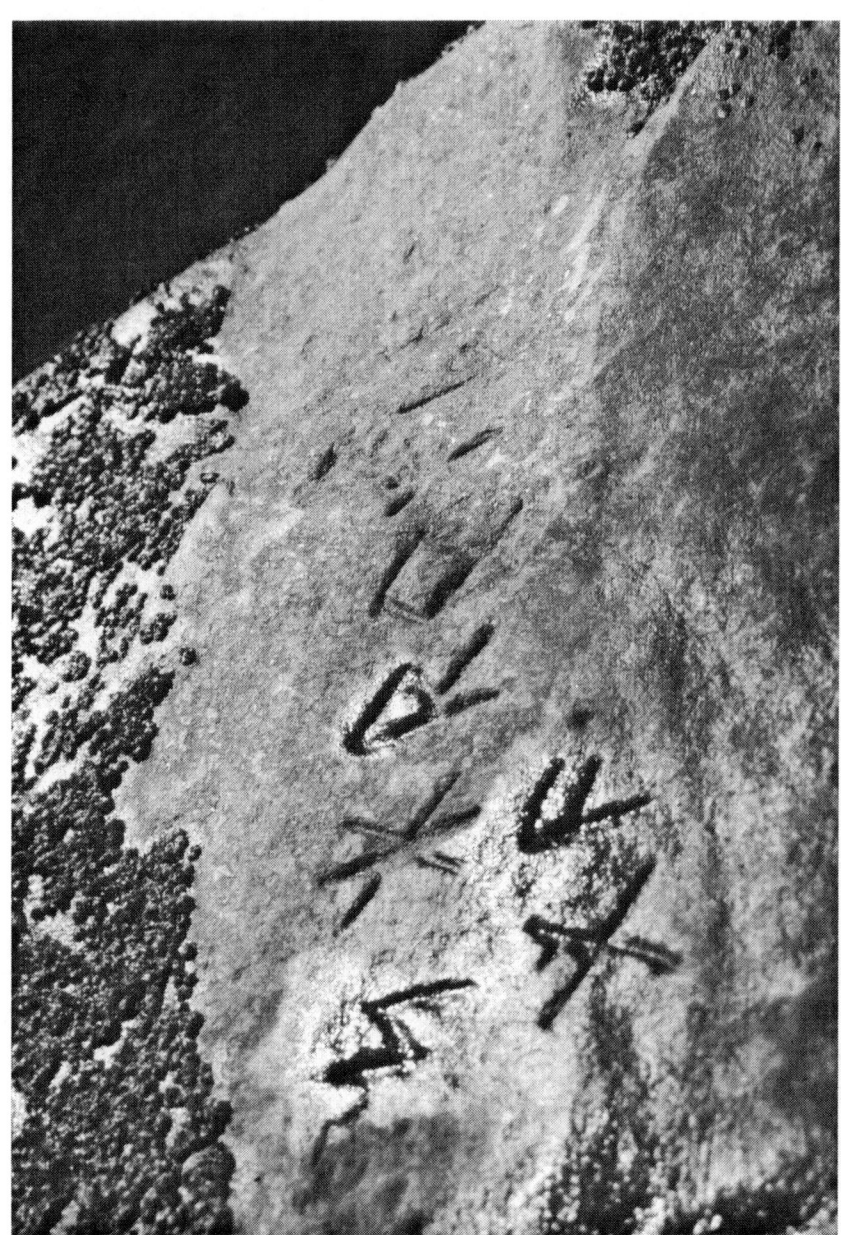

Figure 1: The Narragansett runic inscription

Old English preverbal elements with adverbial counterparts

Michiko Ogura (Chiba, Japan)

A growing tendency to prefer verb-adverb combinations to prefixed verbs from the late tenth century onwards has been reported in Hiltunen (1983) and Niwa (1991 and 1995). It is true that, when a preverbal element is a free morpheme (or, more precisely, when it has an adverbial counterpart), it shows a tendency to move to a postverbal position, unless the element order should involve a semantic change (like PDE *overcome* and *come over*). On the other hand, when the preverbal element is a bound morpheme, what matters is not a postposition but the interchangeability of the preverbal element under semantic (e.g. PDE *come* and *become*) or dialectal/scribal (e.g. *onsacan* and *ætsacan*) condition.

Since I have already reported on the case of bound-morph prefixes in Ogura (1995), I focus on the free-morph prefixes here in this paper. My aim is to propose some patterns of the basic element order in Old English and then to examine Old English renderings in the three versions of the Gospels in comparison with Old High German renderings on the use of verbs with free-morph prefixes in order to see if Old English renderings follow the basic patterns or if they faithfully follow the Latin order.

1. Basic element orders in Old English

I propose the following patterns of element order, not as rules but as strong preferences.
    (a) V_{imp} + Partic.
    (b)   (ɟ/ac +) Partic. + V (+ {Prep + N})
            (ɟ/ac +) V + Partic. (+ {Prep + N})
            (ɟ/ac +) Partic. + {Prep + N} + V
            N.B.{Prep + N}+ V + Partic. and {Prep + N} + Partic. + V are less frequent and V + {Prep + N} + Partic. is unattested
    (c)   gif/ þe + Partic. + V (+ Aux)
    (d)   Partic. + to + V_{-enne}

Pattern (a) means that, when a verb is in the imperative (or optative or hortative), a particle or an adverbial element is to be postposed. Example (1) illustrates an imperative and (2) a hortative.

(1)   *BlHom* 15 187.35 Rære *up* þin heafod & geseoh þis þæt Simon deþ
        'Raise up thy head and see this that Simon does'

(2) *BlHom* 15 181.19 *Cuman* nu myccle hundas *forþ* & hine abitan beforan þyssum casere
'Let great dogs now come forth and bite him before this emperor'

Exceptions to this pattern are found with the verbs with bound-morph prefixes, as in

(3) *ÆCHom* I,39 523.98 *Ymbscrydað eow*
'Clothe yourselves'.

Pattern (b) shows the possible choice of the element order in the principal or ʒ/*ac*/*ne* clauses. In the first type a particle is preposed to the verb and in the second type it is postposed, which means that a tendency towards the postposition is not notable at all in these clauses. At times, however, as illustrated by example (4), the preposition and the postposition can tell a semantic difference: the postposed *of* 'off' should be stressed so as to emphasize the action of striking something, while the preposed *of*- may focus on the completed action of killing.[1]

(4) *Or* 4 5.90.14-15 ærest hiene mon swong, þa sticode him mon þa eagan ut, ⁊ siþþan him mon *slog* þa handa *of*, þa þæt heafod, ⁊ eall his cynn mon *ofslog*
'first they scourged him, then put his eyes out, and afterwards struck off his hands, then his head, and slew all his kin'

A preposed element and a postposed element can be different even if they denote much the same. In example (5) *onfeng* and *feng to* can be compared (since there is no instance of *feng on or *tofeng).[2]

(5) *Chron* A 560(18.1-2) Her Ceawlin *feng to* rice to Wesseaxum, ⁊ Ælle *feng to* Norþanhymbra rice
'In this year Ceawlin succeeded to the kingdom in Wessex and Ælle succeeded to the kingdom of the Northumbrians'
Chron E 560(19.1-2) Her Ceawlin rice *onfeng* on Weast Seaxum, ⁊ Ælle *feng to* Norðhymbra rice

In example (6) we find a combination of an adverbial element and a verb in different orders with the same sense.

(6) *Chron* A 734(44.14) Her wæs se mona swelce he wære mid blode begoten; ⁊ *ferdon forþ* Tatwine ⁊ Bieda
'In this year the moon was as if it were covered with blood and Tatwin and Bede died'

Chron E 734(45.14) Her wæs se mona swilce he wære mid blode begoten. ⁊ Tatwine *forðferde* erceb. ⁊ eac Beda.

When a prepositional phrase with a close connection to both the verb and the particle is involved, it is more often postposed than preposed to the combination of the other two elements. But it may also follow a particle and, as a result, come between the particle and the verb. In example (7) the two verbs show two different orders; the first one is also an example of pattern (a).

(7)   *ÆCHom* II,12 114.132-3 *Astih* ðu eft *up to me*, and aaron samod; Moyses ða godes hæse gefylde. and *eft up to him astah*
'Come again up to me, and Aaron as well; then Moses fulfilled God's command and again went up to him'

Thus, such element orders as *astigan up to him, up to him astigan, upastigan to him, to him upastigan* and *to him astigan up* can be found, but **astigan to him up* is not attested.[3]

Pattern (c) illustrates the order in the subordinate clause, as in examples (8) and (9); when an auxiliary cooccurs, it comes at the end of the clause, as in (8).

(8)   *Or* 2 5.48.19 Morþonius, Xersis þegn, forlet þa scipa þe hie *on farende wæron*
'Mardonius, Xerxes' general, left the ships in which they had been sailing'
(9)   *ÆCHom* I,37 500.111 swa þ ða cristenan bealdlice *ineodon*
'so that the Christians boldly went in'

Pattern (d) is an order with inflected infinitives. A particle, if a free morpheme, stands before *to*, as in example (10).

(10)   *Chron* A 669 (34.10) (=B, C, F) Her Ecgbryht cyning salde Basse mæsseprioste Reculf mynster *on to timbranne*
'In this year king Egbert gave Reculver to Bass the priest to build a monastery'
Cf.   *Chron* E 669 (35.11) Her Egbriht cining sealde Basse preost Raculf, mynster *to tymbrianne*.

If a prepositional phrase cooccurs, it can be a strong cause of the postposition of a particle, as in

(11)   *ÆCHom* II,22 207.38 He geceas him timan to acennenne on menniscnysse. to ðrowigenne. to arisenne of deaðe. *to astigenne up to heofenan.* mid þam lichaman ðe he middanearde gefette

'He chose time to bring forth in incarnation, to suffer, to rise from death, to ascend up to heaven, with the body which he obtained in the world'

2. A comparison between Old English and Old High German versions of the Gospels

Are the basic patterns found in original prose in the previous section relevant to Old English versions of the Gospels? It is obvious that interlinear glosses are materials improper to an investigation of syntax. The *Lindisfarne* version is expected to represent Latin element orders, even though it sometimes violates the element-for-element translation. The *Rushworth 1* version appears more independent than *Rushworth 2*, a closer copy of *Lindisfarne*, in addition to the dialectal difference, though the latter does not always follow the model. The *West Saxon* version (here I use MS CCCC 140)[4] is much freer and similar to the contemporary prose and more proper to a syntactic investigation. The reason for the comparison between these three Anglo-Saxon versions and the Old High German Tatian is that, in order to examine linguistic development and find a clue to an earlier form of Anglo-Saxon, this ninth-century version is the most reliable material among the related languages and, if the basic element order patterns are similar in both languages, we may tell the difference between a native grammar and a Latin-based syntax in a more convincing way than we have done with Anglo-Saxon versions alone. The comparison between the three Anglo-Saxon versions is useful for making dialectal and stylistic differences clear and, adding an Old High German version, we may see which Anglo-Saxon version is closer to the Old High German one in syntax and translation style and whether the similarity and/or the difference is thoroughgoing or not.

As an appendix, I give two tables. Table 1 illustrates the lexical comparison of the renderings of Latin verbs of motion. All types of verbs are investigated, then the Old English verbs with free-morph prefixes are chosen, and finally, the verbs whose preposed elements (i.e. apparent prefixes) can be postposed so as to prove their independence are left for illustration. Mt., Mk., Lk. and Jn. in brackets mean that the lexeme is found especially (if not exclusively) in the Gospel of Matthew, Mark, Luke or John. Only the major counterparts are cited in the table, which means that the one-to-one lexical correspondence is rather rare. Among the Latin prefixes, *in-* (and *intro-*) seems to be translated faithfully with the exception of *WSCp*, but *ex-* and *ad-* are not always rendered *ut-* and *to-* respectively. *Trans-* is rendered *ofer-* and *de-*, *ofdune-*, in *Li* and *Ru1* & *2*, but *WSCp* prefers simple verbs. The lexical choice is more strict in Tatian than in Old English versions, but still three to five counterparts are regularly found in rendering one particular Latin verb.

Table 2 shows the number of occurrences of the preposition and the postposition of a free-morph prefix or an adverbial element. *Intrare* and *introire* are likely to be rendered with a preposed element except *WSCp*, a fact that is also attested in Table 1. The choice of a simple verb (sometimes with a bound-morph prefix, as in *astigan*) is preferred in most instances. Tatian shows a preference for the preposition in rendering *exire* (*ûzgangan*), *intrare* and *introire* (*ingangan*), *descendere* (*nidarstigan*) and *accedere* (*zuogangan*). The postposition of the adverbial element is not so frequent, but in translating *exire*, *intrare*, *descendere* and *egredi* (and *abire*, especially in *Ru*), each version tries the syntax. (Asterisks on some of the numbers in *Li* denote the translations of Latin adverbs: * means *foras* and ** *intro*.)

Examples (12) and (13) are chosen to illustrate the basic pattern (a). In the optative construction in (12), *Li* and *WSCp* use an obvious preposition, while *Ru1* alone has the postposed *to*. Since *cuman* and *becuman* are synonymous, the choice between the two (including cognates in other languages) does not matter much. Imperative forms in (13) show postposition except *Li*.

(12) Mt. 6.10 [*aduentat* regnum tuum]
 Gothic: *qimai* þiudinassus þeins
 Li: to-cymeð ríc ðin
 Ru1: *cume to* þin rice
 WSCp: *to-becume* þin ríce
 Heliand: *Cuma* thîn craftag rîki
 Tatian: *queme* thín rihhi
 Otfrid: *Biquéme* uns thinaz ríchi
 (*AV*: Thy kingdome come)

(13) Mt. 7.13 [*Intrate* per angustam portam quia lata porta et spatiosa uia quæ ducit ad perditionem et multi sunt qui intrant per eam]
 Li: *inngeonges* ðerh nearuo port 1 dure 1 gæt forðon ðiu wide geat ㄱ rumwelle weg ðiu lædas to lose 1 losing ㄱ monigo sint ða ðe inngeongas ðerh ða ilco
 Ru1: *gaþ inn* þurh naarwe geate for þon wíd geatte ㄱ rúm weg þe lǽdeþ to forwyrde 1 forlore ㄱ monige sindun þa þe in-gan þurh þære 1 þæne
 WSCp: *Gangað inn* þurh þ nearwe geat. forþon þe þ geat is swyþe wíd. ㄱ se weg is swiþe rum þe to for-spillednesse gelæt ㄱ swyþe manega synt þe þurh þone weg farað
 Tatian: *Gét in* thuruh enga phorta, uuanta breit phorta inti uúit uúeg thie thar leitit zi furlore, inti manage sint thie thuruh thie gangent
 (*AV*: Enter ye in at the strait gate, for wide is the gate, and broad is the way that leadeth to destruction, and many there be which goe in thereat)

Examples (14) and (15) contain negation. Since the negative particle *ne* is regularly put immediately before the verb, an adverbial element may occupy the position that either precedes or follows '*ne* + V'. The order '*ne*+ P + V' can be, when P is a free-morph prefix, a slavish translation of Latin. In (14), *Li* has '*ne* + P + V' and *WSCp* 'P+ *ne* + V', while *Ru1* and Tatian have '*ne*/*ni* +V + P'. We cannot say the same thing for (15); *Li* has '*ne* + P + V' and *Ru2* follows it, while *WSCp* shows '*ne* + V + {Prep + N}' and Tatian 'P + *ni* + V'. In the latter example, two prepositional phrases following are involved in the choice of element order in *WSCp*.

(14) Mt. 23.13 [quia clauditis regnum caelorum ante homines uos enim *non intratis* nec intro-euntes sinitis intrare]
Li: forðon gie tyndon ríc heofna before ł aer monnum gie forðon *ne inn-eadege* ne ða inngeongende gíe letas inn-geonga
Ru1: þe gelucaþ rice heofona beforan monnum ge þonne *ne gǽþ* inn* ne þa ingangende letaþ ingangen (*gangǽþ, alt. to *gǽþ*)
WSCp: forþam ge belucað heofona rice. beforan mannum; Ne gé *in ne gaþ* ne ge ne geþafiað þ oðre ingan
Tatian: inti bisliozet himilo richi fora mannon: ir *ni get in* noh thie inganganton ni lazet ingangan
(*AV*: for yee shut vp the kingdom of heauen against men: For yee neither goe in your selues, neither suffer ye them that are entring, to goe in)

(15) Jn. 10.1 [qui *non intrat* per ostium in ouile ouium sed ascendit aliunde ille fur est et latro]
Li: seðe *ne Inn-gaas* ł ðerh duru in scipa plett ł locc ah astiged ofer on oðre halfe ł ðe ðeaf is ꝺ settere ł sceacere
Ru2: seðe *ne ingœð* ðerh dura hiorde is (*sic*) scipa ah astigeð oðre hwoena he scead ł ðæf is ꝺ sceaðo
WSCp: se þe *ne gǽð* æt þam gete *into* sceapa falde. ac styhþ elles ofer he is þeof ꝺ sceaða
Tatian: thie thar *in ni gét* thurah duri in then euuist thero scapho, oh gistigit allesuuanan, ther ist thíob inti scaheri
(*AV*: He that entreth not by ye doore into the sheepefold, but climeth vp some other way, the same is a theefe, and a robber)

In (16) the case ending is reconfirmed by a preposition, except the slavish *Li*.[5]

(16) Mk. 5.18 [Cum *ascenderunt nauem* coepit illum deprǽcari qui dæmonio uexatus fuerat ut esset cum illo]
Li: ꝺ miððy *astigon ðæt scip* ongann hine gebidda seðe from diowle auæled ł gebered wæs þte were mið him

Ru2: ⁊ miððy *astigun in þ scip* ongan hine gibidda seðe from diowle awæled wæs þte were mið him
WSCp: Þa he *on scip eode* hine ongan biddan se ðe ǽr mid deofle gedreht wæs. þ he mid him wære
Tatian: Mit thiu her tho *arsteig in skef*, ...
(*AV*: And when hee was come into the ship, he that had bene possessed with the deuill prayed him that hee might bee with him)

When the Latin version has a prefixed verb and a prepositional phrase following, it is rendered either 'P + V + {Prep + N}' or 'V + P + {Prep + V}', as in

(17) Jn. 4.30 [*exierunt* de ciuitate et ueniebant ad eum]
      Li: *út eadon* of ðær byrig ⁊ ge-cuomon to him
      Ru2: ⁊ *ut-eodun* of ðær byrig ⁊ gicomon to him
      WSCp: Ða *eodon* hi *ut* of ðære byrig ⁊ comon to him
      Tatian: Tho *giengun* sie *uz* fon dero burgi inti quamun zi imo
      (*AV*: Then they went out of the citie, and came vnto him)

When the Latin version has *foras* (Mt. 10.14, 21.17 and 26.75 (= Lk. 22.62)) or *intro* (Mt. 26.58) that follows a verb, even *Li* can show postposition in faithfully translating Latin adverbs.

(18) Mt. 10.14 [Et quicumque non receperit uos neque audierit sermones uestros *exeuntes foras* de domo uel de ciuitate excuitite puluerem de pedibus uestris in testimonium eorum]
      Li: ⁊ suæ hua ne onfoas iuh ne héres worda Iuera *geongas úut* of hus ł of ceastræ sceaccas ða asca of fotum Iurum in cyðnisse ł in gewitnisse hiora ł ðara
      Ru1: ⁊ swa hwilce swa nyle onfo eow ne heran wordum eowrum *gáð ut* of þæm huse oþþe þære cæstre ascákeþ dust of fotum eowrum in cyþnisse heora
      WSCp: And swa hwa swa eow ne under-fehð ne eowre spræca ne gehyrð. þonne ge *út-gan* of ðam huse oððe of ðære ceastre asceacaþ þ dust of eowrum fotum
      Tatian: Inti so uúer iuuih ni inphahit noh ni horit iuuaru uuort, *úzgangante* fon themo hús odo fon theru burgi árscutet then melm fon iuuaren fuozin ín zi giuuiznesse
      (*AV*: And whosoeuer shall not receiue you, nor heare your wordes: when yee depart out of that house, or city, shake off the dust of your feete)

(19) Mt. 21.17 [Et Relictis illis *abiit foras* extra ciuitatem in bethaniam ibique mansit]
      Li: ⁊ forletno weron ða *ge-eade uta* buta ceastra in bethania ⁊ ðer wunade
      Ru1: ⁊ forletende hiæ *eode ut* of þara ceastræ in bethaniæ ⁊ þær wunade
      WSCp: ⁊ he forlet hi þa ⁊ *ferde* of þære byrig to bethania. ⁊ lærde hi þar be godes rice

Tatian: Inti in tho forlazenen, ..., *gieng uz* fon thera burgi in stat thiu Bethania heizit, inti thar uuoneta
(*AV*: And he left them, and went out of the citie into Bethany, and he lodged there)

(20) Lk. 22.62 [et *egressus foras* petrus fleuit ámare]
Li: ꝥ *foerde uta* petrus geweap bitterlice
Ru2: ꝥ *foerde utt* petrus weop biterlice
WSCp: Ða *eode* petrus *út* ꝥ biterlice weop
Tatian: Inti *uzgangenti* Petrus uuiof bittaro
(*AV*: And Peter went out, and wept bitterly)

(21) Mt. 26.58 [et *ingressus intro* sedebat cum ministris ut uideret finem]
Li: ꝥ *eode Inn* gesætt mið ðæm ðegnum þte he gesege ðone ende
Ru1: ꝥ *ingangende* gesæt betwih mið þæm þægnum þ he gesæge endunge
WSCp: ꝥ he *in-eode* ꝥ sæt mid þam þenum þ he ge-sawe þone ende
(*AV*: and went in, and sate with the seruants to see the end)

In (18) and (20) Tatian uses *uzgangan* and in (21) *Ru1 ingangan*, ignoring Latin order. In (19) *WSCp* chooses a simple verb *feran*. In (20) *WSCp* has '*þa* V S P' order, in contrast with *Li* and *Ru2*. *Þa* 'then' + VS order is also found in (17), where Tatian takes the same order, and later in (27), where Tatian has 'V *tho* P S'; in these two examples a prepositional phrase follows the particle.[6] There are two dubious instances in which *Li* shows postposition. One is Jn. 10.1 in (15), where *aliunde* 'from some other direction' may correspond not to one word but to *ofer on oðre halfe*. The other is (22), where *contra* corresponds to *togægnas*, and *ofer* might have been a prefixed element, as *transire* is often rendered *oferfaran*, but is postposed owing to the hortative construction (see the basic pattern (a), though *WSCp* free translation chooses '*uton* + infinitive').

(22) Mk. 4.35 [Et ait illis illa die cum sero esset factum *transeamus contra*]
Li: ꝥ cwæ[ð] to him on ðæm dæge miððy efern ł smyltnis were awordæn *fære wæ ofer togægnas*
Ru2: ꝥ cwæð to him on ðæm dæge miððy efern wæs giworden *fære we ofer togægnes*
WSCp: ꝥ sæde him þonne æfen bið *uton faran agen*
(*AV*: And the same day, when the Euen was come, he saith vnto them, Let vs passe ouer vnto the other side)

Let us look at some more examples of Latin verbs whose Old English counterparts may, if not translated as simple verbs, show either preposition or postposition of the adverbial element. Both *ascendere* and *descendere* can be rendered *astigan*; the downward movement, however, is often emphasised by *ofdune* or *niþer*, while the upward movement can be expressed without *up*. Thus in (23), '*astigan* + *of*-phrase' is enough to denote the upward movement but *ofdune* or *niþer* is used for the downward movement. Tatian uses prefixed verbs for either direction. In (24) *descendere* occurs twice; *Li* tries to avoid choosing the same lexeme and uses a double gloss, in which *foerde in* should be considered an unexpression of the prepostional object rather than postposition. *Ru2* does not follow *Li* faithfully but alters the syntax. Instead of *feran*, *WSCp* uses *cuman* and makes full use of prepositional phrases. Tatian uses two different prefixes. In (25), postposition is chosen except *Li*, probably owing to the command to the third person.

(23) Mt. 3.16 [Baptizatus autem confestim *ascendit* de aqua et ecce aperti sunt ei caeli et uidit spiritum die *descendentem* sicut columbam uenientem super sé]
Li: mið ðy wæs gefulwad ueototlice hraðe ł sona *astag ł aras* of wætre ꝫ heonu untyned weron him heofnas ꝫ gesæh gast godes *of-dune stigende* suelce culfre cymmende ofer him
Ru1: þa gedeped [wæs] se hælend hræþe *ástág* of þæm wættre ꝫ henu him weron ontynde heofunas ꝫ he gesæg godes gast *niþer-stigendne* swa culfre cumende ofer hine
WSCp: Soþlice þa se hælend gefullod wæs. hrædlice he *astah* of ðam wætere. ꝫ him wurdon þærrihte heofonas ontynede ꝫ he ge-seah godes gast *niþer-stigende* [*WSH*: *niþer-astigende*] swa swa culfran. ꝫ wunigende ofer hine
Tatian: ... inti themo heilante gitoufitemo inti betontemo, sliumo *úfarsteig* fon themo uuazzare. Senu thô aroffonota uuarun imo himila, inti gisah gotes geist *nidarstigantan* lichamlichero gisiuni samaso tubun, quementan ubar sih
(*AV*: And Iesus, when hee was baptized, went vp straightway out of the water: and loe, the heauens were opened vnto him, and he saw the Spirit of God descending like a doue, and lighting vpon him)

(24) Jn. 5.4 [angelus autem domini secundum tempus *descendebat* in piscinam et mouebat aquam qui ergo primus *descendisset* post motum aquae sanus fiebat á quo-cumque languore tenebatur]
Li: engel uutudlice drihtnes æfter tid *of-dune astag* in þ uoel ł in þ fisc-pol ꝫ ymbcerde ł þ uæter seðe forðon ærist *ofdune stagade ł foerde in* æfter styrenise ł uætres hal son uere ł from suæ–huælc un-hælo ł adle uere ahaldan ł
Ru2: engel wutudlice drihtnes æfter tide þ ymb-cerde ðæt wæter swa hwælc swa forðon ærist *of-dune astag ł foerde of-dune astag* in ða burg æfter styrenisse wætres hale wosa from adle swa hwelc were gihalden
WSCp: Drihtenes engel *com* to his timan on þone mere ꝫ þ wæter wæs astyred. ꝫ se þe raþust. *com* on þone mere æfter þæs wæteres styrunge weraþ gehæled fram swa hwylcere untrumnysse swa he on wæs

Tatian: Gotes engil after ziti *nidarsteig* in den uuiuuari inti ruorta thaz uuazzar. Der dar erist *ingisteig* aftter giruornisse thes uuasseres, heil uuas uon so uuelichero suhti uuas bihabet.
(*AV*: For an Angel went downe at a certaine season into the poole, and troubled the water: whosoeuer then first after the troubling of the water stepped in, was made whole of whatsoeuer disease he had)

(25)   Mt. 24.17 [et qui in tecto non *descendat* tollere aliquid de domo sua]
Li: ⁊ seðe in hrof ł in hus ne *ofstiges* genioma huot-hwoego of hus hiora
Ru1: ⁊ seþe on þæce siæ ne *stigað* he *niðer* to genimanne owiht of hi huse
WSCp: ⁊ seþe ys uppan hys huse ne *gá* he *nyþyr* þ he ænig þing on his huse fecce
Tatian: Thanne ther der in theki ist ni *stigit nidar* zi nemanne uuaz fon sinemo huse
(*AV*: Let him which is on the house top, not come downe, to take any thing out of his house)

Three examples are given for *ingredi* and *egredi*. In (26) a pair of inward and outward movement is represented by the alteration of preposed elements in all versions except *WSCp*, which uses *gan* once and postposes the pair *in* ⁊ *út*. (For *introire* that precedes these verbs, *WSCp* alone use *gan* without *in*, while the other versions use prefixed verbs, as is basic for *gif*-clauses.) In (27) postposition is found in *WSCp* and Tatian, a prefixed *utgangan* in *Ru1*, and *geferan* in *Li*.[7] In (28) Tatian alone chooses postposition.

(26)   Jn. 10.9 [ego sum ostium per me si quis introierit saluabitur et *ingredietur et egredietur* et pascua inuenieet]
Li: ic am duru ðerh mec gif huælc inngaeð ł gehæled bið ⁊ *inn-fœreð* ⁊ *ut-fœreð* ł ⁊ lesua ł gemoetað
Ru2: ic am duru-word ðerh mec gif hwelc in-gæð gi-hæled bið ⁊ *in-fœreð* ⁊ *utt-fœreð* ⁊ leswe gemoeteð
WSCp: ic eom geat swa hwylc swa þurh me gæð byþ hal. ⁊ *gæð in* ⁊ *út* ⁊ fint læse
Tatian: Ih bim duri. Thurah mih oba uuer ingengit, ther ist giheilit, inti *inget inti úzget* inti findit fuotrunga
(*AV*: I am the doore; by me if any man enter in, he shall be saued, and shall goe in and out, and find pasture)

(27)   Mt. 22.10 [et *egressi* serui eius in uias congregauerunt omnes quos inuenerunt malos et bonos]
Li: ⁊ *gefoerdon* ða ðegnas his on wegum gesomnadon alle ðaðe onfundon yfelra ⁊ godra

Ru1: ⁊ þa *utgangende* þa eesnas on weogas somnadun alle þa þe hi gemettun gode ⁊ yfle
WSCp: Ða *eodon* þa þeowas *út* on þa wegas ⁊ gegaderedon ealle ða þe hig gemetton góde ⁊ yfele
Tatian: *Giengun* thô *úz* sine scalca in uuega inti samanotun alle thie sie fundun, ubile inti guote
(AV: So those seruants went out into the high wayes, and gathered together all as many as they found, both bad and good)

(28)   Mk. 5.40 [ipse uero eiectis omnibus adsumit patrem et matrem puellae et qui secum erant et *ingreditur* ubi erat puella iacens]
Li: he hueðre miððy fordrifenum allum ł miððy alle ute fordraf genom ðone fader ⁊ moder ðæra maedne ⁊ ðaðe mið him weron ⁊ *infoerde* ðer wæs ðæt mæden licende
Ru2: he hweðre mið fordrifnum allum ginom ðone fæder ⁊ moder ðæs mægdnes ⁊ ða ðe mið him weron ⁊ *in-foerde* ðer wæs ðæt mægden licgende
WSCp: He þa eallum út adrifenum. nam petrum ⁊ þæs mædenes modor. ⁊ þa ðe mid him wæron. ⁊ *inn-eodon* suwiende þar þ mæden wæs
Tatian: Hér thó allen úzaruuorphanen, ginomanemo fater inti muoter thes magatines inti then mit imo uuarun, *gieng in* thar thaz magatin lág
(AV: But when he had put them all out, he taketh the father and the mother of the damosell, and them that were with him, and entreth in where the damosell was lying.)

(29) is an example of *introire* with negation; postposition is chosen in WSCp and Tatian, in contrast with the slavish order of Li and Ru2.

(29)   Jn. 20.5 [et cum sé inclinasset uidet posita linteamina non tamen *introiuit*]
Li: ⁊ miððy hine gebég gesæh gesettedo ða linnin hrǽglo nó huoeðre ł suæðæh *inn-eode*
Ru2: ⁊ miððy hine gibeg gisæh gisette ða lineno hrægl ne hweðre *in-eode*
WSCp: ⁊ þa he nyðer-abeah he geseah þa linwæda licgan; ⁊ ne *eode* þeah *in*
Tatian: Inti mittiu her sih nidarheldita, gisah thiu lininun lachan gilegitíu, ni *gieng* thoh uuidoro *in*
(AV: And he stouping downe and looking in, saw the linnen clothes lying, yet went he not in)

(30) and (31) are given for *abire*. In (30), though preposed elements differ, Li and Ru1 prefer preposition, while WSCp and Tatian use simple verbs. (In Tatian, *thana* 'from there' can be an alternative of a prefixed element.) In (31), Ru1 and WSCp show postposition, while Li and Tatian use simple verbs.

(30)   Mt. 27.66 [illi autem *abeuntes* munierunt sepulchrum signantes lapidem cum custodibus]
Li: ða ilco uutedlice *from eodon* gefæstnadon þ byrgenn mercande ł gemercadon ðone stán mið haldendum
Ru1: hiæ þa *awæg gangende* mid heordum geoldun (sic) þa byrgenne gemerkade þon stan mid heordum
WSCp: Soþlice hig *ferdon* ⁊ ymbe-trymedon þa byrgene ⁊ inn-seglodon þone stan mid þam weardum
Tatian: Sie tho thana *gangenti* festinotun thaz grab biinsigilenti then stéin mit bihalterin
(AV: So they went, and made the sepulchre sure, sealing the stone, and setting a watch)

(31)   Mt. 22.22 [et audientes mirati sunt et relicto eo *abierunt*]
Li: ⁊ gehercnadon ł mið ðy geherdon wundrigendo sint ł ge-uundradon ⁊ mið ðy forleorton hine *ge-eadon*
Ru1: ⁊ hiæ geherende wundradun ⁊ forleten hine *eodun awæg*
WSCp: Þa hig þ ge-hyrdon þa wundrodon hig ⁊ forleton hyne ⁊ *ferdon onweg*
Tatian: Thaz thô gihorente vvuntorotun, inti imo furlâzanemo *fuorun*
(AV: When they had heard *these wordes*, they marueiled, and left him, and went their way)

In (32) *accedere* is rendered by a simple verb in all versions except Tatian.[8]

(32)   Mt. 25.20 [et *accedens* qui quinque talenta acceperat optulit alia quinque talenta dicens]
Li: ⁊ *geneolecde* seðe ða fif cræfto onfeng gebrohte oðero fif cræfto cuoeð
Ru1: ⁊ þa *cumende* seþe fif ... onfeng brohte oþre fif cweþende
WSCp: Ða com seþe ða fif pund underfeng ⁊ brohte oþre fife ⁊ cwæð
Tatian: Inti *gieng zuo* therde fimf talenta intfieng, brahta andero fimf talenta quedenti
(AV: And so hee that had receiued fiue talents, came and brought other fiue talents, saying)

3. Conclusion

To sum up, *Li* is most faithful to the Latin and most reluctant in accepting postposition, and *Ru2* follows it, though they do not always translate Latin prefixes but at times use simple verbs (or *ge-/a*-verbs). *Ru1*, on the other hand, shows independent renderings with occasional choice of postposition. *WSCp* in its free translation either shows postposition or uses a simple verb with a prepositional phrase. Tatian is somewhere in between *Ru1* and *WSCp*, and the basic patterns of element order are nearly the same as those of Old English. The increasing use of prepositional phrases after late Old English has given English a new way of syntactic development besides the alternative set of preposition and postposition of the adverbial element. The threshold of the verb-adverb combination found in *WSCp* might be, at the same time, the departing point of English from German in their linguistic history.

Notes

[1] This is not a rendering faithful to Latin. See the commentary of Bately's edition, p. 276: "90/13-15.ærest ... heafod. Hanno's end was in fact much more unpleasant: see OH IV. vi. 19 'primo uirgis caesus, deinde effossis oculis et manibus cruribusque fractis, uelut a singulis membris poena exigeretur, in conspectu populi necatus est'."

[2] *On-* in *onfon* is a bound-morph prefix and cannot be postposed, and *tofæncge*, a noun with a bound-morph prefix found in a double gloss in the *Lambeth Psalter* 123.6, should be read as *to fæncge* (rendering *captionem*). Three examples of *onfeng to rice* are found in Chronicles (*Chron* A II (6.3); *Chron* E 39 (7.15), 784 (53.33-34) but only one example of *on rice feng* (*Chron* D (cf. Classen 1926) 972.1).

[3] I have gone through the examples in the *Microfiche Concordance* for the constructions with *astigan*, *up* and *to*-phrase (both *to* a person and *to* a place) and got this result.

[4] For the other manuscripts of the West Saxon version and their differences, see Liuzza 1994: Introduction.

[5] In Mt. 26.42 *from me* is written independently in *Ru1*:
[pater mi si non potest hic calix *transire* nisi bibam illum fiat uoluntas tua]
Li : fader min gif ne mæge ðes cælc oferliora nymðe ic drinca hine ł ðene sie willo ðin
Ru1: fæder min gif ne mæge þeos cælic *leoran from me* nymþe þ ic of him drince beo hit þin willæ
WSCp: Min fæder gyf þes calic ne mæge *gewitan* [*WSH: witen*] buton ic hyne drince gewurþe þin willa
Tatian: min fater, oba bi mag these kelih *furifaran* nibih in trinke, uuese thin uuillo
(*AV*: O my father, if this cup may not passe away from me, except I drinke it, thy will be done)

[6] Cf. Example (4), *Or* 4 5.90.14 *þa sticode him mon þa eagan ut*, which is not an example of the postposition but *ut* occurs independently at the end of the clause.

[7] In sixteen instances of *egredi*, *(ge)feran* is chosen eight times, i.e. 50%.

[8] *Therde* is a compound relative (i.e. *ther* + *the*), which corresponds to Anglo-Saxon *seþe*.

References

Editions

Behaghel, Otto (ed.)
1948 *Heliand und Genesis.* (6th edition.) Halle: Niemeyer.

Classen, Ernest *et al.* (eds.)
1926 *An Anglo-Saxon chronicle, from British Museum, Cotton MS, Tiberius B. IV.* (Modern language texts: English series.) Manchester: Manchester University Press.

Sievers, Eduard (ed.)
1962 *Tatian.* Paderborn: Schöningh.

Studies

Hiltunen, Risto
1983 *The decline of the prefixes and the beginnings of the English phrasal verb.* Turku: Yliopisto.

Lucas, Peter (ed.)
2002 *Middle English from tongue to text.* Dublin: Dublin University Press.

Niwa, Yoshinobu
1991, 1995 *The function and development of prefixes and particles in three Early English texts.* (vols. I & II) Tokyo: Kinseido.

Ogura, Michiko
1995 "The interchangeability of Old English verbal prefixes", *Anglo-Saxon England* 24: 67-93.

2002 "*On the way, on way* and *away* in Old and Middle English", in: Lucas (ed.): 71-82.

Robinson, Orrin W.
1992 *Old English and its closest relatives.* London: Routledge.

Venezky, Richard L. -- Antonette diPaolo Healey (ed.)
1980 *A microfiche concordance to Old English.* Toronto: Pontifical Institute of Medieval Studies.

116 Michiko Ogura

Table 1: Renderings of Latin words in each version

	Li	Ru	WSCp	Tatian
uenire	cuman gecuman	cuman	cuman gan	quëman biquëman
ire	gan gangan	gan gangan	faran gan feran (Lk.)	faran gangan
abire	gan gangan (Mt.) feran	gan feran (Lk., Jn.)	feran faran (Jn.) gan	gangan faran
exire	gan gangan (Mt.) feran (Lk.)	gan feran (Lk.) utgan (Mt.)	gan utgan (Mt.) feran	angan
transire	oferferan oferfaran	gelioran (Mt., Mk.) oferferan	faran feran gewitan	faran furifaran
introire	in(n)gan in(n)gangan	ingan inferan	gan	ingangan
intrare	in(n)gan in(n)gangan	ingan ingangan	gan ingan	ingangan
ambulare	gangan gan	gangan gan	gan gangan	gangan
vadere	gan gangan	gan gangan	faran (Mt., Jn.) gan	faran
ascendere	astigan	astigan	astigan faran (Jn) feran	arstigan stigan
descendere	ofdune astigan (Lk.) ofdune stigan (Jn.) ofstigan	astigan ofdune astigan (Jn.)	cuman (Jn.) faran feran (Lk.)	nidarstigan
accedere	geneolecan	geneolecan gan (Mt.) cuman (Mt.)	genealæcan cuman (Mt.)	gangan zuogangan

Table 2: Positions between the verb and the free-morph prefix or an adverbial element

	Li	Ru	WSCp	Tatian
Partic. + V	6	7	2	
abire V	77	67	76	54
V + Partic.	1*	5	2	1
Partic. + V	18	26	33	44
exire V	101	70	70	11
V + Partic.	1*	8	17	9
Partic. + V	72	35	21	30
intrare V	5	21	44	14
V + Partic.		5	6	3
Partic. + V	46	39	10	16
introire V	3	8	35	7
V + Partic.			3	
Partic. + V	3	2	3	5
ascendere V	54	49	50	25
V + Partic.	1	1	3	2
Partic. + V	39	17	7	18
descendere V	6	11	28	3
V + Partic.		4	4	3
Partic. + V	19	16	19	8
ingredi V	1	2	10	
V + Partic.	1**			
Partic. + V	1	2	9	9
egredi V	25	16	12	
V + Partic.	2*	2	4	1
Partic. + V	8	4	1	14
accedere V	57	58	61	21
V + Partic.		1		4
Partic. + V	28	16	2	4
transire V	13	23	40	19
V + Partic.	1	1		

N.B. V simple verb with or without a bound-morph prefix

Old English words for people in the *Épinal-Erfurt glossary*

Hans Sauer (Munich, Germany)

1. Introduction

If we can call a glossary a text – this is what, for example, Henry Sweet did in his edition[1] – then the *Épinal-Erfurt glossary* (*ÉpErf*) is certainly the oldest English text of any length that we have. Therefore, it is invaluable for studying the earliest stage of the English language, especially its spelling, phonology, morphology, in particular word-formation, and its vocabulary.[2]

In the present paper, I shall look more closely at the Old English names for people (persons) which *ÉpErf* contains; of course, their Latin lemmata will also be taken into account. There are c. 64 such Old English names in *ÉpErf*. This is not a very large number, especially when compared with the number of plant names in *ÉpErf* (more than 120) and the names for animals (more than 110).[3] Moreover, for several reasons no precise number of names for people can be given (see 3. below), but this is true of the animal and plant names as well. Nevertheless, the names for people offer several interesting aspects. In particular, I am going to analyse their etymology (see 5. below), their morphology (with a special view to word-formation, see 6. below) and their meaning (see 7. below). This is the centre of the investigation. To start with, however, I shall briefly present the manuscripts (see 2. below), discuss the question of words to be included and to be excluded (see 3. below), and sketch the nature of the Latin lemmata and the problems they posed to the Old English glossator(s) (see 4. below). To conclude, I shall look at the question of survival (see 8. below) and, in the ninth section, add a few final remarks. The basis of the investigation, the list of the Old English names for people in *ÉpErf* is given in section 10 (section 10 also provides a list of Latin lemmata plus their Old English glosses), and a bibliography (see References).[4]

2. The *Épinal-Erfurt glossary*

2.1. The manuscripts

ÉpErf is transmitted in two manuscripts, which are obviously derived from a common ancestor. Strangely enough, one of the extant manuscripts of the oldest English text was written on the continent, and both are now located on the continent. These manuscripts are:

(1) Épinal, Bibliothèque municipale 72 (2), fols. 94-107, written in England by an English scribe in the late 7th or early 8th century (Ép);
(2) Erfurt, Wissenschaftliche Allgemeinbibliothek, Codex Amplonianus F.42, fols. 1a1-14va33, written in Cologne by a German scribe in the late 8th or early 9th century (Erf).

The common ancestor of *ÉpErf* has been dated c. 670-690, i.e. the time when Theodore of Tarsus (602-690) and Hadrian (c. 636-709/710) taught at Canterbury (i.e. from 669 onwards), and it may be connected with Theodore's school at Canterbury.[5]

ÉpErf has been described and edited several times.[6] The most recent edition is Pheifer (1974), which I have used for the present article, and all line references are to Pheifer's edition. The most recent facsimile edition is the one by Bischoff et al. (1988).[7]

2.2. The structure of *Épinal-Erfurt*

Épinal-Erfurt is a Latin glossary in a rough alphabetical order, mostly in a-order, i.e. with the Latin lemmata arranged only according to their first letter, with some parts in ab-order. It contains more than 3280 Latin lemmata. Most of them have Latin glosses, but c. 1100, roughly a third, are glossed in Old English.[8] Many of the Latin words are common words, but some are relatively rare (see also 4.1. below). The nouns are often given in the nom. sg., but sometimes in inflected cases, e.g. *adsaeculam* 101 (acc. sg.), *coniurati* 201 (nom. pl.), *censores* 197 and *gladiatores* 481 (both nom. and acc. pl.), *gregariorum* 479 (gen. pl.), *stipatoribus* 929 (dat. pl.), *foederatas* 436 (acc. pl.), etc. This probably reflects the fact that originally the lemmata were taken from texts and were only arranged alphabetically later. The inflected cases are often imitated in the Old English glosses, as far as this is possible in the Old English inflexional system, e.g. *gimodae* 201, *giroefan* 197 and *caempan* 481 (nom. and acc. pl.),[9] *aedilra* 479 (gen. pl.), *ymbhringendum* 929 (dat. pl.), etc.

Compounds are often written as two words in *ÉpErf* (on word-division in the manuscripts, cf. Pheifer 1974: xxiii = § 4); in the present study, I have often inserted a hyphen between the elements of compounds in order to make the morphological structure clear. In the list in section 10, the spellings of both Ép and Erf are given if they differ; otherwise, the spelling of Ép is normally quoted, unless Erf has the better (i.e. more original) spelling or is the only witness.

3. The word-field 'people': Its delimitation and its subdivisions

3.1. Inclusions and exclusions

As stated in section 1, a precise number of the names for people attested in *ÉpErf* cannot be given. There are several reasons for this, in particular:
(1) Names for people/persons can be regarded as a semantic field (word-field), but semantic fields are often difficult to define and to delimit, and there are different ways of doing this. With many semantic fields there is a group of words which belong to the core of the field, whereas others belong to the margin.[10] The words collected here as representing the concept 'people, person' are listed in different sections of Roberts -- Kay (1995), to give just a few examples: *burgleod* 'citizen(s)', *dweorg* 'dwarf', *fostorcild* 'foster-child', *steopfæder* 'stepfather' and others are presented under 'Humankind' (02.03), whereas *cempa* 'warrior, fighter, man' is listed under 'War' (13.02.10.01), and *gerefa* is listed several times, once also under 'War' (section 13.02.10.01.01) and once under 'Social Interaction' (e.g. 12.01.01. 05) – polysemous words obviously often have to appear in different sections. *Grima* 'spectre, ghost' and *orc* 'demon' at best belong to the margin of the field 'people', but I have still included them here; Roberts -- Kay list them under 'Religion: the extrasensorial world' (16.01.03). Strite (1989) has a different division: among other fields, he distinguishes between terms for 'Deity', for 'Kinship', for 'Male and Female', for 'Monster' and for 'Nobility'. Some words in the *ÈpErf* refer to attributes of people rather than to people themselves, e.g. *sceol(h)egi* 'squinting' 981 or *felospraeci* 1009 'talkative'; I have excluded those. For my tentative subdivision of the semantic field, see 3.2. below.
(2) The borderline between present participles (normally ending in *-ende* in the nom. sg.) and agent nouns (normally ending in *-end* in the nom. sg.) is also not always easy to draw.[11] As a rule, I have included forms which translate Latin agent nouns (esp. in *-or, -ator*), e.g. *baedendrae* for *inpulsore* 539, *bisuicend* for *impostorem* 545 or *ymbhringendum* for *stipatoribus* 929 (see further section 6.6.1. below), but I have mostly excluded Old English forms that translate Latin participles, e.g. *tilgendum* 78 (for *tiliendum*) for *adnitentibus*. A dictionary such as ClH seems to follow the same principle: it lists *bǣdend, beswicend* etc. as a separate words (in addition to their bases *bǣdan, beswican*), but not *tiliend*.
(3) Some words are ambiguous or polysemous and might or might not refer to persons. Thus, *actuaris* 87 (probably a form of *actuarius*) might refer to a ship or to a person ('scribe');[12] the same applies to its Old English gloss

uuraec: it could refer to a ship or to a person ('persecutor'), cf. Pheifer (1974: 64). *Uuildae* 'wild ones' 99, glossing *agrestes*, could refer to 'wild people', i.e. 'inhabitants of the countryside'. According to Pheifer (1974: 65) it rather refers to 'wild plants'; a decision seems, however, difficult.

(4) Occasionally a Latin lemma containing no personal name is rendered with an Old English gloss containing a personal name (*uia secta* – *iringaes uueg*, 1050), and conversely, occasionally a Latin lemma containing a personal name is not rendered with a personal name in the Old English gloss (*pliadas* – *sifunsterri*, 762).

3.2. Semantic subgroups

I have tentatively subdivided the Old English names for people into five subgroups. Although female terms are included in groups 1-2 and 4-5, I have in addition also set up a subgroup 6 'women'. The number of clearly marked names for women (circa six) is much smaller than that of the names for men, although some names are perhaps really neutral and might include men as well as women (e.g. *burg-leod, cneorissa, fostor-bearn, grima, scin, uuildae* etc.). It is also striking that relatively many of the names for women have a negative denotation or connotation (*cebisae, haegtis, mera*). Some of the groups seem relatively self-evident (1 and 2), whereas others are more mixed (4 and 5). Moreover, there will always be words which are difficult to assign: for example, the distinction between occupation and profession on the one hand and status on the other is not always certain. Thus, I have put *mundbora* into the status-group (4), but *raedbora* into the occupation group (2); see further section 7.3 below. The lists also show that *ÉpErf* is not a systematic guide to the (Latin or Old English) vocabulary and its semantic structure in our sense of a dictionary: among the kinship terms, for example, basic terms such as 'father, mother, brother, sister, husband, wife' etc. are missing, whereas more marginal terms such as 'stepfather' and 'concubine' are included.

(1) Kinship: (i) general and neutral: *cneorissa, fosturbearn, meeg*; (ii) men: *steup-faeder, sueor* (2x), *gesuirgion*; (iii) women: *cebisae, nift*.
(2) Profession and occupation: *byrgere, edisc-ueard, egdere, flitere in ebhatis, gibuur, haetend, hors-thegn, hrof-uuyrcta, lecea, ledir-uyrcta, leuuis, orit-mon, roedra, red-bora, giroefa, scinlaeca, scinnere, scyend, teblere*. Among these *red-bora* and *giroefa* could be singled out as having a political and administrative function.
(3) Warlike or destructive occupation: *caempa, ferhergaend, strael-bora, uuicing-sceadan*.

(4) Status, social relation and interaction: *aedil, aeldor (ealdor), baedend, bisuicend, burg-leod, byrgea, ceap-cnext, dweorg, fultumend, gimodae, gidopta, mundbora, sigiras, gitreeudae, thegan, tyctaend uuildae, uuoda, uuoedendi, uuraec, ymbhringend(um)*.
(5) Mythology, extrasensorial and extraterrestrial world:[13] (i) Gods: *tiig, orc*; female: *burg-runae, uuyrdae*; (ii) demons, spectres, witches etc.: *grima, egisi-grima, scina*; women: *haegtis, mera, uuydu-mer*; (iii) stars: *iringaes uueg*; *sifun-sterri*.
(6) Women, females: (i) kinship: *cebisae* (for *pelices*); *nift* (for *priuigna*); (ii) Gods, mythology: *burg-runae* and *uuyrdae* (for *parcae*); (iii) demons, witches: *haegtis* (*striga*), *incuba* (*mera*); (iv) stars: *sifunsterri* (*pliadas*), i.e. the woman's name is only expressed in the Latin lexeme, but has not been translated into the Old English one.

4. The nature of the Latin vocabulary and the problem of how to render it into Old English

4.1. The origin of the Latin lemmata

Most of the Latin words in *ÉpErf* referring to persons were inherited from classical Latin (about three quarters);[14] a quarter (c. 18), however, seem to be post-classical. Many of the latter are also rare, and some seem to be corrupt. Moreover, sometimes the original gender and inflexional class were changed.[15] Postclassical are: *arcister* 'archer' (according to Pheifer [1974: 5] a corruption of *arcites*, and used instead of the more common *sagittarius*; cf. *DMLBS*); *broel(l)arius* 'park-keeper' (derived from *broilus* 'park', a Late Latin [Gallo-Latin] loan from continental Celtic); *byrseus* 'tanner' (from Greek); *commentariensis* 'clerk of a law-court, registrar of public documents'; *contribulus* 'of the same tribus' (for *contribulis*); *dromedarius* 'camel or camel-driver' (from Greek); *ephilenticus* 'epileptic' (probably for *epilepticus* from Greek); *erpicarius* 'harrower'; *incuba* 'female incubus'; *inpostor(em)* 'impostor'; *larbula* (first recorded in Aldhelm), *mascus* 'ghost, spectre' (normally *masca*; chronologically one of the latest elements: ultimately from Arabic, borrowed into Medieval Latin in the 7th century; the origin of PDE *mask*, G *Maske* etc.); *maulistis* 'seducer, pimp' (from Greek); *nitatio* 'shining, ghost' (perhaps from *niteo* 'shine' or rather **nitito / *nititare* 'shine repeatedly'); *phisillos* (perhaps for *physicus* or for *physiologus*, originally 'natural philosopher' etc.; the meaning 'physician' of *physicus* is late); *via secta* 'milky way' (rare); *vispell(i)o* 'a thief who robbed corpses of their grave-clothes', and, at least with a post-classical meaning, *vetellus* (for *vitellus*) 'father-in-law'.[16]

4.2. The character of the Latin lemmata

What is more important and interesting, however, is the character of the Latin words for people or persons used in *ÉpErf*. Predominantly they refer to men, females occur much more rarely (see section 3.2). Perhaps even more surprisingly, no specifically Christian terms occur, although *ÉpErf* obviously originated in the context of a Christian school in Anglo-Saxon England (perhaps Theodore's school at Canterbury). On the other hand, many of the Latin words (and especially some of the classical ones) specifically refer to Roman or late antique culture, institutions, occupations and professions, mythology etc., e.g. *actuaris* 87 (if for *actuarius* 'a short-hand writer'); *censores* 197 'Roman magistrats responsible for the citizens' morals'; *commentariensis* 223 'registrar of public documents'; *contribulus* 164 'a member of the same tribe'; *dromidarius* 320 'dromedary, dromedary-driver'(from Greek); *gladiator* 481'gladiator, fighter in a public circus'; *iurisperiti* 557 'the learned in the law, legal expert'; *Mars* 663; *mulio* 658 'mule-keeper, muleteer'; *orcus* 698; *parcae* 761 and 764 'goddesses of fate'; *pleiades* 762 'the seven stars' (from Greek); *rabulus* 854 'a brawling advocate, pettifogger'; *scaenicus* (*scienicis*; from Greek) 952 'player, actor on the stage'; *vispellones* 760 'thieves who robbed corpses of their grave-clothes'.

4.3. The problem of how to render them into Old English

Due to their partly culture-specific character it is not surprising that the glossator(s) sometimes had difficulties in translating these and similar terms, and they applied different strategies to cope with the task.
(1) On the whole the Old English renderings are quite adequate, e.g. *burg-leod* for *municeps* 'citizen'; *ceap-cnext* for *empticius* 'bought' (i.e. 'bought slave)'; *dweorg* 'dwarf' for *nanus uel pumilio*; *fer-hergend* for *grassator*; *fostur-bearn* for *alumnae*, etc. How far these renderings are native words and how far they represent loan-formations or loan-meanings (semantic loans) is sometimes difficult to decide and will be discussed later (see section 5.6.).
(2) In three or four instances the renderings are even quite ingenious and represent a kind of cultural transposition or substitution: a Latin word or phrase is rendered by an Old English word or phrase that replaces the classical concept with a native concept. (i) *uuicing-sceadan* for *piraticum*, *piraticam* 736; (ii) *iringaes uueg* for *uia secta* 1050, (iii) *tiig* 'Tiw, Germanic god of war' for *Mars* 663;[17] for an explanation of *uuicing-sceadan* and *iringaes uueg* see 6.5.4. below. (iv) *Parcae* was apparently a

little more difficult. It occurs twice within a few lines (761, 764) and is translated differently on those two occasions (*burg-runae* and *uuyrdae*). Whether the use of *uuyrdae* for *parcae* suggests that there may have been goddesses of fate in Germanic mythology, or whether this is just an attempt at translating an unfamiliar Latin term (and is basically integrated into the Christian world-picture), has been hotly disputed.[18] The fact that *uuy[r]d* is also used in *ÉpErf* to translate *sortem, condicionem* (980) seems to speak against a 'Germanic' interpretation of *wyrd*; apparently it was semantically relatively open and could translate various Latin words – *wyrd* also renders *fatum, fortuna* etc. in Old English literature, see, e.g., BT s.v. 'wyrd',[19] so there does not seem to be a connection to Germanic godesses of fate. The literal meaning of *burg-runae* for *parcae*[20] seems to be something like 'counsellors in a town'. The second element *–rune* 'one who knows or tells secrets' is related to *rūn* 'counsel, mystery, secret, letter, runic letter', but apparently it does not occur independently in Old English, only as a second element of combinations (compounds), see BT and BTS s.v. '-rune'.

(3) In at least one instance, the Old English glossator even tried to paraphrase a Latin term, namely *flitere in ebhatis* (*ebhat(is)* is a form of *eofot* 'crime, sin, guilt') 'a disputer, quarreller in lawsuits' for *rabulus* 'cheap lawyer, pettifogger, demagogue' (854); see Pheifer (1974: 116).

(4) Occasionally the Old English translation is more general and less specific than the Latin term, e.g. *giroefa* (*gerēfa* > PDE *reeve*) 'high official' for *censores* as well as for *commentariensis* – apparently *(ge)refa* was often used for translating titles of non-English officials (see Pheifer 1974: 73; *BTS*, s.v. 'gerefa II'); less specific translation equivalents are also *byrgeras* 'corpse-bearers, lit. 'buriers' for *uispellones* (see section 4.2.); *oritman* (for *eored-mon*) 'horse-man, rider' for *dromidarius* 'camel-driver'; *thegan* 'servants, warriors, noblemen' for *adsaeculam* 'follower, attendant' (according to Lewis & Short, s.v. 'assecla', the latter was often used contemptuously; thus *thegan* was probably more positive). More negative than its Latin lemma is probably *scinneras* 'magicians, illusionists' for *scienicis* (prob. for *scaenicis*) 'players, actors'.[21]

(5) Not quite correct is *hors-thegn* 'ostler, groom, lit. horse-servant' for *mulio* 'mule-keeper, muleteer' (658); as with *dromidarius* (rendered more vaguely as *oritman*, see above), the Old English glossator apparently had problems in rendering names of animals that he did not really know. *Dromedarius* is actually attested in the Bible (e.g. Is. 60.6), but much more rarely than *camelus*; *mulus, mula* is also attested, e.g. 2Kgs. 18.9; 1Prov. 12.40. By glossing *gregarius* (*gregariorum* 479) 'belonging to a flock or herd, of the common sort' with *aedil(ra)* 'noble, aristocratic', the glossator apparently

changed the meaning presented by the Latin lemma into its contrary (antonym); perhaps he thought of the contrast between common soldiers and noblemen presented in some of the apparent sources and chose the wrong member of the pair (cf. Pheifer 1974: 91).[22] *Mund-bora* 'protector, guardian etc.' also is rather the opposite of *suffragator* 'supporter' (934).[23]

5. Etymology and loan-influence

With regard to etymology, one basic distinction is between native words and loan-words, another is according to chronological layers. The distinction between native words and loan-words is, however, blurred by hybrid formations, loan-formations and semantic loans. Both hybrid formations and loan-formations are English formations, but hybrid formations use loan-words as their basis, whereas loan-formations imitate a foreign, in our case usually a Latin model with native material. Semantic loans are also native words, but their meaning has been taken over from a foreign, in our case also usually a Latin word, e.g. PDE *hell*, G *Hölle* < Gmc **xaljō*, originally probably 'a hidden place', the later, Christian meaning taken from Lat (*loca*) *inferna*. Loan-formations, of course, usually also entail a loan-meaning. With loan-words, a distinction also has to be made between immediate origin and ultimate origin: *byrseus*, e.g., is a Latin word in the context of *ÉpErf*, but ultimately it comes from Greek.

Chronologically, several layers can be distinguished: layers usually recognized are Indo-European (IE), Germanic (Gmc), West-Germanic (WGmc) and Old English (OE); sometimes still finer distinctions are made. Etymological dictionaries and studies do not always agree on the chronological labelling, however, and they often use different conventions for rendering the reconstructed Indo-European and Germanic forms. Another complication is that sometimes a root or base or word goes back to an earlier stage, but the derivation from it was coined at a later stage: this is the case, for example, with many of the agent nouns in *-end* and *-ere*: they were formed in Old English, but the underlying verb (or noun) is often older (see section 6.6.1.-2.).

Words can usually be labelled as IE or Gmc or WGmc because they have cognates in related languages; conversely, words are labelled as OE when they have no cognates. But even here, problematic cases occur: Carr (1939: 129) for example, regards a number of compounds which have related forms in Old English, Old High German etc. as independent parallels and not as going back to Germanic or to West-Germanic – I am not sure whether his reasons are always convincing, but I follow his classification here. In the following, I shall deal first with the native words and then with loan-words, hybrid formations, loan-formations and semantic loans. Although the compounds dealt with here are usually nouns, they are listed separately from the simple nouns.

5.1. Indo-European

Of the c. 64 words for people in *ÉpErf*, only c. four can be traced back to Indo-European; all of them are simple nouns, namely (i) *dweorg* 'DWARF' < Gmc **dwerg-az* (cf. G *Zwerg*) < IE **dwergwk-os* 'dwarf'; (ii) *lecea(s)*, *lǣce* < Gmc **lǣkjaz* < IE **legios*; (iii) *nift* 'niece' < Gmc **nefti-* (cf. G *Nichte*) < IE **nepti*; (iv) *sweor* 'father-in-law' < Gmc **swehura-* (cf. G arch. *Schwäher*) < IE **swekura* (Lat *socer*). No compounds can be traced back to Indo-European.

5.2. Germanic

Among the c. 14 words inherited from Germanic, there are eight nouns, two adjectives and three verbs, furthermore one compound and one prefix-formation which was perhaps originally a compound.
(1) Nouns: (i) possibly *geswirgion* (*geswiria*) 'cousin'; (ii) *grima* 'ghost, spectre'; (iii) *mare* (written *mera* in *ÉpErf* 558) < Gmc **maron, maron* 'female incubus', which survives in PDE *nightmare* < possibly even IE, cf. OI *mor, morrigain* 'queen of nightmares'; (iv), *mǣg* 'relative, kinsman' < Gmc **mǣga-*; (v) *tiig* 'Germanic god of war'; (vi) *þegn* < Gmc **þegna-*, which survives in PDE arch. *thane* (cf. arch. G *Degen*); (vii) *wyrd* < **wurð-i-* (see further section 6.7.); (viii) *wrǣc* 'ship' or 'persecutor'.
(2) Adjectives: (i) *wild* < Gmc **swelþija-*; (ii) *wod* < Gmc **wōda-*.
(3) Verbs: (i) *bǣdan* 'to urge, incite'; (ii) *hǣtan* (weak 1) 'to heat, to make (or be or become) hot' < **hait-jan* (> OE **hāt-jan* > *hǣtan*; cf. G *heizen*); (iii) *treowian* (wk. 2) 'trust', derived from *treow* (cf. G *trauen*).
(4) Compound nouns: Whereas apparently no compounds were inherited from Indo-European (at least not among the names for persons), one clear and one questionable compound go back to Germanic: (i) *burg-lēod* 'inhabitants'; cf. Toth (1980: 271-273; Carr 1939: 129); (ii) *steop-fæder* < Gmc **stiup-faðer* (> PDE *stepfather*; cf. G *Stiefvater*); see Carr (1939: 52). It was perhaps originally a compound, but is here regarded as a prefix-formation, because *steop-* existed not even in Old English any longer as an independent word (see section 6.5.4.).

5.3. West-Germanic

The West-Germanic layer is apparently slightly smaller than the Germanic layer; it consists of c. ten words, c. six nouns, one adjective, two verbs, and one compound nouns.
(1) Nouns: (i) *gebūr* < WGmc **ga-būr-, gi-būr-*, which survives in PDE *neighbour* (cf. G *Bauer, Nachbar*); (ii) *byrgea* 'one who gives bail' < WGmc **burg-jōn* (cf. G *Bürge*); (iii) *cebisae* 'concubine' < WGmc **kabiso* (cf. G *Kebse*); (iv) *gidopta*: perhaps a variant of *ge-dohta*, formed on the adj. *dohtig* > PDE *doughty* (cf. G *tüchtig*) or its basis *dugan (dohte)* (cf. G *taugen*); (v) *haegtis* 'witch' (G *Hexe*), see section 6.6. (3); (vi) *roedra* (ClH *rēðra*) < WGmc **rōþr-i*, derived from *rōðor* 'rudder' (cf. G *Ruder*).
(2) Adjectives: (i) *aeðele* (*ÉpErf aedilra* 479) < WGmc **aþl-ja-* (cf. G *edel*, related to *Adel*).
(3) Verbs: Possibly (i) *forhergian* (cf. G *verheeren*) and (ii) *ymbhringan* (cf. G *umringen*), since both also occur in German.
(4) Compound nouns: (i) *mund-bora* 'protector, lit. protection-bearer' 934, see Carr (1939: 102, no. 77).

5.4. Old English

The majority of the native names for persons attested in *ÉpErf* are Old English formations (c. 27); most of them apparently arose through word-formation processes. Some are possibly loan-formations, see section 5.5.
(1) Nouns: (i) c. nine derivations in *-end*, see section 6.6.1. The underlying verbs are usually older; (ii) c. five derivations in *-ere* (see section 6.6.2.): *byrgere, egderi* (possibly WGmc), *flitere, scinnere, teblere*; (iii) c. five others: *ealdor, giroefa, leuuis, scina, scinnlæca*.
(2) Adjectives used as nouns: *gemod* (*ÉpErf gimodae*).
(3) Compound nouns: These form the largest group (c. 15); in the *ÉpErf* spelling they are: *burg-leod, burg-runae, edisc-ueard, egisi-grima, fostur-bearn, hors-thegn, hrof-uuyrcta, ledir-uuyrcta, orit-mon* (for *eored-mon* according to Pheifer 1974: 80), *red-bora, sifun-sterri, strel-bora, uuicing-sceadan, uuydu-mer, Iringaes uueg*. For their subdivision see section 7.1.

5.5. Loan-words and hybrid formations

There is just one simple loan-word among the names for persons in *ÉpErf*, that is *orc* (borrowed into Old English from Lat *orcus* originally 'underworld', then also 'God of the underworld'),[24] but there are a few hybrid formations, namely

(i) *caempa* 'warrior, fighter' (< WGmc **kamp-jon*), a West-Germanic formation (cf. G *Kämpe*) based on the Latin loan-word OE *camp* (G *Kampf* < Lat *campus*); (ii) *teblere* 'gambler', based on the Latin loan-word *teblae/tefil* < Lat *tabula* (in the meaning 'game of dice') – Lat *tabularius* also existed, but it had a different meaning, 'registrar'; thus it is unlikely that *teblere* is an immediate borrowing from Latin and more likely that it was newly formed in Old English from *teblae*; (iii) the OE compound *ceap-cnext*, the first element of which is *cēap* 'bargain' < Lat *caupo* (cf. G *Kauf*), > PDE *cheap*.

5.6. Loan-formations and semantic loans

Old English adopted not only loan-words from Latin, but also created a number of loan-formations based on Latin models,[25] as well as some semantic loans (loan meanings). The number of loan-formations was probably even higher than the number of loan-words.[26]

5.6.1. Subgroups within loan-formations

Within the loan-formations ('Lehnbildungen') a threefold subdivision is often made between loan-translations ('Lehnübersetzungen'), loan-renditions ('Lehnübertragungen') and loan-creations ('Lehnschöpfungen').

(1) Loan-translations are usually complex words (compounds or prefix- or suffix-formations) and they follow their Latin model most closely by rendering it morpheme by morpheme, e.g. *hǣlend* – *salvator*, where the stem of *salvare* is rendered by the stem of *hǣlan* 'HEAL', and the agent suffix *-(a)tor* is rendered by the agent suffix *-end*.[27]

(2) In loan-renditions only one element of the Latin model is translated literally and one is rendered more freely. For example, in *ceap-cnext* 'bought slave', perhaps modelled on *empticius*, the first element *emere*, *emptus* is translated relatively literally by *ceap*, but whereas in Latin the second element *-icius* is a suffix, in the Old English the second element (*cnext*) is a word.

(3) Loan-creations are still freer: They show no formal correspondence with their Latin model. This is also the reason why loan-translations are easiest and loan-creations are most difficult to recognise. But even loan-creations normally use the same word-formation processes as native words and therefore cannot always be distinguished from native formations at first sight (and sometimes not at all).

(4) Loan-formations can also be hybrid, i.e. they can contain a loan-word. This is the case with *ceap-cnext* and probably also with *teblere*, see sections 5.5. and 6.4.2. (2).

5.6.2. Criteria for loan-formations and semantic loans

In order to classify an Old English word as a loan-formation, it should be certain or at least likely that this word did not exist before as a parallel but independent Old English formation; in order to classify it as a semantic loan (loan meaning), it should be certain that it had another meaning before it took over its new meaning from Latin. A number of criteria have been suggested for the distinction between loan-formations and semantic loans on the one hand and parallel but independent native words or native meanings on the other.[28] But none of the criteria proposed so far is sufficient to decide all problematic cases, and even if they are combined they are not always decisive. Some of these criteria are:

(1) The concept or thing was not known to the Anglo-Saxons before they came into contact with the Christian missionaries, nor to their Germanic ancestors before they came into contact with the Romans. This is generally likely for most of the specifically Christian concepts (e.g. *almighty, gospel, hell, sin*). As we noted above, some words for 'people' attested in *ÉpErf* are quite general and the concepts probably also existed in Anglo-Saxon England, but a number of the Latin words for persons in *ÉpErf* also stand for specifically Roman or late Antique concepts and the glossators sometimes had difficulties in translating them (cf. section 4). This does not mean, however, that all of the Old English words used to render them are loan-formations or have a loan-meaning;[29] as we pointed out above (see section 4.3), in a number of cases we may simply have to do with imprecise translations that give only a very rough Old English equivalent of the Latin word or transpose it into the Anglo-Saxon world, e.g. *censores* and *commentariensis – giroefa(n)* 'REEVE'. We also do not know whether the Anglo-Saxons had separate professions for all the kinds of workers and artisans that are referred to in the Latin lemmata and that are given Old English equivalents (*byrgere, egderi, hors-thegn, hrof-uuyrcta, lediruuyrcta* etc.): Harrowing (*egðan*) was certainly done by the farmers, but probably just as one of many things a farmer had to do (cf. also section 7.3.).

(2) There is a close morphological correspondence between the Latin model and its Old English counterpart; this applies in particular to loan-translations and partly also to loan-renditions. This does not mean,

however, that all Old English words which are morphologically similar to corresponding Latin words are loan-translations or loan-renditions based on these Latin words; the parallels might be accidental.
(3) The Old English word is rare or even a hapax legomenon, and/or it occurs only in glossaries. But some words which in Old English are attested only in glossaries must have been common, as is clear from their later use.
(4) The glossators apparently had no fixed Old English equivalent for a certain Latin word and therefore they had to experiment, using different Old English formations for the same Latin word.[30]

It has also to be kept in mind that, once they are created, loan-formations lead an independent life and do not necessarily gloss or translate the Latin word which triggered off their coinage; see, e.g. the remarks on *strel-bora* and *hrof-wyrcta* below.

5.6.3. The status of the Old English names from *ÉpErf*

Taking these points into consideration, I would very tentatively suggest the following classification:
(1) Native words are certainly or probably: *æðele* (*aedilra*), *byrgea, cebisae, dweorg, ealdor, flitere, gidopta, fostur-bearn* (although attested only in glossaries), *grima, haegtes, hors-thegn, leceas, meeg, mera* (for *mare*), *mund-bora, nift, red-bora, roedra, scina, seofon-sterri, sigiras, steop-faeder* (*steup-faedaer*; orthographic variants), *sueor(as), gesuirgion, teblere* (a hybrid formation), *tiig, wild(ae), wod(a), wraec*.
(2) The following are imprecise translations for persons and offices connected with the Roman or Late Antique world, but they are also native words or formations: *cempa – gladiator* 481 (hybrid, i.e. a native formation based on a loan-word); *flitere* (*in ebhatis*) – *rabulus* 854; *gebur – colonus* 163; *giroefa(n)* – *censores* 197, *commentariensis* 223; *red-bora(n)* – *iurisperiti* 552; *thegn – adsaeculam* 101 etc.
(3) The following might be semantic loans (i.e. have a loan-meaning): *Gimodae* 'of one mind' for *coniurati* (cf. BT, BTS s. v. 'gemōd', adj.). *Uuyrdae* for *parcae* (764) can also be regarded as having a loan-meaning. *Burg-leod* (see above) is a Germanic compound; according to Toth (1980: 271-3) it has a loan-meaning when translating *civis*; this probably also applies to Ép 620, where it glosses *municeps*.
(4) Loan translations: (i) The eight agent nouns in *-end* attested in *ÉpErf* (see also section 6.6.1.) are based on native verbs, but as agent nouns they could be loan-translations, rendering Latin agent nouns in *-(a)(t)or* (and sometimes also Latin (present) participles): *baedend(rae) – inpulsor(e)* 539;

bisuicend – inpostor(em) 545; *ferhergaend – grassator* 467; *fultumend(i) – adstipulatus* 95; *hætendae – calentes* 206; *scyhend – maulistis* 654; *uuoedend(i) –* Lat *lymphatico*; *ymb-hringend(um) – stipator(ibus)* 929. According to Kärre (1915: 229) most Old English agent nouns in *-end* were "exclusively literary words"; they were occasional formations and are attested very rarely.[31] This is also true of the formations attested in *ÉpErf*.
(ii) Apart from the group consisting of agent nouns in *-end*, there are relatively few examples among the names for persons in *ÉpErf* which could be regarded as loan-translation. A possible case is *egderi (egðere)* 'harrower' for *erpicarius* (normally *herpicarius*) 396, which occurs only in glossaries (but is a WGmc formation, attested also in OHG & OLG).

(5) Loan renditions: To this group belong perhaps: (i) *ceap-cneht* for *empticius* 349, which is rare and mainly attested in glossaries, apart from an occurrence of *cype-cniht* in Ælfric; (ii) *edisc-uueard* (hapax legomenon) for *broelarius* 'park-keeper' 148, which was perhaps not a profession or occupation in Anglo-Saxon England; (iii) *hrofwyrcta* (literally, 'roofmaker') for *tignarius* ('carpenter, builder' cf. Klump 1908: 120); according to Pheifer (1974: 127) it is, however, modelled on *sarcitector* rather than on *tignarius*. *Ledir-wyrcta* (for *byrseus*), on the other hand, might be native; (iv) *strel-bora* (hap. leg.) 'archer', lit. 'arrowbearer' for *arcister* 114 – if this is a loan rendition, it is, however, modelled on *sagittarius* rather than on *arcister* (cf. Pheifer 1974: 65); (v) *uuicingsceadan* for *piraticum/piraticam* 736: *uuicing* is a name for persons (see further section 6.6.4.), but whereas Lat *piraticum (piraticam)* is originally an adj. (*piraticus* 'pertaining too pirates', the agent noun is *pirata*), in OE *sceaða(n)* there may have been a confusion between the action noun *sceaðe* and the agent noun *sceaða*, with the glossator substituting the more frequent *sceaða* 'enemy, warrior' etc. for the rarer *sceaðe, sceaða, sceþþu* 'crime'. In all the cases mentioned so far, the Latin lemma is a suffix-formation, whereas its Old English rendering is a compound; (vi) *gitreeude – foederatas* is perhaps also a loan-formation; here, both the Latin and the Old English word are suffix-formations.

(6) Loan creations: To this group belong perhaps: (i) *burg-runae* for *parcas* 761 – *burg-runae* is a hapax legomenon; moreover, the *glossator(s)* apparently experimented and within a few lines used once *uuyrdae* 764 and once *burg-runae* 761 for *parcae, parcas*; see also section 4.3.2.; (ii) *byrgeras* for *uispellones* 760 is rare and only occurs in glossaries; (iii) *egisi-grima* 'ghost', lit. prob. 'terror mask' – *larbula*; (iv) *orit-mon* for *dromidarius* is a hapax legomenon (prob. for *eored-mon*) – camel-drivers were certainly not a usual feature in Anglo-Saxon England (but see section

4.3.5.); (v) *scinneras* for *scienicis* (prob. for *sc[ae]nicis*) is rare and occurs in glossaries only. (vi) *uuydu-mer* – Echo.

6. Morphology, especially word-formation

6.1. Theoretical and methodological questions

6.1.1. The area of word-formation

Within morphology, inflexion can be regarded as the creation of different forms of the same word (lexeme), whereas word-formation can be regarded as the creation of new words. This distinction is fairly straightforward in many cases, but there are also areas where word-formation is not so easy to separate from inflexion. We mentioned the sometimes problematic distinction of agent nouns and present participles (see section 3.1.2 and also 6.6.1.); another unclear area is the substantivization of adjectives (see section 6.8.). The latter is often regarded as an inflexional or syntactic phenomenon, but since the word-class changes in the process, it could also be mentioned in the context of word-formation. With other patterns, such as the bahuvrihi nouns and zero-derivation (conversion) it has been disputed whether we have to do with word-formation or with a purely semantic process.

6.1.2. Simplexes, complex words and their distinction

Apart from the distinction between word-formation and inflexion it is, of course, also important to separate complex words (consisting of two or more morphemes), from simplexes (monomorphemic words). The former belong to the field of word-formation, whereas the latter do not.[32] Thus, *burg-leod*, *teblere* and *ceap-cnext* are clearly complex words, whereas *dweorg*, *meeg* (*mæg*), *grima*, *sweor*, *þegn* etc. are simplexes, at least from an Old English point of view. On the whole, there are relatively few simplexes among the names for persons in *ÉpErf*.

The structure of words can change in the course of time, however. A number of words were originally complex (i.e. in Indo-European or in Germanic or even in very early Old English), but, mainly due to phonetic and phonological processes were later obscured into simplexes. To give a few modern examples: *lord*, *lady*, *gospel*, *sheriff*, *woman* are simplexes (monomorphemic words) in Modern English, but they were compounds in Old English (*hlāf-weard*, *hlǣf-dige*, *gōd-spel*, *scīr-gerefa*, *wīf-man*). This is, of course, connected with the question of whether one should attempt a diachronic analysis (in our case reaching back into reconstructed Germanic or even Indo-European forms) or a strictly synchronic analysis (taking only Old English forms into account that are motivated in Old English), and it is also connected with the question of productivity and analysability. Basically, I shall attempt a synchronic classification of the complex words although it is often difficult not to get involved in etymological considerations. I shall also sketch the history of the compounding patterns and the etymology of the prefixes and suffixes. Since there are many borderline cases, a strict division of synchrony and diachrony is not always possible. Thus, there are many formations showing i-mutation in their stem-vowel, such as *byrgea* (ClH *byrga*), *caempa*, *giroefa*, *roedra*, *wyrd* (to take just the examples from *ÉpErf*). These are monomorphemic forms from a strictly synchronic point of view (even at the time of *ÉpErf*), but they were originally formed with a suffix *-i, -j* etc.; they form a relatively large and conspicuous group, therefore they are included here and dealt with in section 6.7. See further Kastovsky (1992: 357-61).

6.1.3. A model for describing word-formation

There is no commonly accepted model for describing word-formation processes and complex words which have been created through such processes. Consequently, schemes of classification vary. One of the most elaborate models was developed by Marchand (1969: esp. chapters 1-2). Basically, it still seems useful although it has to be modified and supplemented. Here, I can sketch the model only very briefly, although there are problems of analysis on all levels and, accordingly, all levels have been the subject of extensive discussion.[33]

(1) Morphological shape describes the word-class and the morphological status of the elements: *burg-leod* consists of two nouns; *teblere* consists of a noun (*tebl*) and a suffix (*-ere*). The word-class and the morphological status are not always clear, however.

(2) Morphological structure: Here it is assumed that complex words as a rule consist of two immediate constituents, the determinant (dt) and the determinatum (dm); in other terminologies: the modifier and the head. The determinant (modifier) specifies the determinatum and restricts its range of reference (semantically speaking, the compound is a hyponym of its determinatum); the determinatum (head) dominates grammatically, i.e. it indicates the word-class and the semantic category. Thus, *burg* is the determinant in *burg-leod* and *leod* is the determinatum; in *teblere*, *tebl* is the determinant and the suffix *-ere* is the determinatum, indicating the agent in this case – but there are also cases where the dt and the dm are more difficult to establish. The combination of morphologic shape and

morphologic structure yields the the types and subtypes of word-formation as dealt with here; see sections 6.2ff.

(3) The syntactic paraphrase[34] provides a sentence which contains the elements (constituents) of the complex word and explains their relation: *burg-leod* 'people [leod] who inhabit, live in a town [burg]'; *teblere* 'someone who [-ere] gambles or has to do with gambling [tebl]'. The syntactic paraphrase thus also is a kind of semantic analysis. One problem of the syntactic analysis is that in compounds without a verbal element sometimes different verbs can be inserted (see above: 'inhabit' or 'live in'); another, that for us it is, of course, difficult if not impossible to form correct Old English sentences. If it is not possible to paraphrase a complex word with the help of its elements, then this word is probably idiomatized or lexicalized; see under 5.iv below.

(4) The type of reference forms a bridge between morphological structure and syntactic paraphrase; it states which part of the sentence (subject, object, adverbial, verb or rather the verbal action indicated by the verb) has been topicalized and becomes or corresponds to the determinatum of the complex word. Thus, both *burgleod* and *teblere* are subject-types ('people live in a town'; 'someone is connected with gambling'); *ceap-cnext* is an object-type ('someone has bought the slave' or 'someone has acquired the slave through buying', see section 6.2.2.(4)). As these examples show, in order to allow comparison, the type of reference must be established from a full, declarative sentence in the active voice, which is still open as to the types of reference – a relative clause (as given in section 3) or a passive clause has already been topicalized and the type of reference has been fixed.

(5) Semantic structure (meaning): This is probably the most complex level and thus also most difficult to describe in a systematic and satisfactory way. In the case of complex words, at least a threefold distinction can be made, that is between reference, sense (meaning) and the internal relation of the constituents. In addition to this, the question of idiomatization and lexicalization comes into play. (i) Reference: Most of the words discussed here refer to persons/people (often to quite specific kinds of people); (ii) Sense: One distinction is according to broad semantic categories such as agent nouns, experiencer nouns and patient (passive) nouns. Thus, *teblere* is an agent noun, because it implies an activity; *burg-leod* is an experiencer noun, because living somewhere is not really an activity; *ceap-cnext* is a patient noun, because its meaning is 'slave or servant who has been bought'; see further section 7.1. Another distinction is between several semantic fields (word-fields), such as names of relation, occupational names etc.; see section 3.2.; (iii) Internal structure: Complex words are

morphologically motivated, i.e. dt (A) and dm (B) stand in a relation to each other; most generally this can be described as 'B has something to do with A', or 'B is somehow connected with A'. The precise connection must then be specified. This can be done with the help of a syntactic paraphrase of the kind mentioned above under (3) and (4); it can also be done by assigning semantic roles to the constituents, e.g. *burg-leod* [PLACE/INHABITANT]; *teblere* [ACTIVITY/AGENT]; *ceap-cnext* [ACTIVITY/ PATIENT];[35] (iv) Idiomatization and lexicalization: What has been said so far refers to complex words with regular semantic structures, which can be paraphrased with the help of their elements relatively easily or can be assigned semantic roles. If a paraphrase with the help of the elements is unsatisfactory or impossible, then the complex word is probably idiomatized or lexicalized. In cases of idiomatization or lexicalization the meaning of the entire word is different from the sum of the meanings of its constituents; often semantic features have been added, or sometimes also lost. Thus, *iringaes uueg* refers to the Milky Way, which is not apparent from *iring* plus *way*. If a distinction between idiomatization and lexicalization is made, then lexicalization refers to a later, diachronic change of meaning (and sometimes also of form), whereas idiomatization refers to a synchronic process, to complex words which had semantic peculiarities from the moment of being coined. Sometimes the distinction is difficult to make. *Iringaes uueg*, however, seems to be a clear case of idiomatization: probably, it did not have an earlier meaning, but was coined with the meaning 'Milky Way'.

6.1.4. Recursivity of word-formation processes

Word-formation can be recursive, that is a word can undergo a sequence of several word-formational processes (occasionally, processes also seem to work simultaneously). To give a Modern English example, *friend* (noun) can be suffixed to yield *friendly* (adj.); this can be prefixed to yield *unfriendly* (adj.), this can be suffixed again to yield *unfriendliness* (noun). Words which have undergone two (or more) processes are accordingly listed twice (or several times). Thus, for example, *bisuicend* is discussed under the prefix *be-*, *bi-* and under the suffix *-end*; *iringaes uueg* is discussed under the noun + *s* + noun compounds and under the suffix *-ing*.

6.1.5. The structure of the entries

With compounding types, the following information is given: (a) definition; (b) attestation in *ÉpErf*; (c) problems, e.g. distinction from other types; (d) history (prehistory and later development) and productivity; (e) syntactic-semantic subclassification; (f) literature. Similarly, with prefixes and suffixes, the following information is given: (a) form, i.e. first the 'normal' Old English form (i.e. form in Late West Saxon), then the form in *ÉpErf*, followed by the PDE form (if the prefix or suffix survives) and the basic meaning; (b) attestation in *ÉpErf*; (c) problems, e.g. distinction from other affixes, question of affix family; (d) history (etymology and later development) and productivity; (e) gender and inflexional class; (f) function, derivation, meaning(s) and semantic subgroups; (g) literature.

6.2. Compounds (compound nouns)

6.2.1. The range of compounds

Compounds are sometimes difficult to distinguish from syntactic groups on the one hand and from affix (prefix and suffix) formations on the other, but we need not discuss this question here (cf., e.g., Sauer (1992: 57-124, 221-41, 298-309).

6.2.2. The types of compounds

Among the compound nouns, several subtypes can be distinguished. The following are certainly or possibly attested among the names for people in *ÉpErf*: noun + noun; noun in the genitive + noun; numeral + noun; verb + noun; noun + deverbal (agent) noun without a suffix; noun + deverbal (agent) noun with suffix *-t*. Others are missing, such adjective + noun, but this is probably due to the limited scope of the material in *ÉpErf*. The productivity of these types varies: Noun + noun is the strongest type in *ÉpErf* (see further below). Noun + deverbal agent noun is also well attested, whereas the others are rare in *ÉpErf* and generally rarer than noun + noun.
Literature: See, e.g., Kastovsky (1992: 362-76); Sauer (1992: 125-48).

(1) **Noun + noun**:
(a) In noun + noun compounds, both elements are primary nouns, i.e. there is no verbal element on the surface; compounds where one element is deverbal are here assigned to other types, see especially (4)-(6) below.

(b) About nine noun + noun compounds are attested among the names for people in *ÉpErf*: *burg-leod, burg-runae, edisc-ueard, egisi-grima, fostor-bearn, hors-thegn, orit-mon* (for *eored-mon*), *uuicing-sceada(n), uudyu-mer*.
(c) Of course, it is not always easy to be certain whether an element should be labelled as primary or as deverbal. (i) For a discussion of *ceap-cnext*, see (4) below; (ii) Kastovsky (1968: 235-8) apparently regards *weardian* as primary and *weard* as derived (deverbal), but here *weard* is regarded as primary and *weardian* as derived, following the rule of thumb that strong verbs are primary and related nouns are derived, whereas weak verbs are secondary and in their turn derived from nouns, adjectives or other verbs; (iii) Moreover, sometimes a noun is originally deverbal but functions as primary in the compound, e.g. *sceada* (*sceaða*) 'criminal, robber etc.' (or *sceadu* etc. 'crime, robbery', see section 5.6.3. (5)) is derived from the verb *scieððan, sceaððan* (strong VI),[36] but *uuicing-sceada* 'pirate' is a copula compound meaning something like 'the criminal is a viking';[37] (iv) *Haegtis* is re-garded as an obscured compound by some, but it is here classified as a suffix formation, see section 6.6 (3); (v) *-runae* (< *rūno*) 'the woman who knows/tells secrets', connected with *rūn* 'mystery, secret etc.', apparently is not attested independently (but cf. *gerūna*).
(d) The type noun + noun is an old composition type, going back to Indo-European.[38] The earliest formation in our corpus goes back to Germanic, namely *burg-leod*.[39] The others are apparently Old English formations. Throughout the history of English, noun + noun has apparently always been the most productive composition type.[40]
(e) Noun + noun has many syntactic-semantic subgroups. As far as the sense is concerned: Among the names for people there are three subgroups (from the point of view of semantic roles): agent nouns (e.g. *hors-thegn*), experiencer nouns (e.g. *burg-leod*), and patient (passive) nouns (e.g. *fostur-bearn*); see further section 7.1. As far as the relation of the elements is concerned: A basic distinction is between copula compounds (where a form of 'to be' has to be supplied) and rectional compounds (where another verb has to be supplied). The only possible copula compound is *uuicing-sceada(n)*, if *sceada* is regarded as an agent noun: 'a viking is a criminal'.[41] The others are rectional compounds. Syntactically, both the agent and experiencer nouns are subject-types, e.g. *hors-thegn* 'B looks after A', *burg-leod* 'B inhabits A' (subject – object in the paraphrase sentence; object – subject in the compound), whereas the patient nouns are object types, e.g. *fostur-bearn* 'someone gives A (food, maintenance

[fostor]) to B (bearn)' (i.e. subject – direct object – indirect object in the paraphrase sentence; direct object – indirect object in the compound).
(f) Literature: Marchand (1969: 45-53 and 60-3); Koziol (1972: 48-58 = §§ 69-97); Kastovsky (1992: 365-9); Sauer (1992: 148-51 and 389-420).

(2) **Noun in the genitive + noun** (genitival compounds):
(a) Both elements are also primary nouns, but the first noun is in the genitive.
(b) There is just one example of a noun in the genitive + noun compound among the names for persons in *ÉpErf*, i.e. *iringaes uueg*, lit. 'Iring's way', i.e. 'the Milky Way' (which contains a personal name as first element, but does not refer to a person as a whole; for *iring*, see section 6.6.4.).
(c) Genitival compounds are not always easy to distinguish from syntactic genitive groups; see, e.g., the discusssion in Sauer (1992: 152-5). Basically, a syntactic genitival group has a very specific (specifying) reference, e.g. PDE *my father's car* is only my father's car if my father actually owns it, whereas a genitival compound has a more general (classifying) reference, e.g. PDE *the driver's seat* refers to the seat behind the steering wheel where the driver habitually sits, even if this seat is empty at the moment, or if it is occupied, e.g., by a child that cannot drive.
(d) Genitival compounds are apparently a relatively young type; sometimes they are also called "secondary compounds", see Carr (1939: 309ff.). Perhaps originally they coalesced from the corresponding syntactic genitival groups (in German, they are therefore sometimes called 'Zusammenrückungen'). At least, the names of the days of the week, however (e.g. *Tuesday, Wednesday, Thursday*), go back to West-Germanic, and they are usually regarded as loan-translations from Latin. *Iringaes uueg* may even be Germanic, because *Irings vegr* is also attested in Old Norse. Genitival compounds have always been of limited productivity in the history of English.
(e) Literally, *iringaes uueg* can probably be explained as 'This way has been named after Iring' (perhaps more specifically because according to legend he was the first to walk on it [metaphorically]). This compound is certainly idiomatized, because it refers to the 'Milky Way'.[42]
(f) Literature: Carr (1939: 309-18); Marchand (1969: 65-9); Koziol (1972: 60-2 = §§101-3); Kastovsky (1992: 369-70); Sauer (1992: 152-63).

(3) **Numeral + noun**:
(a) The first element is a numeral, the second a noun.
(b) There is just one example, *sifunsterri*, which is not a personal name, but glosses (translates) a Latin name (*pliadas* < Gk *pleiades*) in *ÉpErf*.

(c) *Sifunsterri* is actually quite complex because it also has the suffix *-i* (< *-ja*) which indicates collectivity (cf. G *Berg* – *Gebirge*; *Schwester* – *Geschwister*; *Stern* – *Gestirn(e)*); the normal OE form is *steorra*. *Sifunsterri* thus belongs to a type which combines compounding with suffixation. Whereas compounds with a numeral as a first element are here set up as a separate type, they are sometimes subsumed among other types in the literature, e.g. among adjective + noun compounds; formations such as OE *seofonleaf* rather belong to the bahuvrihi compounds (cf. Carr 1939: 164-70; Sauer 1992: 241-6).
(d) The type has apparently always been rare.
(e) Syntactically-semantically, *sifun-sterri* could be analysed as a copula compound, 'the(se) stars are seven'.
(f) Literature: Kluge (1926: 35 = § 66); Marchand (1969: --); Koziol (1972: 63f. = § 108); Kastovsky (1992: --); Sauer (1992: 171-4, 241-6).

(4) **Verb + noun** (verbal stem + noun):
(a) The first element is a verb or, in Old English (as well as in Modern German), rather the stem of a verb; the second element is a noun.
(b) There is also just one possible example, namely *ceap-cnext* 'bought servant or slave' (349).
(c) It is sometimes difficult to decide whether a given compound should be analysed as noun + noun or as verb + noun. This is also true of *ceap-cnext*, which could be analysed as noun *cēap* (a loan-word from Lat *caupo*, cf. G *Kauf*) + noun *cnext* 'servant [cnext] who has been acquired by bargain [ceap]', or as *cēap-*, stem of *cēapian*, (weak 2; in its turn derived from *cēap* noun), + noun cnext 'servant [cnext] who has been bought [ceap-]'. The fact that the verb was derived from the noun suggests that *ceap-* in *ceap-cnext* should perhaps rather be analysed as a noun; on the other hand, the more natural syntactic paraphrase (at least in Modern English) would be 'a slave who has been bought' rather than 'a slave who has been acquired by trading, purchase'. The formation is here listed as an example of the verb + noun compounds mainly to show that this type existed in Old English.
(d) This type was perhaps developed in West Germanic. It arose from formations where the first element "was a deverbal noun which was formally identical with the verb stem" (Kastovsky 1992: 370f.); the deverbal noun could then be interpreted as the verb stem. The type has been moderately productive from Old English to Modern English.
(e) Semantically, *ceap-cnext* represents a patient noun, and syntactically, an object type, 'servant, slave [cnext] who has been bought' < 'Someone has bought the slave'.

(f) Literature: Carr (1939: 175-96); Marchand (1969: 72-4); Koziol (1972: 65f. = § 113); Kastovsky (1992: 370-1); Sauer (1992: 185-94).

(5) **Noun + deverbal noun with suffix -*t***:
(a) The first element (dt) is a noun, the second (dm) is a deverbal noun with the suffix -*t*.
(b) The element -*wyrhta* (see Klump 1908: 42-9), which contains the suffix -*t*, is attested as second element in two compounds in *ÉpErf*, namely *hrof-uuyrcta* 996 (for Lat *tignarius*) and *ledir-uuyrcta* 155 (for Lat < Gk *byrseus*) – both occur in glossaries only, see Klump (1908: 64 & 119-20).
(c) Compounds with a second element (dm) containing the suffix -*t* are here set up as a separate type of compounds. -*wyrcta*/-*wyrhta* is derived from the present stem of the weak verb (class 1) *wyrcan* – *worhte* – *geworht* (see also under section d); *wyrhta* was also commonly used as an independent noun.
(d) In the suffix -*t*, several Gmc suffixes fell together, e.g. -*ti*, -*tjo*. *Wyrhta* is a Gmc formation (< *wurh-tjo* < weak verb 1 *wurk-jan* or immediately from the stem Gmc *wurk-* < *werk-am*, > OE *weorc* > PDE *work*). Some compounds of the type noun + deverbal noun with suffix -*t* also seem to go back to Germanic, e.g. *neawist* (cf. Carr 1939: 58, no. 4), or to WGmc, e.g. *man-sli(e)ht* (cf. Carr 1939: 101, no. 70). *Hrof-uuyrcta* and *ledir-uuyrcta* are OE formations. The suffix -*t* lost its productivity in Middle English.
(e) The suffix -*t* derived deverbal nouns.
(f) The suffix -*t* derived mainly names of things, e.g. *ǣht* 'property', *gift* 'GIFT' – *wyrhta* is thus a bit unusual in being a name for persons and an agent noun 'B works [i.e. makes] A (e.g. a roof, leather)'; in both compounds (*hrof-uuyrcta*, *ledir-uuyrcta*) the object is an effected object.
(g) Literature: Klump (1908: esp. on -*wyrhta*); Kluge (1926: 66 f. = § 127 f.); Marchand (1969: --)[43]; Koziol (1972: 207f. = § 485f.); Kastovsky (1992: 358-60 & 384); Sauer (1992: 207-10).

(6) **Noun + deverbal (agent) noun (without a suffix)** = noun + verb$_{\emptyset\text{ noun}}$
(a) The first element is a noun, the second is a deverbal agent noun without a suffix. The word class of the second element changes from verb to noun.
(b) There are c. four compounds referring to persons the second element of which is clearly deverbal: in three, the second element is -*bora*, in one, -*laecea*: *mund-bora*, *red-bora*, *strel-bora*; *scinn-laecea(n)*.
(c) Although the handbooks do not always clearly separate noun + deverbal noun compounds from noun + noun compounds (often subsuming the former among the latter), both should be kept apart. The deverbal agent nouns can be derived from strong and from weak verbs: -*bora* is derived

from the past participle stem of *beran* (strong IV; OE *beran – bær – bǣron – (ge)boren*).[44] The basis of *laecea-* is doubtful. Possible candidates are *lǣcan* 'spring up', *gelǣcan* 'emulate, join with' (or even the noun *gelǣca* 'rival'), but all of these words were rare; moreover, the semantic connection with *laecea* is unclear. As the form *-bora* shows, derivation from strong verbs was not always made from the present stem, but often from one of the past stems or the past participle stem. Derivation from a "low ablaut grade" even seems to have been the original pattern (Carr 1939: 216), which also suggests that derivation from strong verbs was older than derivation from weak verbs. The deverbal noun is often also used as an independent word, but it does not have to be; *-bora* and *-(ge)laeca* almost always occur as second elements of compounds. But even elements such as *-bora* and *(ge)laeca* should not be regarded as suffixes, but rather as potential words, derived from another word (cf. Kastovsky 1992: 365).

(d) The composition type noun + deverbal agent noun is an old pattern and goes back at least to Germanic (see Carr 1939: 216). *Mundbora* 'guardian' is a West-Germanic formation (Carr 1939: 102, no. 77), the others seem to be Old English. As the examples show, the type was fairly productive in early Old English; later, its productivity diminished. Many of the Old English formations died out in Middle English, but there were also some new formations; Sauer (1992: 202-5), still has more than 40 noun + deverbal agent nouns attested in Early Middle English. Competing types were formations in *-end* and *-ere*, see section 6.6.

(e) The deverbal noun normally is a weak (consonantal) masculine (n-stem; cf., e.g., Campbell 1959: 249 = § 618). All of these formations are agent nouns; a rough general paraphrase would be 'B performs the action indicated by the underlying verb on A', e.g. 'B bears [i.e. gives] rǣd [counsil]'; 'B bears [i.e. carries] stræl [an arrow]' (idiomatized or lexicalized for 'archer'). Syntactically they are subject types, i.e. the second element (dm) corresponds to the subject of the sentence. The first element corresponds to the object; in *strel-bora* it is an affected object. In *mund-bora* and *red-bora*, literally and syntactically the object is an affected object ('B bears, i.e. carries protection, advice'), but semantically the object is an effected object ('B gives protection, advice'). Whereas in *-bora* the original meaning of the verb can still be seen ('someone who bears = carries something'), the connection of *-laecean* with *lǣcan* 'to spring up, rise, flare up' or *gelǣcan* 'to emulate' is more difficult to establish, see above. Possibly *scinn-laecea* was formed in Old English in analogy to the noun OE *scīn-lac* 'magic', a West-Germanic formation (Carr 1939: 107, no. 23; cf. also Sauer 1992: 235-7).

Old English words for people   143

(f) Literature: Kärre (1915: --); Carr (1939: 5f. & 216-9); Koo (1946: 16-8); Marchand (1969: 79-80); Koziol (1972: 58f. = § 98); Kastovsky (1992: 365 & 367-9); Sauer (1992: 198-207).

6.3. Combinations with locative particles

6.3.1. General remarks

The first element is a locative particle; the second element is a noun. Locative particles can be used as prepositions (e.g. OE *ymbe*) or adverbs (e.g. OE *ūt* > PDE *out*) or both (e.g. OE *ofer* > PDE *over*). They are sometimes also used in transferred meanings, e.g. temporal; *over* and *under* are often used in the meaning 'too much, more than should be', resp. 'too little, less than should be'; this is a meaning which they do not have in independent use. In the literature on word-formation, locative particles are often silently subsumed under the prefixes (e.g. by Koziol 1972: 89-127), but since particles also occur as independent words, combinations with them should be kept separate and classified as compounds. Nevertheless there seems to be a widespread feeling that locative particles are more like prefixes than like words.[45] Perhaps this has to do with the fact that they are function words belonging to the closed word-classes, and not content-words belonging to the open word-classes (cf. Sauer 2000: 112 & 132).
Literature: Carr (1939: --); Marchand (1969: 108-21); Koziol (1972: 89-127); Kastovsky (1992: --); Sauer (1992: 176-85).

6.3.2. The particles

There is only one example in our material.
(1) *ymb(e)-*
(a) *ymb(e)* occurs independently as a preposition and as an adverb meaning 'around, about' (cf. G *um*); in compounds, the *-e* is often omitted.
(b) *ymbhringendum* (Ép 929) or *ymbdringendum* (Erf 929), lit. 'surrounders', for Lat *stipatoribus* 'attendants'; (possibly a loan translation, see section 5.6.3.4.).
(c) The Ép form *ymbhringend(um)* and the Erf form *ymbdringend(um)* probably represent different verbs, *ymbhringan* and *ymbdringan* – not quite consistently, ClH lists the verbs and the agent noun *ymbhringend* as separate words, but the agent noun *ymbdringend* only as a variant of *ymbhringend*. The forms *ymbhringend(um)* and *ymbdringend(um)* are here

regarded as agent nouns formed from the verbs (theoretically, they could also be present participles), see section 3.1.(2).

(d) *Ymb(e)* developed from Gmc **umbi-* (cf. G *um*). Combinations with *ymbe-* were quite frequent in Old English; judging from ClH, there were c. 130 different formations. There were far fewer even in Early Middle English.[46] In the course of Middle English, *ymb(e)* changed into *umb(e)*, *emb(e)*, but then it died out as well as all the combinations formed with it. It survives in German as *um-* (*um das Haus herum, umgeben, umringen* etc.).

(e) *Ymb(e)-* has the meaning 'around'. It is combined with verbs.

(f) Literature: *MED* s.v. 'umbe', adj, adv, prep, pref; *OED* s.v. 'umbe-'; Marchand (1969: --); Koziol (1972: 126f. = § 289); Kastovsky (1992: --); Sauer (1992: 182).

6.4. Prefix- and suffix-formations (affix formations)

6.4.1. General considerations

(1) Definition: Affixes, i.e. prefixes and suffixes are defined as bound morphemes, as elements that do not occur independently. Prefixes are attached in front of a word; suffixes are attached at the end of a word.

(2) Distinction from words: The distinction between words and affixes (prefixes and suffixes) is not always clearcut, especially since a number of prefixes and suffixes developed from words.[47] As stated above, locative particles are here not regarded as prefixes, nor are deverbal agent nouns such as *-bora*, *-wyrhta* regarded as suffixes (even if they rarely occur independently); members of both groups are regarded as words (or at least as potential words).

(3) Variation, its reasons and its classification: Some prefixes and suffixes occur in a number of spellings in Old English as well as in Middle English (e.g. *be-* and *bi-*; *for-* and *fer-* etc.). There can be several reasons for such variation, in particular: (i) There was no standardized spelling in Old English yet (nor in Middle English); (ii) There were stressed and unstressed variants; see, e.g. Campbell (1959: 30-5 = §§ 71-92), and the remarks on *be-*, *bi-* below; (iii) The prefixes and suffixes in question go back to Germanic or even Indo-European prefixes or suffixes which occurred in variant forms (see, e.g., below on *for-*, *fer-*). The question arises whether such variant forms should be regarded as variants (spelling variants, pronunciation variants, allomorphs) of the same prefix or suffix or as different prefixes or suffixes. This question has to be considered for each

group of variants separately. Sometimes it is useful to regard such a group as a prefix- or suffix-family (following Kastovsky 1992: 384).

6.4.2. Prefixes

(1) *be-. bi-*
- (a) *ÉpErf* still has the earlier form *bi-*, see (d) below; in later Old English as well as in Modern English (and in Modern German), the usual form is *be-* (PDE *be-* /bɪ/). The meaning is basically 'by, around, about, near etc.'.
- (b) The only form attested in *ÉpErf* (among the names for persons) is *bisuicend* 'deceiver, impostor' for Lat *inpostor(em)* (545), the agent noun formed from the verb (strong I) *bisuican (beswican)* 'deceive'.
- (c) The prefix *bi-* is related to the particle (preposition, adverb) *be* (> PDE *by*; cf. G *bei*), but is nevertheless treated as a prefix here, because it often has a different meaning, and partly also a different form. On the question of stress, see the following section.
- (d) *bi-* comes from the Germanic prefix **bi-*, which is the unstressed form of the particle Gmc **bi*, the latter in its turn was often lengthened: OE *bī* > PDE *by* /baɪ/, OHG *bī* > G *bei*. In Old English, however, unstressed (*be-*) and stressed (*bi-*) forms of the prefix apparently also co-existed. According to Campbell (1959: § 73), the stressed (and lengthened) form was used with nouns, the unstressed with verbs. Since in *ÉpErf bi-* precedes a noun derived from a verb, however, it seems more likely to me that the *bi-* in *ÉpErf* simply represents the older form. The unstressed form of the prefix *bi-* was weakened/lowered to *be-* in the course of Old English (and also in the course of German: *be-*, e.g. *betrügen*), but raised again in PDE *be-* /bɪ/. *Be-* was productive in Old English (see ClH). *Beswican* is an Old English formation, which, however, died out later. *Be-* still exists in Modern English.
- (e) --
- (f) *be-* is basically a verbal prefix, which then also occurs in nouns and adjectives derived from verbs with *be-*. *Be-* has basically the meaning 'by, around, about, near etc.', but since in *bisuican* the basic verb *swican* also means (among other things) 'abandon, deceive', the *bi-* (*be-*) in *bisuican* (*beswican*) probably just has an intensifying meaning 'to deceive (thoroughly)'. According to ClH (s.v. 'be-'), one of the functions of *be-* is to make intransitive verbs transitive (including *beswican*), but since the simplex *swīcan* could also be used transitively, this function does not seem to apply here.

(g) Literature: *EWDS*, s.v. 'be-, bei'; *ODEE*, s.v. 'be-, by'; Lenze (1909); Campbell (1959: 31 =§ 73 f.); Marchand (1969: 146-8); Koziol (1972: 95-7 = §§209-16); Kastovsky (1992: 379).

(2) *for-, (fer-)*
(a) The normal Old English form is *for-* (which is still the Modern English form: *for-* /fɔː/, /fə/), but *ÉpErf* also has the variant form *fer-* (cf. G *ver-*), cf. (d) below.
(b) The only form attested among the names of persons in *ÉpErf* is *ferhergaend* 'ravager' for Lat *grassator* (467), the agent noun formed from the weak verb 2 *forhergian (ferhergian)* 'to ravage, plunder, destroy'.
(c) The prefix *for-, (fer-)* is different from the particle *fore-*, which is also often used in word-formation.
(d) The prefix OE *for-, fer-* can ultimately be traced back to IE **pro-, *per-* (cf., e.g., Lat *por-, pro, per*), i.e. there have always been variant forms, which can be regarded as members of a prefix family. The corresponding German prefix is *ver-* (as in *verbieten, verlassen* etc.). *For-* was productive in Old English (see ClH) and formations with *for-* still exist in PDE (*forbid*), but *for-* does not seem to be productive any longer. *Ferhergian* is possibly a West-Germanic formation, cf. G *verheeren* (OHG *firherion*).
(e) *For-, fer-* was mainly a verbal prefix, but it was also used with adjectives and adverbs and, of course, it occurs in nouns derived from verbs with *for-* (as in *ferhergaend*).
(f) *For-, fer-* had several meanings; in *ferhergian*, there is the sense of 'destruction', but since the underlying verb *hergian* (OHG *herion*) had the same meaning ('ravage, plunder', originally 'to ravage, destroy with an army [here]'), the function may be intensifying.
(g) Literature: *EWDS*, s.v. 'ver-'; *ODEE*, s.v. 'for-1'; Marchand (1969: --) (Marchand deals only with *fore-*); Koziol (1972: 99f. = §§ 221-2); Kastovsky (1992: 379-80).

(3) *ge-, gi-* (and **ge- + -ja*)
(a) The usual Old English form was *ge-*, but *ÉpErf* uses mainly *gi-* (Ép has *ge-* just once, 214; Erf has *ge-* slightly more frequently). The prefix no longer exists in English.
(b) Six formations with *ge-, gi-* are attested among the names for persons in *ÉpErf*: *gibuur* 'farmer' for Lat *colonus* (163); *gidopta (gidogta)* 'comrade' for Lat *contubernalis* (189); *gimodae* 'of one mind' for Lat *coniurati* (201); *giroefa(n)/geroefa(n)* 'high officials, REEVES' for Lat *censores* and

commentariensis; *gisuirgion* 'cousin (nephew, sister's son)' for Lat *consubrinus*; *gitreeudae* 'federates' for Lat *foederatas*.
(c) For problematic aspects, see section (f) below.
(d) *ge-*, *gi-* goes back to a Germanic prefix **ga-*. It was very productive in Old English; but in Middle English, it was weakened to *y-*, *i-* and died out in Late Middle English / Early Modern English, leaving few traces (see, e.g. *ODEE*, s.v. 'y-'), which suggests that it had lost all its original functions in English. It lives on in German as *ge-* (*Gebirge, Gebrüder, Geschwister* etc.) and was grammaticalized for the past participle (*gearbeitet, gegangen*).
(e) --
(f) *ge-*, *gi-* had two main functions: a) It was a verbal prefix expressing perfectivity and was accordingly frequently used for the past participle (but often also for the present forms); b) it was a nominal prefix expressing collectivity. Here we are concerned with the nominal prefix which expresses collectivity and associativity. All the formations listed above under (b) have this meaning, at least originally. (i) *gibuur* (which is preserved in PDE *neighbour*, cf. G *Nachbar*; the basic word lives on in PDE *bower*) is a West-Germanic formation **gi-bur* or **ga-bura* (cf. G *Bauer*), originally meaning 'the fellow occupier of a dwelling' (*ODEE*). Whether it was still transparent in Old English is another question. The other formations are morphologically a bit more complex; (ii) *giroefa(n)* (ClH *(ge)refa*) and *gisuirgion* (ClH *geswigra*) show a combination of the prefix *ge-* and an original suffix *-ja*, which caused i-umlaut before disappearing (cf. Kluge 1926: 35 = § 66 *ga- - -ja*): *giroefa* (< **gi-rōf-ja*) is doubly lexicalized: a) because the underlying noun *rōf* 'number, enumeration' is no longer attested independently in Old English (but cf. *secg-rof, stæef-rof* and OHG *ruova, ruoba*), and b) because its meaning 'high official' is no longer connected with the meaning 'number'; (iii) *Gisuirgion* is derived (with metathesis) from *sweger* 'mother-in-law' (Gmc **swegro* < IE **swekru*, cf. Lat *socer, socrus*; G arch. *Schwieger*, later expanded to *Schwiegermutter* (and *Schwiegervater*)), which in its turn is related to OE *sweor* (< Gmc **swehura-* < IE **swekuro*; G arch. *Schwäher*); (iv) *Gimodae* seems to be a bahuvrihi-adjective, i.e. a noun used as an adjective (in this case as nom. pl. m. of the strong adjective declension): *gi- + mod* 'having one mind, being of one mind'; (v) *gitreeudae* was probably derived from the past part. of the weak verb *treow(i)an* 'to trust in, confederate with', or it could be an extended bahuvrihi-adjective formed from the noun *treow* 'truth, promise, treaty'; (vi) *gidogta* (Erf) seems to be the more original form than *gidopta* (Ép); *gidogta* (nom. sg. m. of the weak

adjectival declension) could be derived from the adj. *dohtig* 'valiant', which in its turn goes back to the pret. pres. verb (II) OE *dugan*, *dēag*, *dugon*, *dohte* (cf. G *taugen* and the adj. *tüchtig*).

(g) Literature: *EWDS*, s.v. 'ge-'; *ODEE*, s.v. 'y-'; Kluge (1926: 35 = § 66, *ga- - -ja*); Marchand (1969: --) ; Koziol (1972: 102-4 = § 227); Kastovsky (1992: 380).

(4) *steop-*, *steup-*

(a) The usual Old English form was *steop-*, but Ép has the earlier form *steup-* and Erf has *staup-*; the PDE form is *step-* as in *stepfather* (G *Stief-* as in *Stiefvater*).

(b) Attested in *ÉpErf* is *steup-fædaer* 'STEPFATHER' for Lat *uitricius* 1070.

(c) Status of *steop-*: The status of *steop-* has been disputed. For example, the *ODEE* s.v. 'step-' calls it an element prefixed to terms of relationship, the *EWDS* s.v. 'Stief-' calls it a prefixoid (Präfixoid), whereas Carr (1939: 52) lists combinations with *step-* among the compounds. In my opinion, for Old English (as well as for PDE), *step-* should be labelled as a prefix because it does not occur independently in Old English. The related verb OE *astiepan*, *astypan* etc. 'to deprive, bereave', which is adduced by the proponents of the word-status of *steop-* was apparently derived from *steop-* before the latter died out in independent use; in any case *astiepan* does not prove the word-status of *steop-* in Old English.

(d) *steop-* is apparently a Germanic prefix (Gmc **steup-*; not attested in Gothic); it is attested, for example, in German (G *Stief-* < OHG *stiof-*) and Old Norse (*stjup-*); to judge from OE *steop-*, Ép *steup-* has preserved the original Germanic form. Many combinations (including *stepfather*) are also Germanic, see Carr (1939: 52). The prefix lives on as *step-* in PDE (and as *Stief-* in G), but, due to its function and meaning, is of limited productivity. OE forms are *steop-bearn* and *steop-cild* 'step-child' (also 'orphan'), *steop-fæder* 'stepfather', *steop-moder* 'stepmother', *steop-sunu* 'stepson' and *steop-dohtor* 'stepdaughter'. Late Middle English formations are *stepbrother*, *stepsister* and *stepdame*.

(e) *steop-* is prefixed to nouns, more precisely to nouns of relationship.

(f) *steop-* has a clearly defined meaning, which is, however, not easy to paraphrase: according to the *ODEE*, s.v. 'step-', it "designate[s] a degree of affinity resulting from the remarriage of a widowed parent", i.e. the relation is no blood-relation, but acquired through remarriage of a parent. Marchand (1969: 193) explains stepfather as 'father to a bereaved child' (perhaps this should be rather 'someone who acts like a father to a bereaved child').

(g) Literature: *EWDS*, s.v. 'Stief-'; *ODEE* s.v. 'step-'; Carr (1939: 52, nos. 62-5); Marchand (1969: 193); Koziol (1972: 114 = § 252); Kastovsky (1992: --).

6.5. Suffixes

(1) *-end*

(a) The usual Old English form of this suffix, which formed agent nouns, was *-end*; this is also the normal form in *ÉpErf*. Ép once has *-aend* (*ferhergaend*, 467). The suffix no longer exists in English.

(b) About nine agent nouns with the suffix *-end* are attested in *ÉpErf*:[48] (i) *baedend(rae)* 'inciter, one who urges' from *bǣdan* for Lat *inpulsore* 539; (ii) *bisuicend* 'deceiver' from *beswican* for Lat *inpostor(em)* 545 (on *be-*, see above); (iii) *ferhergaend* 'ravager' from *forhergian* for Lat *grassator* 467 (on *for-*, see above); (iv) *fultemend* (2x) 'helper' from *fultumian* for Lat *adstipulatus* and Lat *adsessor(e)* 95; (v) *haetend(ae)* 'those who heat' from *hǣtan* for Lat *calentes* 206; (vi) *scyhend* 'seducer, pimp' from *scȳan* 'to persuade, incite, tempt' for Lat (< Gk) *maulistis*; (vii) *tyhtend* from *tyhtan* 'invite, incite etc.' for Lat *inlex* 509; (viii) *uuoedend(i)* (= *wēdend*) from *wēdan* 'to rave, be mad' for Lat *lymphatico* (*wēdan* in its turn is derived from *wōd*, cf. *wōda* 383 for *ephilenticus*, probably an error for *epilepticus*); (ix) *ymb-hringend(um)* 'surrounder(s)' from *ymbhringan* (with the variant *ymbdringendum* from *ymbðringan*) for Lat *stipator(ibus)* 929.

(c) As stated above (cf. 3.1.2.), agent nouns with the suffix *-end* and present participles with the ending *-ende* are not always easy to separate. Here, I have included among the agent nouns mainly those forms which translate a Latin agent noun in *-or, -(a)tor*.[49] Although there were also compounds with the deverbal agent nouns in *-end* as second element, *ÉpErf* has only uncompounded forms.

(d) The suffix *-end(e)*, used for the present participle of verbs and then also for agent nouns, goes back to Germanic (and ultimately to Indo-European); as the examples show, it was quite productive in Old English (it is preserved in German as *-end* for the present participle, e.g. *gehend, stehend*, and – no longer productive – as *-and* for the agent noun, e.g. *Heiland* or names such as *Weigand*). All the forms listed under (b) above seem to be Old English formations, and all of them may be loan-translations (see section 5.6.3.4). In connection with the loss of the present participle ending *-end(e)* and its substitution by *-ing* in the course of Middle English, however, the agent noun-suffix *-end* also died out and with it also most of the words formed with it (with the exception of *fiend, friend*, which were no longer

transparent). As Koziol (1972: 188) points out, -*ing* could not be used as a suffix for agent nouns because it was (and still is) used for action nouns. -*end* was replaced by other agent noun suffixes, in particular by -*er(e)*.
(e) -*end* formed agent nouns from verbs. Whereas the present participle in -*ende* was mainly inflected according to the adjectival declension, agent nouns in -*end* were mainly inflected according to the Gmc a-stems (strong masculines), but there was some overlap in inflexion.
(f) -*end* had a competitor in -*er(e)*, which eventually supplanted it; on -*er(e)*, see below. -*end(e)* apparently always derived present participles and agent nouns from verbs, whereas -*ere* apparently initially derived nouns from nouns, but then increasingly also derived nouns from verbs; this may have been an additional reason why -*er(e)* ousted -*end(e)*.
(g) Literature: Kärre (1915: 77-233); Kluge (1926: --); Koo (1946: 44-63); Marchand (1969: --); Koziol (1972: 188 = § 446); Pheifer (1974: lxxvii = § 65.1); Kastovsky (1992: 385).

(2) -*ere*
(a) The usual Old English form of this suffix, which forms agent nouns, was -*ere*; this is also the usual form in *ÉpErf*. Ép once has the older form -*eri* (*egderi* 396). The suffix lives on as PDE -*er* and is still very productive.
(b) Five derivations in -*ere* are attested in *ÉpErf*: (i) *byrgere* (*byrgeras*) 'burier, corpse-bearer' for Lat *uispellones* 760; (ii) *egderi* 'harrower' for Lat *erpicarius* 396, cf. also *egdae* – *erpica* 395; (iii) *flitere* (*in ebhatis*) 'quarreler (in lawcourts)' for Lat *rabulus* 854; (iv) *scinneras* 'magicians' for Lat *sc[ae]nicis*; (v) *teblere* 'gambler' for Lat *aleator* 7, cf. also *teblae*, *tefil* – *alea* 6. On *sigiras* see section 6.8.
(c) --
(d) The suffix -*ere* is an early loan-suffix; it was probably borrowed into Germanic from the Latin suffix -*arius* (or rather from loan-words containing this suffix).[50] The Germanic form *-*arjaz*, *-*ærjaz* developed into the OE form -*eri* (see above) and the into -*ere*. As can be seen from the attestations in *ÉpErf*, it was productive even in early Old English and is still productive today in its PDE form -*er* /ə/.
(e) -*ere* derived masculine nouns inflected according to the Gmc (strong) a-declension (cf. Brunner 1965: 202 = § 248.1).
(f) -*ere* (> PDE -*er*) derived and still derives mainly agent nouns; to a smaller extent, also instrument nouns; all the formations in *ÉpErf* belong to the agent nouns. Marchand (1969: 273) gives the basic meaning as 'someone or something connected with what the basis denotes'. In Latin, -*arius* derived agent nouns from nouns (i.e. denominal nouns), as can also be seen

from several Latin lemmata in *ÉpErf*, where the basic noun more or less immediately precedes the derived noun in *-arius*: *broel* 147 – *broelarius* 148; *dromidus* – *dromidarius* 320; *erpica* 395 – *erpicarius* 396 (for *herpica* and *herpicarius*); cf. further *gregarius* (*gregariorum*, 479) from *grex*; *tignarius* 996 from *tignum* (and *alea* 6 – *aleator* 7). Derivation from nouns also seems to have been the original function in Germanic and early Old English; later, derivation from verbs became more frequent. Apparently, when the first element (the basic word) could be regarded as a primary noun or as a verb (stem of a verb) or a deverbal noun, it was later connected with the verb. In *ÉpErf*, too, several formations allow of a double explanation. All examples can be explained as denominal nouns, but most could also be deverbal nouns: *byrgere* could be derived from *byrgen* (noun) or *byr(i)an* (verb; cf. also *byrgend* 'gravedigger'); *egdere* (ClH *egðere*) from *egðe* (noun) or *(ge)egðan* (verb); *flitere* from *(ge)flit* (noun) or from *(ge)flitan* (strong verb I); *taeflere* from *taefl* (*tebil*) (noun) or from *tæflian* (verb). Only *scinnere* can apparently just be derived from the noun *scinn* (the verb *scīnan* has long *i* and a different meaning). *Taeflere* could be a loan-word from Lat *tabularius*, but in Classical Latin *tabularius* meant 'registrar, keeper of archives etc.' and not 'gambler', whereas Lat *tabula* 'table' among other meanings also had the meaning 'a board to play on'; thus, OE *teblere* should probably be regarded as a hybrid Old English formation, i.e. as an Old English formation which used a loan-word from Latin as its basis.[51] On the question of how far the *-ere* formations attested in *ÉpErf* could be loan-formations (possibly *egderi*), see section 5.6.3 (4). Since both *-end* and *-ere* formed agent nouns, they became competing suffixes (cf. also formations such as *-bora* and *-wyrhta*). Originally, however, they had different bases for derivation, see above. Occasionally there were formations from the same basic word with both suffixes, e.g. *byrgere* (*ÉpErf* 760) and *byrgend* (both of which were rare, however). There are, however, no directly competing formations attested in *ÉpErf*; see further Koo (1946: 354-62).

(g) Literature: *EWDS* s.v. '-er'; *ODEE* s.v. '-er¹'; Kärre (1915: --); Kluge (1926: 6f. = §§ 8-11); Koo (1946: 64-82 and 354-62); Marchand (1969: 273-81); Kastovsky (1971: 285-325); Koziol (1972: 188-91 = §§ 447-52); Kastovsky (1992: 385-6).

(3) *-es(s)* etc.
(a) This suffix appears in Old English in several forms: *-es(s)*, *-is(s)*, *-ys(s)*, *-isn* etc. Apparently, *-is(s)* is the earlier form, whereas *-es(s)* is the later

weakened form. *ÉpErf* has the earlier form -*is* (Ép -*isae* and -*issa*, Erf -*issae* are probably inflected forms), see below.

(b) Three words certainly or possibly containing this suffix are attested among the names for persons in *ÉpErf*: (i) *cebisae* (probably pl.) 'concubine(s), kept mistress(es)' (G *Kebse*) for Lat *pelices*; (ii) *cneorissa* 'generation, family, tribe' etc. for Lat *sanguinis*; (iii) *haegtis* 'witch' for Lat *strig(i)a*.

(c) The different forms can probably be regarded as variants of the same suffix (or as a suffix family). The suffix, however, seems to have been rare in Old English, and many formations with it are problematic from a morphologic or semantic point of view (or both); see (f) below. It has nothing to do with the PDE suffix -*ess* (as in *actress, heiress, stewardess* etc.), which was borrowed from French into English in the 13th century. Handbooks of English word-formation often ignore it, whereas some Old English grammars mention it.

(d) The suffix goes back to a West-Germanic suffix *-*isjō*- (or *-*isi* according to Campbell 1959: 238 = § 592.d). *Cebisae* is a West-Germanic formation (**kabisō*) and exists in German as *Kebse* (archaic); *haegtis* is also a West-Germanic formation and exists in German as *Hexe* (cf. Carr 1939: 99, no. 38 and *EWDS* s.v. 'Hexe'). *Cneorissa* seems to be an Old English formation which was frequently used. Campbell (1959) and Brunner (1965) list just eight formations between them, apart from *cebisae* (*ciefes, cefes*), *cneoriss* and *haegtess* also *byres* 'chisel', *forleges* 'adulteress, harlot', *ides* 'female', *Lindis* (the county of Lincoln) and *lynis* 'linchpin' (G *Lünse*). The suffix probably lost its productivity even in Old English. With it, practically all formations died out as well.

(e) -*is* apparently derived mainly strong feminine nouns (Gmc *jō*-stems) from nouns, i.e. denominal nouns. Ép *cebisae* probably is the nom. pl. (Érf *caebis* seems to have lost the ending), *cneorisae* Erf reflects the gen. sg., and *cneorissa* Ép is the old gen. sg. ending (Brunner 1965: 205 f. = § 252).

(f) The suffix appears to have had the basic meaning 'belonging to, pertaining to'. Four of the eight formations refer to women, three of which have a negative connotation or denotation (*cebisae, forleges, haegtess*; *ides*), two to instruments (*byres, lynis*), one to a place or rather area (*Lindis*), and one to an abstract, *cneoris* (which is, however, here listed among the names for people). All three formations attested in *ÉpErf* are problematic from an Old English point of view: (i) The noun underlying *cebis(ae)* apparently no longer existed even in Old English; thus *cebisae* is an obscured formation (the underlying noun seems to have been a loan-word meaning 'bed', taken from Lat *cavea*; *cebisae* thus originally seems to have meant something like 'one who shares the bed'); (ii) *Cneorissa* 'generation' was perhaps

formed from *cneo(w)* 'KNEE' in its meaning 'generation, step in a pedigree'. But if this is the case, it seems to be tautological semantically, whereas formally the <r> is difficult to explain (a case of dissimilation?);[52] (iii) The first element of *hægtis* is OE *hæg, haga* 'hedge, enclosure' (cf. G *Hag*), but the second element *-tis* poses a problem. It has been reconstructed as a word **tusjo* which, however, is not attested independently in Old English nor in Old High German (and the meaning of which also seems to be unclear) – this would make *haegtis* an obscured compound. Here, however, it has been classified as a derivation with the suffix *-ess, -iss* (following the Old English grammars) – but if this is the case, then the inserted <t> is difficult to explain. The original meaning seems to have been something like 'someone/a female who is active in hedges'.[53] For a survey of opinions, see Jente (1921: 295-9 = § 168).
(g) Literature: *EWDS* s.v. 'Hexe', 'Kebse'; Kärre (1915: 40-1); Jente (1921: 295-9 = § 168); Kluge (1926: 25 = § 46); Marchand (1969: --); Koziol (1972: --); Kastovsky (1992: --); Campbell (1959: 238 = § 592.d); Brunner (1965: 209 = § 258(c), note 6).

(4) *-ing*[1]
(a) The normal Old English form of this suffix was *-ing*, more rarely *-ung*; *-ing* is also used in *ÉpErf*.
(b) Two formations are attested among the names for people, both as parts of compounds (which do not refer to people as a whole), see section 6.2.2. (1–2): (i) *iring* (personal name) in *iringaes uueg* 1050 for Lat *uia secta*; (ii) *uuicing* 'VIKING' in *uuicing-sceada(n)* 736 for Lat *piraticum, piraticam*.
(c) Here we have to do with the denominal suffix *-ing*, not with the deverbal suffix *-ing*.
(d) The suffix goes back to a Gmc *-inga*, *-unga* > OE *-ing* (*-ung*); for its ultimate origin, see, e.g., Kluge (1926: 12 = § 23). It was fairly productive in Old English; later, its productivity was largely lost (in contrast to the deverbal suffix *-ing*) – very few new formations seem to have been coined in the Modern English period, and none in the 20th century.
(e) *-ing*[1] typically derives masculine nouns (Gmc a-stems) for persons from nouns (or adjectives), i.e. denominal nouns; cf. Campbell (1959: 228 = § 574.6).
(f) One basic meaning of *-ing* is 'belonging to, coming from, descending from'. This was orginally apparently also true of the two words attested in *ÉpErf*. Both are, however, difficult to explain: (i) *Iring* is perhaps a West-Germanic patronymic 'son or descendant of Ir-'; *Ir-* however, is probably an obscured form of the underlying noun (apparently not mentioned by

Munske 1964); (ii) The etymology of *wicing* has been disputed: By some it has been regarded as a loan-word from Old Norse (< *vikingr*). Since, however, the first attestation of *uuicing* in *ÉpErf* precedes the first Viking raids on the English coast (from 793 onwards) by c. hundred years, the explanation as a native English formation seems more likely (see, e.g. *ODEE*, s.v. 'Viking'): *wic* 'camp' + *-ing*, i.e. originally meaning 'someone who lives in/comes from a (temporary) camp'.[54]

(g) Literature: *EWDS*, s.v. '-ing'; *ODEE*, s.v. '-ing³' and 'Viking'; Kluge (1926: 11-6 = § 22-7); Munske (1964); Marchand (1969: 305); Koziol (1972: 195 = § 463, -ing¹); Kastovsky (1992: 386).

(5) *-or*
(a) *-or* forming masculine names of persons is a rare suffix in Old English.
(b) The only attestation in *ÉpErf* is *aeldor* (ClH *ealdor*) in: *bituicn aeldrum* for *inter primores* 546.
(c) The *-or* discussed here is not identical with the suffix *-or* as in *actor*, *inventor* etc., nor with the comparative suffix OE *-ra* (> PDE *-er*). In the *ÉpErf* form *aeldrum* (dat. pl.) the vowel of the suffix has been syncopated.
(d) The suffix seems to go back to an IE *$-ter$ (Kluge *$-t\mathring{r}$). According to Kluge it was widespread in the Indo-European languages, but apparently it was rare even in Germanic and also in Old English. *Baldor* 'prince' is the only other formation mentioned by Kluge for Old English. *Aeldor* (*ealdor*) goes at least back to WGmc, it is derived from the adj. *ald* (*eald*); the compound *ealdorman* (> PDE *alderman*) has corresponding forms in other West-Germanic languages, but Carr regards these as independent parallels. *-or* apparently became unproductive even in the Old English period.
(e) *-or* apparently derived weak masculines (n-declension).
(f) *-or* derived names of persons (masculines), originally apparently agent nouns.
(g) Literature: Kluge (1926: 17 = § 30); Carr (1939: 149); Marchand (1969: --); Koziol (1972: --); Kastovsky (1992: --).

6.6. Derivation with change of stem-vowel

(a) Many words do not have a suffix in their attested Old English form, but they have i-umlaut in the stem, which shows that originally (i.e. in Germanic or in West-Germanic or in preliterary Old English) they were derived with a suffix that consisted of or contained an *-i-* or *-j-* (Gmc *$-i-$ or *$-ja-$ or *$-jan-$ or *$-j\bar{o}n$).

(b) About six nouns from our *ÉpErf* material belong to this group: (i) *byrgea* 921 'one who gives bail, trustee' (G *Bürge*) for Lat *sequester*; (ii) *caempa(n)* 481 'fighter(s), warrior(s)' for Lat *gladiator(es)*; (iii) *giroefa(n)* (ClH *gerefa*) 223 'high official(s), REEVE(S)' for Lat *censor(es)* and *commentariensis* (see section 4.3.4.); (iv) *roedra* (ClH *reðra*) 875 'rower (sailor)' for Lat *remex*; (v) *gisuirgion*; (vi) *uuyrd*. On **ge-...-ja* (*giroefa* and *gisuirgion*), see section 6.5.3.; on *uuyrd*, see 5.2.
(c) These formations cannot be explained strictly synchronically, but because they form a relatively large and conspicious group, they are dealt with here.
(d) This pattern goes back to Germanic and was still productive in (early) Old English, but died out later. *Cempa* is probably a Germanic formation (**kamp-jan*) from the Latin loan-word OE *camp*, G *Kampf* (< Lat *campus*), cf., e.g. G *Kämpe* (and *Kämpfer*). *Wyrd* (*uuyrd*) is probably also a Germanic formation from an ablaut grade (preterite pl. stem) of the strong verb of class III OE *weorþan* – *wearþ* – **wurdon** – *geworden* (see Seebold 1970: 559-61). *Byrgea* is a West-Germanic formation (< **burg-jōn*; cf. G *Bürge*), probably derived from the strong verb of class III OE *beorgan* – *bearg* – **burgon** – *(ge)borgen*.[55] As pointed out in 6.5. (3) above, *giroefa(n)* was formed in Old English from the combination prefix *ge-* plus suffix *-ja*. *Rēðra* was apparently also formed in Old English, from *rōðor* 'oar, scull, RUDDER' + **-ja*.
(e) The derivations in **-ja(n)* belong to the weak masculines (n-stems). In our material, there are derivations from nouns (denominal derivations), i.e. *caempa, giroefa, roedra, giswirgion*, and derivations from verbs, i.e. *byrgea, wyrd*. Derivation from verbs was not always from the present stem, but often from a past stem (cf. above (d) and 6.2.2.5.).
(f) Most of the formations listed here are agent nouns; whether *wyrd* was originally also an agent noun or rather an action noun ('that which happens') is unclear (see 4.3. (2) above).
(g) Literature: Kluge (1926: 4ff. = §§ 5,7,12-14); Campbell (1959: 250 = § 619(2)); Kastovsky (1968); Marchand (1969: --); Koziol (1972: --); Kastovsky (1992: 360-1, 382-3, 392ff.).

6.7. Adjectives used as nouns

(a) Most adjectives could be used as nouns in Old English.
(b) The examples from *ÉpErf* among the material relevant here are (i) *uuildae* 99 for Lat *agrestes*; (ii) *uuoda* (ClH *woda*) 'madman' 383 for Lat *ephilenticus* (probably for *e[p]ile[p]ticus* < Gk); (iii) possibly *aedil(ra)* for *gregariorum*.

(c) Whether the substantivization of adjectives should be regarded as an inflexional, a syntactic, or as a word-formational phenomenon is open to dispute. It is often regarded as an inflexional (grammatical) phenomenon because it was a fairly regular process in Old English and because it is often connected with a change of inflectional class; it could, however, also be regarded as a word-formational phenomenon (a case of conversion or zero-derivation) because a change of word-class is involved.[56] For the latter reason it is mentioned here.
(d) The use of adjectives as nouns was inherited from Germanic; it was common in Old English and is still common in German. This use has become rather restricted in Modern English (*the blacks, the whites* with plural *-s*; *the poor, the rich, the beautiful, the ugly* without plural *-s*); often, prop-words such as *one* or *-man* have to be added (*the good ones*).
(e) When adjectives are used as nouns, they are inflected according to the weak or consonantal (n-)declension if they are preceded by a demonstrative pronoun (definite article), and according to the strong (vocalic) declension if they are used on their own.
(f) --
(g) Literature: Brunner (1962: 73-8 = § 14); Marchand (1969: --); Koziol (1972: 282f. = § 666).

6.8. Difficult and unclear cases

We have several times pointed out that a number of apparently complex words are difficult to analyse for a number of reasons; see, e.g., *ceap-cneht, haegtis* etc. Two words have not been assigned to a specific word-formation type here: (i) *leauuis* for Lat *scurra*. A number of explanations have been put forward, see Pheifer (1974: 125). Pheifer himself suggests to analyse it as a compound adj. **lea-wis* 'scurrilous'. This would explain it as a bahuvrihi adjective with *-wis* 'having a certain way' as second element (cf. *riht-wis* 'RIGHTEOUS' and see Sauer 1992: 308-9), but an OE **lea* 'glad, scurrilous' does not seem to be attested; (ii) *sigir(as)* 'glutton(s)' for Lat *lurcones auidi*: *sigir* might be a derivation with the suffix *-ere* (see above), but the form *-ire* (nom. acc. pl. *-iras*) would be very unusual. Moreover, the underlying verb is unclear: Pheifer (1974: 96) posits an unattested weak verb 1 **sigirjan*; the attested verb *sigan* (strong I) 'sink' does not seem to fit semantically.

6.9. Morphological variants and peculiarities

6.9.1. Formations with blocked (unique) morphemes

In some compounds one constituent does not (or no longer) occur independently; also, in some prefix- and suffix-formations the basic word no longer exists independently even in Old English. Examples from our material are: Compounds: (i) *burg-runae* (*-runae* does not occur independently); prefix-formations: (ii) *giroefa* (ClHall *gerēfa*), see sections 6.4.2 (3) and 6.7; suffix-formations: (iii) *cebis(ae)*, *Iring*, see sections 6.5. (3) & (4).

6.9.2 Obscured compounds

In obscured compounds, one or both constituents have developed differently in the compound than in independent use; usually one or both have been weakened, shortened, and assimilated, so that they can no longer be recognized. There is a scale from slight to heavy obscuration; heavily obscured compounds have become monomorphemic (e.g. PDE *gospel, lammas, lord, lady, sheriff, woman* etc.). Since there was no standardized spelling in Old English, it is sometimes difficult to tell whether a given form is just a spelling variant or an obscured form. Obscuration can be regarded as an advanced form of lexicalization (see 6.1.2.5 above). An example is *orit-mon*: *orit* seems to be a variant of *eored*, see Pheifer (1974: 80) and 6.2.2.(1) above; another example may be *leuuis* 977a, see section 6.9.

7. Semantic structure

As indicated in sections 3. and 6.1.2 (5), there are several ways of looking at and classifying the meaning of words. Unfortunately for the analyst, there is no one to one correspondence between word-formation types and semantic patterns: A given word-formation pattern can exhibit several semantic patterns (see, e.g. section 6.2.2.(1) on noun + noun compounds); conversely, a given semantic pattern can be expressed by several word-formation patterns. Here, I concentrate on the distinction between agent nouns, experiencer nouns and patient (passive) nouns. The agent nouns are by far the largest group.

7.1. Agent nouns, experiencer nouns, patient nouns

7.1.1. Agent nouns

In agent nouns, the second element (dm) indicates a person who performs some activity with respect to the first element (dt). Syntactically, agent nouns represent a subject type, i.e. the second element (dm) is the subject in the underlying or paraphrase sentence; the first element (dt) often is the object. The object can be the affected object or the effected object. Agent nouns occur among: (i) The noun + noun compounds: *edisc-uueard, hors-thegn* (both with affected object) 'B deals with, takes care of, guards A'; *egisi-grima* 'B causes A'; (ii) The noun + deverbal noun compounds, e.g. *mund-bora, hrof-wyrcta, scinn-laeca,* see further section 6.2.2.(5). The first element in *hrof-wyrcta* is an effected object; whether the first element in *mund-bora* and *scinn-laeca* is affected or effected, is more difficult to tell; (iii) The suffix formations in *-end*, e.g. *ferhergaend*, see further 6.6.(1) above; (iv) The suffix formations in *-ere* listed under 6.6.(2) above, e.g., *flitere*. Actually, all formations of the types mentioned under (ii), (iii) and (iv) are agent nouns (or were at least originally agent nouns); (v) Some of the derivations with change of stem-vowel, e.g. *caempa, roedra,* see section 6.7. Here, the original meaning may have been 'someone who has to do with a camp [combat, battle]', 'someone who has to do with a *roðor* [oar]', but the actual meaning 'warrior, fighter' and 'oarsman' (cf. G *Ruderer*) is that of an agent noun.

7.1.2. Experiencer nouns

Experiencer nouns are rarer; they indicate persons who do not really perform an activity, but are rather in a (often permanent) state. Syntactically, they also represent a subject type, e.g. *burg-leod* 'B inhabits, lives in A'. Experiencer nouns, too, occur within several morphological types, in particular: (i) Noun + noun compounds, e.g. *burg-leod, burg-runae* and *uuydu-mer* 'B lives in A, inhabits A', perhaps also 'B is active in A', which would, however, make them an agent noun; *orit-mon* 'B belongs to, is a member of A'; (ii) formations with the prefix *steop-*: *steop-faeder* 'B is not the real father, but the mother's second husband'; (iii) formations with the suffix $-ing^1$, e.g. *iring, uuicing*, which indicate descent or origin ('B comes from A') – later, *wicing* was probably rather seen as an agent noun; (iv) bahuvrihi adjectives, e.g. *gimodae* 'those who have the same mind [mod]'; (v) simplexes such as *dweorg*.

7.1.3. Patient (passive) nouns

Nouns expressing a passive relationship are still rarer (which is also the case in PDE). They indicate a person on which a certain action is or has been performed, e.g. among the verb + noun compounds *ceap-cnext* 'servant, slave [cneht] who has been bought, has been acquired through trade [ceap]'; *fostur-bearn* 'child [bearn] that is given or receives food, sustenance [fostor]'. The passive sentence has, however, already been topicalized. To ensure comparability the basic syntactic paraphrase has to start from an active sentence, too; this reveals the patient nouns from a syntactic point of view as object types (with a direct or a prepositional object): 'Someone buys /has bought this servant/slave'; 'someone gives sustenance to this child (or 'someone provides this child with sustenance').

7.2. Other structures

The complex words which do not refer to a person (although some of them contain a word for a person) cannot be analysed in terms of agent or experiencer nouns. Thus, *iringaes uueg* probably has to be paraphrased as 'the way which Iring has gone/has taken'; *sifun-sterri* as 'the stars are seven' (a copula compound); *uuicing-sceaðe* as 'harm, damage which is/has been done by vikings' (but possibly also as a copula compound 'a viking is a harmful person', see section 6.2.2.1.).

7.3. Idiomatized and lexicalized formations

Some formations cannot be (or can only partly be) explained with their elements; they are idiomatized or lexicalized (see section 6.1.2.5). Idiomatization and lexicalization can be seen as a scale: there is a cline from formations which are not idiomatized or lexicalized, formations which are just slightly idiomatized or lexicalized (see on *hors-thegn* below), formations which are more strongly idiomatized or lexicalized (e.g. *fostur-bearn*; see below) and formations which are heavily or totally idomatized or lexicalized (e.g. *Iringaes uueg*). It has often been said that the addition of fairly general semantic features (such as [+habitual], [+professional]) leads to slight idiomatization or lexicalization, whereas the addition of more specific features (such as [+not one's own child]) leads to stronger lexicalization. Where exactly idiomatization begins, however, is not easy to tell; thus *sifun-sterri* can still be paraphrased as 'seven stars'; it does not refer to any seven stars, however, but to a specific constellation; thus it is perhaps slightly idiomatized. The names for occupations or professions attested in *ÉpErf* do not always reveal how far these occupations were done professionally or habitually, or just occasionally, or, to put it differently, whether the person in question did this activity as his (or her) main or only occupation or just occasionally as one of several occupations; this applies, e.g., to *hors-thegn, hrof-uuyrcta, bisuicend, ferhergaend*. From a cognitive point of view it could be said that these formations conceptualize a typical occupation or activity of the person concerned. Compounds with blocked morphemes, i.e. where one element does not (or no longer) occur independently, can also be regarded as lexicalized; the same applies to prefix- and suffix-formations where the underlying word (basic word) no longer occurs independently: *cebisae, giroefa*. Other clearly idiomatized or lexicalized complex words are: (i) Noun + noun: *fostor-bearn* can still be explained as 'child [bearn] that is given sustenance [fostor]' (see above), but the implication is that it is not one's own child, but an adopted child; (ii) Noun + *s* + noun: *iringaes uueg* is clearly idiomatized, see above; (iii) Numeral + noun: on *sifunsterri*, see above; (iv) Verb + noun: *Ceap-cnext* is interesting because it implies tense. Normally, tense is neutralized in compounds, but *ceap-cnext* apparently refers to a 'servant/slave who has been bought' (and not to a servant who is being bought or who will be bought); (v) Prefix formations: *gebur* 'farmer' etc. was probably no longer associated with its underlying noun *bur* 'dwelling, cottage, BOWER'.

8. Survival, or: Looking ahead

Just as it is interesting to look at the origin (etymology) of the words (see section 5.), it is also interesting to look at their survival. But the further fate of the words is also not easy to classify. Apart from words which clearly died out (see 8.1.) and words which clearly survive (see 8.2.), there are also complex words which do not survive as such but where one or both elements survive (see 8.3); more rarely, there are words which survive only as parts of compounds or complex words (see 8.4). Moreover, some words survive formally, but have clearly changed their meaning (8.5); in other cases, one form was substituted by a related, but morphologically distinct form; e.g. *wyrhta* (< *wyrcan*) has been replaced by *worker* (< *work*), or the basic word survives, but not the derivation (e.g. *bear* < *beran*, but not *-bora*) – but I did not want to set up too many subdivisions here. In any case it is striking that among the words for people attested in *ÉpErf*, the large majority has died out, i.e. c. 52 (if 8.1 and 8.3 are taken together), whereas only c. 14 survive (if 8.2 and 8.4-5 are taken together) – even if 8.2-5 are taken together, only c. 29 survive, whereas c. 37 (see 8.1) have died out.

8.1. Words which have died out (c. 37)

aedil, baedend, bisuicend, byrgea, cebisae, caempa, cneorissa, egdere, egisigrima, flitere, fultemend, gibuur, gidogta, grima, haegtes, meeg (ClH *mǣg*), *leuuis, mundbora, nift, orc, redbora, roedra* (ClH *rēðra*), *scyhend, scinn, scinnlaeca, scinnere, sigir(as), strelbora, sueor(as), gesuirgion, gitreuudae, uuoda, uuoedendi* (*wēdend*), *uuraec, uuyrd, ymbhringend, ymbdringend*.

8.2. Words which have survived (c. 8)

dweorg (> *dwarf*); *ealdor* (> *elder*); *giroefa* (> *reeve*); *haetendae* (> *to heat*); *steup-faedaer* (> *stepfather*); *thegn* (> *thane*; archaic); *uuicing* (> *Viking*); *wilde* (> *wild*).

8.3. Complex words which have died out but where one or both constitutents survive (c. 15)

burg-leod and *burg-runae* (but *borough, -burgh*); *byrgere* (but *to bury*; as a possible word: *burier*); *ceap-cnext* (but *cheap* and *knight*, see 8.5.); *ediscuueard* (but cf. *warden*, a later loan word); *ferhergian* (but *to harrow*); *fosturbearn* (but *to foster*); *gimodae* (> *mood*, see 8.5.); *hors-thegn* (but *horse* and archaic *thane*); *hrof-uuyrcta* (but *roof*); *Iringaes uueg* (but *Iring* and *way*); *oritmon* (but *man*); *sifun-sterri* (but *seven* and *star(s)*); *teblere* (but *table*); *uuydumer* (cf. *nightmare*).

8.4. Words which have survived as parts of compounds or complex words (c. 3)

mera (*mare*) in *nightmare*; *gebur* in *neighbour*; *Tiig* in *Tuesday* (*Tues-* is a blocked morpheme in Modern English).

8.5. Words which have survived but have clearly changed their meaning (c. 3)

ceap (noun) (> *cheap* adj.); *cnext* 'servant, slave' (> *knight*); *gimodae* (cf. *mood*).

8.6. Latin lemmata which were borrowed into English after the Old English period

In c. seven cases, the Old English gloss died out, but the Latin lemma was taken over into English after the Old English period:
Bisuicend – inpostorem (PDE *impostor*); *caempan – gladiatores* (PDE *gladiator*); *cneorissa – sanguinis* (cf. PDE *consanguinuity*); *fostur-bearn – alumnae*; cf. PDE *alumni*; *mascus – grima* (cf. PDE *mask*); *mera – satyrus, saturnus* (cf. PDE *nightMARE*, but also *satyr, Saturn*); *orit-mon – dromidarius* (cf. PDE *dromedary*); *gitreeudae – foederatas* (cf. PDE *federates*); *uuoda – ephilenticus* (prob. for *epilepticus*; cf. PDE *epileptic*).

9. Conclusion

I hope to have shown that all the aspects of the names for people we have looked at, especially the questions of word-field, etymology, word-formation, semantics, and survival show a rich internal structure and subdivision. Clearly, some patterns were more productive and prominent than others, e.g. as regards word-formation compounds consisting of noun + noun and of noun + deverbal agent noun without a suffix as well as agent nouns in *-end*; as regards semantics agent nouns (as opposed to experiencer and patient nouns). Eventually, this study could be expanded into a more comprehensive survey of the areas mentioned as attested in *Épinal-Erfurt*, but especially as far as word-formation is concerned. It has become clear that the word-formation processes and the prefixes and suffixes dealt with here are unevenly represented in the handbooks on English word-formation. Those that were productive in Old English and are still productive (such as noun + noun, *be-, -ere, -ing*[1]) are usually discussed in the handbooks; those that were rare in Old English or have a doubtful status and died out later or even in the Old English period (such as *-ess/-iss*) are often ignored in the handbooks, but sometimes information on them can be found in the grammars and dictionaries.

Old English words for people 163

10. Word-lists

10.1 List of the Old English names for people in *Épinal-Erfurt*

The entries are arranged as follows:

(a) Late West-Saxon spelling of the word or of its first element according to ClH (the question marks at *gidopta* and *leuuis* indicate that there does not seem to be an entry in ClH).
(b) *ÉpErf* spelling. If the spellings of Ép and Erf differ, usually both spellings are listed, first the spelling of Ép, then the spelling of Erf.
(c) Meaning in ' '; if the Modern English equivalent is the more or less regular descendant of the Old English word, it is given in capitals. If there is an etymologically (and semantically) related German word, this is also given.
(d) Indication, if it is a rare word.
(e) Latin lemma in *ÉpErf*.
(f) Entry number in *ÉpErf* (ed. Pheifer 1974).

For the words beginning with A-F, the entries in the *DOE* were checked.

1. *æðele*: *aedilra* (gen.pl.) 'noble, aristocratic' (cf. G *edel*) – *gregariorum* 'common (soldiers)' (gen.pl.), *ÉpErf* 479; cf. *DOE* s.v. 'æþele 1.e.ii'.
1a. *aeldor* > *ealdor*
2. *bǣdan, bǣdend*: *baedendrae* (Ép), *bedændrǣ* (Erf) 'inciter, instigator, one who urges' – *inpulsore*, *ÉpErf* 539; only under the vb. *bǣdan* in *DOE*
3. *beswīcan, beswicend*: *bisuicend* (Ép), *bisuiccend* (Erf) 'deceiver, impostor' – *inpostorem* Ép, *inposterem*, Erf 545; cf. *DOE* 'be-swīcend'
3a. *-bur*: see *gebur*
4. *burg, burh*: *burg-leod* (*a mu[ni]cipio*) 'citizen, inhabitant' (lit. 'town-people') – *municeps*, Ép 620 (Erf 00)
5. *burg, burh*: *burg-runae* (Ép; nom. and acc. pl.), *burg-runæ* (Erf) 'fates, furies, wise women, sybils' (only in glossaries and glosses) – *parcas* (acc.pl.), *ÉpErf* 761 (Jente 1921: 329)
6. *byrga*: a) *byrgea* 'one who gives bail, guarantor' (cf. G *Bürge*) – *sequester* 'depositary, trustee' *ÉpErf* 921; b) *byrgea – pres et uas* (Ép), *praes et uas* (Erf) 'surety, bondsman' *ÉpErf* 776.
7. *byrgere*: (*þorh*) *byrgeras* (Ép; pl.), (*dorh*) *buyrgenas* (Erf, probably for *b[y]rge[r]as*) 'corpse-bearer', lit. 'burier' (rare; only in glossaries) – *(per) uispellones* 'thieves who robbed corpses of their grave-clothes', *ÉpErf* 760

8. *ceap*: (> PDE *CHEAP*; cf. G *Kauf*): *ceap-cnext* 'bought servant, slave' – *empticius*, Erf 349 (Ép 00); DOE has one entry *cēap-cniht*, *cȳpe-cniht*
9. *cempa*: *caempan* (Ép; nom. and acc. pl. etc.), *cempan* (Erf) 'warriors, champions' (cf. G *Kämpe*, *Kämpfer*) – *gladiatores* 'gladiators, fighters in the public games', *ÉpErf* 481
10. *cifes*: *cebisae* (Ép), *caebis* (Erf) 'concubine, kept mistress, harlot' (cf. G *Kebse*) – *pelices* (sg. *pelex*, *paelex*), *ÉpErf* 745
11. *cneoris(n)*: *cneorissa* (Ép), *cneorissae* (Erf) 'generation, family, tribe, line of descendants etc.' – *sanguinis* (gen. sg.) 'blood, blood-relation, consanguinity', *ÉpErf* 903; DOE has two different entries, *cnēoris* and *cnēorisn*
11a. *-dopta*, *-dohta*: see *gedopta*, *gidopta*
12. *dweorg*: *duerg* 'DWARF' – *nanus uel pumilio* (*punilio* Erf), *ÉpErf* 686
13. *ealdor*: *bituicn aeldrum* (Ép), *bituichn ældrum* (Erf) 'ELDER, chief, leader etc.' – *inter primores* (sg. *primoris*), *ÉpErf* 546
14. *edisc*: *edisc-ueard* (Ép), *edisc-uard* (Erf) (in glossaries only) 'park-keeper' – *broelarius* (Ép), *broellearius* (Erf), *ÉpErf* 148
15. *eges-grima*: *egisi-grima* 'ghost', lit. 'terror mask' etc. – *larbula ÉpErf* 569; cf. *grima*
16. *egðere*: *egderi* (Erf; Ép 00) 'harrower' (in glosses only) (cf. G *Egge*, *eggen*) – *erpicarius* Erf 396 (Ép 00) (for *herpicarius*); cf. *egdae* – *erpica* 395 (for *herpica*; not in Lewis & Short); DOE s.v. 'egeþere'
16a. *eored-*: see *orit-mon*
17. *flītere*: *flitere in ebhatis* 'quarreler in lawcourts' – *rabulus* 'petty advocate', *ÉpErf* 854
18. *for-*, *forhergian*, *forhergend*: *ferhergænd* (Ép), *ferhergend* (Erf) 'ravager' (rare; only in glossaries) – *grassator* 'rioter, street robber', *ÉpErf* 467
19. *fostor* (> PDE *FOSTER*): *fostur-bearn* (Ép), *foetri-barn* (Erf, for *foe[s]tri-barn*) (probably pl.) (rare; in glosses & glossaries) 'foster-child(ren), fosterling(s)' – *alumn(a)e* 'foster-daughters', *ÉpErf* 108[57]
20. *fultum(i)an*, *fultum(i)end*: a) *fultemendi* (dat. sg.) 'helper' – *adstipulatus* (for *adstipulator* 'one who joins another in a stipulation, an assistant in a trial') *ÉpErf* 74; b) *fultemendum* (dat. pl.) 'helpers' – *adsessore* (Ép), *adsessores* (Erf) 'he that sits by one, assessor, assistant of a judge' 95
21. *gebur*: *gibuur* (Ép) 'freeholder, farmer', *uicinus* (Erf) – *colonus* 'tiller of the soil etc.', *ÉpErf* 163
22. ?: *gidopta* (Ép), *gidogta* (Erf) 'comrade' (?) – *contubernalis* 'comrade', literally 'tent-companion', *ÉpErf* 189
23. *gemōd*: *gimodae* (Ép), *gimode* (Erf) (nom. pl.), lit. 'of one mind' – *coniurati* 'conspirators', *ÉpErf* 201

24. *gerēfa*: a) *giroefan* (pl.) (Ép), *geroefan* (Erf) 'high official(s), REEVE(S)' – *censores* 'censors', *ÉpErf* 197; b) *giroefa* (Ép), *geroefa* (Erf) – *commentariensis* 'recorder, the clerk of a law court', *ÉpErf* 223
24a. *ge-*: see further *sweor*, *treowan*
25. *grima*: a) *grima* 'mask, ghost, spectre' – *mascus*, Ép 646; *marcus* (probably for *ma[s]cus*) Erf 638a; b) *grima* (*ÉpErf*) – *scina*, *ÉpErf* 904; c) *nitatio uel grima* (*ÉpErf*) – *scina*, *ÉpErf* 953[58] (cf. also *egisi-grima*, no. 15 above)
26. *hægtes(se)*, *hægtis*: *haegtis* (Ép), *hegtis* (Erf) 'fury, witch' (G *Hexe*) – *strigia* Ép, *striga* Erf 'witch (screech-owl)' (< Gk *strix*), *ÉpErf* 913 (Jente 1921: 295–299 = § 168)
27. *hǣtan* (> PDE *HEAT*): *haetendae* (pres. part. pl.) (Ép), *hattendae* (Erf) 'those who heat' – *calentes*, *ÉpErf* 206
28. *hors*: *hors-thegn* 'ostler, groom', lit. 'horse-servant' – *mulio* 'mule-keeper, mule-driver etc.', Ép 658 (Erf 00)
29. *hrōf*: *hrof-uuyrcta* (Ép), *hrof-huyrihta* (Erf) 'roofmaker' – *tignarius* (Ép), *trigrarius* (Erf, for *t[i]g[n]arius* 'carpenter, builder'), *ÉpErf* 996
30. *Iring*: *iringaes uueg* (Ép) – *iuuuringes uueg* (Erf) 'Milky Way', lit. 'Iring's Way' – *uia secta* (apparently not in Lewis & Short), *ÉpErf* 1050
31. *lǣce*: *leceas* (*ÉpErf*, nom. and acc. pl.) 'physician, doctor, LEECH' – *phisillos* (for *physiologos* or *physicos*? < Gk) 'people with a knowledge of nature', *ÉpErf* 746
32. *leðer-*: *ledir-uuyrcta* (Ép), *ledir-uyrhta* (Erf) (hapax legomenon) 'tanner', literally 'LEATHERmaker' – *byrseus* (Ép), *byrreus* (Erf) (< Gk, not in Lewis & Short), *ÉpErf* 155
33. ?: *leuuis* (*ÉpErf*) – *scurra* originally 'elegant man', later 'city buffoon, jester', *ÉpErf* 977a – the interpretation of *leuuis* is difficult, see (Pheifer 1974: 125): suggestions include *leas* 'false, deceitful'; *lews(a)* 'misery' (less convincing); **leawis* 'scurrilous'
34. *mǣg*: *meeg* (Ép 164 – Erf has *consanguinis*) 'kinsman, relative' – *contribulus* 'of the same tribus' (rare according to Lewis & Short), *ÉpErf* 164
35. *mare*, *mera*: *mera* (*uel satyrus*) (Ép), *merae* (*uel saturnus*) (Erf, probably for *sat[y]r[u]s*) 'female incubus', cf. PDE *nightMARE* – *incuba*, *ÉpErf* 558 (cf. *uuydu-mer*, no. 62 below)
35a. *-mod*: see *gemod*
36. *mund* 'protection': *mund-bora* 'protector, guardian, prefect, advocate' – *suffragator* 'supporter', *ÉpErf* 934; cf. *mundbyrd* 'protection, help' – *suffragium* Ép, *subfragium* Erf 935 'voting tablet, vote, favorable decision'

37. *nift*: *nift* (*ÉpErf*) 'niece, stepdaughter, granddaughter' (cf. G *Nichte*) – *priuigna filia sororis idest nift*, *ÉpErf* 734 (Lat *priuigna* strictly speaking means only 'stepdaughter'; 'granddaughter' is *neptis*; 'niece' is *filia fratris* or *filia sororis*)
38. *orc*: *orc* (*ÉpErf*) 'God of the underworld, demon' – *orcus* 'abode of the dead, god of the infernal region, death' Ép, *orci* Erf 698. *Orc* is probably a loan-word from Lat *orcus* (see section 5.5.; Jente 1921: 137 = § 97)
39. ?: *se orit-mon* (probably for *eored-mon*, ClH *ēoredmann*) 'horse-man, member of a troop of riders' – *dromidarius* 'camel-driver', Erf 320 (Ép 00)
40. *rǣd*: *red-boran* (nom. and acc. pl.) 'advisers, counsellors' – *iurisperiti* 'those skilled in the law', *ÉpErf* 552
41. *rēðra*: *roedra* 'rower, sailor' – *remex*, *ÉpErf* 875
41a. *-rēfa*: see *gerefa*
42. *scīn*, *scinn*, *scina* 'spectre, illusion, evil spirit', *ÉpErf* 904, 953: see *grima*, 25 above with footnote 58 (Jente 1921: 155 = § 108; cf. § 169)
43. *scinnere*: *scinneras* (Ép), *scineras* (Erf) 'magicians' – *scienicis* (probably for *sc[ae]nicis* < Gk), *ÉpErf* 952 (Jente 1921: 157 = § 108; cf. § 169)
44. *scinnlǣca*: *scinlaecean* (Ép; gen. sg.), *scinlecan* (Erf) 'wizard, magician' – *nebulonis* (gen. sg. of *nebulo* 'worthless fellow, rascal'), *ÉpErf* 681 (Jente 1921: 160 = § 108; cf. § 169)
45. *scȳan* (?) 'persuade, tempt': *scyhend* (Ép; 00 Erf) 'seducer, pimp' (hapax legomenon) – *maulistis* (< Gk *maulistes*), Ép 654 (not in Lewis & Short)
46. *seofon*: *sifunsterri* (Ép), *funsterri* (Erf, for *[si]funsterri*) 'the seven stars' – *pliadas* (for *Pleiades* < Gk), *ÉpErf* 762
47. *siger*: *sigiras* 'gluttons' – *lurcones auidi uel sigiras* (Ép), *lurcones sigiras uel auidi* (Erf), 568
48. *steop-*: *steup-faedaer* (Ép), *staup-fotar* (Erf) 'STEPFATHER' (G *Stiefvater*) – *uitricius*, *ÉpErf* 1070 (for *vitricus*)
49. *strǣl*: *strel-bora* (hapax legomenon) 'archer, bowman', literally 'arrow-bearer' – *arcister* (probably for *arcites*), *ÉpErf* 114
50. *swēor*: a) *suehoras* (Ép), *sueoras* (Erf) 'fathers-in-law' (G *Schwiegerväter*) – *uitelli*, *ÉpErf* 1062; b) *sueor* 'father in law' – *uetellus* (probably for *u[i]tellus*, literally 'little calf'), Erf 1099 (Ép 00)
51. *geswiria*: *gesuirgion* (Ép), *gisuirgian* (Erf) 'cousin (father-in-law)' – *consubrinus* (for *cons[o]brinus* 'cousin'), *ÉpErf* 214
52. *tǣfl*: *teblere* (Ép), *tebl.re* (Erf) 'gambler' – *aleator*, *ÉpErf* 7 (cf. also *teblae*, *tefil* – *alea*, *ÉpErf* 6)
53. *Tīw*: *tiig* (*ÉpErf*) 'Tiw, Germanic god of war' (cf. OE *Tiwesdæg* > PDE *TUESDAY* for Lat *Martis dies*) – *mars martis*, *ÉpErf* 663 (Jente 1921: 86 ff. = § 59)

54. *treowian*: *gitreeudae* (nom. and acc. pl.) (Ép), *getreudæ* (Erf) 'federates' – *foederatas*, *ÉpErf* 436
55. *tyhtan*: *tyctaend anb* [for *ab*] *inliciendi* (Ép), *tychtend ab inliciendo* (Erf) 'inciter, instigator' – *inlex*, *ÉpErf* 509
56. *þegn*: *thegn* (Ép), *degn* (Erf) 'servant, vassal, warrior, nobleman, THANE' – *adsaeculam* (Ép), *adsexulam* (Erf) 'follower, attendant', *ÉpErf* 101 (see also *hors-þegn*)
57. *wicing*: *uuicing-sceadan* (Ép), *uuicing-scadae* (Erf) 'pirate' or 'piracy' (?) – *piraticum* (Ép), *piraticam* (Erf) 'piracy', *ÉpErf* 736
58. *wilde*: *uuildae* (*ÉpErf*) 'wild' (could refer to wild people or to wild plants) – *agrestes*, *ÉpErf* 99
59. *wēdend* (from *wēdan*): *uuoedendi* (Ép), *uuodenti* (Erf) 'raving, mad' – *lymphatico* 'distracted, panic-struck', 575; cf. *wōda*, no. 60.
60. *wōda*: *uuoda* (Erf; 00 Ép) 'madman' – *ephilenticus* (probably for *e[p]ile[p]ticus* < Gk), Erf 383
61. *wræc*: *uuraec* (Ép), *uraec* (Erf) 'ship' or 'persecutor' (normally in OE 'misery, persecution') – *actuaris* (for *actuari[u]s*?) 'swift sailer' or 'scribe', *ÉpErf* 87 (*uuraec* 90 for *aegit* is a form of *wrecan* 'drive' etc., also *uuraec* 1002 for *torquetur*)
62. *wudu-mǣr*: *uuydu-mer* 'wood-sprite' ('wood-nymph') – *Echo*, *ÉpErf* 347; cf. *mare, mera*, no. 35 above
63. *wyrd*: a) *uuyrdae* (*ÉpErf*; nom. pl.) 'the Fates' – *parcae* Ép, *parce* Erf 764 b) *condicionem id uuyd* (Ép; probably for *uuy[r]d*), *conditionem id uyrd* (Erf) 'fate, fortune, chance, event etc.' – *sortem*, *ÉpErf* 980 (Jente 1921: 199–208 = § 128)
64. *ymbe-*: *ymb-hringendum* (dat. pl.) (Ép), *ymb-dringendum* (Erf), literally 'surrounders' – *stipatoribus* 'attendants, members of a retinue', *ÉpErf* 929

10.2. The Latin names for people in the *Épinal-Erfurt* Glossary

(1) List of the Latin names:
This list of Latin lemmata is mainly given to provide cross-references to the Old English glosses; not all the spelling variants are therefore given.
1) actuaris (for actuarius?) – uuraec
2) adsaecula(m) (assecla) – thegan
3) adsessor(e) – fultemend(um)
4) adstipulatus (for adstipulator?) – fultemend(i)
5) agrestes – uuildae
6) aleator – teblere
7) alumn(a)e (alumna, alumnus) – fostur-bearn

8) arcister (not in Lewis & Short; late?) – strel-bora
9) broel(l)arius (not in Lewis & Short; late) – edisc-u(e)ard
10) byrseus, byrreus (not in Lewis & Short; not in *DMLBS*; late?) – lediruuyrcta
11) calentes (from caleo) – haetend(ae)
12) censor(es) – giroefa(n)
13) colonus Ép (Erf: uicinus) – gibuur
14) commentariensis – giroefa
15) coniurati – gimodae
16) consubrinus (probably for consobrinus) – gesuirgion
17) contribulus – meeg
18) contubernalis – gidopta
19) dromedarius, dromidarius – orit-mon
20) Echo – uuydu-mer
21) empticius – ceap-cnext
22) ephilenticus (probably for epilepticus < Gk) – uuoda
23) erpicarius (for herpicarius) – egderi
24) foederatas (from foederatus, foederata) – gitreeudae
25) gladiator(es) – caempa(n)
26) grassator – ferhergaend
27) gregariorum (gregarius) – aedilra
28) incuba – mera (uel satyrus Ép, uel saturnus Erf)
29) inlex – tyctaend
30) inpulsor(e) – baedend(rae)
31) inpostor(em) – bisuicend
32) iurisperiti (juris-peritus) – red-bora(n)
33) larbula (not in Lewis & Short; late: first recorded in Aldhelm) – egisigrima
34) lurco(nes) – sigiras
35) lymphatico – uuoedendi
36) Mars martis – tiig
37) mascus (7th century) – grima
38) maulistis (< Gk; post-classical) – scyhend
39) mulio – hors-thegn
40) municeps – burgleod
41) nanus (classical but vulgar according to Lewis&Short), pumilio (classical) – duerg
42) nebulo(nis) – scin-laecea(n)
43) orcus – orc (Latin loanword into Old English)
44) a) parca(s) – burg-runae; b) parca(e) – uuyrdae

45) pelices (pelex, paelex) – cebisae
46) phisillos (for physiologos or physicos?; < Gk) – lece(as)
47) piraticum, piraticam – uuicing-sceada(n)
48) pliadas (for Pleiades; < Gk) – sifunsterri
49) primor(es) – aeldrum
50) priuigna – nift
51) pumilio: see nanus
52) rabulus – flitere in ebhatis
53) remex – roedra
54) sanguinis (sanguis) – cneorissa
55) scienicis (probably for sc[ae]nicis from scaenicus) – scinneras
56) scina (possibly an Old English word) – a) grima; b) nitatio uel grima
57) scurra – leuuis
58) sequester – byrg(e)a
59) stipator(ibus) – ymbhringend(um), ymbdringend(um)
60) strig(i)a (cf. strix) – haegtis
61) suffragator – mund-bora
62) tignarius – hrof-uuyrcta
63) uia secta (post-classical?) – Iringaes uueg
64) uispello(nes) – byrgeras
65) a) uitelli (uitellus) – sue(h)or(as); b) uetellus (probably for uitellus) – sueor
66) uitric(i)us – steup-faedaer

(2) A few etymological notes:
(a) The following ultimately go back to Greek:
byrseus < βύρσευς
dromedarius < δρομεδάριος
Echo < ἠχώ
ephilenticus (probably for epilepticus) < ἐπιλέπτικος
lymphaticus: cf. νυμφολεπτός
maulistis < μαυλίστης
phisillos (for physiologos or physicos?) < φυσιόλογος
piraticum, piraticam < πειράτικος
pliadas (for Pleiades) < πλειάδες
satyrus (see incuba) < σάτυρος
scienicis (probably for scaenicis from scaenicus) < σκηνικός
strig(i)a (cf. strix, strigis) < στρίγξ

(b) Of Celtic origin is:
broelarius

(c) Of Arab origin is:
mascus

(3) The following suffixes occur among the Latin lemmata (cf. Leumann 1963):
-alis: contubernalis
-ans, -ens (present participles): calentes
-arius: actuaris (if for actuarius); broel(l)arius; dromedarius; erpicarius; gregariorum; tignarius
-atus, -itus (past participle): adstipulatus (perhaps for adstipulator); coniurati; foederatas; iurisperiti
-estis: agrestes
-ensis, -iensis: commentariensis
-ester: sequester
-ex: remex
-icius: empticius; uitric(i)us
-icus: ephilenticus (probably for epilepticus); piraticum, piraticam; scienicis (probably for scaenicis from scaenicus)
-inus: consubrinus
-ister: arcister
-istis (from Gk): maulistis
-o, -io, -ilio: mulio; nebulo(nis); pumilio; uispello(nes)
-or, -tor, -ator: adsessor(e); aleator; censor(es); gladiator(es); grassator; inpulsor(e); inpostor(em); primor(es); stipator(ibus); suffragator
-ulus, -ellus: contribulus; rabulus; uitelli (from uitellus or uetellus?)

(4) Spelling:
Strikingly, with prefix-formations usually the original non-assimilated form is given in *ÉpErf*: *adsaecula(am)* (cf. *assecla*); *adsessor(e)* (cf. *assessore*); *adstipulatus* (cf. *astipulatus*); *inlex* (cf. *illex*); *inpulsor(e)* (cf. *impulsor*); *inpostor(em)* (cf. *impostor*) – but *suffragator* (however, *suffragium* Ép, *subfragium* Erf 935); cf. further, e.g., *adnitentibus* (78).

Notes

[1] Cf. Sweet (1885). Greenfield -- Robinson (1980), on the other hand, do not regard glossaries as literature and accordingly (and unfortunately), exclude them from their *Bibliography of publications on Old English literature*. For brief surveys of the Old English glossaries, see, e.g. Gneuss (1987-1989); Lendinara (1999).

² The evidence of *ÉpErf* for inflexional morphology is limited (but see 2.2. below), and there is hardly any evidence for syntax.

³ On these, see Sauer (1999a) and (1999b).

⁴ For help with the present article and critical comments, my thanks are due to Christian Heimerl, Wilhelm Heizmann, Michael Herren and Ursula Lenker.

⁵ Cf. Pheifer (1995: 329-333); see also Lapidge (1996: esp. 154). By some, it has also been connected with the school of Aldhelm (c. 640-709/710) at Malmesbury – Aldhelm was a student of Theodore and Hadrian. On the sources of *ÉpErf*, see Lindsay (1921).

⁶ For descriptions see, e.g., Ker (1957: no. 114 and App. no. 10); Pheifer (1974, xxi-xxviii, §§ 1-13)

⁷ Earlier facsimiles are Sweet (1885) and Schlutter (1912). One of the earlier editions is Sweet (1885).

⁸ Pheifer (1974) edits only those Latin lemmata which have Old English glosses, but the facsimile by Sweet (1883), for example, has a transcription of all the lemmata and glosses, including the Latin – Latin ones. See also Goetz (1881-1923: 5, 337-401).

⁹ Theoretically, *caempan* and *giroefan* could also represent other inflected cases, but not the nom. sg.

¹⁰ Cf. Sauer (2001: 254-255).

¹¹ See, e.g., Brunner (1965: §§ 286, 305); Campbell (1959, § 632).

¹² More probably to a ship, if *wraec* is derived from *wrecan* 'drive, impel'.

¹³ On this aspect of *ÉpErf*, see Herren (1998: esp. 97-99).

¹⁴ Strikingly, with prefix-formations the original non-assimilated forms are often given; see section 10.2 (4).

¹⁵ To start with, I checked Lewis&Short and labelled as post-classical those words which are not listed there. A further check of the *ThLL* usually confirmed this. Among the classical as well as among the post-classical Latin words, several directly or ultimately go back to Greek; see section 10.2 (2).

[16] The bases from which *vispell(i)o* and *vetellus/vitellus* are derived are unclear: *Vetellus* (Erf) literally is 'a little old man'; possibly, this is a misspelling of *vitellus* (Ép), lit. 'little calf' (from *vitulus*) – a connection with the Roman emperor Vitellius seems doubtful. The normal Latin word for 'father-in-law' was *socer, socrus*.

[17] The replacement of the Roman gods by their Germanic equivalents was common practice in the days of the week (e.g. *dies martis – tiwesdaeg > Tuesday*), which are loan-translations going back to the 2nd or 3rd century A.D., i.e. to the West-Germanic period.

[18] On the meaning of OE *wyrd*, see, e.g. Weber (1969) and Stanley (1975) with reference to earlier discussions; see also Strite (1989: 70f.) for references.

[19] On the etymology of *wyrd*, see section 6.7.

[20] Thus the same Latin word is rendered by two different Old English words (*parcae*: *uuyrdae, burgrunae*); conversely, the same Old English word renders two (or three) different Latin words: *uuyrd*: *parcae, condicio(nem), sort(em)*. Cf. also *giroefa*: *censor(es), commentariensis*.

[21] Perhaps a reflex of the fact that the church had never liked the Roman theatre and its plays.

[22] Another possible explanation would be that the glossator read *egregius*.

[23] Outside the word-field 'people', a nice case of translating a Latin word with its Old English antonym (and simultaneously a case of cultural adaptation/substitution) is: *res puplica – cynidom* 859.

[24] Cf. also *orcneas* 'monsters', *Beowulf* 112. *Orc* 'pitcher, cup, flagon', a loan-word from Lat *orca, urceus* is less likely, but cf. Pheifer (1974: 106).

[25] Usually through word-formation processes, especially compounding, and, probably to a lesser degree, derivation. Although most histories of the English language stress this fact, the only extensive study of this phenomenon (at least as far as Old English is concerned) is still Gneuss (1955). Cf. also, e.g., Kastovsky (1992: 300, 309-317).

[26] See Gneuss (1955).

[27] Irrelevant features are, e.g., the position of the elements and their inflection: whereas Lat *liber evangelii* is a genitival phrase with the noun in the genitive following the noun

in the nominative, the Old English loan-translation *godspellboc* has changed the order of elements as well as substituted the genitive by a nominative.

[28] See, e.g., Gneuss (1955); Toth (1980: 23-28).

[29] This is what Kastovsky (1992: 310) seems to suggest.

[30] See footnote 18 above.

[31] Apart from a few which were used frequently, in particular *hælend*, *scieppend*, *wealdend* and a few others. But even those which then became popular were probably originally loan-translations (*hælend* < *salvator*, *scieppend* < *creator*).

[32] For the purpose of distinguishing complex words from simplexes, we disregard inflexional endings. Simplexes can, of course, be useful for the semantic analysis.

[33] See, e.g., Sauer (1992); Stekauer (2000). For a recent introduction to English word-formation, see Schmid (2005). I disregard the question of accent here.

[34] In transformational terms, one could speak of an underlying sentence. For our purpose, we can disregard the question whether the sentence is just a paraphrase or whether it actually underlies the complex word and whether the complex word was derived from it.

[35] For a relatively consistent attempt to analyse English word-formation with the help of semantic roles, see Hansen *et al.* (1982).

[36] See Seebold (1970: 408); Kastovsky (1968: 144-145).

[37] A problem here is that *sceada* refers to a person, whereas the Latin lemmata in *ÉpErf piraticum, piraticam* rather refer to an action – perhaps the glossator confused *sceaða* with *sceaðe*, see further section 5.6.3. (5).

[38] In Indo-European, compounding consisted of a combination of stems rather than of a combination of words, however.

[39] See Carr (1939: 129 no. 13). In this as in other cases, Carr regards the OE, OHG and OLG parallels as "parallel and independent formations in the West Germanic languages", and not as inherited from West-Germanic – whether he is right here is another question.

[40] If other types, such as noun + deverbal noun, are subsumed under it, it obviously becomes an even stronger type.

[41] It is a rectional compound, however, if *sceade* is regarded as an action noun: 'damage done by vikings' < 'vikings do damage, commit crimes'.

[42] According to Pheifer (1974: 131; quoting earlier sources), Iring was a Germanic hero who slew Theoderic the Frank and escaped with the help of his sword; *Iringaes uueg* seems to imply (by way of exaggeration) that he escaped via or to the Milky Way. See now Heizmann, forthcoming.

[43] Marchand (1969: --) etc. indicates that there is no information on the pattern or affix in question.

[44] Cf. Seebold (1970: 104-106); Kastovsky (1968: 148f).

[45] Carr (1939) does not include compounds with locative particles in his treatment.

[46] See Sauer (1992: 182), who lists three formations, two of which, however, were newly formed in Early Middle English.

[47] For example, PDE *-hood* developed from the noun OE *hād*, which died out in ME; OE *dōm* split up into the PDE noun *doom* /du:m/ and the PDE suffix *-dom* /dəm/.

[48] My list differs slightly from the one in Kärre (1915: 228), probably due to the difficulty of separating agent nouns from present participles.

[49] Of the ten Latin nouns ending in *-or, -tor, -ator* (cf. section 10.2.3.), five have been glossed with Old English nouns in *-end(e)*: *adsessor(e)* – *fultemend(um)*; *grassator* – *ferhergaend*; *impulsor(e)* – *baedend(rae)*; *inpostor(em)* – *bisuicend*; *stipator(ibus)* – *ymbhringend(um)*; four have been glossed with Old English nouns ending in other suffixes or with Old English compounds: *aleator* – *teblere*; *censor(es)* – *giroefa(n)*; *gladiator(es)* – *caempa(n)*; *suffragator* – *mund-bora*. On the other hand, some Old English formations in *-end* render Latin words not ending in *-(a)(t)or*.

[50] Among the Latin lemmata in our material, the following five or six nouns in *-arius* occur:
actuaris (for *actuarius?*) – *uuraec*; *broelarius* – *edisc-u(e)ard*; *dromedarius* – *orit-mon*; *erpicarius* (for *herpicarius*) – *egderi*; *gregariorum* – *aedilra*; *tignarius* – *hrof-uuyrcta* – only one of them (*erpicarius*) has been glossed with an Old English noun ending in the suffix *-ere*.

[51] See section 5.6.1. An alternative, but less convincing explanation would be to regard *teblere* as a loan-word with a change of meaning, influenced by one of the meanings of *tabula*.

[52] According to Campbell (1959: 238 = § 592.d) *cneoriss* is "of uncertain formation", whereas Pheifer (1974: lxxvii, fn. 3) explains the second element as *rysi* < **runsiz* (without giving a meaning), which would exclude it from the derivations in *-ess, -iss*.

[53] Herren (1998: 99) explains *haehtisse* (glossing *Eumenides*) as a corrupt form of *Hecates* 'of Hecate' (< **Hecatissa*).

[54] Munske (1964: 125), however, does not believe this explanation.

[55] *Byrgea* 'trustee' (G *Bürge*) is probably homonymous with (but not directly related to the stem of) *byrg(e)an* 'to bury' and *byrgere* 'burier'.

[56] Similar considerations apply to the question of whether the formation of adverbs (with *-lice* > *-ly*) belongs to grammar or to word-formation.

[57] *Alumnis* Ép 115a, glossed by *aelifnae*, is a different word, see Pheifer (1974: 65f.: *alum*).

[58] Although given as a Latin lemma twice in *ÉpErf* (904, 953), *scina* is possibly not a Latin word, but OE *scīn, scinn, scinna* 'spectre, illusion, evil spirit', see Pheifer (1974: 123f.) and no. 42 in section 10.1.

References

(Many of the dictionaries, handbooks and editions have often been reprinted; of the *LexMA* there is also a CD-ROM edition.)

Bischoff, Bernhard et al. (eds.)
  1988 *The Épinal, Erfurt, Werden, and Corpus glossaries.* (Early English Manuscripts in Facsimile 22.) Copenhagen: Rosenkilde and Bagger.

Brunner, Karl
  1960-62 *Die englische Sprache: Ihre geschichtliche Entwicklung.* 2 vols. (2nd edition.) Tübingen: Niemeyer.

  1965 *Altenglische Grammatik nach der Angelsächsischen Grammatik von Eduard Sievers.* (3rd edition.) Tübingen: Niemeyer.

Campbell, A[listair]
    1959   *Old English grammar*. Oxford: Oxford University Press.

Carr, Charles T.
    1939   *Nominal compounds in Germanic*. (St Andrews University Publications 41.) Oxford: Oxford University Press.

Conrad O'Briain, Helen *et al.* (eds.)
    1999   *Text and gloss: Studies in insular learning and literature presented to Joseph Donovan Pheifer*. Dublin: Four Courts.

Falkner Wolfgang -- Hans-Jörg Schmid (eds.)
    1999   *Words, lexemes, concepts: Approaches to the lexicon: Studies in honour of Leonhard Lipka*. Tübingen: Narr.

Gneuss, Helmut
    1955   *Lehnbildungen und Lehnbedeutungen im Altenglischen*. Berlin: Schmidt.

    1987-1989   s.v. 'Glossen, Glossare: IV', in: *LexMA*.

Goetz, Georg
    1881-1923   *Corpus Glossariorum Latinorum*. 7 vols. Leipzig: Teuber.

Greenfield, Stanley B. -- Fred C. Robinson
    1980   *A bibliography of publications on Old English literature to the end of 1972*. Toronto: University of Toronto Press.

Hansen, Barbara *et al.*
    1982   *Englische Lexikologie*. Leipzig: VEB Verlag Enzyklopädie.

Heizmann, Wilhelm
   (forthcoming) s.v. 'Thüringische Heldensagen', in: Hoops (ed.).

Herren, Michael W.
   1998 "The transmission and reception of Graeco-Roman mythology in Anglo-Saxon England, 670-800", *Anglo-Saxon England* 27: 87-103.

Holthausen, Ferdinand
   1934 *Altenglisches etymologisches Wörterbuch.* Heidelberg: Winter.
   1974 3rd edition.

Hoops, Johannes (ed.)
   1973- *Reallexikon der germanischen Altertumskunde.* (2nd edition.) Berlin: de Gruyter.

Jente, Richard
   1921 *Die mythologischen Ausdrücke im altenglischen Wortschatz.* (Anglistische Forschungen 56.) Heidelberg: Winter.

Kärre, Karl
   1915 *Nomina agentis in Old English.* Part I. Doctoral dissertation. Upsala [only part I published]: University Press.

Kastovsky, Dieter
   1968 *Old English deverbal substantives derived by means of a zero morpheme.* Unpublished doctoral dissertation. University of Tübingen.

   1971 "The Old English suffix *-ER(E)*", *Anglia* 89: 285-325.

   1992 "Semantics and vocabulary", in: *CHEL* 1, 290-408.

Ker, N.R
1957 *Catalogue of manuscripts containing Anglo-Saxon.* Oxford: Oxford University Press.
1990 Reprinted edition with supplement.

Kluge, Friedrich
1886 *Nominale Stammbildungslehre der altgermanischen Dialekte.* Halle: Niemeyer.
1926 3rd edition. Ed. Ludwig Sütterlin -- E. Ochs.

Klump, Wilhelm
1908 *Die altenglischen Handwerkernamen.* (Anglistische Forschungen 24.) Heidelberg: Winter.

Koo, Zung-Fung Wei
1946 *Old English living noun-suffixes exclusive of personal and place-names.* Unpublished doctoral dissertation. Radcliffe College, Cambridge, Mass.

Koziol, Herbert
1937 *Handbuch der englischen Wortbildungslehre.* Heidelberg: Winter.
1972 2nd edition.

Lapidge, Michael (ed.)
1995 *Archbishop Theodore: Commemorative studies on his life and influence.* (CSASE 11.) Cambridge: Cambridge University Press.

1996 *Anglo-Latin literature 600-899.* London: The Hambledon Press.

Lendinara, Patrizia
1999a s.v. 'Glossaries', in: *BEASE*.

1999b *Anglo-Saxon glosses and glossaries.* (Variorum collected studies series.) Aldershot: Ashgate.

Lenze, Josef
1909   *Das Präfix bi- in der altenglischen Nominal- und Verbalkomposition.* Doctoral dissertation. University of Kiel.

Leumann, Manu
1963   *Lateinische Laut- und Formenlehre.* (= Leumann -- Hofmann -- Szantyr, *Lateinische Grammatik* I.) München: Beck.

Lewandowska-Tomaszczyk, Barbara -- Irena Czwenar (eds.)
1999   *A new curriculum for English studies.* Piotrków Trybunalski: Naukowe Wydawnictwo Piotrkowskie przy Filii Akademii Swietokrzyskiej.

Lindsay, W.M
1921   *The Corpus, Épinal, Erfurt and Leyden glossaries.* (Publications of the Philological Society 8.) Oxford: Oxford University Press.

Marchand, Hans
1960   *The categories and types of Present-Day English word-formation.* Wiesbaden: Otto Harrassowitz.
1969   2nd edition. München: Beck.

Munske, Horst Haider
1964   *Das Suffix *-inga/-unga in den germanischen Sprachen.* Marburg: Elwert.

Pheifer, Joseph Donovan (ed.)
1974   *Old English glosses in the Épinal-Erfurt glossary.* Oxford: Oxford University Press.

1995   "The Canterbury bible glosses: Facts and problems", in: Lapidge (ed.), 281-333.

Roberts, Jane -- Christian Kay
1995   *A thesaurus of Old English.* 2 vols. London: King's College.

2000	2nd edition. Amsterdam: Rodopi.

Ryder, Mary Ellen
1994 *Ordered chaos: The interpretation of English noun-noun compounds.* Berkeley: University of California Press.

Sauer, Hans
1992 *Nominalkomposita im Frühmittelenglischen.* (Buchreihe der Anglia 30.) Tübingen: Niemeyer.

1999a "Old English plant names in the Épinal-Erfurt glossary: Etymology, word-formation and semantics", in: Falkner -- Schmid (eds.), 23-38.

1999b "Animal Names in the Épinal-Erfurt Glossary", in: Conrad O'Briain *et al.* (eds.), 128-58.

2000 "Time words and time concepts in Anglo-Saxon prose: The *Theodulfi Capitula*", in: Lewandowska-Tomaszczyk -- Czwenar (eds.), 251-74.

2003 Revised reprint, in: *Prospero: Rivista di culture anglo-germaniche* 10: 247-71.

Schlutter, Otto Bernhard
1912 *Das Epinaler und Erfurter Glossar:* Vol. 1: *Faksimile und Transliteration des Epinaler Glossars.* (Bibliothek der angelsächsischen Prosa 8.) Hamburg: Grand.

Schmid, Hans-Jörg
2005 *Englische Morphologie und Wortbildung.* (Grundlagen der Anglistik und Amerikanistik 25.) Berlin: Schmidt.

Seebold, Elmar
1970 *Vergleichendes und etymologisches Wörterbuch der germanischen starken Verben.* (Janua Linguarum ser. pract. 85.) The Hague: Mouton.

Stanley, Eric G
1975 *The search for Anglo-Saxon paganism.* Cambridge: Brewer.

Stekauer, Pavol
1998 *An onomasiological theory of English word-formation.* Amsterdam: Benjamins.

2000 *English word-formation: A history of research (1960-1995).* Tübingen: Narr.

Strite, Vic
1989 *Old English semantic field studies.* (American University Studies. IV.100.) New York: Lang.

Sweet, Henry (ed.)
1883 *The Épinal glossary, Latin and Old-English.* (EETS o.s. 79b) Photo-Lithographed from the original MS by W. Griggs. London: Humphrey Milford, Oxford University Press.
1936 Reprinted edition.

1885 *The oldest English texts.* (EETS o.s. 83.) London: Oxford University Press.

Toth, Karl
1980 *Der Lehnwortschatz der althochdeutschen Tatian-Übersetzung.* Würzburg: Königshausen & Neumann.

Tournier, Jean
1985 *Introduction descriptive à la lexicogénétique de l'anglais contemporain.* Paris: Champion-Slatkine.

Weber, Gerd Wolfgang
1969 *Wyrd: Studien zum Schicksalsbegriff der altenglischen und altnordischen Literatur.* Bad Homburg: Gehlen.

The assize of bread (1256)

Claire Fennell (Trieste, Italy)

1. Introduction

In their Introduction to Book I (1235-1377) of the *Statutes of the realm*, printed in 1810, the editors found that the extant statutes of Henry III (1216-72) were written almost entirely in Latin, whereas the statutes of Edward I (1272-1307) and Edward II (1307-27) were written in both Latin and French. The editors wrote:

> It seems on the whole to be highly probable that for a long Period of Time, Charters, Statutes and other Public Instruments were drawn up indiscriminately in French or Latin, and generally translated from one of those Languages into the other, before the Promulgation of them, which in many Instances appears to have been made at the same Time in both Languages. (Record Commission 1831: xlii)

The editors merely took note, *en passant*, of a "very ancient [English] Translation of some of the Statutes of the Time of Henry III and Edward I" (Record Commission 1831: xlii).

One of these statutes, known as the *assisa panis et ceruisie*, laid down the "method by which the price of ale and bread was to be fixed" (Salter 1921: 130), and also established the profit and reimbursement to which the baker was entitled, known as the *lucrum pistoris*. The *assisa panis et ceruisie* is extant in many manuscripts; I can mention only five here (cf. 4. Edition: list of manuscripts). In a footnote placed at the beginning of their text, based on Cotton Claudius, MS D II (C), the editors of the *Statutes of the realm* observed that "[t]he Printed Copies give this as a Statute of 51 Hen. III" (Record Commission 1831: 199), but prudently write *Temp. Incert.* above it (Record Commission 1831: 200). Nevertheless, until recently the statute was generally assigned by scholars to the 51st year of Henry III's reign (1266/7). In his introduction to the records of courts held in Oxford in connection with the assize of bread and ale between 1309 and 1351, Salter took issue with the dating of the statute to 1267, for, he maintained,

> [t]he Statute [...] is really of uncertain date; and in any case it is certain that the assize was much older [... it] was nothing more than recognizing what existed already, and ordaining that the same scale should be used throughout the realm (Salter 1921: 130).

It is certainly true that few of the many extant versions of the Assize are provided with a dating clause, and that the assize *per se* was nothing new (Cunningham 1910: 567-9). What is new, however, is the price-weight relationship of wheat and bread which is the basis for the calculations in C. This arithmetical relation is not applied in an incomplete *assisa panis*, contained in MS Peterborough 1 (P), fol. 85ᵛ, preceded by the dating clause "die Mart*is* pr*oximo* tres sept*imanas* pasche Anno d*o*m*ini* m°. cc° .L.iij. [iij] yd*us* Maii" (Tuesday 13th May 1253) – but is applied in an undated version of the statute written out on the page facing the 1253 assize, virtually identical to the text in C. In 1963 Betty Hill was able to show that under the year 1256 the annals of Burton Abbey (Staffordshire), having stated that "justices were sent throughout the country to reform the measures, *qui etiam per loca assisam panis, vini et cervisiae sub forma tradiderunt subsequenti*" (Hill 1963: 204), gave a text using the method adopted in C. An Anglo-Norman assize, Huntingdon, 31911, fol. 264, using the same calculations, is followed by the date clause, "anno regni regis henrici filii Regis Iohannis xlv°'" – that is, 45 Henry III 1(261/2). So I think the promulgation of the assize can be assigned with a fair degree of certainty to 1256.

The meaning of *assize* (Latin *assisa*, Anglo-Norman *assise*, Middle English *assise*) as it is used in the *assize of bread and ale* is 'ordinance...regulating quality, weight, size, price, etc., of commodities' (*MED*, s.v. 'assise' 3 [a]). From the regulation of size to the (statutory, or standard) size itself the step was evidently short, and today the aphetic form of the word, *size*, is there to remind us of an ordinance that "as a control on the charges of bakers...would presumably have been useful to virtually any consumer" (Cartlidge 1997: 259), and would remain unrepealed until 1836. In truth, although the word *assise* exists in Old French, with various meanings deriving from the fundamental one of 'session', I have found the meaning given to it in the *Assize of bread* only in the *AND*, not in the Old French ones I consulted. The *OED* (s.v. 'assize'), takes note of a suggestion made by Stubbs that the meaning 'ordinance' assumed by *assisa/assise* in trilingual England might have come about by the word being used to render Old English ȝesetnes, Middle English *isetnesse* 'statute, ordinance'. At this point, it is perhaps worth quoting Plucknett (1922: 12) on the non-technical uses of such terms as *statute, ordinance* and so forth in the period to which our assize belongs: "[certain] passages [...] suggest that the word 'statute' means the provision made rather than the instrument embodying it [...]" ... "there is no contrast expressed or distinction visible between statutes and ordinances. Neither of these words was as yet a technical term, and neither had any special meaning" (Plucknett 1922: 33).

I should like now to consider four versions of the assize, or rather, of a part of it (the *Assize of bread*), none of which, as far as I know, has been printed before, and which I print in section 4 of this paper. Two are written in Latin, in P, fol. 86^r, and Oxford, Jesus College, MS 29 II (J), fol. 195^r; one in Anglo-Norman, in London & Oslo, The Schøyen Collection, MS 563 (S), fol. 76; and one in Middle English, in Oxford, Rawlinson, MS B 520 (R), fols. 43^v-44^r. The manuscripts that contain them were all compiled around the turn of the thirteenth century, that is, during the reign of that "great legislator [...] great administrator [...] great organizer" (Maitland 1908: 20), Edward I, when collections of the statutes begin to appear.

The weights and measures we shall find in the Latin versions of the assize of bread are *quarterium. libra, solidus, denarius, obolus* and *quadrans*, in the Anglo-Norman version *quartier, liuere, sou, dener, obole, ferlink/quadrant*, and in the English *quarter, pound, silling, peni, halpeni* and *furþing*. Before outlining the arithmetic involved in the assize of bread, I shall briefly refer to part of a constitution of weights and measures that is contained in both S (fol. 76^r) and R (fol. 42^v), which I also print in section 2. The basic unit of weight (and price) is the silver penny. Thirty-two average grains of wheat make a penny, 20 pence an ounce, 12 ounces or 20 shillings a pound, 8 pounds a gallon, 8 gallons a bushel, and 8 bushels a quarter. Although to our way of thinking we have here a mixture of weights, measures and prices, it is not hard to calculate that the weight of a quarter of wheat, on which the price of bread is based, is 512 lb. Our two lists do not spell out how many pence make a shilling, but given that there are 20 pence to the ounce, and 12 ounces to the pound, it follows that there are 240 pence to the pound; and since the pound weighs 20 shillings, there are, indeed, 12 pence to the shilling. Prices in the *Assize of bread* are in terms of weight – starting with the pennyworth of silver – but the weight will be expressed in pounds, shillings, pence, halfpence and farthings (with 12 pence to the shilling and 20 shillings to the pound).

Now for a brief summary of the mathematics involved in the assize of bread. The assize started by establishing the relation between the price of a quarter of wheat (512 lbs.) and the price of a loaf of bread, or rather, between the price of a quarter of wheat and the weight of the standard farthing loaf, the wastel (the same lexeme as modern French *gâteau*). The price of the loaf remained constant, but its weight decreased or increased as the price of wheat rose or fell. Alan Ross has investigated the "arithmetical relation between the price per quarter of corn (p) and the weight of the unit, the farthing-wastel-loaf (w)" (Ross 1956: 340). In the earlier assizes, according to his calculations, for every increase of a penny in p, there was a decrease of a shilling in w, expressed in the relation $w=12$ $(7-p)$ (and this method was still being applied in the 1256 version of the assize to prices of corn ranging from 3 s. to 4 s. 6 d. So it is in all our versions of the assize: for instance when $p=12$d., $w=12$ $(7-3)=12 \times 4=48$s., or 2 lb. 8 s.). In the 1256 assize, however, the relation of w to p was calculated according to the principle of inverse proportion, expressed in $wp=136$ (Ross 1956: 340). In all our versions, except R, which omits the "16 shillings", when $p=12$ d., $w=136$ s., that is, 6 lbs. 16 s., and so on.

Space does not allow me to go through each and every variation in the price of a quarter of wheat from one to twelve shillings to see how our four versions agree with each other and with the correct weight of the farthing-loaf according to Ross's calculations. What does seem to emerge, however, is that the mistakes, of which there are several, usually involve either an omission, or the addition or subtraction of a unit, which given the use of the minim to express one, and four minims to express number four, is a fairly easy slip to make.

Having set the lowest price for the quarter of wheat (12 d., or 1 s.), and the heaviest weight for the standard, or wastel, loaf (6 lb. 16 s.), the assize went on to establish the relative weights of six other qualities of bread from which a farthing loaf might be made. These were listed in descending order of quality, with one apparent exception. After the wastel came the cocket (two qualities), the simnel, whole wheat bread, treat bread and meal bread. The poorer the quality of the bread, obviously, the heavier the loaf. The first type of cocket weighed 2 s. more than the wastel, the second type 5 s. more; the simnel weighed 2 s. less (this is the exception), the whole wheat loaf one and a half cockets, the treat loaf two wastels, and the meal loaf two cockets.

We can make out a list of the weight in the 1256 assize of a farthing loaf of the various types of bread when a quarter of wheat cost 12 d.:

12 d.	*wastel*		6 lb 16s.
12 d.	*first cocket*	[wastel + 2 s.]	6 lb. 18 s.
12 d.	*second cocket*	[wastel + 5 s.]	7 lb. 1 s.
12 d.	*simnel*	[wastel – 2 s.]	6 lb. 14 s.
12 d.	*whole wheat*	[1.5 cockets]	10 lb. 11 s. 6 d.
12 d.	*treat*	[2 wastels]	13 lb 12 s.
12 d.	*meal*	[2 cockets]	14 lb. 2 s.

It is apparent from this list that I have calculated the weights of the *panis integer* and the *panis de omni blado* on the basis of the weight of the second, heavier, inferior cocket loaf. None of the texts considered in this paper tells us which of the two cockets is meant, but an assize of bread contained in the roughly contemporary *Oak Book of Southampton* calls the second cocket *cocketus maior* and stipulates that the *panis integer* should weigh "cocketum et dimidium maioris ponderis" (Studer 1910-11: 29) and the *panis de omni blado* "ij cocketos maioris ponderis" (Studer 1910-11: 31). Since the prices in general coincide with those of our assizes, I think we can follow the *Oak Book* on this.

After establishing the weight of the standard farthing loaf and of the other six types of bread when a quarter of wheat cost twelve pence (or *denarii* or *deners*), that is, a shilling (or *solidus* or *sou*), the assize went on to calculate the weights of the wastel farthing loaf for wheat prices ranging from 1 s. 6. d. to 12 s. a quarter, going up by 6 d. a time. In our assizes, these are written out consecutively, that is, they are not entered as tables, and in each assize the exact words used to express the relationship vary somewhat before the most economical formula is found and then kept to, generally at the point in which a quarter of wheat costs 2 s. 6 d. I have stopped printing each text when this happens. As a matter of fact, the English version never does hit on a single formula, so I have reproduced it in full. Since the English version, unlike the Anglo-Norman and especially the Latin versions, also hardly ever resorts to abbreviations, and indeed sometimes writes out numbers in full, it appears to be quite a bit longer than the others.

2. The manuscripts and their versions

Each of our four versions of the *Assize of bread* is different as regards the part or parts of the *Assize of bread and ale* that appear(s) in the manuscript, and the order in which they are set out. Of the Latin versions, P has no rubric, and contains the *assisa panis* and the *lucrum pistoris*, but not the *assisa ceruisie*; J, which is not complete, contains only the assize of bread, under a centred heading "Ass[isa] panis Anglie". The English and Anglo-Norman versions both contain all three parts of the statute. The English version has first a general heading, "Here biginnez þe Assise of bred ant of Ale", and ends with "Here hendez þe assise of bred ant of ale". However, whereas the assize of bread is followed by the *lucrum pistoris* without a break, the assize of ale begins a new line, and space is made at the end of that line to write, in red, "Assise of ale". In the Anglo-Norman version, in which the *lucrum pistoris* follows the assize of ale, the three parts of the assize are each given as separate instruments, with a separate rubric, respectively "Incipit assisa panis", "Incipit assisa Ceruisie", and "Incipit lucrum pistoris".

I shall now take a brief look at the manuscripts in which our four assizes appear. P is a cartulary of the Abbey of Peterborough, written mainly in Latin, with some Anglo-Norman texts, at present housed in Cambridge University Library. The manuscript originally belonged to Robert Swapham, successively pittancer and cellarer of the Abbey, who died in 1273. The first 350 leaves (which incidentally include the best Latin version of the story of Hereward the

Exile – later to be known as the *Wake* – on fols. 320-339) were "compiled in the end of the thirteenth and beginning of the fourteenth centuries" (Hardy -- Martin 1888: xlvii). It is immediately preceded by the imperfect 1253 version of the statute we noticed earlier; this is written in a rather cramped hand below the closing lines of a constitution, in Anglo-Norman, of weights and measures, which lacks the beginning, the very part that concerns the *Assize of bread* (fols. 85); before that by an Anglo-Norman glossary of English legal terms (fol. 84), and a list in Latin of the counties and bishoprics of England (fol. 83^v-84^r). Our assize, which is written out in a rather informal hand, is followed by three blank pages (fols. 86^v. and 87), then by a list of *Privilegia apostolica* (fol. 88).

The second Latin assize is the only piece of Latin in J (the *The owl and the nightingale*-MS), presently housed in the Bodleian Library, which otherwise contains virtually nothing but literary works, written in English before the *Assiza* and in Anglo-Norman after it. The *Assize* occupies sixteen and a half lines, with seven lines left blank at the end of the page. It is preceded on the same page by the closing lines of a description, in English, of the shires and bishoprics of England – the only other work "of general reference" in the manuscript (Cartlidge 1997: 259) – and before that by a verse homily on "soþe luue" (fols. 193^r-194^r), an "orison of our lord" (fols. 192^r-193^r) – each headed "Tractatus quidam", and the *Proverbs of Alfred* (fols. 189^r-192^r) headed "Incipiunt documenta Regis Aluredi". It is followed on folio 195^v by an Anglo-Norman poetic work entitled "Ici comence de Tobye". It is the date of our *assisa* which provides the date *post quem* for the manuscript.

S is at present in Oslo, in the custody of its owner, Martin Schøyen. This codex, like R, is a collection of statutes. Of these collections Woodbine (1990: 9) observed that

> one of the most interesting of the many types of manuscript volumes from the thirteenth and fourteenth centuries is that which was compiled for the use of English lawyers during the period of the first three Edwards... it contained, if not the whole, at least a large part, of the library of the lawyer who owned it. The volume usually begins with a collection of the Statutes which goes down to about the time the book was written. Following this come a number of tracts and treatises... [o]ften a Register of Writs complete the volume [...].

The first of the Statutes was considered to be Magna Carta. S begins with an early *inspeximus*, dating back to 1225, the ninth year of Henry's reign; the latest dateable statute goes back to 1293. The assize is preceded by that part of a long description of weights and measures (fol. 76^r) which is to be found in section 2 below, and before that by a statute known by its first words as "Circumspecte agatis" (fols. 75ᵛ-76ʳ), promulgated in 1285. It is followed on fol. 76ᵛ, after the *assisa ceruisie* and the *lucrum pistoris*, by an *extenta manerii* (fol. 76ᵛ-77ʳ), a series of instructions, formulated in 1276, on making a correct survey of manors.

R is the collection of statutes noted by the editors of the *Statutes of the realm*. It also begins with Magna Carta, in this case Edward I's *inspeximus* of 1297 or 1300 (all but the first folio of the charter is missing, so we have no dating clause). The latest dateable statute is from 1299. The *Assize of bread and ale* is preceded on fols. 42ᵛ-43ʳ by a complete constitution of weights and measures, before that by instructions on the "maner to maken homage ant feoutee"; it is followed by the 1276 Statute of Exeter (fols. 44r-45r), erroneously entitled "Here...biginnez þe statut of Oxeneforde".

3. The description of the types of bread

I would now like to make a comparison of the way in which our four versions indicate and describe the various types of bread, to see if this suggests anything about the relationships between the four texts as regards content and language. P tells us that the *wastell[us]* is "bene coctus", J that the *wastellus* is "albus et bene coctus"; S that the *wastel* is "bien buletee e bien quyt"; R that the standard loaf is "þe furþing of wite bred ant alse þe wastel". The wastel was obviously a well baked loaf made of white, finely boulted wheat flour. Each of our texts concentrates on different characteristics of the loaf, its whiteness, the length of its baking, the fineness of the flour. The English text actually pairs the wastel with "wite bred", as if they were two different types of loaf, of equal value. Whether the wastel was actually what we would call bread, or rather something more similar to a brioche, with the addition of eggs, butter, milk and/or sugar, is one of the many questions I have not the time to pursue in this paper.

Of the next type of bread, which was only slightly heavier than the wastel – 138 shillings as against 136 – three texts give us the same information. P and J inform us that the *koket[us]* was made "de eodem blado et de eodem bultello" as the wastel, S that the *coket* was "de meme le blee e de meme le buletel" (The grain was of the same quality, and the sifting as fine; could it have been slightly less well done, and therefore heavier?). In R we read that the *coket* is "of þilke sulue corne ant bussel". Evidently, the scribe either misread or misunderstood the word *bul(e)tel(lus)* in some exemplar – <lt> in some scripts does look very similar to <ss>. In the context, at any rate, the word *bussel* makes some sort of sense, because we could take the relative phrase to mean "of the same grain and of the same batch". What is not certain, of course, is what language the potential exemplar was written in, since *bultel* is one of those words that were lifted straight from one language into the other.

As for the second kind of cocket, the assize in P specifies that it is "de blado minoris precii", and the *Assisa panis anglie* in J adds "& de grossiori bultello", than the wastel. In S we read that it is "de blee de mendre pris", and in R "of corne of lasse pris". The words might be construed to mean that the flour was not wheaten – each version uses its indigenous word for corn, which can mean any type of grain, not only wheat – but I am inclined to think that the grain was in fact wheat, albeit from an inferior batch, and was less finely sifted than the wastel and cocket 1, which meant that more bran was left in.

We now come to the apparent exception in our list, the simnel – (P *simenell[us]*, J *symenel*, S *simenel*, R *siminel*), which is listed after the two cockets but weighs two shillings less than the wastel. None of the texts I have selected gives any description of the simnel, or the reason for this apparent anomaly. However, the assize in C (fol. 252^v) explains that simnel bread weighs less than the wastel "quia bis coctus est". In other words, it is lighter because having been baked twice it contains a lower percentage of humidity.

The last type of bread for which the same lexeme appears in all the versions is treat bread, (*tret* in P and S, *trait* in R; there is a line missing here in J). *Trait/tret* was the name given in Anglo-Norman to the second, middling coarse quality of bran, so treat bread – which is worth half the wastel – would be made of middling coarse wheat bran. It is worth 25% less than whole-wheat bread, so maybe there was virtually no flour in it at all.

We do have two kinds of bread that are described by each language in its own words, the third to last and the last quality. Like treat bread, they are only described, not given a name. The first is described as *integer de frumento* in P and J, *enteer de furment* in S, *al hol* in R. This is pretty clearly 'whole-wheat', made, that is, of wheat flour together with the bran, perhaps the finer bran, since it is worth 25% more than treat bread. The second, which is the cheapest bread of all, is described as being made *de omni blado* in P and J, *de tuz blez* in S, *of alle kunne corne* in R, that is, from any type of meal: rye, barley, oats or even peas (in later English versions of the assize we find it being called *horse bread*!).

I think we may now make a few observations about the assize of bread as it appears in our four selected versions. Our assizes represent something like 4 % of all the extant versions we know of, but there are probably many more we are not aware of. Even as far as these four versions are concerned, given the space at my disposal, I have been able to take only a most cursory look at their content, context, and language. As regards the content, we have seen that the assizes show a great deal of freedom in the way they are written down, the way they describe certain types of bread, the order in which they present their information, even their formulation of the relationship between the price of corn and the weight of the farthing loaf. Before drawing any serious conclusions from these data, we should have to examine most if not all of the extant assizes. It might be argued by some, for instance, that the various forms of the assize we have here, as well as others we have not considered, might fall into some recognizable pattern; or that all the Latin versions might turn out to share certain characteristics as against the Anglo-Norman ones – of the English versions, I know only of the existence of R.

What we have said about the content of the assizes is true of the context in which we find them. Two manuscripts (R and S) are collections of statutes: R is written entirely in English, S is written almost indiscriminately in Anglo-Norman and Latin, though the rubrics are all in Latin. One manuscript is a cartulary (P), written mainly in Latin, with some Anglo-Norman, but contains an explanation in Anglo-Norman of some English legal terms. And finally, J is an almost exclusively poetic compilation, in which there is "little to suggest a subordinate status for any of the three languages" (Scahill 2003: 29). We have seen that the *assisa* is preceded by a list, in English, of the shires and bishoprics of England, a useful guide for lawyers when planning eyries. The list, this time in Latin, also precedes the assize in P, though not immediately, while it is absent from the two collections of statutes. We saw that three of our assizes are immediately preceded by a description of weights and measures, of which the one in P, without a heading, lacks the begininning, the very part that would have been useful for the assize; R is complete, and is headed "composicion of mesures", S has the beginning only, the part that concerns the assize of bread, under the rubric "composicio monete & mensure". Each of our assizes is followed by a different text, and we may note that there is no chronological order to be perceived in the arrangement of the datable texts within the codices. The grouping of the texts seem rather to reflect a similarity of subject – for instance, in our case, numbers and lists – whereas the choice of what statute or tract to include in the collections of statutes seems to be dictated rather by the interests of a given individual.

Finally, as regards the linguistic aspect of the assizes, we have seen how some terms are lifted straight from one language to another, for instance the designations of certain types of bread. The language most often borrowed from seems to be Anglo-Norman, and for our assizes we may well appropriate Studer's comments on an entry in a roughly contemporary collection of municipal ordinances, the *Oak book of Southampton*: "the language [...] is Norman French (or, as it is now often called, Anglo-French); other entries are in mediaeval Latin, which often is but thinly disguised French or English" (Studer 1910-11: I, vii), and again "some of the words have not even been translated into Latin, but appear in their French form, though occasionally the scribe has adorned them with a Latin termination" (Studer 1910-11: II, vi). In P, in fact, not once are the endings for *wastell, simenell* or *koket* written out in full, though they are for other words, and the form of the word *treat*, that is, *tret*, reflects Anglo-Norman phonology. We have noticed that some of these words are peculiar to the French of England, and that the extension of the possible meanings of *assisa/assise* to include regulation of the price of bread and ale might have been influenced by English usage. Furthermore, our Anglo-Norman assize (though not the two Latin ones!) actually adopts the English lexeme *furþing*, for it refers to the wastel farthing loaf as *le wastel de ferlink*, whereas when giving the weight of the loaf it always uses the abbreviation *q.* (Anglo-Norman or Latin?) for the farthing. Apart from these cases, the names of the weights are Latin in the Latin texts, romance in the Anglo-Norman texts, and English in the English text. In other words: each language seems to have gone its own way as far as expressing the meaning of the statutes was concerned, each borrowing from the other whenever convenient. Finally, what are we to make of R, the – as far as I know – solitary extant English collection of statutes dating from the time of Edward I? Were the editors of the *Statutes of the realm* wrong to consider only Anglo-Norman and Latin as the languages in which the statutes were promulgated during his reign? If not, then the existence of this English collection of statutes, compiled for the use of an English lawyer so soon after the promulgation of the statutes themselves, might still be one more instance of some "higher local status of written English" (Scahill 2003: 31).

4. Edition

In printing the texts below I have expanded all the abbreviations (which appear in italics), in order to facilitate the reader. Sometimes I have had to guess at the intentions of the scribe; I feel sure that on more than one occasion he had no particular idea in his own mind as to what the expanded version of his abbreviations might be.

I have maintained the punctuation of the scribe, though I have sometimes had to make my own decisions. Where he placed full stops at various distances from the words that preceded and followed them, especially when writing numbers, I have made a choice and applied it throughout. In the case of certain letters, such as <w>, it is virtually impossible to distinguish upper from lower case.

The symbol { represents the paragraph mark in P, R and S. Words placed between square brackets are my own proposed additions or emendations.

List of manuscripts mentioned or edited here:
1. C: London, British Library, MS Cotton Claudius D ii (Middle English; not edited here; edition: Record Commission, *The Statutes of the Realm*, I)
2. J: Oxford, Jesus College, MS 29 (II) (Latin; edited below)
3. P: Peterborough, MS 1; housed in Cambridge, University Library (Latin; edited below)
4. R: Oxford, Bodleian Library, MS Rawlinson B 520 (Middle English; edited below)
5. S: London & Oslo, The Schøyen Collection, MS 563 (Latin and French [Anglo-Norman]; edited below)

P: Peterborough, MS 1
[fol. 86^r] {Quando quart*erium* fr*umenti* venditur pro .xij. denarios. tunc Panis Wastell*i* pond*erabit* .vj. Li*bras* .xvj. Panis aute*m* de koket de eode*m* blado & de eode*m* bultell*o* ponderabit plus qu*a*m Wastello .ij. solidos. et de blado minor*is* precii ponderabit plus qu*a*m Wastello .v. solidos. Panis vero *S*imenell*i*. ponderabit minus Wastello .ij. solidos & pan*is* integ*er* de q*u*adrante de fr*umento* ponderabit. Coket & dim*i*dium. Panis vero de Tret ponderabit .ij. Wastell*os*. Panis vero de om*n*i Blado ponderabit .ij. Coke*tos*. {Quando qu*a*rterium frumenti venditur pro .xviij. denari*i*s. Tunc panis de wastello bene coctus ponderabit .iiij. Libras .x. solidos .viij. denarios. {Qu*a*ndo venditur pro .ij. solidis. Tunc pan*is* de quadrante ponderabit .Lxviij. solidos. {Quando venditur pro .ij. solidis .vj. denariis. Tunc pan*is*. quadrantis. ponderabit .Liiij. solidos .iiij. denarios. obolum. quadrantem [...]

J: Oxford, Jesus College, MS 29 (II)
[fol. 195^r] Ass*isa* panis Anglie
Qvando frume*n*tum venditur pro .xij. denariis. tu*n*c wastellus de quadrante. alb*us* & bene coctus. po*n*derabit sex libras. & sexdecim solidos. Panis aute*m* de koket. de eode*m* blado & de eode*m* Bultello. ponderabit plu*s* wa[s]tello .ij. solidos. & blado minor*is* precii & de grossiori bultello plus qu*a*m wastello [.v. solidos]. Panis de symenel min*us* de wastello ponderabit .ij. solidos. Panis integ*er* [de q*u*adrante de fr*umento* ponderabit. Coket & dim*i*dium. Panis vero de Tret] ponderabit .ij. wastellos. & panis de om*n*i blado .ij. kokes.
Qvando q*u*arterium de frume*n*to vend*itur*. pro .ij. solidis. tu*n*c ponderabit wastell*us* .lxviij. sol*idos*. Qva*n*do pro .ij. solidis. & .vi. denariis: tu*n*c po*n*derabit .Liij. solidos .iiij. denarios. & .iij. quadrantes.

S: London & Oslo, The Schøyen Collection, MS 563
[fol. 76ʳ] *Incipit Composicio monete & mensure.*
Per discrecionem totius Regni Anglie fuit mensura d*omi*ni Reg*is* co*m*posita videlicet quod denarius anglican*us* qui vocat*ur* sterlingus rotundus sit & sine tonsura et ponderabit .xxxij. grana frum*e*nti rubei in medio spice. {Et .xx. denar*ii* faciunt vnciam Et .xij. vncie faciunt libram. scil*ice*t .xx. solid*os*. Et .viij. libre faciunt gallonem vini & octo gallones vini faciunt bussellum london*iensem* Hoc est octauam p*ar*tem qu*ar*terii. {*Explicit Composicio monete & mensure. Incipit assisa panis*
Qaunt le quarter de furment se vend pur .xij. den*ers* donc peysera le Wastel de ferlink bien buletee e bien quyt. vj liueres e .xvj. souz. Payn Coket de meme le blee e de meme le buletel peysera plus ke le Wastel de deus souz. E de blee de mendre pris peysera plus ke le Wastel de. iiij Souz. le Simenel peysera meyns du wastel de deuz souz le Payn enteer de furment peysera Coket e demy. payn de tret peysera deus Wasteus. {E payn de tuz blez peysera deus Cokes. {Qaunt pur .xviij. deners donk peysera le wastel de ferlink .iiij. liueres .x souz. e viij. deners. {Qaunt pur. deus souz donk peysera. lxviij. souz. {Qaunt pur .ij. souz e .vj. den*ers* donk liiij. souz. iiij. d*e*n*ers*. ob*ole*. qu*adrant*......

R: Oxford, Bodleian Library, Rawlinson, MS B 520
[fol. 42ᵛ] Here...biginnez þe composicion of Mesures
Þoru þe discrecion of al þe reaume of yngelonde was þe king-ges mesures imade. þat is to wite þat te Englisse peni. þat is cleoped sterling round ant biþoute clippinge sal pisen tuuo ant þritti greines of wete. amidde þe pis. {Ant .xx. panes makez an vnze. ant tuuelfe vnzene makiez a pound .xx. sillinges. ant Eȝtte pound makez a galon. ant Eȝtte galons makez a bussel of Londone þe Etteþe del a quarter...
[fols. 43ᵛ-44ʳ] Here biginnez þe Assise of bred ant of Ale.
Wan me sullez þe quarter of ȝwete for .xii. panes. þanne sal þe furþing worth bred. weie .vj. pond [ant xvj sillinges] ase of wastel. þe furþing worth bred of Coket. of þilke sulue corne. ant bussel. sal weie more þan þe wastel. bi .ij. sillinges. ant of corne of lasse pris. þe coket sal weien more þan þe wastel bi .v. sillinges. þe bred of siminel sal weie lasse þan þe wastel bi .ij. sillinges. Of al hol bred þe furþingwort sal weie a Coket ant an half. Bred of trait sal weie tuuei wasteles. Bred of alle kunne corne. sal weie. tuuei cokettes. {Wan þe quarter of wete is isold for .xviij. panes. þanne sal. þe furþing of wite bred ant alse þe wastel. weien .þre [iiij] pond. ant .x. sillinges. ant .viij. panes. Wan þe quarter wete. is at .ij. silling. þanne sal þe furþingworth weie eȝtte ant sixti sillinges. Ant wan. þe quarter is at tuuei sillinges ant .vj. panes. þanne sal þe furþingworth. weie .iiij. ant vifti sillinges. ant .iiij. panes ant halfpeni. ant a furþing. Ant wan he

is at. þre sillinges. þanne þe bred of a furþing. sal weien .viij. ant .xl. sillinges. Wan he is at þreo sillinges ant .vj. panes. þanne sal þe furþingworth weie tuuo ant forti sillinges. Wan he is at .iiij. sillinges. þanne sal þe furþing weie .vj. ant. þritti sillinges. Wan he is for .iiij. sillinges ant .vj. panes. þanne sal þe furþingworth weie. þritti sillinges . Wan he is for vif sillinges. þanne sal þe furþing bred weie .vif. ant .xx sillinges ant .ij. panes ant an half peni. Wan for .vif. sillinges. ant .vj. panes. þanne sal þe furþing bred weie .iiij. ant .xx. sillinges ant .viij. panes ant a furþing. Wan for .vj. sillinges. þanne is a furþing bred .xxij. sillinges. ant viij. panes. Wan for .vj. sillinges ant .vj. panes. þanne þe furþing bred sal weie .xx. sillinges ant .xi. panes. Wan for .vij. sillinges. þanne þe furþing bred sal weie .xix. sillinges ant .v. panes. Wan for .vij. sillinges. ant .vj. panes. þanne sal þe furþing bred weie .xviij sillinges ant a peni ant halpeni. Wan for .viij. sillinges. þanne þe furþing bred sal weie xvij sillinges ant vj panes. Wan for .viij. sillinges ant .vj. panes. þanne sal þe furþing bred weie .xvij. sillinges. Wan for nine sillinges. þanne sal þe furþing bred weie viftene sillinges ant a furþing. Wan for nine sillinges ant .vj. panes. þanne sal þe furþing bred weie .xiiij. sillinges ant .iiij. panes ant an halpeni. ant. a furþing. Wan for .x. sillinges. þanne sal þe furþing bred weie .xii. sillinges ant .vij. panes ant a furþing. Wan for .x. sillinges ant .vj. panes. þanne þe furþing bred sal weie .xi. sillinges ant .iiij. panes ant a furþing. Wan for .xj. silling. [fol. 44^r] ant .vj. panes. þanne þe furþing bred sal weie .xii. sillinges ant x. panes. Wan for tuuelf sillinges. þanne þe furþing bred sal weie .xi. sillinges ant .iiij. panes ant an halpeni.

References

Cartlidge, Neil
    1997   "The composition and social context of Oxford, Jesus College, MS 29(II) and London, British Library MS Cotton Caligula A.ix", *Medium Ævum* 66: 250-69.

Cunningham, W.
    1910   *The growth of English industry and commerce.* (5th edition.) Cambridge: Cambridge University Press.

Hill, Betty
    1963   "The history of Jesus College, Oxford, MS. 29", *Medium Ævum* 32: 203-13.

Hardy, Thomas Duffus -- Charles Trice Martin (eds.)
    1888   *Lestoire des Engles solum la translacion Maistre Geffrei Gaimar.* (Rolls Series 91) Vol. I. London.

Maitland, Frederic W.
    1908   *The constitutional history of England.* Cambridge: Cambridge University Press. [many reprints]

Plucknett, T.F.T.
    1922   *Statutes and their interpretation in the first half of the fourteenth century.* Cambridge: Cambridge University Press.

Record Commission (ed.)
    1831   *The statutes of the realm: Printed by command of His Majesty King George the Third in pursuance of an address of the House of Commons of Great Britain from original records and authentic manuscripts.* Vol I. n.p.: Record Commission.

Ross, Alan S.C.
    1956   "The assize of bread", *Economic history review* (2nd series.) 9: 332-42.

Salter, Herbert Edward (ed.)
    1921   *Mediaeval archives of the University of Oxford.* Vol. II. Oxford: Clarendon.

Scahill, John
    2003   "Trilingualism in Early Middle English miscellanies. Languages and literature", *The year book of English studies* 33: 18-32.

Studer, Paul (ed.)
    1910-11   *The Oak Book of Southampton of c. A.D. 1300.* 2 vols. Southampton: Cox and Sharland.

Woodbine, George Edward
    1910   *Four thirteenth century law tracts.* Oxford: Oxford University Press.

Revising the Wyclif Bible

Conrad Lindberg (Linköping, Sweden)

1. Introduction

The Wyclif Bible exists in two versions, one more literal, one more idiomatic. Forshall -- Madden printed them in 1850 in parallel columns; in the present article, I have combined the two (see below), using the first text as a base and marking deviations from the second text by underlinings for additions, square brackets for omissions, a double apostrophe " for transpositions, numbered in footnotes in complex cases, and raised Arabic numerals for substitutions explained in footnotes. By thus giving the two texts together, I hope to make the changes from one version to the other more visible.

The process of translating the Bible is set out in the so-called *General Prologue* to the versions. The author, probably John Purvey, mentions four steps taken by someone he refers to as *he*, not improbably Wyclif himself: first to make a Latin bible sufficiently true, then to examine the text by using commentaries etc., thirdly, to consult others as to hard words and passages, and fourthly, the translation, that is the final version, not the preliminaries. A fifth step is suggested by his using competent men to correct, or revise the translation.

What we have now is a revised text of an original version. We can see how literal Latinisms were gradually eliminated in favour of more English phrasing. This process probably started from the very beginning, perhaps first by glossing the Latin text established, then extracting the first English rendering and making the literal text readable. The final step, or steps, meant a virtual re-translation of the earlier text, using guidelines set out in the *Prologue*: to translate after the sense and not only after the words, to resolve Latin constructions as the ablative absolute and participial constructions, also relative pronouns, to add (or omit) things understood in the text, to change the order of words, and to use connecting words freely.

2. Baruch 3.20: "risen. The ȝunge"

At this point (Bar. 3.20), two manuscripts of the earlier version break off abruptly, one (MS Bodley 959) at the end of a recto, and the other (MS Bodley Douce 369 1st part) with a note following: "here ends the translation of Nicholas of Hereford". A third manuscript (MS CUL Ee. Is. 10) says here: "here ends the translation of N and begins the translation of J".

Forshall -- Madden (1850) believed the first manuscript to be the original copy of the translator and the second to be a later copy. They do not mention the note in the third manuscript. They even went so far as to date the making of the first text to 1382 when Hereford was called away to the Blackfriars' synod in Rome. Fristedt (1953) showed in his thesis that Forshall -- Madden (1850) were wrong in thinking the break to be the end of the original translation, since the manuscript shows signs of having been copied from an even earlier text.

And yet, the agreement of the three manuscripts at this point must have a significance. It is reasonable to assume that the archetype behind these manuscripts was an unfinished original which was revised in the copying out of MS Bodley 959, which has many instances of original corrections and revisions. The date 1382 may not be far wrong, as Hereford was one of Wyclif's closest disciples in Oxford in the 1370s.

The J. mentioned in the Cambridge manuscript has been diversely interpreted: Margaret Deanesly might have thought it meant John Purvey; Forshall -- Madden (1850), who do not mention the note, may have thought it meant John Wycliffe; I, myself have thought of John Ashton, another close disciple of Wyclif's. The crucial question in this connection is how to interpret the word *translation*: is it meant to signify a version or can it stand for a revision? Let us consider the rest of the chapter.

There is a difference between the two halves of the third chapter of Baruch. Although mainly translated in the same fashion, the two versions tend to converge more, the number of changes are smaller as can be seen from the number of footnotes and notes. Is this the result of a change of translators or of a change of revisers? A change of translators would rather increase the differences, a change of revisers would be noticeable more in details, such as personal preferences.

This tendency in the two versions to converge is even more apparent in books coming after Baruch, sometimes, as in the Book of Jonah, so predominant that one may think of just one translation with minor modifications. I think this is the result of extensive revision undertaken with the aim of producing a uniform text, which was probably the ultimate aim from the very beginning. The preliminary steps taken were inevitable: first the gloss-like Latin-based turning of the Bible text, then the smoothing out of this crude version in a literal type of text, revised and approved before the final translation, using the earlier efforts, could be undertaken. This late version was copied extensively (there are more than 150 MSS extant of it, whereas the early version exists in less than 50 MSS), and in this process further revision was introduced, taking into account both of the existing texts.

Revising the Wyclif Bible then meant a scrupulous refinement of the text, constantly referring back to the Latin original and comparing variants of translation in order to arrive at a satisfactory version of the Bible. To be satisfactory, it had to be true to the Word and yet easy to read. We can understand the various attempts from this double aim.

A modern researcher should proceed in much the same fashion: always consult the Latin Vulgate, test the literal possibility and draw on the idiomatic resources of the language. Thus, a study of revision becomes a clue to understanding this monumental bible.

3. The text: Baruch 3

	And now, Lord [almiȝti] God of Irael, the[1] soule in anguysshes,
2	and the[1] spirit tormentid[2] crieth to thee. 'Heere [thou] " Lord, and haue mercy; for God " thou art merciful'. And haue [thou]
3	mercy of[3] vs, for wee han synned bifor thee, that sittist 'in to euermor[4], and wee shul not pershe 'in to the spirituel during[4].
4	Lord God al myȝti, God of Irael, here [thou] now the orisoun[5] of the deade men of Irael, and of the sonus of hem, 'for thei han synned[6] bifor thee, and thei herden not the vois of the Lord " ther
5	God, and ioyned[7] " ben " to vs " euelis. 'Wile thou not[8] han mynde of[3] the wickenesse of oure fadris, but haue [thou] mynde of[3] thin
6	hond and of[3] thi name in this tyme; for thou art Lord " oure God,
7	and 'wee shul preise[9] the " Lord. 'For that[10] thou hast ȝoue thi drede in oure hertes, that wee inwardli[11] " clepe thi name', and preise[9] thee in oure caitifte; for wee shul be turned[12] fro the
8	wickenesse of oure fadris, that synneden in[13] thee. And lo! wee 'in oure caitifte " ben to dai, 'that vs thou hast scatered[14], in to repref[15], and in to cursing, and in to synne, after[16] alle the wickidnessis[17] of oure fadris, that wenten[18] awei fro thee,
9	[thou] Lord " oure God. 'Here thou " Irael, the [co]maundemens of lif; ' with eres " parceyue [thou]', that thou wite[19] prudence.
10	'What is [it] " Irael, that 'in the lond of the enemys " thou
11	art'? Thou 'hast eldid[20] in an alien lond, thou art defoulid with deade men, thou art set[21] with men goende[22] doun in to helle?

12, 13	Thou hast forsake the welle of wisdam; for [whi] if 'in the weies of God " thou haddest go', 'thou 'shuldist han²³ dwellid " for-
14	sothe²⁴ in pes <u>vp</u> on erthe. Lerne [<u>thou</u>], wher be²⁵ prudence²⁶, wher be²⁵ vertue, wher be²⁵ vnderstonding, that thou wite togidere, wher be²⁵ long abiding²⁷ of lyf and <u>of</u> liflode, wher be²⁵
15	liȝt of eȝen, and pes. Who fond 'his place²⁸? [and] who entride in
16	to 'his tresores²⁹? Wher ben the princes of Jentilys³⁰, and that
17	lordshipen³¹ of³² [<u>the</u>] bestes, that ben <u>vpon</u> erthe? That³³ 'in³⁴
18	the briddis of heuene " pleien; that³³ siluer " tresoren and gold, in whiche trosten " men, and <u>ther</u> is " noon ende' of the purchasing of hem? That³³ siluer " forgen³⁵, and ben besy, ne³⁶ <u>ther</u> is "
19	finding of 'the werkus of hem³⁷? Thei ben outlawid³⁸, and 'to helle³⁹ " thei wente¹⁸ doun'; and othyr men 'in the place of hem"
20	risen. The ȝunge men of hem sawen liȝt, and dwelten on erth. Sothely⁴⁰ thei knewen
21	not the wei of disciplyne⁴¹, nether vndirstoden the pathis 'of it⁴²; nether the sones of hem resceyueden it. 'Fro the face of hem
22	" it is⁴³ maad fer'; it is not herd in the lond of Canaan, nether
23	<u>it</u> is seen in Theman. And⁴⁴ the sones of Agar, that souȝten out prudence that³³ is of erth, the marchauntis of erth, and [<u>of</u>] Theman, and the 'fablers, <u>or ianglers</u>⁴⁵, and seekers out of prudence, and of vnderstondinge; sothely⁴⁰ thei knewen not the weie of
24	wysdam, nether hadden mynde of³ the paathis therof. O! Yrael, '<u>hou</u>⁴⁶ grete " is " the hous of God⁴⁷, and '<u>hou</u> grete " [is] " the
25	place of his possessioun⁴⁷; [<u>it is</u>] gret and 'not hauynge⁴⁸ eende,
26	heeȝ and 'with outen mesure " grete. 'Ther " weren " named gyauntis⁴⁹; tho⁵⁰ that 'fro⁵¹ the bigynnynge " weren in⁵² grete stature',
27	witynge⁵³ bataile. The Lord chese not these, nether thei founden
28	the weie of discipline⁴¹; therfor thei pershiden. And for thei

Revising the Wyclif Bible   201

29   hadde not wijsdam, thei pershiden for her vnwijsdam. Who
                stei3ede in to heuen, and toke it[54], and ledde[55] it doun fro [the]
                cloudis?
30   Who passide ouer the se, and foonde it, and brou3t it to, vpon[56]
31   chosen gold? Ther is " not[57], that may wite[58] the waies therof,
32   nether that sekith out the pathes therof; bot he that wote[59] alle
                thingis, knew3 it, and foond it by his prudence. The whiche
                maade redy the erth in euerlastynge tyme, and fulfilled it with
                feeld[60]
33   bestes, and four footid bestis. The whiche sendith out li3t, and
                it goth; and he clepid it, and it obeischide[61] to hym in tremb-
34   lynge. Forsoth sterris 3auen li3t in her keepyngus, and
                gladiden[62];
35   thei[63] ben[64] clepid, and thei[63] seiden, We 'cumen to[65]; and thei[63]
36   shyneden to hym with mirth, that maad hem[63]. This is our God, and
37   'other shal not[66] ben gessid a3enis hym. He this foonde al[67]
                weie of disciplyne[41], and bitoke[68] it to Jacob, his child, and to
                Yrael,
38   his derworth[69]. After these thingus he was seen in erthis[70], and
                lyued with men.

Notes on the Middle English text (variants in the versions)

[1]a [2]anoied [3]on [4]withouten ende [5]preier [6]that synneden [7]fastned; 4+2+1+3
[8]Nyle thou [9]herie [10]For whi for this thing [11]to help [12]conuertid [13]a3ens
[14]whidur thou scateridist vs [15]schenschipe [16]bi [17]wickidnesse [18]3eden
[19]kunne [20]wexidist eld [21]arettid [22]hem that goon [23]haddist [24]sotheli [25]is
[26]wisdom where is prudence [27]duryng [28]the place therof [29]the tresouris therof
[30]hethene men [31]ben lordis [32]ouer [33]which/e [34]with [35]maken [36]and no
[37]her werkis [38]distried [39]hellis [40]But [41]wisdom [42]therof [43]was [44]Also
[45]tale telleris [46]ful [47]3+2+1 [48]hath noon [49]3+2+1 [50]thei [51]at [52]of [53]and
knewen [54]that wisdom [55]brou3te [56]more than [57]noon [58]knowe [59]kan (han)
[60]twei footid [61]obeieth [62]weren glad [63]tho [64]weren [65]ben present [66]noon
other schal [67]ech [68]3af [69]derlyng [70]londis

Notes on the underlying Latin text

1 Domine /omnipotens/ [2]anxius 2 Audi Domine quia Deus es misericors [3]miserere nostri 3 [4]in sempiternum; in aevum 4 [5]orationem [6]qui/a/ peccaverunt Domini Dei sui [7]agglutinata sunt nobis mala 5 [8]Noli meminisse iniquitatis, memento manus tuae et nominis tui 6 Dominus Deus noster [9]laudabimus te Domine 7 [10]quia propter hoc [11]ut invocemus nomen tuum [9]et laudemus [12]quia convertemur [13]in te 8 nos in captivitate nostra sumus [14]quo (qu/i?/a) nos dispersisti [15]in improperium [16, 17]secundum omnes iniquitates [18]qui recesserunt Domine Deus noster 9 Audi Israel mandata auribus percipe [19]ut scias prudentiam 10 Quid est Israel quod in terra inimicorum es 11 [20]inveterasti [21, 22]deputatus es cum descendentibus 13 [23, 24]Nam si in via Dei ambulasses habitasses utique in pace super terram 14 [25, 26]Disce ubi sit prudentia, ubi sit virtus, ubi sit intellectus [27]ubi sit longiturnitas 15 [28, 29]locum eius; in thesauros eius 16 [30]gentium [31, 32]dominantur super bestias 17 [33, 34]Qui in avibus caeli ludunt 18 [34]qui argentum thesaurizant in quo confidunt homines et non est finis [33, 35]qui argentum fabricant [36, 37]nec est inventio operum illorum 19 [38]Exterminati [39, 8]et ad inferos descenderunt et alii loco eorum surrexerunt

20 [40]autem [41]disciplinae 21 [43]a facie ipsorum longe facta est 23 [44]quoque [45]fabulatores [40]autem [3]commemorati sunt semitas eius 24 [46, 47]quam magna est domus Dei et ingens locus 25 [48]Magnus /est/ et non habet finem excelsus et immensus 26 [49]Ibi fuerunt gigantes nominati [50, 51]illi qui ab initio fuerunt [52]statura magna [53]scientes 27 [41]disciplinae 29 [54]accepit eam [55]et deduxit eam 30 attulit illam [56]super aurum electum 31 [57, 58]Non est qui possit scire vias eius exquirat 32 [59]scit [60]replevit eam pecudibus 33 [61]obaud/iv/it 34 [62]laetatae sunt 35 [63, 64]/et/ vocatae sunt et dixerunt [65]Adsumus [63]qui fecit illas 36 [66]/et/ non aestimabitur alius 37 Hic [67]omnem viam disciplinae [68]tradidit [69]dilecto suo 38 [70]in terris

Notes on vocabulary items

Bar. 3.1	tormentid[2] - [2]anoied: anxius; 'tormented' Pss.101.1 EV, 'anguished' LV, ELV Ecclus.5.10, 'annoyed' LV Bar.3.1
Bar. 3.3	'in to euermor[4] - [4]withouten ende: in sempiternum; '/for/ evermore' EV Gen.13.15; I Kgs.27.12, '/into/ without end' LV Gen.13.15, ELV Deut.5.29
Bar. 3.3	'in to the spirituel during[4] - [4]withouten ende: in aevum; LV 'without end' Ecclus.41.16 - EV 'spiritual world' Ecclus.18.8, 'spiritual time' 38.39

Bar. 3.4	orisoun[5] - [5]preier: orationem; 'orison' EV III Kgs.8.28, LV 'prayer', ELV Tob.6.18
Bar. 3.4	ioyned[7] - [7]fastned; agglutinata; 'join /fast/' ELV Ecclus.25.16, Jer.13.11, EV Bar.3.4, 'fasten' LV Bar.3.4, 'glue /tog./' ELV Ezek.29.4
Bar. 3.6	preise[9] - [9]herie: laudabimus; 'praise' EV I Pss.29.13, ELV II Pss.5.13, 'hery' LV I Pss.29.13, ELV Dan.2.23
Bar. 3.7	inwardli[11] - [11]to help: in-voc.; 'inwardly clepe' ELV Gen.4.26, EV 48.16, LV Rom.10.12, 'cl. inw.' Zeph.3.9 LV, 'clepe' LV Gen.48.16, 'clepe /in/to help' LV Ecclus.36.14, 46.6, 'in-clepe' Dan.9.18 EV
Bar. 3.7	turned[12] - [12]conuertid: convertemur; 'convert' EV Lev.19.4, 'turn' LV, v.v. III Kgs.8.47
Bar. 3.8	repref[15] - [15]schenschipe: inproperium; 'reproof' EV Wisd.5.3, ELV Rom.15.3, 'shendship' LV Tob.3.4, Ecclus.22.27 ('despite' EV)
Bar. 3.11	'hast eldid[20] - [20]wexidist eld: inveterasti; 'eeld' EV II Esd.9.21, 'wax old' LV, 'inw. eeld' Pss.6.8., 'be old' LV Is.65.22
Bar. 3.11	set[21] - [21]arettid: deputatus; 'set' EV Bar.3.11, 'aret' LV Est.14.8, 'ordain' ELV II Macc.4.19
Bar. 3.14	prudence[26] - [26]wisdom (prudence): prudentia; 'wisdom' EV Deut.32.28, 'prudence' LV, ELV Prov.2.3
Bar. 3.14	abiding[27] - [27]duryng: longiturnitas; cf. longiturnus: 'long during' EV Bar.4.35, 'full long' LV
Bar. 3.16	Jentilys[30] - [30]hethene men: gentium; 'Gentiles' Gen.10.5 EV, ELV III Esd.1.49, 'heathen /men, folk/' LV Gen.10.5, ELV IV Kgs.16.3, EV Dan.3.37
Bar. 3.16	lordshipen[31] - [31]ben lordis: dominantur; 'have lordship' EV Gen.1.28, 'be lord/s' LV, ELV both III Esd.4.3 and Gen.45.26, 'lordship' EV Num.24.19, ELV III Esd.2.27
Bar. 3.18	forgen[35] - [35]maken: fabricant; 'forge' EV II Esd.4.11, 'make' LV, ELV Num.32.16
Bar. 3.19	outlawid[38] - [38]distried: exterminati; 'destroy' LV Esd.30.33 ('put out' EV), ELV Judith 5.22, 'outlaw' ELV III Esd.4.8, Judith 3.13 EV
Bar. 3.20	disciplyne[41] - [41]wisdom: disciplinae; 'discipline' EV Lev.26.23 ('doctrine' LV), 'wisdom' LV Wisd.1.5, 'prudence' LV Job 33.16

Bar. 3.23	'fablers, or ianglers[45] - [45]tale telleris: fabulatores; no other instance indexed
Bar. 3.24	hou[46] - [46]ful: quam; 'how' ELV Gen.28.17, EV T.7.2, 'full' LV III Esd.3.18, ELV D.A.17.15
Bar. 3.29	ledde[55] - [55]brouʒte: de]duxit; 'lead down' EV Gen.42.38, LV Tob.13.2, ELV Jer.14.17, 'bring down' EV I Kgs.2.6, LV Jer.9.18
Bar. 3.35	'cumen to[65] - [65]ben present: adsumus; 'be present' LV Gen.4.7, ELV D.A.10.33, 'come' LV Jgs.14.15, ELV II Kgs.24.8
Bar. 3.37	bitoke[68] - [68]ʒaf: tradidit; 'give' LV Gen.9.2, ELV 29.29, 'betake' LV Gen.14.20, ELV 21.14
Bar. 3.37	derworth[69] - [69]derlyng: dilecto; 'dearworth' EV II Esd.13.26 ('loved' LV), 'darling' LV Pss.28.6, ELV both Mt.17.5 and 12.18
Bar. 3.38	erthis[70] - [70]londis: terris; 'earth' EV Gen.2.11, 'land' LV, v.v. I Kgs.14.32

References

Deanesly, Margaret
    1920   *The Lollard Bible.* Cambridge: Cambridge University Press.

Forshall, Josiah -- Madden, Frederic (eds.)
    1850   *The Holy Bible.* (Wycliffite Versions.) Oxford: Oxford University Press.

Fristedt, Sven
    1953   *The Wycliffe Bible.* (Part I.) Stockholm: Stockholm Studies in English.

Chaucer's Latinity

Michael W. Twomey (Ithaca/NY, USA)

The English word *Latinity* of course derives from the Latin third-declension noun *Latinitas*, referring to Latin style. It is a Classical Latin word that was not anglicized until after the Middle Ages. Its earliest attestation in the *OED* is from the seventeenth century, and in its traditional sense, it refers almost exclusively to 'pure' Latin – classical Latin as opposed to Vulgar Latin or Medieval Latin.[1]

Whereas virtually every other aspect of Chaucer has been discovered, covered, and recovered, the Latin in Chaucer's works has received only passing scholarly attention. Nevertheless, students must learn to read Chaucer's Middle English aloud, and Chaucer's texts include words, phrases, even entire sentences in Latin.[2] The first bit of Latin in the *Canterbury tales* is the inscription on the Prioress's brooch: *Amor vincit omnia*. Should we use classical, ecclesiastical, or some other pronunciation?[3] The question of how to pronounce Chaucer's Latin leads to questions about the nature and significance of Chaucer's use of Latin. As we know, unlike his friend John Gower, who appealed to posterity in French and Latin as well as in English, Chaucer left behind works only in English; and yet we know that Chaucer was at least comfortable reading and translating Latin, French, and Italian. His grasp of scientific Latin was secure enough to enable him to translate the *Treatise on the astrolabe*, and he probably read the Roman authors Virgil, Ovid and Statius in Latin; but in composing works such as the *Clerk's tale* and *Boece*, Chaucer seems to have used a French translation, which he checked against the Latin when necessary.[4] Ultimately, for as much as has been written about Chaucer's Latin sources, we still lack a systematic study of the kinds of Latin that Chaucer knew, and the role that Latin plays in Chaucer's works.

In this essay, I want to outline some of the main questions such a study might address:
- Which Latin is Chaucer's?
- What are the registers of Chaucer's Latin?
- How was Chaucer's Latin pronounced?
- And of course, what does Chaucer's usage of Latin 'say' about his literary aims and the expectations he might have held of his reader, and how his use of Latin might illustrate the state of late Anglo-Latin before humanism and the state of English before its final adoption as the prestige language of Britain?

To begin, we have to ascertain when Chaucer is 'speaking' to us in Latin. A lot of what Chaucer does with Latin falls under the heading of ' Latinism' – words that are morphologically Latin rather than English or French – but the italicized Latinisms in the *Riverside Chaucer* tend to be the ones signaled by Chaucer as such, and Chaucer's Latinisms are not equal in status. There are broadly speaking two kinds of Latinisms in Chaucer. The first kind are words and phrases spoken by Chaucer's narrators and characters, such as the Prioress's "Alma redemptoris mater" (VII, 641). I call these intra-textual Latinisms. The other kind are those written into the manuscripts as textual markers: explicits and incipits between sections of works like the *Knight's tale* and *Troilus and Criseyde*, epigraphs, and glosses. I call these extra-textual Latinisms. We can safely assume that intra-textual Latinisms are from Chaucer's own pen; but we cannot assume the same of extra-textual Latinisms, which at least sometimes must be scribal, unless they were done at Chaucer's instruction in some lost manuscript predating Hengwrt and repeated by subsequent scribes.

Intra-textual Latinisms are superficially the easiest to identify. Most if not all of them can be described as what Chaucer himself called *terms*, which are given a very useful general treatment in Burnley (1983: chapter 7). As Burnley shows, the Middle English word *term*, which refers to the specialized vocabulary and style of a defined sphere of usage, such as law, hunting, or war, closely approximates the modern linguistic concept of register. In the years before the rise of an English standard, an English-speaker would display both copiousness and propriety by using terms correctly. In the *Canterbury tales*, Chaucer refers often to the use of *terms*.[5] The word *term* came to English via French, but it can refer to specialized language in Latin. Examples of terms would be the Friar's pleasant "in principio" (*CT* I.254) from the gospel of John, a term that was used apotropaically even after the Reformation (cf. Bloomfield 1955), and the term *Fortuna Major*, the name of the constellation that rises on the morning after Troilus and Criseyde make love for the first time (*Troilus and Criseyde* III, 1420). The Summoner had a few terms, "two or three / That he had learned out of some decree" (*CT* I, 639-40), one of which was "questio quid iuris" (*CT* I, 646). Except for the Wife of Bath and the Canon's Yeoman, the secular members of the Canterbury pilgrimage generally profess not to know any terms. The Franklin feigns ignorance of astrological terms (*CT* V, 1266), which would have been in Latin. After hearing the *Physician's tale*, Harry Bailly avers that he cannot speak "in terme" (*CT* VI, 311), and he enjoins the Clerk to avoid terms, colors, and figures of rhetoric (*CT* IV, 16) in his tale. But Chaucer's Latin goes beyond terms to oaths and ejaculations, such as the many *benedicites* and the many variations on God's *corpus* (e.g. *CT* I, 3743) that color the speech of the Canterbury pilgrims. And let us not forget the Wife of

Bath's infamous "quoniam" (III, 608). One part of a study of Chaucer's Latinity will be to classify the varieties of Latin reflected in these Latinisms.

With one exception, none of Chaucer's intra-textual Latin is longer than a phrase. The exception is the twelve-line Latin summary of Statius's *Thebaid*, book by book, that follows line 1498 in Book V of *Troilus and Criseyde* in all but two of its sixteen manuscripts.[6] The lines are in randomly mixed unrhymed hexameters and pentameters,[7] they come at the beginning of Cassandra's rehearsal of Theban history, and they are echoed in a general way by the English text that follows them. Skeat is the only modern editor who treats the lines as part of Chaucer's text. Some of the lines have been traced to prefaces in manuscripts of the *Thebaid*,[8] and scholars tend to regard them as notes from which Chaucer translated Cassandra's speech, but ultimately we do not know whether the lines are Chaucer's or not. If they are Chaucer's, why did Chaucer leave them in the text? If they are not Chaucer's, then why did scribes so faithfully reproduce them?

Extra-textual Latinisms occur as epigraphs, textual links, and glosses. Unlike intra-textual Latinisms, they are unprotected by the surrounding English text, and in Chaucer manuscripts and incunabula they are sometimes changed and sometimes omitted entirely, which casts some doubt on their authorial status – although it is well to remember that scribes did not always copy Chaucer's English texts accurately or completely, either.

The epigraphs are most likely to be Chaucer's. In *Riverside*, the *Knight's tale* is prefaced with a heading and an epigraph, both italicized. First, in English, "Heere bigynneth the Knyghtes Tale", and after that, an abbreviated quotation in Latin from Statius's *Thebaid*. *Riverside's* italics separate these statements from Chaucer's text. Now *Riverside*, like Robinson's 2nd edition before it, is based on the Ellesmere manuscript (El) with supplementary readings provided from Hengwrt (Hg), both widely regarded as the two earliest surviving manuscripts of the *Canterbury tales*, as well as from other manuscripts.[9] The English incipit, "Heere bigynneth the Knyghtes Tale", seems to function as a textual boundary that keeps the Statian epigraph inside the text of the *Knight's tale*. And yet, the incipit is not enough of a boundary to protect the epigraph fully, since the epigraph is missing from three of the nine manuscripts used in *Riverside*.[10] Caxton's 1483 edition (*STC*, no. 5094) of the *Canterbury tales* leaves it out, and some of the major modern editions, such as Baugh's, relegate it to the notes. In contrast, the Latin epigraph from Jeremiah 6.16 that begins the *Parson's tale* is successfully protected by an English heading in all nine manuscripts used in *Riverside*, as well as in Caxton.

Chaucer was among the first English writers whose works were formally divided with Latin textual markers in the manuscripts (Butterfield

1996: 60-61). This so-called *ordinatio* had long been used for authoritative texts in Latin, and so the use of these textual markers in fifteenth-century manuscripts of Chaucer is one sign of Chaucer's status as an *auctor*. But are these textual markers scribal or authorial? The Latin incipits and explicits that divide sections of some of the *Canterbury tales* and works like the *House of fame* [three books], *Troilus and Criseyde* [five books], and the *Legend of good women* are also unprotected in the manuscripts. Consequently, they are reproduced erratically both in manuscripts and in print. Once again, Hg and El often agree on these, but because textual markers are formulaic, and because they are a standard part of the *ordinatio* of a manuscript, the scribes observe neither the same word order nor the same vocabulary.[11] Even if in fact they were authorial, the textual markers in the manuscript would have been regarded as instructions from the author, but not as part of the author's text. They were optional and malleable. This is true even of the colophon for the *Canterbury tales*, which follows Chaucer's Retraction. Some manuscripts (e.g. El) give an English colophon reading, "Heere is ended the book of the tales of Caunterbury, compiled by Geffrey Chaucer, of whos soule Jhesu Crist have mercy. Amen." Others (e.g. Ad^1) have a Latin colophon with some variation of *Hic capit Auctor licenciam* – "Here the author takes his leave".[12]

Another kind of extra-textual Latin comes in the form of marginal glosses. There are glosses from the *Thebaid* in the *Knight's tale*, from Petrarch in the *Clerk's tale*, from Jerome's *Adversus Jovinianum* in the *Wife of Bath's prologue* and the *Franklin's tale*, and from Innocent III's *De miseria humanae conditionis* in the *Man of law's tale* and the *Pardoner's prologue and tale*. The few scholars who have worked on these glosses consider them to be Chaucer's, inserted either as reminders about source-materials to be used in revising the English text, or as source-acknowledgments.[13] I see no reason to argue against this hypothesis. However, in the transmission history of Chaucer manuscripts, the glosses, like the rubrics, were textually unprotected, and therefore they were not systematically copied, when they were copied at all. Although Chaucer's English text too was subject to scribal change, the glosses were even more so, because they are not part of a systematic program anchored to the English text, such as the program of Latin verses, commentaries, glosses, and colophons in manuscripts of Gower's *Confessio amantis* (Pearsall 1989: 14-15). A problem similar to that of the glosses is the phrase "radix Chaucer", referring to the beginning point for astrological calculations about (or perhaps by) Chaucer, which was written in a fourteenth- or early fifteenth-century hand into a set of tables in Cambridge MS Peterhouse 75. I, fol. 5^v. John North (1988: chapter 4, esp. 170-80) has argued that the phrase was written into the manuscript by Chaucer himself, while I have counter-argued that it is not possible to know.

The Latin in Chaucer's Retraction might be considered both intra- and extra-textual. The Retraction ends with an English prayer to Christ "that I may been oon of hem at the day of doom that shulle be saved", to which is attached the liturgical Latin colophon *Qui cum patre et spiritu sancto vivit et regnat Deus per omnia secula*, which lacks the final word *seculorum*. The Retraction occurs in only 28 of the 82 or 83 manuscripts of the *CT*,[14] and in some manuscripts only the first few words of the Latin prayer are given. Again, the Latin prayer may be Chaucer's, but it could just as easily be scribal.

One striking fact that emerges from this brief survey of Chaucer's Latin is that unlike Gower and other contemporaries and followers, Chaucer did not compose an original text in Latin. His Latin occurs either as single Latin words, as quotations, or as formulas. Chaucer uses Latin *as* Latin, but he does not seem to have attempted to speak in his own voice in Latin. Assuming that the Retraction is meant to be his literary farewell, Chaucer's last words are a formulaic Latin prayer. Chaucer's voice, so seemingly modern and individual, merges in the end with all the other voices that have ever spoken or written that prayer. What is more, Latinisms are much rarer outside the *Canterbury tales*. *Troilus and Criseyde* has perhaps three, which is one less than the number in just the *General prologue*.[15] The only other work in which there is more than one or two Latinisms is the *Treatise on the astrolabe*, where Chaucer uses the imperative *nota* to call attention to important points and where he uses several terms in Latin rather than translate them into English. As if we needed any more confirmation of the achievement of the *Canterbury tales*, Chaucer's Latinisms in the *Canterbury tales* imply an audience far more learned than even the sophisticated court audience that we presume for *Troilus and Criseyde*, or the scientific audience that we presume for the *Treatise on the Astrolabe*. The presumed audience of the *Canterbury tales* would have to be familiar with both French and Latin and know a number of registers of each.

One question is whether to consider **loanwords and Latin names** as Latinisms, or whether these should be regarded as English words. The problem with loanwords is that it is not always possible to tell whether the word is morphologically English or Latin. A famous example is the word *ambages* from *Troilus and Criseyde* (V, 897).[16] As a Latin word, *ambages* would be a third-declension noun with singular and plural in *-es*, like *vulpes* 'fox'. As an English word, it would be the plural of a presumed French loan, *ambage*. Chaucer immediately glosses the word, which suggests that *ambages* is a term he does not expect his reader to know: "That is to sayn, with double wordes slye". However, this gloss does not tell us anything about the origin of the word. Likewise, with names whose morphology is Latin, we cannot be sure whether the name counts as English or Latin, since so many classical names retained their original forms – as witness the name of the goddess Venus in Modern English.

The problem of loanwords and names is complicated by **pronunciation**, which helped to blur the lines between English and Latin. Whereas the picture of Chaucer's Latinity that I have been drawing emphasizes the compartmentalization and specialization of Latin that characterizes Latinity in England at the end of the Middle Ages, Chaucer's Latin pronunciation, as I have reconstructed it, suggests the extent to which the English language had assimilated Latin, and it forecasts the increased borrowing from Latin into English that was to take place after the Reformation. The explanation for this assimilation is, simply stated, that by the fourteenth century, Latin pronunciation reflected the norms of Middle English.

By all accounts, the pronunciation of medieval Latin in England was always influenced by the pronunciation of the vernacular – Anglo-Saxon before the Norman Conquest, Middle English and Anglo-Norman French after the Conquest, and Middle English after the fourteenth century, when English superseded French as the dominant vernacular.[17] The situation seems simple, but it is complicated by the presence, late into the Middle Ages, of Latin verse composed according to the classical rules of scansion – such as John Gower's Latin verses in the *Confessio Amantis* – which indicates a knowledge of quantitative distinctions and possibly of other features of classical pronunciation.[18] It seems safer to suppose two styles of Latin pronunciation – one, more formal, that aspired to classical norms, and the other, less formal, that was pulled into the orbit of vernacular norms. However, the distinction between the two styles is chiefly vowel quantity, which is important for composing verse in classical meters (Rigg 1996: 80-1).

The problem lies in determining just what the influence of the vernacular would have been. Because of the Norman Conquest, England lay along the fault line that divided northern and southern pronunciation of Latin – that is, Germanic-speaking countries vs. Romance-speaking countries. Before the Norman Conquest, England was in the Germanic camp. Under the apparent influence of the Germanic Stress Rule, the Anglo-Saxons would lengthen vowels in the initial syllable of disyllabic words such as *pater* whose classical pronunciation calls for a short vowel. Under the influence of their own vernacular practices, the Anglo-Saxons would pronounce *g* before a front vowel as a semi-vowel [y] and they would voice intervocalic *s* to [z].[19] After the Conquest, when Latin was taught by French schoolmasters, French pronunciations began to be introduced. For example, *g* before a front vowel now became the affricate [dʒ] as in Modern English *gem* and *gin* (Allen 1978: 102, Fowler 1937: 100, 104). Despite this French influence on Anglo-Latin, for the twelfth and thirteenth centuries, it is not always clear whether to use Middle English or Anglo-Norman pronunciation for Anglo-Latin. For example, the Latin relative pronoun *qui* might be French [ki:] or English/classical Latin [kwi:].

From the fifteenth century through the Reformation, the situation is also complex. During the period of the Great Vowel Shift, which was underway by the mid fifteenth century, Latin long vowels must have kept pace with English long vowels, since at the end of the shift the Latin long vowels are pronounced as English long vowels, i.e., as in 'old Latin' and legal Latin. For example, after the Great Vowel Shift, "Deus hic" in the *Summoner's tale* (*CT* III, 1770) would be pronounced [di:ʊs haik]. But the Great Vowel Shift is only one of several influences on English pronunciation of Latin in this period. In the sixteenth-century, the Reformation dispersed English Catholics to various Continental lands where they would have acquired Continental Latin pronunciation, including the reformed classical pronunciation promoted by Erasmus.[20] When these Catholics brought their Continental Latin back to England under Queen Mary, there would have been a number of competing systems in play.

The fourteenth century, in contrast, poses fewer problems, and so we can ascertain the Latin pronunciation of fourteenth-century England with a little more confidence than we can ascertain the Latin pronunciation of the periods before or afterwards. The end of the fourteenth century, the period of Chaucer's literary career, is the period of greatest certainty for Anglo-Latin pronunciation. At around 1400, the Great Vowel Shift had not yet begun – or at least we are fairly sure that Chaucer's conservative pronunciation does not give evidence of it (cf. Smith 1996: 86-111). Hence, as a general rule, we can probably pronounce Chaucer's Latin as if it were Chaucer's Middle English – i.e., the two languages are allophonic. Here are some examples of Latinisms cited earlier in this essay:

- The Prioress' brooch: *Amor vincit omnia* [ˈamɔr ˈvɪnsɪt ˈɔmnɪa] (*CT* I, 162).
- The Summoner's cry: *Questio quid iuris* [ˈkwɛsti·ɔ: kwɪd ˈʤyrɪs] (*CT* I, 646).
- Nicholas's song: *Angelus ad virginem* [ˈanʤɛlʊs at ˈvɪrʤɪnɛm] (*CT* I, 3216).
- The Wife of Bath's prized bodily part: her *quoniam* [ˈkɔnɪ·am] (*CT* III, 608).

The question of how to pronounce Chaucer's Latin is in effect a synecdoche of the whole problem of Chaucer's Latinity. In the fourteenth century, Latin was being absorbed into English, a process that accelerated into the early modern period. As A. G. Rigg argues in his *History of Anglo-Latin literature*, fourteenth-century Latin in England was a language that increasingly was acquiring a strong English 'flavour'. If in the fifteenth century it would undergo the influence of humanism and "the establishment of Classical Latin Standards" (Rigg 1992: 242), in the fourteenth century Anglo-Latin was becoming fragmented into numerous specialized varieties.[21] This is the condition represented by Chaucer's use of what I earlier referred to as *terms*.

And yet, despite this absorption of Latin into English, histories of English language and literature often see English as a language struggling against French and Latin for authority. Most recently, in the Introduction to part one of the *Cambridge history of medieval English literature*, the editor, David Wallace, calls "Latinitas" a "hegemonic force" of such power that, together with French, it "rendered the native population mute" in the years after the Norman Conquest, and in the prefaces to later sections of the *Cambridge History*, Wallace extends the hegemony of Latinity down through the end of the Middle Ages.[22] Wallace is not alone in characterizing Latinity as an oppressor, nor am I singling him out, since there has long been a tendency to see the career of English in the fourteenth century in chauvinistic terms. To some extent, this is due to a misreading of the chronicle record. As Thorlac Turville-Petre and Steven Justice have separately observed, accounts of English and English literature from the Norman Conquest through the English Rising of 1381 fail to realize the element of nationalist polemic in medieval chronicles, and they erroneously pit English against Latin in a struggle for political power.[23] Postcolonialism and cultural studies ironically seem to be the new home for a very old form of linguistic chauvinism in which the English language rises up against its oppressors, French and Latin.

Chaucer is often enlisted in this struggle via his still-popular role as the putative originator of English poetry, but as Christopher Baswell has argued in *The making of Chaucer's English*, Chaucer's English may be a good deal less original than we might think. What we consider 'English' is so because of our regard for his poetry, not because Chaucer single-handedly forged the English language out of ruder – or nobler, as the case may be – elements. Middle English scholarship's concern with 'vernacularity' too often emphasizes the political at the expense of the literary and linguistic. In narrating the rise of English, it is well for us to remember that in the Middle Ages and through the Reformation, Britain was a polyglot island where one could hear Latin, English, French, Scots, Welsh, and Cornish. Not only were there many voices speaking in many languages, but within each language there were various registers, and this is as true of Latin as it is of the other languages of Britain. In the *Cambridge history* itself, this point is made by Baswell, whose fittingly-titled essay "Latinitas" neatly summarizes the view taken in Rigg's *History of Anglo-Latin literature*: that in England, Latin is "a language regularly contested by other languages of real or putative authority", and that ultimately Latin itself devolved into "an array of increasingly disparate, specialized language practices" (Baswell 1999: 123).[24] In his paper at the 19th Triennial Conference of IAUPE (12 August 2004), Richard Bailey, reporting about a book in progress, made a case for considering English in Britain as part of a multilingual environment, and I would suggest that a study of Chaucer's Latinity would help to fill in our understanding of that environment from a perspective that avoids linguistic chauvinism. Terms such as triglossia or even polyglossia seem more accurate for describing Chaucer's linguistic environment than metaphors of struggle against a Latin hegemony that for Chaucer almost certainly did not exist.

In this essay, I have outlined some issues regarding Chaucer's use of Latin, in hopes of making a start towards an understanding of the place that Latin occupies in Chaucer's vocabulary, in his literary language, and in manuscripts of his work. I have suggested that Chaucer's Latin occurs both intra-textually and extra-textually, in the form of Latinisms, formulas, and quotations – but not as Latin that is original to Chaucer. The question of the Latin in Chaucer manuscripts that occurs as textual markers and glosses remains open, but even if these are also Chaucerian, they too are Latinisms, formulas, and quotations from sources, thus they too are not original to Chaucer. Chaucer's Latin is less a *langue* than a set of pre-existing *paroles*, less a system from which new Latin utterances are produced than a closed set of utterances that have always already been produced. This Latin was often highly specialized terms. Chaucer's Latin illustrates the changes taking place both in Anglo-Latin and in English that culminated in what linguistic chauvinists call "the triumph of English". But I would like to suggest that teleological and political models are inadequate for describing the day-to-day understanding of usage that guided Chaucer in his linguistic choices. If, as Rigg says, Anglo-Latin was fragmenting into diverse areas of specialized use, far from being a "hegemonic force", Anglo-Latin in Chaucer's time is being absorbed into English. If there is a hegemony, it must be the hegemony of English.

Notes

[1] *OED*, s.v. 'Latinity': "1. The manner of speaking or writing Latin; Latin (with reference to its construction or style). In the first quot. the sense of the word is doubtful, and the text insecure. 1619 in Crt. & Times Jas. I (1848) II. 172 One Shingleton..who preaching in Pauls..glanced, they say, scandalously at him [Bacon], and his Latinities, as

he called them. a1656 HALL Rem. Wks. (1660) 241 The Romans expressed the womans marriage by, nubere, which signifies to vail... Neither doubt I but before all Latinity was hatched this was alluded to by Abimelech, Genes. 20. 16. 1661 BOYLE Style of Script. (1675) 148 That cardinal..that said, that once indeed he had read the Bible, but if he were to do it again, 'twould lose him all his Latinity. 1781 GIBBON Decl. & F. xlvii. II. 738 His Latinity is pure. 1826 MISS MITFORD Village Ser. III. (1863) 519 [He] used to..growl as he compounded the medicines over the bad Latinity of the prescriptions. 1831 CARLYLE Sart. Res. (1858) 81, I undertook to compose his Epitaph..which, however, for an alleged defect of Latinity..still remains unengraven. 1865 MERIVALE Rom. Emp. VIII. lxiv. 100 The last remains we possess of classical Latinity are the biographies of the later emperors."

[2] My essay, "Reading Chaucer's Latin aloud" (Twomey 2005), describes phonetic rules for Chaucer's late fourteenth-century Anglo-Latin.

[3] From the *General prologue* (I, 162). All citations from Chaucer are according to *Riverside*.

[4] For summaries of scholarship, see *Riverside's* "Explanatory notes", pp. 1092 (*Treatise on the astrolabe*), 1003 (*Boece*), and 880 (*Clerk's tale*).

[5] Among other examples, Burnley cites: "termes of astrologye" (*CT* V, 1266), "scole-termes" (*CT* IV, 1569), "termes queinte of lawe" (in some MSS.; *CT* II, 1189), "termes of phisik" (*Troilus and Criseyde* II, 1038), "termes of philosophie" (*House of fame*, 857).

[6] According to both *Riverside*, p. 1177, and Robinson (1957: 921).

[7] For a summary of medieval Latin forms, see Rigg (1992: 316). The metres of the 12-line epitome of the *Thebaid* are randomly mixed, not elegiac couplets.

[8] See Magoun (1955), Clogan (1964), and more generally, Windeatt (1992: 123).

[9] MS Ellesmere 26 C 9, ca. 1400, formerly in the possession of Lord Ellesmere, now at the Henry E. Huntington Library, San Marino, California; MS Hengwrt 154 (Peniarth 392D), ca. 1400.

[10] See textual notes to the *Knight's tale* in *Riverside*, p. 1122.

[11] For example, *Clerk's tale* after IV, 448: "Incipit pars tercia" (Hg) vs. "Incipit tercia pars" (El); *Clerk's tale* after IV, 784: "Incipit pars quinta" (Hg) vs. "Sequitur pars quinta" (El). Text: Ruggiers (1979).

[12] Cf. Textual notes in Robinson (1957: 898).

[13] Cf. Dempster (1943-4), Silvia (1965), Lewis (1967), Caie (1975-6). These glosses were first noticed in Manly -- Rickert (1940: 3, 483-527).

[14] My count of the MSS is from *Riverside*, pp. 1118 and 1135.

[15] In *Troilus and Criseyde*: "bendiste" (I, 780), "mea culpa" (II, 525), "Fortuna Major" (III, 1420). In the *General prologue*: "Amor vincit omnia" (I, 162), "in principio" (I, 254), "Questio quid iuris" (I, 646), "Significavit" (I, 662).

[16] [Diomede to Criseyde]: "'And if but Calkas lede us with ambages – / That is to seyn, with double wordes slye, / Swich as men clepen a word with two visages –'." Burnley (1983: 137) locates the Latin term *ambages*, meaning a deliberate ambiguity, in medieval Latin sources.

[17] The scheme of Latin pronunciation in England that is used in the present essay is based on the following: Allen (1978: Appendix B, 102-10), Fowler (1937), (Rigg 1992: "Appendix: Metre", 313-29; 1996a; 1996b). Rigg (1996a: 47-56) discusses several forms of evidence that we can use to reconstruct the pronunciation of Latin in England: rhyme, alliteration, spelling, loan-words, comparative analysis, post-Reformation authorities, and modern legal Latin (which reflects post-Reformation, post-Great Vowel Shift pronunciation).

[18] Latin scansion is summarized in Rigg (1992: 313-29). An excellent study of Gower's verses in particular is Echard -- Fanger (1991).

[19] The Germanic Stress Rule describes the tendency in Germanic languages to stress the initial syllable in polysyllabic words (cf. Lass 1992: 85-90). On Anglo-Saxon pronunciation of Latin, see Allen (1978: 102) and Fowler (1937: 104).

[20] Erasmus, *De recta latini graecique sermonis pronuntiatione* (1528). Erasmus was responding not to the Counter-Reformation but to the linguistic confusion resulting from the plethora of Latin pronunciations in use on the Continent by the early sixteenth century. On the rise and fall of Erasmus's reformed pronunciation at Cambridge University in the sixteenth century via John Cheke, the first Regius Professor of Greek, and Thomas Smith, the first Regius Professor of Civil Law, see Allen (1978: 103-05).

[21] Without counting literary Latin, no less than three dozen kinds of Latinity are listed in Mantello --- Rigg (1996: "Varieties of medieval Latin", part two, section D-E-F).

[22] Wallace (1999: 5, 4); specific instances from the prefaces (Wallace 1999: 314, 485, 486, 637) are critiqued by Somerset (2001: 489-90). As counter-examples, Somerset cites the essays by Christopher Baswell, Winthrop Wetherbee, Glending Olson, and Andrew Galloway in Wallace (1999), to which I would add Galloway's forthcoming essay, "Latin England". As a group, the essays in the *Cambridge history* share the view that Latinity was a linguistically and culturally unifying influence that remained associated with power and authority throughout the Middle English period. A good example is Winthrop Wetherbee's essay on Gower, which calls the *Vox clamantis* "a clear expression of a class-based anxiety" about the uprising in 1381 (Wetherbee 1999: 594). Outside of the *Cambridge history*, another example would be Gellrich (1995: esp. chapters 2, 3, 5).

[23] Turville-Petre (1996: 181, 227), Justice (1994: 17, 225). Among histories of the language, I list Cottle (1969) and the mass-market *Story of English*, by Robert McCrum, William Cran, and Robert MacNeil. On the English Rising of 1381, see Gellrich (1995: chapter 5).

[24] Cf. Rigg (1992: e.g., 242).

References

Allen, W. Sidney
    1978   *Vox latina: The pronunciation of classical Latin.* (2nd edition.) Cambridge: Cambridge University Press.
    1999   Reprinted edition.

Baswell, Christopher
    1999   "Latinitas", in: Wallace (ed.), 122-51.

Bloomfield, Morton W.
    1955   "The magic of *In principio*", *Modern language notes* 70: 559-65.

Burnley, David
    1983   *A guide to Chaucer's language.* Norman: University of Oklahoma Press.

Burton, T.L. -- John F. Plummer (eds.)
2005 *'Seyd in forme and reverence': Essays on Chaucer and Chaucerians in memory of Emerson Brown, Jr.* Provo: Chaucer Studio Press.

Butterfield, Ardis
1996 "*Mise-en-page* in the *Troilus* manuscripts: Chaucer and French manuscript culture", in: Lerer (ed.), 49-80.

Caie, Graham D.
1975-6 "The significance of the early Chaucer manuscript glosses (with special reference to the *Wife of Bath's prologue)*", *Chaucer Review* 10: 350-60.

Clogan, Paul M.
1964 "Chaucer and the *Thebaid* scholia", *Studies in philology* 61: 599-614.

Cottle, Basil
1969 *The triumph of English 1350-1400.* London: Blandford.

Dempster, Germaine
1943-4 "Chaucer's manuscripts of Petrarch's version of Griselda's story", *Modern Philology* 41: 6-16.

Echard, Siân -- Claire Fanger
1991 *The Latin verses in the* Confessio amantis*: An annotated translation.* With a preface by A.G. Rigg. East Lansing: Colleagues Press.

Fowler, G. Herbert
1937 "Notes on the pronunciation of medieval Latin in England", *History*, new series 22: 97-109.

Galloway, Andrew
n.d. "Latin England", in: Lavezzo (ed.), 39-95.

Gellrich, Jesse M.
1995 *Discourse and dominion in the fourteenth century: Oral contexts of writing in philosophy, politics, and poetry*. Princeton: Princeton University Press.

Justice, Steven
1994 *Writing and rebellion: England in 1381*. (The new historicism 27.) Berkeley: University of California Press.

Lass, Roger
1992 "Phonology and morphology", in: *CHEL* 2, 25-155.

Lavezzo, Kathy (ed.)
n.d. *Medieval English nation*. Minneapolis: University of Minnesota Press.

Lewis, Robert E.
1967 "Glosses to the *Man of law's tale* from Pope Innocent III's *De miseria humane conditionis*", *Studies in philology* 64: 1-16.

Lerer, Seth (ed.)
1996 *Reading from the margins: Textual studies, Chaucer, and medieval literature*. San Marino: Huntington Library.

Magoun, F.P.
1955 "Chaucer's summary of Statius' *Thebaid* II-XII", *Traditio* 11: 409-20.

Manly, John M. -- Edith Rickert
1940 *The text of the Canterbury tales, studied on the basis of all known manuscripts*. 8 vols. Chicago: University of Chicago Press.

Mantello, F.A.C. -- A. G. Rigg (eds.)
1996 *Medieval Latin: An introduction and bibliographical guide*. Washington, D.C.: Catholic University of America Press.

McCrum, Robert -- William Cran -- Robert MacNeil
1992 *Story of English*. (Revised edition.) London: Faber and Faber.

McGee, Timothy J. -- A.G. Rigg -- David N. Klausner (eds.)
1996 *Singing early music: The pronunciation of European languages in the late Middle Ages and the Renaissance*. Bloomington: Indiana University Press.

Minnis, A.J. (ed.)
1989 *Latin and vernacular: Studies in late-medieval texts and manuscripts*. Wolfeboro: Brewer.

North, John
1988 *Chaucer's universe*. Oxford: Oxford University Press.

Pearsall, Derek
1989 "Gower's Latin in the *Confessio amantis*", in: Minnis (ed.), 13-25.

Rigg, A.G.
1992 *A history of Anglo-Latin 1066-1422*. Cambridge: Cambridge University Press.

1996a "Anglo-Latin"; in: McGee -- Rigg -- Klausner (eds.), 46-61.

1996b "Orthography and pronunciation", in: Mantello -- Rigg (eds.), 79-82.

Robinson, F.N. (ed.)
1957 *The works of Geoffrey Chaucer*. (2nd edition.) Boston: Houghton Mifflin.

Ruggiers, Paul G. (ed.)
1979 *A facsmile and transcriptions of the Hengwrt manuscript, with variants from the Ellesmere manuscript.* (Variorum Chaucer 1.) Norman: University of Oklahoma Press: Wm. Dawson & Sons.

Silvia, Daniel S.
1965 "Glosses to the *Canterbury tales* from St. Jerome's *Epistola adversus Jovinianum*", *Studies in philology* 62: 28-39.

Smith, Jeremy
1996 *An historical study of English: Function, form, and change.* London: Routledge.

Somerset, Fiona
2001 "*The Cambridge history of medieval English literature* on 'Latinitas'", *Studies in the age of Chaucer* 23: 489-93.

Turville-Petre, Thorlac
1996 *England the nation: Language, literature, and national identity, 1290-1340.* Oxford: Clarendon.

Twomey, Michael W.
1991 Review of John North, *Chaucer's universe. Anglia* 109: 186-90.

2005 "Reading Chaucer's Latin aloud", in: Burton -- Plummer (eds.), 181-90.

Wallace, David (ed.)
1999 *The Cambridge history of medieval English literature.* Cambridge: Cambridge University Press.

Wetherbee, Winthrop
1999 "John Gower", in: Wallace (ed.), 589-609.

Windeatt, Barry
1992 *Troilus and Criseyde.* (Oxford Guides to Chaucer.) Oxford: Clarendon.

Chaucer's *Troilus* in a new comparative context

Saburo Oka (Tokyo, Japan)

1. Introduction

It is certain that Chaucer's *Troilus* as well as his *Canterbury Tales* are the subject of such a flood of print that a justification is needed by anyone who adds to it. To complete my topic, I should need a whole book; the most important previous attempt in almost the same line of research is, without doubt, *The European tragedy of Troilus*, edited by Piero Boitani in 1989, which is a collection of thirteen articles on the topic by distinguished Chaucerian scholars. All big and significant topics, however, leave room for further extension or more detailed exploration. Chaucer criticism has, if we count the contemporary fourteenth century, a history of seven centuries, and we can say that each of these centuries has a remarkably distinctive characteristic. At the beginning of the new century, therefore, we must have an expectation of something new in Chaucerian studies.

In the so-called 'whetstone stanza' in Book One of *Troilus*, Chaucer's Pandarus gives his proverbial advice to his young friend Troilus, saying "By his contraire is every thynge declared." (637)[1] In fact, the comparative method is one of the most efficient ways of human thinking. And in the last two centuries the comparative method has produced many monumental achievements in almost all fields of science and scholarship. As for Chaucerian studies in the 20th century, we can certainly say that remarkable research has been done in a broader perspective, that is to say, extending the perspective from English to European. Now, after the European perspective, which should come next?

2. Chaucer's portrait of Troilus in European classical and medieval contexts

Story-telling is, indeed, a human characteristic. In other words, a human being can be defined as *homo narrans* and it has always two tasks: first, how to preserve the preceding stories and presentations, which makes him *homo conservans*, and secondly, how to transform the accumulated materials, by which he can be *homo ludens*. Many methods of such transformations have been tried, including focalization, simplification, or amplification.

As an example of these conservations and transformations, we can mention Chaucer's portrait of *Troilus* in Book Five, which was made according to the medieval formulaic phrase, "as bokes us declare" (V, 799).

And Troilus wel woxen was in highte,
And complet formed by proporcioun
So wel that kynde it nought amenden myghte;
Yong, flessh, strong, and hardy as lyoun;
Trewe as stiel in ech condicioun;
Oon of the beste entecched creature
That is or shal whil that the world may dure.

And certeynly in storye it is yfounde
That Troilus was nevere unto no wight,
As in his tyme, in no degree secounde
In durryng don that longeth to a knyght.
Al myghte a geant passen hym of myght,
His herte ay with the first and with the beste
Stood paregal, to durre don that hym leste. (827-840)

We can hardly get any vivid portrait of Troilus in Classical Literature: Homer has left us only one epithet ἱππιοχάρμης ('one who fights from a chariot', or simply, 'a horseman') in the *Iliad*, Bk. 24, 1. 257; Sophocles' *Troilus* is extant in a very fragmentary state, in which Troilus is described as ἀνδρόπαις, 'a youth near manhood' (Lloyd-Jones 1996: 306-7). The first medieval author who gave us a somewhat detailed portrait of Troilus was Dares the Phrygian. In his influential *De Exidio Trojae Historia*, cap. 12, Dares says, "Troilum magnum, pulcherrimum, pro aetate valentem, fortem, cupidum virtutis." ('Troilus, a large and handsome boy, was strong for his age, brave, and eager for glory.')[2]

A slightly different way of representation was adopted by Dictys of Crete in his *Ephemeris Belli Troiani*, Book Four, Section 9:

> Capti etiam Lycaon et Troilus Priamidae, quos in medium productos Achilles iugulari iubet indignatus nondum sibi a Priamo super his, quae secum tractaverat, mandatum. quae ubi animadvertere Troiani, tollunt gemitus et clamore lugubri Troili casum miserandum in modum deflent recordati aetatem eius admodum immaturam, qui in primis pueritiae annis cum verecundia ac probitate, tum praecipue forma corporis amabilis atque acceptus popularibus adolescebat.

> (And two of Priam's sons were captured, Lycaon and Troilus, the throats of whom, when they had been brought forth into the center, were cut, by order of Achilles, who was angry with Priam for not having seen to that business they had discussed. The Trojans raised a cry of grief and, mourning loudly, bewailed the fact that Troilus had met so grievous a death, for they remembered how young he was, who, being in the early years of his manhood, was the people's favorite, their

daring, not only because of his modesty and honesty, but more especially because of his handsome appearance.)[3]

Dictys does depict Troilus from the perspective of the Trojan people. Thus, we can confirm that Dares, Dictys and Chaucer share almost the same references about Troilus: young, strong, brave, and handsome.

On the other hand, in his *Roman de Troie*, Benoît de Sainte-Maure amplifies his portrait of Troilus extensively, beginning from his handsome appearance as follows:

> Troïlus fu beaus a merveille;
> Chiere ot rient, face vermeille,
> Cler vis apert, le front plenier:
> Mout covint bien a chevalier.
> (Troïlus était extrêmement beau. Sa physionomie souriante, son teint vermeil, son visage clair et ouvert, son front haut, tout en lui était digne d'un chevalier.)[4]

Due to the restrictions of space, let us quote the following lines (5397-5446) only in Modern French prose translation by Baumgartner.

> Sa chevelure blonde et naturellement brillante lui seyait particulièrement. Ses yeux pers étincelaient de gaieté: leur beauté était incomparable. Lorsqu'il était de bonne humeur, son regard était si doux que c'était un plaisir de le voir. Mais je peux vous dire en toute vérité qu'il offrait à ses ennemis un tout autre visage! Son nez était long et bien proportionné. L'armure convenait bien à sa stature. Sa bouche était bien faite, ses belles dents plus blanches qu'ivoire ou argent. Son menton carré, son cou, élancé et droit, allaient très bien avec sa cuirasse. Les épaules, d'une belle carrure, allaient en s'affinant. La poitrine était bien formée sous les lacets du haubert. Ses mains étaient bien faites et beaux ses bras. Sa taille était bien prise et ses hanches larges. Ses vêtements lui allaient fort bien. C'était un très beau chevalier. Il avait les jambes droites, la voûte plantaire bien formée, tous ses membres étaient bien faits et son assiette à cheval très solide. Il était très grand mais sa haute stature allait de pair avec les proportions de son corps.
> Je ne pense pas qu'il y ait à l'heure actuelle de par le vaste monde d'homme qui le vaille, qui aime autant la joie et les plaisirs, qui tienne moins de propos désagréables et qui soit aussi valeureux et épris de gloire et de hauts faits. Il n'était ni insolent ni porté aux excès mais joyeux, rieur et enclin à aimer. Il fut aimé et il aima avec passion, et il en éprouva bien des tourments. C'était encore un tout jeune homme, mais il était le plus beau et le plus preux des Troyens, à l'exception de son frère Hector dont la suprématie à la guerre ne fut jamais contestée. Darès nous en est ici garant: Hector fut vraiment la fleur de toute chevalerie et Troïlus fut sur ce point bien digne de son frère. Oui, il était vraiment son frère pour la prouesse, la courtoisie et la générosité. (pp. 106-7)

In his *Historia Destructionis Troiae*, Guido delle Colonne has transformed Benoît's Old French romance style into the historical narrative style in Latin; he has condensed Benoît's detailed description about Troilus as follows:

> Troylus uero, licet fuerit corpore magnus, magis fuit tamen corde magnanimus, animosus multum sed multam habuit in sua animositate temperiem, dilectus plurimum a puellis, cum ipse aliqualem seruando modestiam delectaretur in illis. In uiribus uero et strennuitate bellandi uel fuit alius Hector uel secundus ab ipso. In toto eciam regno Troye iuuenis nullus fuit tantis uiribus nec tanta audacia gloriosus. (liber VIII)

> (Troilus, although he was large of body, was even larger of heart; he was very bold but he had moderation in his boldness. He endeared himself to young girls, since he was pleased to maintain a certain reserve toward them. In strength and valor for fighting he was another Hector, or second to him. Moreover, in the whole kingdom of Troy, no young man was celebrated for such great strength and such great daring.)[5]

It is noteworthy that Guido refers to Troilus's inclination toward young girls in addition to his famous bravery.

Lastly, let us quote from Joseph of Exeter's *Bellum Troianum*, which is said to be 'Chaucer's Dares' by Robert K. Root (1917):

> Troilus in spacium surgentes explicat artus, mente gigas, etate puer, nullique secundus audendo uirtutis opus, mixtoque uigore gratior illustres insignit gloria uultus.

> (Troilus was broad and tall. In spirit he was a giant, but in age he was a boy. He was second to none in venturing upon brave deeds. Pride graced his noble feature, more pleasing because it was blended with manly vigour.)[6]

Nevertheless, it is difficult to say that Chaucer's main source of his portrait of Troilus in this passage is Joseph of Exeter's paragraph quoted above. As a matter of fact, Chaucer does not accept Joseph's "mente gigas", but says "Al myghte a geant passen hym of myght".

In the last century Comparative Literature made a large contribution to literary studies by source hunting, but sometimes failed in finding the undeniable definite source of the literary work, or of its plot, or of some particular passages. That is because any author in any age is always both *homo conservans* and *homo ludens*; it is in extremely rare cases that the author dares to expose his raw materials in his work. In Chaucer's portrait of Troilus, we can confirm his way of mixing materials and adding his own, eventually preserving the fundamental elements.

3. Towards a global perspective

Now if we want to have Chaucer's genuine and unique portrait of Troilus, we must examine *Troilus and Criseyde* as a whole, line by line, or word by word. But we can choose here, at least, a few basic or fundamental problems out of so many textual cruxes and difficulties in the interpretation of the work.

First of all, I would like to confirm the correct and proper title of this work. Among all the editors and critics who call it *Troilus and Criseyde*, Robert K. Root (1926: xi) alone says that "by what title Chaucer wished his book to be known is not clear" in the Introduction to his edition. But it is an indisputable piece of evidence that Chaucer's narrator declares in the opening lines, "My purpos is / The double sorwe of Troilus to tellen". And once more the narrator confirms his *purpos* as follows:

> But for to tellen forth in special
> Of this kynges sone of which I tolde,
> And leten other thing collateral,
> Of hym thenke I my tale forth to holde,
> Both of his joie and of his cares colde,
> And al his werk, as touching this matere,
> For I it gan, I wol therto refere. (260-266)

Certainly, some misleading titles can be found in the colophons of some manuscripts: "Liber Troili et Criseydis" in London, British Library, MS Harley 2280; Morgan Library MS 817; Oxford, Bodleian Library, MS Selden Supra 56; Cambridge, St. John's College L. 1, or "the book of Troilus and of Cresseyde" in Oxford, Bodleian Library, MS Rawlinson Poet. 163. Fortunately, we can find some proper titles in other manuscripts: "the book of Troylus of double sorwe in loving of Cri[seyde]" in Oxford, Bodleian Library, MS Selden B. 24, which is too long as the title, although it certainly echoes faithfully the opening lines of the work; "Liber Troili" in London, British Library, MS Harley 2392, and Cambridge, Corpus Christi College 61; "Troylus" in Cheltenham, Huntington Library, MS Phillips 8250, and London, British Library, MS Harley 3943. Therefore, the correct and proper title of this work must be *The Book of Troilus* or simply *Troilus*.

Before we proceed to the problem of the narrative structure of the work, it may be convenient for us to enter into the problem of whether the work is a tragedy or a comedy. Every human narrative consists of some eventful sequences, which naturally narrate some kinds of changes in the situation or the relationship among the participants in the particular narrative, either from *concordia* to *discordia*, or from *discordia* to *concordia*. Every narrative has its own substantial middle part between the beginning and the ending. The narrator is able to begin his or her narrative either from *concordia* or from *discordia*, and to include many kinds of *concordia* and *discordia* in the middle part, making his or her story more interesting and more thrilling. Whether it is a tragedy or a comedy, or whether the narrative is tragic or comic solely depends upon the ending in either *concordia* or *discordia*.

Therefore, if Chaucer's narrator stops his narrative at line 1785 of Book Five, his *Troilus* is undoubtedly tragic, and there should be no problem when the narrator says in the next stanza, "Go, litel bok, go, litel myn tragedye" (1786). At the same time, it must be noted that the selfsame narrator prays that "Ther God thi makere yet, er that he dye, / So sende myght to make in som comedye!" (1787-8) We can understand that "er that he dye" is almost equivalent to "er that I parte fro ye" (5) in the opening stanza in Book One of the work, because Chaucer's narrator continues his ending not in *discordia* but in *concordia* in a new and significant dimension of Being. Thus, his *Troilus* becomes a comedy finally, or a divine comedy in a sense. It is true that Chaucer's narrator certainly tells us Troilus's "double sorwe" in the substantial middle part of the work, just as he promised to his audience in the opening lines, but in the final stanzas Chaucer's narrator begins to tell us about Troilus after his death, who "ful blisfully is went / Up to the holughnesse of the eighthe spere" (V, 1808-1809). The first sorrow of Troilus was dispersed by the happy consummation of love, which is narrated in Book Three, and now his second sorrow after the departure of Criseyde to the Greek camp has been overcome by his blissful ascending to heaven after his tragic death by Achilles. Therefore, the vector of the narrator's narrative is not how the hero became sorrowful, but how his "double sorwe" has been overcome. Then the extremely important narrative is about the actions of the deceased Troilus in the ending of the work. Indeed, Chaucer's Pandarus said already in Book Two:

> How so it be that som men hem delite
> With subtyl art hire tales for to endite,
> Yet for al that, in hire entencioun
> Hire tale is al for som conclusioun.
> And sithe th'ende is every tales strengthe (256-260)

It is not a mere proverbial wisdom, but offers us a key for the structural interpretation of the work. The ending of any narrative has always a cardinal importance to both the narrator and the audience or the reader. The following twenty one lines tell us all actions and movements of Troilus after death:

> And whan that he was slayn in this manere,
> His lighte goost ful blisfully *is went*
> *Up* to the holughnesse of the eighthe spere,
> In convers letyng everich element;
> And ther he *saugh* with ful avysement
> The erratik sterres, *herkenyng* armonye
> With sownes ful of hevenyssh melodie.
>
> And down from thennes faste he *gan avyse*
> This litel spot of erthe that with the se
> Embraced is, and fully *gan despise*
> This wrecched world, and *held* al vanite
> To respect of the pleyn felicite
> That is in hevene above; and at the laste,
> There he was slayn *his lokyng down he caste*,
>
> And in hymself he *lough* right at the wo
> Of hem that wepten for his deth so faste,
> And *dampned* al oure werk that foloweth so
> The blynde lust, the which that may nat laste,
> And sholden al oure herte on heven caste;
> And forth he *wente*, shortly for to telle,
> Ther as Mercurye sorted hym to dwelle. (1807-1827)[7]

When we find in these stanzas such a set of verbs, especially *despise, lough* and *dampned*, we cannot help remembering the several stanzas in Book One which describe the young Troilus when he appears in the narrative for the first time:

> This Troilus, as he was wont to gide
> His yonge knyghtes, lad hem up and down
> In thilke large temple on every side,
> *Byholding* ay the ladies of the town,
> Now here, now there; for no devocioun
> Hadde he to non, to reven hym his reste,
> But *gan to preise and lakken* whom hym leste.

> And in his walk ful faste he *gan to wayten* –
> If knyght or squyer of his compaignie
> Gan for to syke, or lete his eighen baiten
> On any womman that he koude espye.
> He wolde *smyle and holden it folye,*
> And seye hym thus, 'God woot, she slepeth softe
> For love of the, whan thow turnest full ofte!' (183-196)[8]

Then, the narrator, after severely criticizing "this fierse and proude knyght" Troilus, just like a "proude Bayard" (211-266), continues to follow this Troilus, who "leet hymselven so konnynge, / And scorned hem that Loves peynes dryen" (302-303), or "Repentynge hym that he hadde evere ijaped / Of Loves folk" (318-319). And finally,

> Right with hire look thorugh-shoten and thorugh-darted,
> Al feyneth he in lust that he sojorneth,
> And al his chere and speche also he borneth,
> And ay of Loves servantz every while,
> Hymself to wrye, at hem *he gan to smyle.* (325-329)[9]

As a matter of fact, the narrator says clearly in the opening lines that his *purpos* in this work is to tell 'The double sorwe of Troilus / In lovynge", that is to say, "how his aventures fellen / Fro wo to wele, and after out of joie" (1-5); in later lines that the narrator's tale should be "Both of his joie and of his cares colde; / And al his werk" (264-265). However, we can subsume, according to Troilus's first appearance and his last in heaven, that the narrator tells us the *double smile and despise,* that is to say, how his proud smile and contempt for the men and women in love transform to a new smile and contempt for the mortal world in general from the higher dimension of human knowledge.

Of course, the opening of the work conveys the most important message of the narrator. But it is sometimes necessary to paraphrase it as a result of our interpretation of the work. For instance, Homer begins his *Iliad,* saying: Μῆνιν ἄειδε, Θεά, Πηληϊάδεω ᾿Αχιλῆος ('The wrath dost thou sing, o goddess, of Peleus' son, Achilles.'). As a matter of fact, during his long narratives Homer's narrator focalizes on the wrath of Achilles. But in the last Book of the *Iliad*, we can certainly confirm that a sense of pity has been produced from his fierce wrath against the old Trojan King Priam, as Jinyo Kim argued recently in his *The pity of Achilles* (2000). Likewise, in the *Odyssey,* Homer's narrator says in the first line: ῎Ανδρα μοι ἔννεπε, Μοῦσα, πολύτροπον... ('Tell me, Muse, of the man of many devices, ...') It is certain that the main parts of the work are occupied by the narrative about the adventures of Odysseus, "the man of many devices". But at the same time, we can say that the subject of the work is the story of the family reunion as a result of our interpretations of the whole work.

Returning to Chaucer's *Troilus*, we must not forget the significance of the contrast between the young Troilus in the opening and the deceased Troilus in the end, because the narrator tells us carefully in detail how the young Troilus is maturing as a person by his love experience. Already at the end of Book One, the narrator says as follows:

> And in the town his manere tho forth ay
> So goodly was, and gat hym so in grace,
> That ecch hym loved that loked on his face.
>
> For he bicom the frendlieste wight,
> The gentilest, and ek the mooste fre,
> The thriftiest, and oon the beste knyght
> That in his tyme was or myghte be;
> Dede were his japes and his cruelte,
> His heighe port and his manere estraunge,
> And ecch of tho gan for a vertu chaunge. (1076-1085)

In the soliloquy in the temple in Book Four, the young Troilus, who is now three years older since his first appearance, develops his Boethian meditations on Providence and Free Will. Thus, through "his joie" and "his cares colde", his mind has been prepared to be ascended high up to the heavens.

From the famous opening lines of the work, one may easily suggest the capital letter *W* as the pattern of the narrative structure of the work. But we would like to propose the vertical structure of the narrative, at the bottom of which the young proud Troilus appears, and on the top of which the deceased Troilus peacefully sits; all other substantial narratives on his love affair are included between the bottom and the top.

In order to establish such a vertical narrative structure, the idea of ascending to heaven is indispensable. If we confine our perspective within the European context, we can easily refer to Plato's *Timaeus*, or Plotinus' *Enneades*, or other medieval Platonic authors, or Dante's *Divine Comedy* and Boccaccio's *Teseida*. But, all over the world, there are the countless myths, tales, and legends concerning human and superhuman beings who fly away into Heaven; such a universal diffusion of the symbolism of ascension is based upon the essential longing of human beings for absolute freedom from the inevitable human conditions. The symbolism of ascension has been explored extensively by Mircea Eliade in his monumental writings, and especially in his article, "Symbolisms of Ascension and 'Walking Dreams'" which was included in his

Myths, dreams and mysteries: The encounter between contemporary faiths and archaic realities (1960).

Finally, we can say that, although Chaucer's narrator is undoubtedly Christian, his imagination about Troilus's ascension to heaven is deeply rooted in the human longings since our archaic culture. Troilus's laughing at the grief of those who weep for his death or his despising of this wretched world when he is in heaven must be interpreted as his absolute freedom and transcendence from the inevitable human condition.

Notes

[1] All quotations from Chaucer are from *Riverside*.

[2] The original Latin quotation is from Meister (1873); the English translation from Frazer (1966).

[3] The original Latin quotation is from Eisenhut (1973); the English translation from Frazer (1966).

[4] The original Old French quotation is from Costans (1907); the Modern French translation from Baumgartner (1987).

[5] The original Latin quotation is from Griffin (1936); the English translation from Meek (1974).

[6] The original Latin quotation is from Riddehough (1951); the English translation from Roberts (1970).

[7] Italics are mine.

[8] Italics are mine.

[9] Italics are mine.

References

Baumgartner, Emmanuèle (trans.)
    1987   *Le Roman de Troie de Benoît de Sainte-Maure*. Paris: Union Générale d'Editions.

Boitani, Piero (ed.)
    1989   *The European tragedy of Troilus*. Oxford: Clarendon.

Costans, Leopold (ed.)
1907 *Roman de Troie.* (SATF.) Paris: Libraire de Firmin-Didot.

Eisenhut, Werner (ed.)
1973 *Ephemeridos Belli Troiani libri.* (2nd, revised and enlarged edition.) Leipzig: Teubner.

Eliade, Mircea
1960 *Myths, dreams and mysteries: The encounter between contemporary faiths and archaic realities.* New York: Harper & Row.

Frazer, R.M., Jr. (trans.)
1966 *The Trojan War: The chronicles of Dictys of Crete and Dares the Phrygian.* Bloomington, Ind.: Indiana University Press.

Griffin, N.E. (ed.)
1936 *Historia Destructionis Troiae.* (Medieval Academy of America, Publication 26.) Cambridge, Mass.: Medieval Academy of America.

Kim, Jinyo
2000 *The pity of Achilles: Oral style and the unity of the Iliad.* Lanham, Maryland: Rowman & Littlefield.

Lloyd-Jones, Hugh (ed. & trans.)
1996 *Sophocles Fragments.* (The Loeb Classical Library.) London *et al.*: Heinemann *et al.*

Meek, Mary E. (trans.)
1974 *Historia Destructinis Troiæ [by] J. Guido delle Colonne.* Bloomington, Ind.: Indiana University Press.

Meister, Ferdinand (ed.)
1873 *Daretis Phrygii de Excidio Troiæ Historia.* Leipzig: Teubner.

Riddehough, G.B. (ed.)
    1951   *Bellum Troianum*. PhD dissertation. Harvard University.

Roberts, G. (trans.)
    1970   *Joseph of Exeter: The Iliad of Dares Phrygius*. Cape Town: Balkema.

Root, Robert K.
    1917   "Chaucer's Dares". *Modern Philology* 15: 1-22.

Root, Robert K. (ed.)
    1926   *The book of Troilus and Criseyde by Geoffrey Chaucer*. Princeton: Princeton University Press.

Between penance and purgatory: Margery Kempe's *Pélerinage de la vie humaine* and the idea of salvaging journeys

Liliana Sikorska (Poznan, Poland)

Pilgrims and pilgrimages were one of the most characteristic sights of the medieval world. Treated both literally as a form of penance and metaphorically as life's journey, pilgrimage/travel becomes a literary trope which still continues to occupy the minds of scholars as a psychological as well as sociological phenomenon.

In Catholic Poland, masses of people travel on foot (or even wheelchairs) to the Marian shrine and monastery in Częstochowa, the central place of pilgrimage in Poland, to meet on 15th August, the feast of Assumption. In August, pilgrims and pilgrimages appear in the various news media. The language of the news is that of information; where the pilgrims leave from; how long they will walk and who organized the pilgrimage. Locations and numbers, sometimes short interviews with the participants who verbalize their particular intentions as to what they want to achieve through their 'pilgrimaging' (some are clearly there to have some form of holiday and meet other people). But while August pilgrimages make the news, the spiritual context of the travel apart from singing and loud prayers is by and large neglected from the point of view of the reportage. Still, in some ways, the pilgrims' motives and drive are similar to those of medieval pilgrims, namely to atone for one's sins, to be given the grace of God in particular matters, to pray for themselves and others and, finally, to cleanse themselves of sin.

Called by Clarissa Atkinson (1983) a mystic and a pilgrim, Margery Kempe is one of the most famous medieval pilgrims.[1] The entire Book One of *The book of Margery Kempe* (1438)[2] is permeated with narratives of various journeys, the reasons for which are not always stated; mostly she undertakes various trips abiding by the inner imperative, the voice of Jesus. As Roland Maissonneuve (1982) argued persuasively, her character is akin to the figure of the fool of God, or a perfect fool, always following the will of God while patiently bearing abuse and shame. Yet, in the much less discussed Book Two, Margery becomes concerned with various aspects of her travels besides the spiritual one. She becomes painfully aware of the clash between the spirituality of pilgrimage and the physicality of travelling.

This paper is an attempt to revise Maissonneuve's views and contrast the idea of the fool of God which Margery resembles in Book One with the character of Margery Kempe from Book Two where she becomes a more conscious, or one could even say, archetypal traveler (despite the fact that she herself always feels to be the chosen one, Christ's singular love), whose inner voice compels her to leave her dwelling place and undertake the penitential but at the same time 'purgatorial' journey for the sake of another human being and not herself. Rewriting the pilgrimage of the life of man, she does not pose as an Everyman, although her *Book* is to be an example for others to follow. In Book Two, her trips testify to her 'singular' grace but create the image of Margery Kempe, the textual character, a wandering saint. Early in the *Book*, Kempe abandons the Old Testament ideal of a large family and devotion to family life and embarks on her *iter asceticum*, following the New Testament model of solitary, spiritual life ('life on the road' one almost wants to say), propagated by Jesus and his followers.

St. Paul urged Christians to think about themselves as *peregrini* 'pilgrims'. Christianity perceived pilgrimage as the symbol of an individual life's journey. The motif of a journey-pilgrimage is reiterated in secular and religious literature with its two 'extremes' Chaucer's 'realistic' pilgrims and Lydgate's allegorical Pilgrim. These texts make up the mosaic of medieval *peregrine*, detailing the voyages of the one who wanders the land for his/her penance and edification. In Chaucer's version, we see the micro scale of human life, the penitential journey becomes a pretext to show the panorama of medieval society, whereas in Lydgate's *Pilgrimage of the life of man* (1426) we see pilgrimage on a macro scale: it is life's journey from birth to death, a journey inadvertently leading each and every human being to the last things. After all, even the funeral procession brings to mind, literally and metaphorically, a journey – the final one. The eschatological thinking is present in both Chaucer's and Lydgate's works as both portray pilgrimage as a spiritual and devotional obligation. Both encourage the readers/participants to see pilgrimage as an active ascetic practice in the name of atonement for human weakness. Chaucer supports the view that during such a journey each and every participant is a humble pilgrim whose earthly belongings and status are of no importance for spiritual matters. Lydgate, using personifications of sins and virtues, offers his readers an allegorical representation of life. And it is the allegory that helps to look at one's life from a distance and be ready for a change of heart, while going *per pedes apostolorum*. Lydgate reminds his readers of the necessity to learn the highest truth, namely the fleeting passage of time and the inevitability of death: "Pylgrymes schal the verray trouthe lerne" (Lydgate, 1. 82). There are two prologues in *The pilgrimage of the life of man*. Lydgate's translation of Deguileville's prologue is directed to the reader. In his own prologue, Lydgate recounts how he wrote the first version to his prologue and lost it afterwards, and how he writes another. He tells the readers of his dream of the glorious Jerusalem and promises to take them to the heavenly city. The spirit of penitence occasions a mass pilgrimage in search of Truth in Langland's *Piers Plowman*, but the pilgrims get lost and because of their own ignorance cannot find/see Truth. They meet a professional Pilgrim, whose lack of knowledge of where Truth is expresses Langland's criticism of pilgrims, their motives and the significance of such penitential journeying.

Margery Kempe is never referred to as a pilgrim in the *Book*. She goes on pilgrimages as a penitent with tears of contrition "for hir owyn synnes and sumtyme for oþer mennys synnes also" (*The book*, 61). Although she is frequently drawn towards heavenly things, as Christ promises her bliss in heaven,[3] she is not immune to falling from grace. Her life, just like the allegorical journey of Lydgate's Pilgrim's, is to provide a model. Through its roots in reality of everyday life of late medieval England, it is much more plausible than those of the early Christian saints. In allegorical literature, Man is a pilgrim on earth traveling through the land of exile towards his celestial home. The pilgrimage of the life of Margery Kempe is also to end in heaven as Christ declares in their numerous conversations. Margery's *peregrinatio vitae* is on the one hand reminiscent of the journey each and every fool of God undertakes, a slow progression from one humiliation to another. On the other hand, her pilgrimages are evocative of the purgatorial mortifications, and strengthen her argument about *discretio spirituum*, God's voice inside her consequently reinforcing her claims to holiness. Kempe's motives are akin to the motives of those whose life was devoted to *peregrinatio pro Christi amore*, those specific pilgrimages which link the allegorical and literal dimensions of traveling.

In Book One, Margery travels with her husband a number of times: firstly, to secure for herself the vows of chastity, to which both John and herself have to agree and for which both have to be present in front of the bishop; secondly, to meet various religious people and ecclesiastical authorities including the famous Julian of Norwich and other well recognized persons. Naturally, as a devout woman, she

> had a desyr to se þo placys wher he was born & wher he sufferyd hys Passyon & wher he deyd, wyth oþer holy placys wher he was in hys lyue & also aftyr hys Ressurrexyon (*The book*, 32)

and Christ promises her pilgrimages to Rome and Jerusalem. The pilgrimage to Jerusalem seems to be a particular instance of devotional travel

> [a]lthough the sterner moralists such as Gregory of Nyssa and Anthony the hermit warned against the frivolities of pilgrimage, which easily degenerated into the

love of travel for its own sake, the Christians journeying to Jerusalem increased steadily in numbers. (Barber 1991: 15)

Margery never wants to go on her own account but is fulfilling Christ's will, at the same time satisfying her curiosity to see holy places in foreign lands. Her faith travel responds to the deeply ingrained motifs, impulses, which according to Webb (2002: xv) were older and wider than Christianity. As Margaret Wade Labarge says:

> The desire for pilgrimage was obviously strong among the great as among the simple and continued with quite astonishing force until the end of the Middle Ages and beyond. Pilgrimage in some shape or form has been a constant human passion. By the end of the Middle Ages it seems to have had a strong admixture of wanderlust and curiosity as well. (Labarge 1983: 95)

For some pilgrims, as Langland demonstrated, holy thoughts and penitence could well be balanced by the love of adventures, and the search for Truth is never completed.

While insisting on spiritual marriage, Margery wants to rid herself of conjugal debt but first and foremost her prerogative is to be able to travel without restraint. This is why she wants to be given the ring and the mantle, the symbols of her separation from her husband. Apart from legal there were also financial considerations, which run ever present throughout the entire *Book*. Margery pays the debts of her husband, she also pays her own debts:

> ...sche preyd þe parysch preste of þe town þer sche was dwellyng to sey for hir in þe pulpyt þat, yf any man er woman þat cleymyd any dette of hir husbond or of hir þei xuld come & speke with hir er sche went, & sche, wyth þe help of God, xulde makyn a-seth to ech of hem þat þei schuldyn heldyn hem content. (*The book*, 60)

Paying her and her husband's debts before leaving town is not only an act of Christian justice but first and foremost reveals Margery as an honest businesswoman, who, at the onset of her penitential journey, wants to have a clean account both with God as well as with people (cf. Ellis 1990). Margery willingly gives herself to the care of Christ's mercy, but she is never deprived of financial worries. Such material factors are present in Book Two when she tries to excuse herself from carrying out God's plan and going on a trip with her daughter-in-law:

'I am not purueyd of gold ne of syluer sufficiently for to gon wyth as I awt to be, and, þow I wer & wolde gon, I wote wel my dowtyr had leuar I wer at hom, & perauentur þe schip-maistrys xulde not receyuyn me in-to her vessel for to gon wyth hem' (*The book*, 227)

This, in fact, calls in question Margery's absolute and utter adherence to her inner voice. Although she does show the necessary simplicity of heart, and places the love of Christ above all earthly love, she is also quite a skillful manipulator in creating her self-image or better, the image projected onto the text. As Lynn Staley (1994: 11) asserts:

One of Kempe's most important means of achieving her scrutiny of contemporary institutions is her deployment of the individual, Margery, as both a foil for and a representative of the community that she adumbrates in the numerous episodes that compose the Book.

Practical as ever, Margery takes care of her daughter-in-law who, after the death of her husband (Margery's unnamed son), lives with her for a year and a half before her friends want her to come back to Germany. She has a child in care of some friends in Prussia, no husband in England, and simply wants to return home. Margery cares for her daughter-in-law's well-being, and shows necessary Christian altruism. Still, she deliberates:

'Lord, ȝyf it wer þi wille I wolde takyn leue of my confessowr & gon wyth hir ouyr þe see.' Owr Lord answeryd to hyr thowt, seying, 'Dowtyr, I wote wel, yf I bode þe gon, þu woldist gon al redy. Þerfor I wyl þat þu speke no word to hym of þis mater'. (*The book*, 225-226)

Christ is not anxious for her to go, and she herself begins to feel her age (66), after all, she is now an elderly lady, for whom such trips might be dangerous. Still, she decides to accompany her daughter-in-law to Ipswich as the necessary sacrifice of a wandering saint who exchanges the comforts of home with the inconveniences of exile. Margery does not seem particularly eager to go, perhaps remembering that she was in great peril before. Thus, she is reluctant to put her life in jeopardy once again. And moreover, she has hurt her foot, about which her confessor reminds her. But as a true good Christian, fool of God, she trusts the Lord again, and as the two women walk out of Lynne and stop at a church

þe forseyd creatur, desiryng teerys of deuocyon, not myth purchasyn at þat tyme but euyr was comawndyd in hir hert for to gon ouyr þe see wyth hir dowtyr. Sche wolde a putt it owt of hir mende, & euyr it cam a-geyn so fast þat sche myth not rest ne qwiet han in hir mende but euyr was labowryd & comawndyd to gon ouyr þe see. (*The book*, 226)

Margery is tormented by various worries but she is a true *peregrinus* (or perhaps *peregrina*), whose life is to carry the aura of holiness, because of her ceaseless wandering. Like the knights in chivalric tales, who have to leave Camelot in order to seek adventures and undergo constant testing, Margery puts her body and general well-being in danger in order to save, or rather keep saving, her soul. Such quests never promise the return from wilderness, but always entail the never-ending, self-imposed exile similar to that of medieval monks.[4] Her last pilgrimage, more than any other before, just like for Lydgate's Pilgrim, is a quest for herself.

Kempe's attempts at accomplishing what Christ sets out for her strengthen Maissonneuve's arguments about Margery's holy simplicity. For some theologians, like the fifteenth-century scholar Nicholas of Cusa (1977: 667), the mysteries of faith were to be attained through "not knowing". Nicholas represents the conviction of learned ignorance where faith always takes precedence over knowledge. The medieval idea of the holy fool or the fool of God promoted an image of a human being who gave himself/herself entirely to God's commands. S/he was "to proclaim and live, through his word and daily life, the gospel of the beatitudes, to participate in Christ's *kenosis*, passion and divine folly of infinite love" (Maisonneuve 1982: 1). Maissonneuve stresses the spirit endorsed by Pauline writings, as in some way Christ was a fool of God, the puppet in the hands of the Almighty. One finds similar arguments, although framed in a much more extended medieval context, in Karma Lochrie's work (1991: 156-163). Lochrie concentrates on the spiritual aspect of the idea of excess of love and intensity of religious experience, while Maissonneuve highlights the physical aspects of being a fool of God, such as poverty, peregrinations and withstanding abuse and derision. Holy fools are Christ's chosen people, the choice is not theirs but His. The motto of such behavior is that of *imitatio Christi*. "They do all they can to conform themselves to his total self-surrender. They want to live his mystery of self-emptying and nakedness. They even search for all possible humiliations." (Maissonneuve 1982: 2) In some ways, perfect fools transform themselves into sacred jesters, clowns – not hesitating to perform bizarre or strange actions, if they are convinced God required them to do so. "The fool of God lives as a child, in its simplicity and purity, being the soul of compassion for those less fortunate in the world." (Maissonneuve 1982: 5) Maissonneuve proceeds with presenting Margery as a fool of God, perfect in her blind following of the voice of Christ inside her. Lochrie (1991: 157) maintains that the fool's folly begins with the excess of love, an element common to all mystical texts, which in some way attempt to channel such excess through visions and, consequently, writing.

Kempe's love for Christ, one of the pre-requisites for the fools of God, is contained in her need to experience Him. This in fact, provides yet another form of journeying, that of the mind. In many medieval sources, reading is presented as a journey of the mind. Medieval monks were urged to undertake salvaging peregrinations in their daily contemplations. The spiritual effect of such journeys was that of inward illumination. Margery's contemplations usually take the form of dialogues with Christ. Her inner life as well as her visions evince her literal perception of spiritual matters; still each and every one of her meditations resembles a journey of the mind. The excessive tears remind one of the doctrine of compunction, the pain of the spirit, a suffering resulting simultaneously from two causes: the existence of sin and our own tendency toward sin – *compunctio paenitentiae, timoris, firmidinis* – and the existence of our desire for God and even, our very possession of God. Leclercq (1988: 30) claims that it was St. Gregory who laid stress on this aspect of religious life. If the soul is hardened (*durata*) by sin and egoism, compunction is the process that softens it (*emollitur*), enabling the soul to be cleansed from rust (Leclercq 1988: 31).

> The soul illuminated by God's light, the soul which knows God, perceives in itself all that is impure and contrary to God. Thus, it is confirmed in humility, in the same attitude which had been the point of departure and the fundamental reason for its initial flight toward God. (Leclercq 1988: 33)

Kempe might not be aware of the sophisticated theological doctrine but she is familiar with the existing models of affective piety, as she has various works read to her. Richard Rolle, Bridget of Sweden and Elizabeth of Hungary are her models, undoubtedly emulated only to an extent to which she could follow the teaching of a hermit and imitate the life of aristocratic women. Although she is "not lettyrd", she understands the importance of the written word (sacred biographies that recount the lives of saints were after all passed down in written form). The insistence on textual culture or rather the awareness of the existence and the strength of textual culture is never undervalued in the *Book*. Clumsy as it may seem, Kempe repeatedly asserts her knowledge of the Bible and uses dialogue to dramatize her encounters with Christ. She also mentions a number of female models, out of which only one, Marie de Oigny, is brought up by her scribe.

> Margery seeks to emulate a written tradition which will be accepted by those in her society whom she perceives will be her audience. The purpose of hagiography is to instruct, and, according to the Church fathers, the aesthetic dimensions of hagiographic narratives were less important than the devotion it prompted. (Akel 2001: 11)

The events selected from her daily life even though not presented chronologically, express Kempe's metadesign for Margery's holy living (Akel 2001: 10). Her particular understanding of *imitatio Christi*, as many scholars noticed, is an attempt to balance the personal with the public aspects of her life. At the same time Margery's *imitatio Christi* is shaped by textual tradition of various devotional texts.[5] In a way, she chooses *vita mixta*, the life in the world with the spiritual aim in mind, so aptly summarized by Lucifer in *Wisdom* as the ideal life established by Christ himself:

> And all hys lyff was informacyon
> Ande example to man.
> Sumtyme with sinners he had conversacyon;
> sumtyme with holy also comunycayon;
> Sumtyme he laboryde, preyed; sumtyme tribulacyon;
> Thys was vita mixta þat Gode here began. (*Wisdom*, 1.425-428)

Reporting problems and hesitations about writing her *Book*, Margery is strikingly exact in her account of who wrote what, and how this whole thing came about. In Book Two, she establishes the exact temporal frame of the text. Her second scribe copied the previous manuscript of Book One and began to write Book Two beginning "in þe fest of Seynt Vital Martyr sweche grace as owr Lord wrowt in hys sympyl creatur ʒerys þat sche leuyd aftyr…" (*The book*, 221). No doubt, she is in control of the process of creation and writing. In Book Two, authority and self-definition are of less importance, as Margery feels quite confident in her role of the wandering saint. Lynn Staley notices that Margery's book is less an autobiography,[6] and more of, as Heffernan terms it, a "sacred biography":

> …[a] form increasingly translated into vernacular languages throughout the late Middle Ages. The work of Kempe's fellow East Anglians Osbern Bokenham and John Capgrave provides strong evidence of the growing public for such vernacular lives. By using Margery's life as means of scrutinizing not only the foundations of English society but also the nature of ecclesiastical and political authority, Kempe develops what was nascent in the traditions of sacred biography she would have inherited from Latin and Continental models. She also reveals her shrewd grasp of

the ways in which the issues and the language of her day could be used to signify more fundamental truths about societies; like Chaucer and Langland, she is able to convey a world whose immediacy only appears a reflection of reality. ... Written in English about an English "saint" *The book of Margery Kempe* dramatizes the weaknesses of the social and ecclesiastical institutions of an age whose need for such sanctity is acute. (Staley 1994: 37-38)

The idea of travel, of leaving home and giving herself to the mercy of others, is one of Kempe's assumptions about sainthood, which she consequently accomplishes despite the clerical and secular opposition she encounters everywhere she goes. Her piety frequently earns her people's dislike and she is left alone and exposed to slander. All such instances are patiently endured *pro amore Dei*. Spared the tribulations of early Christian saints, her form of martyrdom, thus, is that "by slander" as Gail McMurray Gibson (1989: 47) observes. I would add that Margery's martyrdom is that "by exclusion" from the various groups and communities she tries to belong to, both at home and indeed the communities of pilgrims. It is Christ's holy word:

> [s]wech holy dalyawns & spechys in hir sowle cawsyd hir to sobbyn ryth boistowsly & wepyn ful plentyuowsly. Þe mor sche wept, þe yrkar was hir man of hir cumpany & þe raþar besyd hym to gon fro hir & leeuyn hir a-lone. He went so fast þat sche myth not folwyn wyth-owtyn gret labowr & gret disese. He seyd þat he was a-ferd of enmyis & theuys þat þei xulde takyn hir a-way fro hym perauentur & betyn hym & robbyn þer-to." (*The book*, 233-234)

That was in Stralsund (Strawissownd as the *Book* names the place). Concurrently, the insults she has to endure provide the necessary amount of suffering on Earth, also indispensable in hagiography. In Book Two, although Kempe is spared the drastic accusations of being a Lollard and other such slanderous remarks, she is nevertheless not spared harsh words:

> Sum seyd it was a womanys witte & a gret foly for þe lofe of hir dowtyr-in-lawe to putte hir-self, a woman in gret age, to perellys of þe see & for to gon in-to a strawnge cuntre wher sche had not ben be-forn ne not wist how sche xulde come a-geyn. (*The book*, 228-229)

This, far from being a particularly harsh opinion, is countered by another view of those who treat the trip as an act of charity:

> Summe heldyn it was a dede of gret charite for-as-meche as hir dowtyr had be-
> forn-tyme left hir frendys & hir cuntre & cam with hir husbond to visityn hir in
> þis cuntre þat sche wolde now halpyn hir dowtyr hom a-geyn in-to þe cuntre þat
> sche cam fro. (*The book*, 229)

The balance of suffering, however, has to be preserved and going back from Germany to England, in Aachen Margery is left alone and is called a hypocrite:

> owr Lord ȝaf hir so mech swetnes & deuocyon þat sche wept and sobbyd wondyr
> sor & not myth restreyn hir-self þerfro. Þe monke was wroth & al hir felaschip for
> sche wept so sor, &, whan þei wer comyn a-geyn to her waynys, þei chedyn hir &
> rebukyd hir, clepyng hir ypocrite & seyd many an euyl worde vn-to hir. (*The
> book*, 235)[7]

Thus, like in Book One, Margery is frequently exiled from her company. The rule for such exile is clear, the more she receives from Christ, the more she is despised by her fellow Christians. What more should a true saint want?

After all, she is called by Christ to the holy life; the rejection suffered from fellow human beings, at least those who do not believe in her, is part of the struggle of the pilgrimage of life of Margery Kempe. But it is Christ himself who strengthens her in her vocation. In Book Two, Margery, a woman past her prime, is still a beloved daughter of God and during her ultimate journey to and from Germany she is repeatedly reassured by Christ:

> 'Dowtyr, þu wist wel a woman þat hath a fayr man & a semly to hir husbonde, ȝyf
> sche loue hym, sche wyl gon wyth hym wher-euyr he wil. And, dowtyr, þer is non
> so fayr & so semly ne so good as I. Þerfor, yf þu loue me, þu xalt not dredyn to
> gon wyth me wher-þat-euyr I wil hauyn þe. Dowtyr, I browte the hedyr, & I xal
> bryngyn þe hom a-geyn in-to Inglond in saf-warde. Dowte it not, but leue it ryth
> wel.' (*The book*, 233)

Such is the representation of Christ's love, "give yourself to me and I will make everything alright for you"; which woman can refuse such a declaration from a man she loves? On a serious level, though, these assertions are reminiscent of the idea of the discernment of spirits, *discretio spirituum*, a medieval ecclesiastical doctrine which validated visionary experience and aimed at distinguishing between true and false visionaries.[8] Hence, the stress Margery places on Christ's voice and will rather than on her own. Rosalynn Voaden (1999: 110) recalls that conflict and controversy surrounded the life of Margery Kempe and as such it is inscribed in the text.[9] In Book Two, Margery fulfills yet another role, that of an intermediary between God and the world, which is the role saints frequently play. In order to become a recognized holy woman, she must almost blindly obey the Church while at the same time obey the voice within her. It seems that Book One never achieves such resolution and Margery is constantly entangled in a conflict between orthodoxy and heresy. Similar to the fashionable *Lives*, such as later John Capgrave's *Life of St. Augustine*, *The book of Margery Kempe* encompasses the two archetypal extremes, a sinner and a saint, thus giving its subject a more life-like dimension of character. While her life's story can be seen as comparable to the story of Lydgate's Pilgrim, the insistence on *discretio spirituum* and Margery's numerous 'good works' maintain equilibrium between rights and wrongs suffered in the hands of others. Even though Margery thrives on expiating on the wrongs done to her by others:

> for les þan sche had an had sweche gostly comfortys it had ben vnpossybyl hir to a boryn þe schamys & wonderyngys þe whech sche suffyrd pacyently & mekely for þe grace þat God schewyd in hyr. (*The book*, 99)

After the death of her son and husband, Kempe devotes herself entirely to the well-being of her daughter-in-law. Her trip to Germany (one should call it a trip rather than a pilgrimage) is not commenced upon because of her own spiritual needs, but for more practical reasons: Her daughter-in-law, which she refers to as "daughter", being in a foreign country, and "[i]t is not goodly þat sche xulde gon so fer with a ȝong man a-lone in strawnge cuntre wher her neiþyr is knowyn" (*The book*, 226). What is voiced here are the real dangers of traveling in the Middle Ages, so aptly outlined by Jean Verdon (2003) and by Diana Webb (1999), the latter being a collection of documents on traveling and pilgrimage, and travelers' and pilgrims' experiences. Natural conditions, the weather, bad roads, thieves on land and pirates at sea provided tangible threats to the well-being of pilgrims. Margery herself articulated such fears frequently:

> many tymes, as sche went be þe wey & in þe feldys, þer fel gret leuenys wyth hedows thunderys, gresely & greuows, þat sche feryd hir þat it xulde a smet hir to deth, & many gret reynes, whech cawsyd in hir gret drede & heuynes. (*The book*, 101)

In Book Two, she is not spared the fear of dying at sea either: "þe tempestys weryn so greuows & hedows þat þei myth not rewlyn ne gouerne her schip" (*The book*, 229). Margery's adventures overseas, her meeting dishonest and evil wishing people are generally similar to what one finds in the accounts of so many of her earlier pilgrimages.[10] Her incessant penance is recognized by those "... which knewe mor of þe creaturys leuyng supposyd & trustyd þat it was þe wille & þe werkyng of al-mythy God to þe magnifying of hys own name" (*The book*, 229). Margery fulfills the will of God but she is not spared human fears and doubts. In Book Two, Christ reproves Margery for losing faith in his power:

> Owr mercyful Lord, spekyng in hir mende, blamyd hir of hyr feerdnes, seying, "Why dredist þe Why art þu so aferd? I am as mythy her in þe see as on þe londe. Why wilt þu mistrostyn me? Al þat I haue hite þe I xal trewly fulfillyn, & I xal neuyr deceyuyn þe. Suffyr paciently a while & haue trost in my mercy. (*The book*, 230)

The idea that Kempe is being chastised by God himself and suffers physical discomfort patiently clearly points to the purgatorial character of her trip. In a rather overlooked episode of a six-week stay in Gdańsk (Danzig), most probably at the end of April/beginning of May 1433, nothing is mentioned of the imminent war between the Teutonic Order Knights and Poland. Throughout the 15th century, Prussia was a tumultuous and dangerous place;[11] notwithstanding the lack of traveling company, Christ "monischyd hir to gon owt of þe cuntre" (*The book*, 231). Left to her own devices, Margery cannot choose with whom to go but simply accepts offers from, sometimes, very suspicious people, who cheat and rob her. In Aachen, she is once again "forsaken" and has to spend a night alone.

> Þe nyght fel up-on [hyr], & sche was ryth heuy, for sche was a-lone. Sche wist not wyth whom sche myth reston þat nyght ne wyth whom sche xulde gon þe next day. Þer cam preistys to hir, þer sche was at oste, of þat cuntre. Þei clepyd hir Englisch sterte & spokyn many lewyd wordys vn-to hir, schewyng vn-clenly cher & cuntenawns, proferyng to ledyn hir a-bowtyn yf sche wolde. Sche had mech drede for hir chastite & was in gret heuynes. (*The book*, 236)

While Margery has finally found lodgings with a "good wife", this was certainly one of her most frightening adventures, *locus horridus*, the sum of all of Margery's fears. Here, the *sacrum* of the pilgrimage is reduced to the *profanum* of the life on the road. In Lydgate's text, the readers become *peregrini*, and pilgrims assuredly are brothers to one another:

> ... a-mong pylgrymes, thys a lawe,
> That, as brother vu-to brother
> Euerych sholde a-byden other. (Lydgate, l. 298-301)

In Margery's case, the brotherhood or even simple Christian charity fails other people too frequently to describe all such instances here. Early medieval literature abounds in stories of expulsions. Various 'wanderers' roam medieval poetic texts lamenting their unjust lot. From the stories of Anglo-Saxon poetry to the medieval Irish Mad-Sweeney legend, exclusion, loneliness and wandering evince the harshness of human destiny of those left unprotected. Having found oneself in an environment hostile to human beings, the chances of survival for a single person in the wilderness were slim, as Margery herself learns many times in the course of her wanderings. After all, a *peregrinus*, was "...literally and originally a foreigner or stranger, and artists represented the stranger with the instantly recognizable attributes of the pilgrim" (Webb 2002: 1661).

If we treat pilgrimages as geared towards contrition and penitence, Margery's sea voyage to the North of Europe is more purgatorial in its character. In Lydgate's works as well as many other medieval works such as morality plays, sins are portrayed as thieves and rascals.[12] Setting aside inconveniences of travel, lack of hygiene and sickness, in the literal as well as metaphorical meaning, pilgrimages were beset with peril. And most commonly, hell, or in this case purgatory was other people. Margery never treats her trips as in any way 'purgatorial', although the doctrine of purgatory is known to her. Until the 12th century, the idea of purgation, *purgatories ignis* was known to the Church fathers, who contributed to the development of the purgatorial imagery. Since the 12th century, purgatory had been understood as a separate place, whose origin was traced by Jacques le Goff (1986). One of the chief issues here is that purgatory exists in time as well as in space, not unlike penitential trips, wherein the primary purpose of a soul was purgation. Grave as the metaphorical baptism in fire is, purgatory afforded temporary suffering. In order to shorten the time one would spend in purgatory, one had to atone for one's sins while still on earth by means of penance. Penance was expressed in terms of pilgrimages both far and near, and indulgences which were also articulated in terms of days, weeks and years (Webb 2002: 21), hence one of the forms of atonement was pilgrimage. Davidson (1994: 10) talks about the widespread belief in the presence of saints and apostles in heaven, as they were the ones who passed through death to bliss, without suffering the fires of purgatory. Margery Kempe is continually assured that Jesus will forgive her sins and she is promised:

> þow schalt neuyr com in Helle ne in Purgatorye, but, whan þow schalt passyn owt of þis world, wyth-in þe twynkelyng of an eye þow schalt haue þe blysse of Heuyn, for I am þe same God þat haue browt þi synnes to þi mend & mad þe to be schreve þerof. And I grawnt þe contrysyon in-to þi lyues ende. (*The book*, 17)

What is more, it is Christ who assures her that the slander she endures on Earth is sufficient purgatorial fire and atonement:

> ...þu xuldyst noon oþer Purgatory han þan slawndyr & speche of þe world, for I haue chastysed the my-self as I wolde be many gret dredys & turmentrijs þat þu hast had wyth euyl spyritys boþin slepyng & wakyng many ȝerys. & þerfor I schal preseruyn þe at þin ende thorw my mercy þat þei schal no powyr haue ouyr þe neyþyr in body ne in sowle; it is gret grace & myracle þat þu hast thy bodyly wyttys for þe vexacyon þat þu hast had wyth hem a-for-tyme. (*The book*, 51)

All the storms and sicknesses that Margery has to endure constitute part of God's grand plan as to her person which can be summarized with the words of Julian of Norwich that in the end "all shall be well".

Here, the confessional pattern which dominated mystical literature is used to stress the interconnection between the life of a(n) (erring) sinner and the life of a (forgiven and blessed) saint, an interconnection which, on a large scale, provided models of moral living by paradoxically creating a model sinner and penitent. A scribe of a holy (recognized) woman whose life was ordinary and extraordinary at the same time must have been aware of the necessary tensions between the sinful and saintly behavior of an individual. Both earlier as well as later 'lives' tend to idealize their subjects in order to grant them unquestionable sainthood.[13] Hence, *exemplar* (the exemplary) takes precedence over *historia* (the factual). The question of historical truth is yet another issue. Most of the early saints' lives blended the historical with the exemplary, offering texts in which legends are most commonly presented as verifiable sources.[14] Leclercq (1988: 162) argues that "[t]he desire to praise God in His saints is conducive to exaggeration: everything becomes admirable, and the narrative turns into a panegyric". As the saint is treated as a model Christian, it was understood that less edifying facts should be "passed over in silence – or altered" (Leclercq 1988: 162). At the time of the great upsurge of female mysticism, the Church acknowledged that the audience sought different, more plausible models.[15] The Christian community then was different from that of the early Christian times, although the demand for edifying books was still great enough to comply with what Duffy (1992: 4) calls "a voracious lay appetite for religious literature".[16]

The pattern of the saint's life includes good works and the conversion of sinners. Throughout her 'career', Margery represents herself as having the gift of foresight which was used for predicting the future and telling people what their deceased spouses do, or in the case of erring religious people, it was used to tell them their sins and call for their reform. In Book Two, Margery performs the ultimate act, that of converting a sinner by praying for (and receiving grace) in the name of her straying son. The words to describe his sin of lechery are not those of spiritual degeneration but rather those of physical ugliness: "... hys colowr chawngyd, hys face wex ful of whelys & bloberys as it had ben a lepyr"

(*The book*, 222). The mysterious sickness "for whech men fleddyn hys company & hys felaschep as for a lepyr" (*The book*, 222) disappears under the strength of Margery's prayer; her son changes. He is reformed and goes on pilgrimages. Then, as we learn, he is forgiven by God and becomes a God-fearing Christian "þe mor reuerent to-owr-Lord-ward" (*The book*, 224). The language of the passages describing his conversion does not concentrate on the son, however, but on Margery's force of prayer and the grace the Lord shows her by fulfilling her desire to change him:

> ...sche openyd hir hert to hym [her son], schewyng hym & enformyng how owr Lord had drawyn hir thorw hys mercy& be what menys, also how meche grace he had schewyd for hir, þe whech he seyd he was vnworthy to heryn. (*The book*, 224)

Again, Margery becomes the intermediary between God and her son, consulting God's will in relation to her son and of course, he "trustyd meche in hys moderys cownsel" (*The book*, 224). Here she achieves two goals: "[s]he thus audaciously promotes herself as a holy woman who is, at once, the mediator of God's mercy, the emblem of his parenthood, and the leading player in His drama of salvation" (Winstead 1994: 12). Margery represents herself as an extraordinary and ordinary person at the same time, someone who is not spared the pains of everyday life, and yet, she is Christ's chosen spouse, as if she was 'the chosen Everyman'. Unfortunately, Margery's blissful relationship with her son does not last long, even though he decides to come back home with his wife. When they arrive in England, Margery's son is overcome by a mysterious sickness and dies a day after their arrival, most probably in 1431 (*The book*, 225).[17] So in literal and symbolic terms, her son comes home. Margery does not show excessive grief, but simply notes that soon after his father followed him to the land of "wher deth xal neuyr aperyn" (*The book*, 225).

Conclusion

Life, as St. Columbán pointed out, is a road to eternity (Bitel 1993: 222). The road is infused with traps in the form of various temptations and transgressions, but at its end there is the promise of redemption and paradise. The pilgrimage of the life of man is an educative and penitential journey of metaphorical Manhood. The trope re-iterates the dramatization of Christian repentance and in a way, rephrases Lydgate's invitation to a journey; an enlightening journey of the mind. The journey itself becomes a metaphor of a change, the transformation of the sinner into the saint, or more commonly the condemned into the saved. Various difficulties awaiting the penitent on the road are chastising hardships s/he has to endure, temptations s/he has to resist and sins s/he has to avoid. Both in Book One as well as in Book Two, Kempe's narrative abounds in edifying examples of penitential voyages and purgatorial adventures. Here, the topos of life's journey is seen through the pattern of pilgrimage, being part of her 'saintly' life. In a way, her journeys are quests of Christ in the world and tests of His unending love for her. Concurrently, they are also journeys of self-discovery despite her rather self-absorbing introspection. Undertaking her pilgrimages in Book One, Margery wants to learn about God through the utmost experience of passion, and visit the places related to Christ's life and death and the places connected with the saints. Resuming her travels in Book Two, Margery Kempe becomes a wandering saint, compelled to fulfill the will of God, to complete her sacred biography. The trips articulate the need of salvation and can be related both to the vision of the medieval world of the fools of God, simpletons, eternal wanderers purging themselves through their 'pilgrimaging' as well as to the vision of the modern secular world in which a non-conforming individual can be an outcast, one who is perpetually trying to find a place in society or the community and for whom travelling/moving is the constant quest and the only form of salvation[18].

Notes

[1] Most of the critical sources on Margery's life and times discuss her pilgrimages in detail, cf. Collis (1983), Gallyon (1995), Goodman (2002).

[2] Hereafter referred to as *The book*.

[3] For the images of bliss, see Sikorska (2004).

[4] Wandering is a particular trait of many Irish saints. Many medieval Irish monks left their home in search of sanctity in foreign lands. They believed that "their deaths in the wasteland would demonstrate God's judgment on a sinner, but that their survival would bring spiritual rewards beyond anything they could find at home" (Bitel 1993: 223). Some historians attribute "the fervor of Irish exiles to genetically inspired wanderlust that drove them to row restlessly away from their rainy island" (Bitel 1993: 223). Yet, Bitel argues that forced exile was a sentence for the crimes against society: aristocratic and ecclesiastical power (1993: 223). The self-imposed exile of the monks functioned as a penitential practice. While criminals were punished by the authorities for their crimes, the monks punished themselves for their sins. The voluntary rejection of civilized life with its entitled protection by the community rendered the exiles vulnerable; but they were convinced of the righteousness of their behavior as the will of God. Such is the meaning of the self-imposed exile of the saint-traveler St. Brendan.

[5] Cf. Lochrie (2001), Staley (1994), Dinshaw (2003) and others.

[6] Because *The book of Margery Kempe* was one of the first of its kind where apart from religious and devotional content one finds a number of details of Kempe's private life, the Book was customarily presented as "spiritual autobiography" in a number of works (cf. Ross 1991 and Dinshaw 2003) to name just a few. Maissonneuve (1982: 14) also sees the text as an autobiography, whose generic specifications strengthen the argument about the depth of Margery's mystical life.

[7] The group of people with whom Margery travels to Aachen can be referred to as God's poor, as they beg their way and "before entering a city deloused themselves, a detail which suggests the appropriateness of the bequest made in 1474 by a widow of Hildesheim for the provision of two 'soul-baths' for pilgrims on their way to and from Aachen" (Webb 1999: 91).

[8] Voaden (1999: 112) argues that "scribes, editors and translators were the church's first line of defense in the battle against promulgation of false revelations".

[9] Voaden (1999: 109-10) presents the critical appraisal of Kempe's text as controversial also in contemporary literary criticism, in which mutually exclusive opinions are not infrequent.

[10] Labarge claims that pilgrimages were great undertakings even for the well-to-do, the greatest of all pilgrimages being the one to the Holy Land. Here, as in any other travel, a pilgrims' "wealth could usually provide rather minor improvements on the general conditions, since it was unwise to appear too wealthy in Moslem territory" (Labarge 1983: 72).

[11] For more on 15th century Prussia, see Carsten (1954: 73-148).

[12] In Book One, Margery was cheated and robbed several times. Once she was robbed by a priest: "...a preste wech was in her cumpany toke a-wey a schete fro þe forseyd creatur & seyd it was hys. Sche toke God to wytnesse þat it was hire schete. Than þe preste swor a gret othe, & be þe boke in hys hand, þat sche was as fals as sche mygth & dispysed hir & alto-rebuked hir" (*The book*, 67).

[13] Early Christianity devised hagiography as a dominant mode of educational literature. The lives of the saints offered supposedly real models and were pillars of the new Christian community. In the later Middle Ages, Christianity was no longer struggling with outside forces (the Roman Empire). Instead, as it spread throughout Europe, Asia and North Africa, it had to contend with infidels as well as various heresies (Cathars, Waldensians, Free Spirits and many others) within its own population. The *Omnis*

utriusque sexus decree was a device in that incessant struggle, yet the confessional manuals or sin manuals, practical as they were, aided the birth of yet another hero of medieval literature, the sinner. Such manuals provided their audience with values and forms of behavior that ecclesiastical authorities considered normative. The Church, which affirmed its authority and gained control over an individual conscience, used confession manuals and works like John Mirk's *Instructions for parish priests* to educate a self-conscious penitent, a penitent who was not only willing to change but first and foremost was aware of his transgressions, as only then was his confession valid.

[14] "The sacred biographers of the Middle Ages considered their work historical insofar as they developed categories which they reserved exclusively for this type of writing. History was a category of writing under the general aegis of grammar and had always been considered as part of the study of rhetoric. Cicero, while commenting on the difference between the annalist and the historian, remarked that the annalist was a mere recorder whose guiding principle was 'brevity without obscurity', while the historian was involved in a literary endeavor. His rhetorical skills were necessary since historical writing was either read or listened to." (Heffernan 1988: 66)

[15] Still, the importance of the biblical paradigm of Christ's life on earth, although here seeming to function in the background, is the prism through which saints' lives are seen and told. "Christ's behavior in the Gospels was the single authenticating norm for all action. For actions (*res*) narrated in the lives of the saints to be binding for the community, they had to be an *imitatio Christi*" (Heffernan 1988: 5). The particular *imitatio Christi* also dominated the reception of any of such lives.

[16] "There are two additional reasons for the primacy of the dramatic deed in medieval saints' lives: the paradigmatic actions of Christ in the New Testament and the illiteracy of the audiences for whom these texts were intended. The lives of the saints were sacred stories designated to teach the faithful to imitate actions which the community had decided were paradigmatic." (Heffernan 1988: 5)

[17] Dates quoted according to Emily Hope Allen's "Introduction" to *The book of Margery Kempe*.

[18] Interestingly, the motif of the pilgrimage as self-discovery but also quite literally as healing was used by David Lodge in the novel ominously called *Therapy*.

References

Akel, Catherine S.
2001 "'... A schort tretys and a comfortybl ..': Perception and purpose of Margery Kempe's narrative", *English Studies* 1: 1-13.

Atkinson, Clarissa W.
1983 *Mystic and pilgrim: The book and the world of Margery Kempe.* Ithaca and London: Cornell University Press.

Barber, Richard
1991 *Pilgrimages.* Woodbridge: Brewer.

Bitel, Lisa M.
1990 *Isle of the saints: Monastic settlement and Christian community in early Ireland.* Ithaca: Cornell University Press.
1993 Paperback edition.

Carsten, Francis L.
1954 *The origins of Prussia.* Oxford: Clarendon.

Cusa, Nicholas, of
1977 "On learned ignorance", in: Ross -- McLaughlin (eds.), 667-75.

Collis, Louise
1983 *The life and times of Margery Kempe.* New York: Harper and Row.

Dinshaw, Carolyn -- David Wallace (eds.)
2003 *Medieval women's writing.* Cambridge: Cambridge University Press.

Dinshaw, Carolyn
2003 "Margery Kempe", in: Dinshaw -- Wallace (eds.), 222-40.

Dyas, Dee
2001 *Pilgrimage in medieval English literature 700-1500.* Woodbridge: Brewer.

Eccles, Mark (ed)
1969 *The macro plays: The castle of perseverance, Wisdom, Mankind.* (EETS o.s. 262.) Oxford: Oxford University Press.

Ellis, Deborah
1990 "The merchant's wife's tale: Language, sex and commerce in Margery Kempe and in Chaucer", *Exemplaria* 2: 295-627.

Gallyon, Margaret
1995 *Margery Kempe of Lynn and medieval England.* Norwich: The Canterbury Press.

Gibson, Gail McMurray
1989 *The theatre of devotion: East Anglian drama and society in the late Middle Ages.* Chicago: The University of Chicago Press.

Glasscoe, Marion (ed.)
1982 *The medieval mystical tradition in England.* Exeter: University of Exeter Press.

Goodman, Anthony
2002 *Margery Kempe and her world.* London: Longman.

Heffernan, Thomas J.
1988 *Sacred biography: Saints and their biographers in the Middle Ages.* Oxford: Oxford University Press.

Kempe, Margery
1940 *The book of Margery Kempe.* Stanford N. Meech -- Hope Emily Allen (eds). (EETS, o.s. 212.) Oxford: Oxford University Press.
1993 Reprinted edition.

Krygier, Marcin -- Liliana Sikorska (eds.)
    2004   *For the loue of Inglis*. (Medieval English Mirror 1.) Frankfurt/M.: Lang.

Labarge, Margaret Wade
    1983   *Medieval travellers*. New York: W.W. Norton & Co.

Leclercq, Jean O.S.B.
    1961   *The love of learning and the desire for God: A study of monastic culture*. New York: Fordham University Press.
    1988   Reprinted edition.

Le Goff, Jacques
    1981   *The birth of purgatory*. Arthur Goldhammer (trans.). Chicago: University of Chicago Press.
    1986   Paperback edition.

Lochrie, Karma
    1991   *Margery Kempe and translations of the flesh*. Philadelphia: University of Pennsylvania Press.

Lydgate, John
    1899   *The pilgrimage of the life of man*. F.J. Furnivall (ed.), with introduction, notes, glossary and indexes by Katherine B. Locock. (EETS, e.s. 77, 83, 92.) Woodbridge: Boydell and Brewer.
    1996   Reprinted edition.

Maissonneuve, Roland
    1982   "Margery Kempe and the Eastern and Western tradition of the 'perfect fool'", in: Glasscoe (ed.), 1-17.

Ross, Ellen, M.
    1991   "Spiritual experience and women's autobiography: The rhetoric and selfhood in *The book of Margery Kempe*", *Journal of the American Academy of Religion* 3: 527-46.

Ross, James Bruce -- Mary Martin McLaughlin (eds.)
    1977   *The medieval reader.* Harmondsworth: Penguin.

Sikorska, Liliana
    2004   "Imagining heaven: Visions of bliss in medieval mystical discourse", in: Krygier -- Sikorska (eds.), 97-132.

Staley, Lynn
    1994   *Margery Kempe's dissenting fictions.* University Park: The Pennsylvania State University Press.

Turner, Victor -- Edith Turner
    1978   *Image and pilgrimage in Christian culture.* New York: Columbia University Press.

Verdon, Jean
    2002   *Travel in the Middle Ages.* George Holoch (trans.). Notre Dame: University of Notre Dame Press.

Voaden, Rosalynn
    1999   *God's words, women's voices: The discernment of spirits in the writing of late medieval visionaries.* York: York Medieval Press

Voragine, Jacobus de
    1993   *The golden legend: Readings on the saints.* William Grynger Ryan (trans.). 2 vols. Princeton: Princeton University Press.

Webb, Diana
    1999   *Pilgrims and pilgrimage in the Medieval West.* (International library of historical studies 12.) London: I.B. Tauris.

    2002   *Medieval European pilgrimage.* Houndmills: Palgrave.

Winstead, Karen A.
1994 "The conversion of Margery Kempe's son", *English Language Notes* 2: 9-13.

Malory's critique of violence before and just after the oath of the Round Table

Carol Kaske (Ithaca/NY, USA)

1. Introduction

Violence in the Middle Ages at large is a huge and complex topic. It is a sometimes contested commonplace that, in life and in literature, chivalry served to circumscribe a violence that had previously ruled almost unchecked.[1] The relation of chivalry and violence in Malory in particular has been much discussed. I will address recent work by Lynch, Whetter, and Kennedy. Kennedy strives for moral closure and hence is more suitable for teaching undergraduates; Lynch and Whetter problematize Malory's attitude toward violence, finding it to be a "strangely double view of war" (cf. Whetter 2004: 181, and n. 43; Lynch 1997: 35) and hence they are better for teaching graduate students; both projects unearth evidence that illuminates Malory's work. All would agree that Malory occasionally expresses criticism of the violence of a particular source-passage by changing it, or of the bloodlust of a particular character by having him rebuked for it or praised for restraining it. Whetter and Lynch scorn these approaches, but obviously sometimes Malory does this, and undergraduates need to cut their teeth on these approaches before proceeding to the high mysteries. My first two examples – *The Tales of Balin* and of Arthur's Roman war – are more or less acknowledged to contain some such critiques of violence, and I have found new and at times peculiar examples of them. My two final examples – Sir Brian of the Isles and horse-replacements – have not to the best of my knowledge been recognized as critiques of violence, and they critique violence in an exaggerated way, thus illustrating what Lynch calls Malory's "split consciousness". Looking for this theme in all four passages can explain peculiar actions on the part of the characters and deviations from the source on the part of the author. The pious tone of the Grail Quest renders restraints on violence less remarkable there, hence I will not talk about it; my examples all occur prior to the Grail Quest; indeed, they come from Caxton's first five books, that is, the Winchester MS's first two.[2] Arthur and Sir Brian of the Isles illustrate long-range character development; and Arthur and Balin bear some relation to the Oath of the Round Table (3.15) – an oath which reads in part:

never to do outrageousity nor murder, and always to flee treason; also, by no mean to be cruel, but to give mercy unto him that asketh mercy, upon pain of forfeiture of their worship and lordship of King Arthur for evermore; and always to do ladies, damosels, and gentlewomen succour, upon pain of death.

The Winchester MS adds "strengthe hem in their rightes, and never to enforce them", that is "rape them".

2. Balin and the Roman war

The above mentioned part of the oath can be seen as belatedly rebuking Balin and altering the character of Arthur and so bringing to these episodes a degree of moral closure that undergraduate readers need in order to find their moral compass in this complex work. It is obvious that the moral, insofar as there is one, of Caxton Book II, the Book of Balin, is 'don't be too quick to act' and 'don't put too much force into your blows'. In Chapter 5, in a fair fight, Balin kills Sir Lanceor, who has been sent from Arthur to bring him back to court; in the process, he occasions the suicide of Lanceor's lover Colombe. It is to highlight these pacifistic morals, I propose, that Malory drags in the seemingly digressive prophecy that Lancelot and Tristram will fight on this very spot, "and yet none of them shall slay other" (Caxton 2.7-8). On the simplest and most moralistic level, they are dragged in because they exhibit more restraint than does Balin, thus functioning as a rebuke to him. In the source, which for Balin is the *Merlin continuation* in the *Post-Vulgate*, the prophecy occurs but it ends with "neither will die" – which lacks the moral point.[3] The rebuke of fighters who kill their opponents and the praise of fighters (including one of the same fighters, Lancelot) who manage not to come up again explicitly in the Grail Quest. So far, the moral is clear. But it is hard to see what Balin could have done differently in this instance, except snatch the sword from the lady while she was in a swoon. A tragic fate also dogs Balin and renders his best-laid plans destructive; Balin is not only sword happy but sword unhappy: almost everyone he strikes, he kills; and to this extent there is no moral and the prophet is just telling us that there are luckier people than Balin who live in a more benevolent universe.

Before the oath, in Book One, in the battle with the eleven kings, Merlin rebukes Arthur as follows:

> Thou hast never done, hast thou not done enough? Of three score thousand this day has thou left alive but fifteen thousand, and it is time to say 'Ho!' For God is wroth with thee, that thou wilt never have done... (Caxton 1.17)

In the French source – "The story of Merlin" in the Vulgate cycle – the condemnation is there, but it is milder and shorter: "King Arthur, what are you trying to do? Isn't it enough that you have thoroughly beaten your enemies? Go back to your land" (cf. Pickens 1993: 233). This is criticism by overt condemnation.

Another vehicle of criticism is praise of restraint. Even Arthur's enemies praise Arthur's restraint in one instance: "Let us put our foot-men from us ... for the noble Arthur will not tarry on the foot-men, for they may save themselves" (Caxton 1.16). Then at the end of Book III, comes the oath, administered by Arthur, but obviously devised by a greater mind than his or at least by a nobler part of himself. Then in Caxton Book V, the account of Arthur's Roman war, after Arthur has been crowned at Rome, he assents to his men's request to go home, saying, "for to tempt God it is no wisdom" even adding temperately in the Winchester MS "enough is as good as a feast". Malory added this to the source, in which Arthur does exactly the opposite. In the *Alliterative Morte Darthur*, Arthur says in effect, "That was fun. Now let's go on a crusade" (Hamel 1984: 1. 3206-3217).[4] Malory's Arthur exhibits that restraint which Merlin and the oath enjoined upon him.

Arthur develops chivalry towards women too, and I submit that this also comes about because of the oath. Back in Caxton Book III, chapter 5 before the oath, Arthur shrugged off a damsel who came to court to complain of an injury, only to suffer a graver injury, and Merlin rebuked him for doing so. Then came the oath. Then in Caxton Book V in the Roman war, as Vinaver and Hamel note, Arthur shows kindness to enemy women and Malory makes their pleas for mercy more philosophically compelling than in the source. The women are trying to dissuade Arthur from razing their city and slaughtering all its inhabitants. They appeal to the rights of innocent bystanders; as they say in the Winchester MS: "for then shal dye many a soule that grevid thee never". In line with the Oath, which of course is not in the source, Arthur consents to receive the keys of the city in peace, assures them that neither they nor the women of their households will be sexually molested, and commands his men accordingly. Even though this book has a different source from the rest, Malory portrays Arthur's character as becoming a bit more pacifistic than he was, and he modifies the source to do so. Incidentally, this gradual development in his character supports Lumiansky's thesis of unity across the boundaries of the tales as against Vinaver's claim that "Arthur and Lucius" is a tale separate unto itself.

Of course, I must admit that Malory harbors another motive for these revisions besides a simple critique of violence. The source shows Arthur degenerating and becoming a warmonger who is recalled from embarking on another war (as mentioned above) only by a premonitory dream (Hamel 1984: 1.

3206-3217) and by news that his caretaker Mordred has taken over his kingdom and his wife. If Malory really wanted to limit violence, someone might object, he could have just have gone along with "the anti-war spirit"[5] of his source. At the end of the *Morte Darthur*, Malory does show some "anti-war spirit" – a spirit deriving indirectly and in part from this source; there his Arthur too will degenerate into a warmonger (in this case under Gawain's influence) and be called home too late by just this turn of events, and as in the *Alliterative Morte Darthur*, he will die attempting to recover his realm and his wife. But Malory does not want to have the catastrophe just yet and he does want to retain the forceful Arthur of the *Alliterative Morte Darthur* without his taint of bloodthirstiness. This is another reason why he chooses to portray Arthur in the Roman war as not too bloodthirsty, occasionally merciful, and knowing when to stop. As we have seen, this Arthur has already manifested the flaw attributed to him by the *Alliterative Morte Darthur* in 1.11, and he has evidently corrected it, I suggest, because of the Oath which he has promulgated and therefore must uphold. Malory made this paragon more interesting by having him start as a potential berserker (1.11) and an insensitive boor about women (3.5) and be educated into restraint by the oath.

If these instances of an Arthur who was selfish before the oath and raising his moral standards after the oath have been convincing, readers might perceive the same selfish Arthur destined to reform in his cruel exposure of the so-called May-day children (1.27), leading to the deaths of all but Mordred. As Kennedy (2003: 164) says, Malory does not mention this act again, let alone present the Fall of the Round Table as its punishment. I suggest that this is so because after the oath's prohibition of cruelty, Arthur learns to rein in such violent tendencies.

3. Sir Brian of the Isles and musical horses

Now let us look at two neighbouring incidents which place limitations on violence even though they occur before the oath and independently of it. They do so in morally complex ways.

In Caxton Book III, chapter 13, right before the oath, Malory portrays a virtual pacifist, someone who not only proleptically agrees with the oath but goes beyond it – an anomaly in Malory's chivalric economy. "There is no trace of this long dialogue in French", notes Vinaver (cf. Malory 1973: 117, MS 43^r). A knight describes the pacifist as follows in the Winchester MS: "my sworne brother, a passynge good knyght, and hys name is Bryan of the Ilis, and he ys full lothe to do ony wronge or to fyght with ony man but if he be sore sought on", and Caxton adds, "so that for shame he may not leave it". Brian's pacifism implies that most chivalric combat is 'wrong'. Yet, the interlocutor does not scorn him as a milksop, but says with modern-sounding casualness, "Bring him to the court ... one of these days". This indicates that Malory adds Sir Brian's pacifism to the French source of Caxton 3.13 in order to make a pacifistic point, and thus was of two minds about knightly combat. This peculiar knight, especially in Caxton where he never recurs and never fights, represents a metapoetic moment, a critique of chivalry itself from a viewpoint so high minded as to be alien to all of Malory's *Morte* except the Grail Quest. He functions as a silent rebuke to the other characters just as Sir Lancelot and Sir Tristram do to Balin. Edmund Spenser inserts such a moment in his chivalric romance *The Faerie Queene* when his Hermit Contemplation says to a young knight, "And [in old age, after a successful chivalric career] wash thy hands from guilt of bloudy field, / For bloud can nought but sin, and wars but sorrow yield" (Spenser 1977: I.x.60). Both virtual pacifists are too good for this world, but their message may be what their authors really believed, at least in some moods. Note that Malory's pacifistic sentiments here are not dictated by Christianity as Spenser's are, and as Malory's will be later in the Grail Quest; Brian's is just another point of view.

In the Winchester MS only, in another part of the work, the Roman war (MS 81^v), Malory provides an interesting development that somewhat reconciles Sir Brian's pacifism with the values of those around him and thus offers the puzzled undergraduate reader some moral closure. He includes an uncharacterized Sir Brian without a toponym in a roll-call of Arthur's knights in his Roman war. He had found this Sir Brian in the source for this part of the work, the *Alliterative Morte Darthur*.[6] This fighter's character is enriched by Malory's having characterized him as a pacifist in Caxton 3.13. The brief mention here indicates what circumstances would drive this pacifist to fight – an international war in a national emergency, triggered by a foreign king's supposedly unjust demand for tribute, backed by threats. Thus, in the Winchester MS, Brian's rejection of chivalry proves to be not so categorical.

For my final example, let us go back to the beginning, to the war with the eleven kings treated in Section I (Caxton 1.14-17): We have seen Arthur's violence overtly criticized and his forbearance overtly praised there. Now let us look at exemplary actions of other knights through which Malory laboriously strives to cast a rosy haze over violence. We are asked to believe that a large proportion of the battle is taken up with a lengthy series of actions so bizarrely repetitive that they sound like something out of *Monty Python and the Holy Grail*: it is the game of musical horses, or rehorsing fallen comrades by unhorsing an enemy. An attacker's first goal is to get a horse for his unhorsed friend. I propose that Malory is trying to portray battle as a matter of helping your friends more than hurting your foes. Indeed, in real life, loyalty, camaraderie, or male bonding is often said to be a principal motive for fighting once men get into any battle.

The first four rehorsings are identical in both the French and Malory's version (see my Appendix, numbers 1-4, and so are both of the numbers 9). But in number 7, Griflet smites an anonymous knight and gives the victim's horse to Sir Lucan, and Caxton's version of Malory adds, departing from the sources (and also as it happens, from the Winchester MS): "For Brastias had slain a knight tofore and horsed Griflet". Malory's number 7 illustrates that you do not have to rehorse the person who rehorsed you; if that is not possible, you should rehorse anybody just to keep the favors circulating. The Winchester MS just says "because Brastias had slain a knight tofore" which makes no sense as a motive; many knights slew other knights. Malory or Caxton must have introduced Brastias's previous rehorsing of Griflet to emphasize that one rescues people because one has oneself been rescued, especially if like Griflet one has been rescued twice, the last time without passing on the favor. Also in a tournament a few pages earlier, Lucan had rehorsed Griflet (1.11) without being rehorsed by him in return. A skeptic would say that Malory mistakenly wrote Brastias here when he meant Lucan; if we were to emend "Brastias" to "Lucan", the pattern of reciprocation would be complete. But there is some evidence of a different sort of pattern subtending the text as we have it. The point is that Griflet has had to be rescued twice in this battle and once in the preceding tournament, never mind by whom. This is because he is portrayed as young and hence not so great a warrior as are his rescuers – Kay, Lucan, and Brastias. This point will be confirmed retrospectively when Griflet will subsequently be involved in a patent youth-age contrast in his fight with Pellenore: Pellenore tries to dissuade him from the unequal contest; once Griflet forces Pellenore to fight him and receives the inevitable defeat, Pellenore does not finish him off but helps him back onto his horse and points him in the direction of home (1.22-23) – another act of charity to the young expressed partly in terms of rehorsing.

Dante said that charity is a good undiminished by sharing, and the same is true of camaraderie. Malory dramatizes that it is in fact increased by it, for Lucan in his turn immediately proceeds to slay two anonymous young knights and rehorse two of his downed comrades, thus showing the productivity of such mutual assistance in the chivalric economy. (Malory, number 8). This is not in the source, where the rehorsed Lucan (French version, number 8) goes on to rescue someone else but nothing is said about horses; then Lucan merely *helps* two comrades hoisting two other comrades back onto their own horses (cf. Pickens 1993: 230-31). This is messy and barely counts as a horse replacement at all, and Malory condenses it meaningfully: he attributes the double rehorsing to Lucan and Lucan alone and makes him in the process kill two of the enemies.

What sounded ridiculous is now emerging as a repetition with significant moral variations on the themes of youth and altruism.

Even Malory's enemies play the horse-replacement game – three of them in one terse and original paragraph (1.14). In the French, only one of the enemies rehorses another (event number 2). Malory adds three other horse-replacements – the King with the Hundred Knights again and King Lot twice – for a total of four (1.16). These horse-replacements on the part of the enemy seem to be one more instance of their general *esprit de corps* which is praised in moving terms throughout this particular war. As Lynch (1997 and 2000) says, the bad guys must not be portrayed as too bad because this is a civil war and all the combatants will live together side by side as one nation later in the book. A contrast proves Malory's purpose. In the next great battle – the Roman war – no horse replacements occur. One reason is that Malory is certainly not eager to praise the *esprit de corps* of the Romans and their Saracen allies. But not even the good guys do it. In the War with the Eleven Kings, Malory was not narrating history but making a point about the possibility of infusing violence with altruism. A similarly rosy view of war was projected in the film *Forrest Gump* with Tom Hanks in the title role. Forrest Gump never attacked an enemy; we only saw him running to the field hospital carrying wounded friends.

Most of these horse-replacements are more or less modeled on the French source (see my Appendix); but Malory not only adds three on the part of the bad guys, as we have seen, and sharpens the double one on our side, but also by his characteristic pruning subtracts so much of the other action that they all stand in high relief.[7] In the French source, Kay snags a stray horse and gives it to his fallen father Ector (whom the French version calls Antor, cf. number 5; see Vinaver's notes to pages 29.23-30 in Malory 1973). The rehorsed Antor smites down Morganor and gives his horse to Brastias (whom the French version calls Bretel, cf. number 6). Malory's Kay obtains a horse for his fallen father Ector in the martial way by smiting down Morganor and taking his (Malory, number 5). Malory even paid a price for this change: because he has already used up Morganor in this way, he has to invent a new enemy, Lardans, whose horse can be given to Brastias (Malory, number 6). Considered in isolation, using a stray horse seems more pacifistic, so am I wrong about the meaning of Malory's changes? Malory dislikes using a stray horse, apparently because it earns no glory. Evidently he is not advocating pacifism here, he is imbricating an altruistic motive with warfare's two selfish motives: winning glory and conquering the enemy. These competitive purposes Malory wants not to eliminate but to gild and temper with his third and somewhat contradictory value, loyalty, camaraderie or fellowship, so he emphasizes and even adds horse-replacements. He is trying here to moderate competitiveness, not eliminate it, much as he did with Arthur's acts of mercy at the siege. With an awkwardness betraying a split consciousness, Malory works some degree of altruism into a violent code which he is unwilling to condemn categorically.

4. Conclusion

Both Malory's tempering of Arthur's violence in the Roman war and his imbrication of violence with fellowship in the musical-horses game illustrates the truth of the conventional wisdom that chivalry in general and Malory in particular tempered violence by attributing to it some social benefits. But the contrast between the intrinsic violence of chivalry and the almost total pacifism of Sir Brian of the Isles indicates that on violence as on love Malory is not consistent. Like Whetter (2004) and Lynch (1997 and 2000), I feel that Malory wanted his work to be somewhat dialogic because this corresponded to his ambivalent view of this topic. Perhaps dialogism also was prized by his audience as an occasion for courtly debates after the nightly reading in the great hall. As Richard Kaeuper (2000: 29, cf. also 33) says in his fine article on violence in the Vulgate cycle: there may well be "an internal debate ... on the causes, scale, and consequences of the knightly prowess so highly prized in high society" analogous to the recognized internal debate about love.

5. Appendix: Horse-replacements in Caxton 1.14-16

Events between ** are not in the French source. Events with the same numbers correspond, sometimes with changes.

5.1. Horses in the French source[8]

1	p. 230: Kay smites King Neutres and rehorses Girflet.
2	King with Hundred Knights smites Kay and rehorses King Lot.
3	Girflet and Lucan smite two anonymous enemies and give one of the horses to Kay. (Who gets the other? We never hear. It is messy.)
4	Arthur smites King Tradelment and rehorses Ulfin.
5	p. 231: Kay captures a riderless horse and rehorses his father Antor (=Ector).
6	Antor smites Morganor and rehorses Bretel (=Brastias).
7	Girflet smites an anonymous enemy and rehorses Lucan.
8	Lucan rescues Malruc of the Rock. Malruc helps two companions helping two other companions back onto their horses. (It is messy, and it hardly counts as a horse-replacement.)

9   p. 233: Arthur kills an anonymous enemy and rehorses Ban.

5.2. Horses in Malory

1   1.14: Kay smites King Nentres and rehorses Griflet, also smites King Lot.
2   1.14: King with Hundred Knights smites Kay and rehorses Lot.
3   1.14: Griflet smites Pinel and rehorses Kay.
           Enemies (King with Hundred Knights again, and Lot twice) rehorse three of their men.
4   1.14: Arthur smites King Cradelment and rehorses Ulfius.
           1.14: *King with a Hundred Knights smites Sir Ector, Kay's father, and rehorses King Cradelment.*
5   1.14: Kay smites Morganor and rehorses his father Ector.
6   1.14: Ector smites *Lardans* and rehorses Brastias.
7   1.14: Griflet smites an anonymous enemy and rehorses Lucan *because Brastias had rehorsed him at some time in the past [this is not in the Winchester MS either].*
8   1.14: Lucan slays two anonymous bachelors and rehorses Bellias of Flanders and Gwinas.
9   1.16: Arthur kills an anonymous enemy and rehorses Ban.

Notes

[1] Contested, for instance, by Kaeuper (2000: 34-5) and Lynch (2000: 24-41; 1997, passim).

[2] For ease of reference, I will cite Caxton unless the Winchester MS presents significant differences; for Caxton quotations, I employ the modernized spelling of Malory (1969). For the Winchester MS, I will cite Malory (1973), with the page of the MS for the benefit of those who are using other editions.

[3] Chapter 9 of Asher (1993: 185-91).

[4] Malory's significant departures from the *Alliterative Morte* include the addition of "Malorian dialogs and name-catalogs"; also "the criticism of Arthur's imperialism is removed and that of his arrogance of character much softened", according to Hamel (1984: 6).

[5] Vinaver's phrase, 1369, quoted from William Matthews (1966).

[6] A Sir Bryane appears as a fighter in the *Alliterative Morte Darthur*, (cf. Hamel 1984: l. 1606 and 1744), again without toponym or characterization. At l. 1606, Hamel's note identifies the Sir Bryane of the *Alliterative Morte Darthur* with the fighter "Sir Bryan de les ylyes" in the Winchester MS's version of the Roman war (Malory 1973, MS 81^v). Furthermore, Vinaver's note to this Sir Bryan who fights (Malory 1973: note to p. 212) suggests that he is the same as Sir Bryan of the Isles in the "story of Merlin" (i.e. Caxton 3.13). Vinaver does not comment on the implied qualification of Bryan's principles (cf. Malory 1973).

[7] Cf. "The story of Merlin" translated by Rupert T. Pickens in Lacy (1993: 1, 231, 233).

[8] = "Histoire de Merlin" translated by Rupert T. Pickens in Lacy (1993: 1, 230-31, 233).

References

Editions

Asher, Martha (trans.)
    1993   "The post-Vulgate, part I: The Merlin continuation", in: Lacy (gen. ed.), vol. 4: 167-277.

Hamel, Mary (ed.)
    1984   *Morte Arthure: A critical edition.* (Garland medieval texts 9.) New York: Garland.

Lacy, Norris J. (gen. ed.)
    1993   *Lancelot-Grail: The Old French Arthurian Vulgate and post-Vulgate in translation.* 5 vols. (Garland reference library to the humanities.) New York: Garland.

Malory, Sir Thomas
    1969   *Le Morte D'Arthur.* Janet Cowen and John Lawlor (eds.). 2 vols. Harmondsworth: Penguin.

    1973   *Works.* 3 vols. (2nd edition.) Eugene Vinaver (ed.). Oxford: Clarendon.

Pickens, Rupert T. (trans.)
    1993   "The story of Merlin", in: Lacy (gen. ed.), vol. 1: 164-424.

Spenser, Edmund
    1977   *The Faerie Queene*. A.C. Hamilton (ed.). (Annotated English Poets.) London: Longman.

Studies

Hanks, Dorrel Thomas (ed.)
    2000   *The social and literary contexts of Malory's Morte Darthur*. (Arthurian studies 42.) Cambridge: Brewer.

Kaeuper, Richard,
    2000   "Chivalry and the civilizing process", in: Kaeuper (ed.), 21-35.

Kaeuper, Richard (ed.)
    2000   *Violence in medieval society*. Woodbridge: Boydell Press.

Kennedy, Edward Donald
    2003   "*Malory's Morte Darthur*: A politically neutral English adaptation of the Arthurian story", *Arthurian Literature* 20: 145-69.

Matthews, William
    1966   *The ill-framed knight: A skeptical inquiry into the identity of Sir Thomas Malory*. Berkeley: University of California Press.

Lynch, Andrew
    1997   *Malory's book of arms: The narrative of combat in Le Morte Darthur*. (Arthurian studies 39.) Cambridge: Brewer.

    2000   "'Thou woll never have done': Ideology, context, and excess in Malory's War", in: Hanks, 24-41.

Saunders, Corinne -- Franciose Le Saux -- Neil Thomas (eds.)
    2004   *Writing war: Medieval literary responses to warfare*. Rochester: Brewer.

Whetter, Kevin
  2004 "Warfare and combat in *Le Morte Darthur*", in: Saunders -- Le Saux -- Thomas (eds.), 169-83.

Observations on the loss of final plosive consonants in late Middle English rhyme-words

Saara Nevanlinna (Helsinki, Finland)

1. Introduction

1.1. Aim of this study

This pilot study is just a series of observations trying to illustrate under what conditions plosives (stops) in final position could be lost in manuscripts of late Middle English verse, and to find out if dialectal or colloquial deletion of final stops could ever be regarded as a regional phenomenon. The terms *loss* and *deletion* are taken in a wider sense, so that this study will also include instances where a final stop is not completely 'lost' but only modified in one way or another.

The period examined covers the years 1350-1500, divided into ME3 (1350-1420) and ME4 (1420-1500). My material consists of fifty-seven late Middle English verse texts collected by scanning a large number of texts that were easily available. Three texts written in contemporary Older Scots were used as comparison material. The data represents the following *prototypical text categories* containing different text types (genres) after the nomenclature used in Kytö (1995).
(i) *religious instruction* (*IR*)15: homily 4, religious treatise 11;
(ii) *non-imaginative narration* (*NN*)11: history 3, biography: saint's life 8;
(iii) *imaginative narration* (*NI*)16: travelogue 1, fiction 3, romance 12;
(iv) *text type not defined* (*XX*)15 : drama, i.e. mystery play and morality play 5, lyric, including carol 7, dialogue 1, Bible paraphrase 2.

1.2. Middle English rhymes

1.2.1. Non-standard pronunciation

Middle English rhyming verse was primarily meant to be presented orally. Differently from vowels, irregularity of consonants in rhyme has rarely been touched upon. Deletion of sounds in words that form good rhymes with forms of the standard language, may be generally regarded as evidence of the poet's dialect. Anyone who has studied early Middle English verse must have observed that absolute consistency in rhyme was not the case at that time. Stanley (1988:

53) points out that especially assonance and impure rhymes were very common in early Middle English. Late Middle English rhymes again seem to have been predominantly pure, and scansion, mostly regular. Penzl (1970: 19) postulates that only poetry with predominantly pure rhymes can reveal phonemic changes when they occur in rhyme position.

Milroy (1992a: 66) points out that "language in use is always observed within a social context of some kind". He seems to imply that non-standard pronunciation is style-bound. We must remember that what is non-standard from the point of the standard language today may have been the "consensus form" in the community to which the speaker belonged. Not all the rhymes in a given text may go back to the poet or versifier. During the late Middle English period, there was no common standard language as yet. Thus, a variety of regional Englishes was used in writing. The evidence of rhyming words is especially useful when studying a period when many extant literary texts were versified (Milroy 1992b: 169).

1.2.2. Scribal translation

If a scribe's or reviser's dialect was different from the original poet's, a certain amount of translation was likely to take place. Where several people speaking different dialects tackled a text successively, impure and corrupt rhymes could easily be produced. With the spread of the developing standard towards the end of the fifteenth century dialectal differences became less frequent in written texts.

Occasional spellings reflecting the loss of a stop cannot be considered to be conclusive evidence on their own, but if consonants omitted reflect change in pronunciation, that implies simplification in colloquial register. Informal spoken language always aims at easy articulation. It follows the "principle of least effort", which is a prime source of variation (Samuels 1972: 17). Milroy (1992b: 197) argues that a number of present-day non-standard speech-forms may be traced back to certain variants in ME spelling. Penzl (1970: 18-22) advocates the important view that evidence through contact between languages can be valuable for phonetic identifications, and that occasional spellings may reveal a dialectal change that is not reflected by the established spelling.

1.3. Technicalities

The regional provenance of each example is given in square brackets by an abbreviation used in the county map of *LALME* (1986, 1: 569; 2: 381; 4: 333). Since many of the MSS included in the data were copied by a succession of different scribes, the language could be mixed, even corrupt. That is probably one of the reasons why their linguistic profiles are not to be found in *LALME*. An asterisk is added to suggested regional references which are not based on a thorough linguistic analysis by the editors of *LALME*.[1] The item reference numbers in *IMEV* (1943) are given for identification of the individual MSS examined.

To create a rough picture of how the data were dispersed, the examples will be presented within the frame of larger ME dialect areas, i.e. Northern, West Midland, East Midland, Southern, and Kent (no examples found), according to the map in Jordan (1974: 5), where the lines are drawn along county boundaries. That will serve the present purpose, though some modern scholars, such as Lass (1992: 34), seem to present more accurately drawn maps.[2]

2. The examples

The late ME evidence that I have collected is for the most part based on rhyming couplets (which metre is not specifically indicated in the examples). Verse texts written in stanzaic form, as lyrics and medieval mystery plays or romances, where two or more lines share the same rhyme, are also included. Since this study does not aim at a literary analysis of the verse, I venture to present some of the longer examples in a fragmentary way in order to save space. Longer passages omitted are marked with three dots. Single lines that have been left out between lines written in full are marked by hyphens between two slashes.

The rhyme-words under discussion have been written in italics, except for the final symbols of sounds that should not be pronounced. I have also tried to provide the reader with some translation of the parts of the text that are to be seen in the examples.

2.1. Loss of final plosive consonants

According to Milroy (1992a: 136), final stop deletion is very common in many varieties of English today. Colloquial loss of final stops, especially in clusters, has been discussed by several twentieth-century linguists, e.g. Dobson (1968: § 398), Milroy (1992b: 197), Romaine (1983), Wyld (1956: 303-304).

2.1.1. Loss of final stops after other stops

Loss of /t/ after voiceless stops is sometimes realised in spelling.

(1)   Als to record in Goddes *wirschip*
How þai war broght out of *Egipt*.
(*The northern homily cycle* (3) 4631)[3]
['Also to record in God's worship how they [the Israelites] were brought out of Egypt.']
[NME] *IMEV* 3166.2. (*IR*)

(2)   Of stedfast man þe wittes *frek*,
And eke of wise corage *effec*
(Castleford, *Chronicle of England* 21678)
['The bold will of a steadfast man, and also the effect of wise courage']
[NME*] *IMEV* 1559.1. (*NN*)

Loss of /d, t/ was seen in weak preterites and past participles of French verbs where the stem ends in *d* or *t*.[4]

(3)   þei dyd als he *commawnd*,
and sone was Amon slayn.
so for fowle luf *in land*
ar men oft put to payn.
(*Middle English Old Testament* 8421) (*XX*)
['They did as he commanded, and soon was Amnon killed. So are men often put to pain because of sinful love in the world.']
[WRY] *IMEV* 944.1. (12-line stz., a b a b a b a b C d C d)

(4)   Thys holy mane of God was *accept*
For whatsoeuer that he ded prayd
Vs frome the daunger conseruyd and *kepte*
Of the ranson we Xuld haue payd.
(*As storys wryght and specyfy*, a carol, stz. 3) (*XX*)
['This holy man was accepted by God for whatever he made accessible to Him, saved and kept us from danger by the ransom that we should have paid.']
[Nfk] *IMEV* 405.1. (A b A b).

In one native verb (*to end*), the assimilated final stop of the stem, representing the weak past participle, rhymes with a French word in *–ent*.

(5) When Agamenoun his tale hath *ent*
Be-fore the lordes that were *present*
(*The 'Laud' Troy book* 15561)
['When Agamemnon had ended his story in front of the lords who were present']
Cf. ibid. 13231:
Vn-to that pes that wolde *assent*
For the batayle was as good as *ent*
['who would assent to the peace, for the battle was almost ended']
[EM*] *IMEV* 249. (*NI*)

2.1.2. Loss of final stops after fricatives

Loss of /t/ could occur after the reflex of the Old English palatal fricative (the *ich*-sound). In the example, the final <t> is seen in writing.

(6) For he was Kyng of Kynges *heghe* / *Rex primus aurum optulit*
And allso Lorde and Kyng ful *rygh*t / *Secundus rex thus pertulit.*
(*As holy kyrke makys*, a macaronic carol of the Nativity, stz. 8)
['For he was King of Kings high / The first king offered gold
And also Lord and King in full / The second king thus persevered to the end.']
[WRY] *IMEV* 340.2. (A b A b) (*XX*)

Where /t/ is lost after the reflex of the OE velar fricative (the *ach*-sound) there may occur reverse spelling to produce an eye-rhyme.

(7) As þey seyd þey dyd þat *wogh*te
þe whyche dede ful soure þey *bogh*te
(Mannyng, *Handlyng synne* 4089)
['As they said, they did that harm (*wough*), for which deed they paid dearly']
[Bck] *IMEV* 778.3. (*IR*)

Final /t/ may be lost even after other fricatives.[5] The writer of the following revised version of Mirk's *Instructions for parish priests* is not very literate, judged by his spelling.

(8) And what þu art gylty *of*
Boldely say it [b]othe styll and *soft*
(Mirk, *Instructions for parish priests* 789)[6]
['What you are guilty of, say it boldly, both still and softly']
[Li] *IMEV* 961.7 (*IR*)
Cf. Mirk, *Instructions for parish priests* [Stf] *IMEV* 961.6.:
... gulty *of* / ... make no *scof*

['...guilty of...do not mock']

Final /k/ may be lost after /s/ in the infinitive *ask*. The form *as(s)* has risen either through assimilation from the metathesised stem *ax*, or it is an analogical form after assimilation of medial /k/ in *askte* (Luick 1964, 2: 916).

(9) O pees I bidde þat no man *passe* / - /
And takes gud hede to hym þat *hasse* / - /
Kyng Pharo my fadir *was* / - /
I am his hayre as elde will *asse*/
(*York cycle, Moses and pharaoh*, XI.1)
['O peace, I tell no man to pass and pay good heed to him that has. King Pharaoh was my father. I am his heir as age will require']
[south of Yk] *IMEV* 1273.1. (*XX*) (A b A b A b A b c d c d)

2.1.3. Loss of final stops after nasals

Loss of /d/ was found in Northern present participles and verbal nouns ending in -*and*.

(10) And yf so be that sche be power
And haue no lame to offer, *than*
Two tyrtle-doves to Godes honoure
To bring with her for her *offrand*.
(*York cycle, The Purification*, XVII. 49)
['And if she be poor and have no lamb to offer, then she should bring two turtle doves with her as her offering in God's honour']
[south of Yk] *IMEV* 1273.1. (*XX*) (quatrains: a B a B)

Final /d/ may be lost in other words ending in vowel plus -*nd*.

(11) þat schal be clepud god of *lon*d
He schal awreke al þy *fon*
(*Kyng Alisaunder* 311) [Sal] *IMEV* 683.3. (*NI*)
['... [a son] who shall be called god of the earth. He shall condemn all your enemies']
Cf. an EME variant *Kyng Alisaunder* 313:
þat shal be cleped god of *londe*.
He shal awreke al þi *shonde*.
['... who will be called god of the earth. He will avenge all your shame.']
[Ex] *IMEV* 683.1.

Loss of /d/ was also seen in participial adjectives and weak past participles after postvocalic *n* when the final vowel before *d* was elided.

(12)   / - / on a day byfore þe *none*
       / - / To pley as þey were *ywon*yd.
       / - / Anone he made hyt stonde *sone*
       / - / & vndede þat Jhesu had *done*/
       (*The apocryphal history of the Infancy* 149)
       ['on a day before the noon ... to play as they were used to ... Immediately he made it [the water] stand still ... and [Judas] undid what Jesus had done.']
       [Cnw] *IMEV* 250.1. (*NI*) (a B a B a B a B c d c d)

(13)   Yea, God give me *pyne*
       and that shalbe *thine,*
       for thou art euer *inclin*d
       to drawe towards thee.
       (*Chester play,* XVI A., *The Passion,* 77)
       ['Truly, God, give me pain, and it will be yours, for you are always inclined to draw [men] towards you.']
       [Chs] *IMEV* 716.1. (*XX*) (a quatrain: A A A b)

Sometimes an excrescent /d/ developed after homorganic *n* (Luick 1964, 2: 1038). In some words, loss of the final dental came to survive in Standard English, e.g. *lawn* (sb.) from OF *lande*. Texts may contain duplicate forms.

(14)   þat þou rise vp hale and *sounde*
       And tell vs what man es *Symounde.*
       (*The northern homily cycle* (1), *Peter & Paul* 179)
       ['that thou may rise up whole and sound and tell us what kind of man Simon is.']
       [NME] *IMEV* 3560.1. (*IR*)
       Cf. ibid. 90:
       His first name es callid *Symone*/ þe toþer Petir, wiþ *resoune*
       ['His first name is Simon, the second, Peter, with reason']

From the fourteenth century on, final /g/ could be lost after *n*. This began in Norfolk and Scotland (Luick 1964, 2: 1044), then moved southwards; *g*-less forms were seen in writing in northern and north-eastern texts and in Scotland. The West Midland forms of the verbal noun ended in *-inge/ -ynge* (*LALME* 1986, 4: 106-108).

Skautrup (1944: 217) maintains that vowels were nasalised before *n* and *m* in early Danish, though this was not seen in the Latin alphabet. Nasalisation in early Middle English rhymes has mostly been ascribed to French influence. See Einhorn (1974: 9).

(15) Behold what lyfe that we ryne *ine*
Frayl to fale and euer lyke to *syne*
Thorow our enmys *entysyn*g
Therfor we syng and cry to the
(*Behold what lyfe*, a carol of Candlemas, stz.1)
['Behold what life we run, being prone to fail, and always likely to sin through our enemy's enticing. Therefore we sing and call to thee']
[Nfk] *IMEV* 508.1. (*XX*) (A A A b + burden)

(16) Thane, fra Sanct Colme had *persawin*g (*IR*)
Hou clerly godis grace cane *shyne*
(*The Scottish legendary, The life of St. Machor* 375).
['Then, from the time that Saint Columba became aware of how clearly God's mercy shone [in Machar]']
[Older Scots*] *IMEV* 842.1.

(17) His heritage if he wyll *wynne*
He behouys to do anoþer *thyn*ge
(*Creation* 199)
['If he wants to win his heritage he needs to do another thing']
[Lei] *IMEV* 1677.1. (*IR*)

Loss of final /k/ after *n* was already seen in early Middle English rhymes. There are parallel rhymes with final *k* either pronounced, or not.[7]

(18) That þey receyueth for to *dryn*ke
After that holy *hoselynge*
(Mirk, *Instructions for parish priests* 252)
['[Wine and water] that they receive to drink after Holy Communion'] Cf. ibid. 1233:
Hast þou I-stole mete or *drynke,*
For þou woldest not þerfore *swynke*?
['Have you stolen food or drink, because you did not want to labour for them?']
[Stf] *IMEV* 961.6. (*IR*)

In the final cluster /mb/, /b/ was assimilated in early Middle English c.1300, but more sophisticated writers, like Chaucer, retained the <b> in writing.

(19) And set þi luf so sad *in him*
 þat þou may euer vpward *clim*
 (Rolle, *Forme of living* 495) (*IR*)
 ['And fasten your love so firmly in him that you are always able to climb upwards']
 [NME] *IMEV* 1442.1.

(20) And I griffed her
 right vp in her *home*
 And by that day twenty wokes
 It was quik in her *wom*b.
 (*I haue a newe gardyn*, a carol, stz. 17)
 ['I grafted her a shoot right in her home. And twenty weeks later it Was alive in her womb']
 [Nfk] *IMEV* 1302.1. (*XX*) (a B c B)

2.1.4. Loss of final stops after vowels

Loss of /k/ after /a/ in the infinitives *take* and *make* was seen in rhymes written in the Northern dialect area (including Scotland). There also occurred variants with *k*. Loss of final /k/ in *take* has a parallel in the Scandinavian dialects. Both in Danish and Norwegian the infinitive has lost its *k*. See Skautrup (1944: 229) and Seip (1955: 134). The Northern second and third person present tense forms *tas(e* and *mas(e* were found as rhyme-words in neighbouring North Midland texts.[8]

(21) / weddid wyffes wolde he *ta* /
 Maydyns, maryage *alswa*/
 (*The wicked knight and the friar* 16) (*IR*)
 ['wedded wives would he [the wicked knight] take, maidens and wives also [would he spoil]']
 [NME*] *IMEV* 1722.1. (12-line stz., a a b C C b d d b e e b)

Where final /k/ was lost in the infinitive *make*, the form *ma* may have risen analogically from a contracted form such as *made* from *makede* (Jespersen 1965: § 250). Jespersen is of the opinion that *ta* was formed on the analogy of *ma*. In MSS written by Southumbrian scribes we may come across the variants *to* and *mo* with the vowel rounded. Skautrup (1944: 276) postulates that in early Danish, long *a* could be rounded in labial neighbourhood. According to Gordon (1981: 322), a rounded long *a* was spelt with <a, aa, o> in Danish by c.1300. In Old Norwegian, long *a* had become identical with long open *o* through lip-rounding by 1250, but the spelling with *a* was retained and stood for both sounds (Gordon 1981: 267).

(22) agaynes hym to *goo* / - / - / - /
And strake hym *thro* / - / - / - /
He strykes the body *fra* / - / - / - /
Mirthe may scho *ma*!
(*Perceval* 1724) (*NI*)
['to go against him ... and struck him fiercely ... He strikes [the sultan's head] from the body ... May she rejoice!']
There is a more corrupt passage, cf. ibid.1891:
Þat will vs bothe *sle*! ... Ne wirke me no *wo*? ... His maistrys to *mo* ... Er þat I hethen *go*!
['Who will kill us both ... Nor do me any harm? ... To behave outrageously ... Before I go from here.']
[NME*] *IMEV* 1853.1. (a a a B c c c B d d d B e e e B)

2.2. Modification of final stops in assonating rhymes

The majority of the types of assonating rhymes to be discussed below seem to be late Middle English copies of older texts from the early Middle English period when that kind of impure rhymes were acceptable.

2.2.1. Glottal replacement of /k/, /p/, and /t/ ?

Where final /k p t/ came to occur in rhyme-words, sometimes after the loss of final *schwa*, words ending in any two of the three voiceless stops would first occur in rhyme with each other in some copies of older texts written by late Middle English scribes. I suggest that such rhymes, which had been legitimate in early Middle English (cf. Einhorn 1974: 5-6), might possibly have become acceptable in oral presentation even after late ME standards. Gimson (1969: 170) postulates that replacement of final /k/ and /t/, and more rarely of /p/, by glottal stop is typical of several kinds of regional speech today. If these final stops had already been replaced by glottal stops in late Middle English casual speech, such rhymes might have sounded 'good' to contemporary audiences when a verse text was spoken or recited.

(23)   / - / Vnblemyst I am, wythouten *blot* / - / Bot "makelez quene" þenne sade I *not*
/ - /A hondred and forty þowsande *flot* / - / Saint John hem sy3 al in a *kno*t / On
þe hyl of Syon, þat semly *clot* / - / Arayed to þe weddyng in þat *hyl-co*ppe / þe
nwe cyte o Jerusalem.
(*Pearl* 781) (*NI*)
['Unblemished I am, without a stain ... But then I did not say " peerless queen" ...
A company of a hundred and forty thousand ... Saint John saw them all in a group
on the hill of Syon, that fine mountain ... Dressed for the wedding on that hilltop,
the new city of Jerusalem.']
[Chs] *IMEV* 2744.1. (12-line stz., a B a B a B a B B c B c)

(24)   Whan Parfory harde *that*
Hym thought hys herte *bra*ke.
(*St. Katherine* (4) 247)
['When Porphyry heard that he thought that his heart broke']
[Lei] *IMEV* 227.2. (*NN*)

(25)   And lewde men þan þer ey3ene *we*pe
That teres fell vndere þer *fe*te.
(*The stasyons of Ierusalem*, a travelogue, stz. 113)
['And then lay people cried their eyes out, so that tears fell down to their feet.']
Cf. ibid. 687:
And than sche praysyd hym all *abou*te
And with hyre pappes gane hym *sow*ke
['And then she praised him [baby Jesus] throughout and fed him from the
breast.']
[Lei] *IMEV* 986.1. (*NI*)

(26)   And anon after, as seynt Wylfride ley in his bed vpone a ny3t –
Bot he nas not fulliche 3et *a-sle*pe:
Hym þou3t þat he sey an angel fulle bry3t
Stondynge at his beddus *fe*te.
(*St. Editha* (Ethelreda) 621)
['And soon afterwards, as Saint Wilfrid lay in his bed one night - but he was not
yet fully asleep: it seemed to him that he saw a very bright angel standing at the
foot of his bed.']
[Wlt*] *IMEV* 3090.1. (*NN*) (quatrains: a B a B)

2.2.2. Assimilation of final stops in the clusters *-nd, -ng,* and *-mb*

Any two words ending in the above clusters could rhyme with each other in early
Middle English, apparently after the model of frenchified nasalised
pronunciation (cf. Einhorn 1974: 9). Some of these rhymes survived in late

Middle English. They were found both south, east, and north. Colloquial loss of final *d* and *g* after *n*, and that of *b* after *m* has been attested above (see 2.1.3.). The combination of vowel and nasal in these rhymes must have resulted in a nasalised vowel and a velar type of nasal consonant sound. Since all the rhyme-words involved in this assimilation in late Middle English texts were of native origin, we must bear in mind that vowels had been nasalised before *m* and *n* in early Danish (Skautrup 1944: 217).

(27)   Wiþ hys ffoot he wolde nouȝt *won*de /
       He slowȝ þe child ryȝt in here *wom*be
       (*Athelston* 273)
       ['With his foot he would not hesitate. He slew the child right in her womb.']
       [Li] *IMEV* 1973.1. (*NI*) (12-line stz., a a b c c b d d b E E b)

(28)   They fare in chyrche as a lyone *stron*g
       And meke in feld as any *lom*b
       (*God of hewine* 174)[9]
       ['They move about in church like a strong lion, and, humbly in field like any lamb.']
       [EM*] *IMEV* 957.1. (*IR*)

2.2.3. De-voicing of final /d/

Wright (1968: 233) argues that de-voicing of final /d/ after /r, l, n/ has often taken place in modern dialects in words of more than one syllable, from Scotland to the South, but not in the eastern and south-eastern counties. The examples in my data are all from the West, where they also apply to mono-syllabics. Eye-rhymes (see no. 31 below) may occur even here.

(29)   And euer haue pete on þe pore
       And part with him þat God þe send
       þou hast no noþer tresoure
       Aȝayns þe day of *iugement*
       I cownsel þe:
       (Audelay, *ffede þe hungere*, a carol, stz. 3)
       ['And have ever pity on the poor one and share with him whatever God may send you. You have no other spiritual goods against the Judgement Day. I advise you:']
       [Stf] *IMEV* 792.1. (*XX*) (a B a B c + burden)

(30) An angel drofe hym yn-to *desert*
Wyth a bry3th brennyng *swerde*.
(*The legend of Ipotis* 233)[10]
['An angel drove him [Adam] into the desert with a brightly burning sword']
[EM*] *IMEV* 220.9. (*XX*)

(31) þus alle men He doþ cumford
And cowncelis 3ou pur charite
Settis no3t be þe ioy of þis *word*
Hit is bot vayn and vanete/
(Audelay, *Saynt ancelyne* 'St. Anselm', lines 27-39) (*IR*)
['Thus he comforts all people and advises you through love. Don't value the joy of this world, it is but vainglory and vanity.']
[Stf] *IMEV* 2853.1. (13-line stz., A b A b b c b c d e e e d)

De-voicing of final /d/ after vowels was found in northerly and eastern texts. Phillipson -- Lauridsen (1982: 12, 24) maintain that those speaking with a Danish 'accent' are not able to make a distinction between voiced and voiceless stops in final position. Before a pause only /p t k/ occurs.

(32) Hast þow any tyme with herte prowd
A-noþeres synne I-spoken owt
(Mirk, *Instructions for parish priests* 1025)
['Have you ever, with a proud heart, made public another man's sin']
[Stf] *IMEV* 961.6.
The rhyme is retained in the Lincolnshire revision (*IMEV* 961.7.) (*IR*).

2.2.4. Final /d/ in rhyme with dental fricative

These rhymes were only found in Scandinavian-influenced areas. Gimson (1969: 162ff.) argues that the English alveolar /d/ is pronounced voiceless in final position. In the Danelaw, final *d* could occur in rhyme with the dental fricative. Skautrup (1944: 222) attests that the fricative could be written <d> in the oldest sources in Middle Danish. Both sounds appear to have been allophones of the same sound. Reverse spelling will occur in the examples.

(33) Kyng Edwarde þan soght aflie *Davide*
He suffred hem haf noþer pes ne *gride*.[11]
(Castleford, *Chronicle of England* 38076)
['Then King Edward tried to put David to flight. He allowed him to have neither peace nor security.']
[WRY*] *IMEV* 1559.1. (*NN*)

(34) 'Osanna' þei sange 'þe sone of *Dauid*' / - /
And poure folke fecched floures of þe frith
(*York cycle*, XXX. 343.)
['Hosanna', they sang, 'Son of David' ... And poor people brought flowers of the meadow']
[south of Yk] *IMEV* 1273.1. (*XX*) (A b A b c d d d c)

(35) Of þe shall be sore *aferd*
When þey come yn-to myddul *erþe*.[12]
(*The legend of Ipotis* 311)
['[And all those who see] you [Satan] will be very frightened when they come to mid-earth.']
[EM*] *IMEV* 220.9. (*XX*)

(36) He wente forth yn þat *tyde*
Walkynge by þe *see-syþe*/
(*Emare* 685.) (*NI*)
['He went along at that time, walking by the sea-side']
[EM*] *IMEV* 1766.1. (12-line stz., a a b C C b d d b e e b)

(37) No thynge that of hym *sterde*
/ - / - / Hymselff was the *fovrthe*[13]
/ - / - / And euery man drew his *swerd*
/ - / - / And bare them to the *erthe*.
(*Ipomadon* (1) 8418)
['[there was] nothing that moved him off ... he himself was the fourth ... And every man pulled his sword ... and struck them [Cabanus' men] down']
[EM*] *IMEV* 2635.1. (*NI*) (12-line stz., a a B c c B d d B e e B)

3. The Findings

The editors of *LALME* must have had their reasons for making a distinction between MSS written in the mixed dialect of the West Riding of Yorkshire (WRY) and the more or less mixed language of a number of other texts written elsewhere in Yorkshire which are referred to by the general term NME (Northern Middle English) but not entered on maps. A map presented by Skautrup (1944: 97) shows that the North was first occupied by East Norse (Danish) invaders at the time the Vikings settled down in Britain, but that West Norse (Norwegian) settlements spread from the north-western counties sporadically all over the West Riding (cf. the maps in Gilbert 1985: 11-14).

Table 1: Temporal and regional distribution of the manuscripts

Subperiod	NME	WRY	EM	WM	South	Totals
ME 3	12	2	11	5	4	34
ME 4	5	3	10	5	---	23
Totals	17	5	21	10	4	57

Table 1 shows that the MSS assigned to ME3 take up nearly 61 per cent of the data. The ratio of Northern Middle English texts to East Midland and West Midland texts is 12: 11: 5. The four Southern, and the two West Riding MSS seem to exhibit later copies of early Middle English texts. In ME4, the East Midland MSS outnumber the others. The NME and WM texts amount to half of their number. There were only three MSS assigned to WRY, and none to the South.

Table 2: Distribution of prototypical text categories among the regions

Dialect region	IR	NN	NI	XX	Totals
NME	8	3	5	2	18
WRY	-	2	---	3	5
EM	3	4	7	6	20
WM	3	---	3	4	10
South	1	2	1	---	4
Totals	15	11	16	15	57

As seen in Table 2, all the four prototypical text categories represented in the data were found in Northern and East Midland manuscripts. In West Midland and Southern texts, three text categories were represented, and in texts written in the West Riding, only two.

4. Conclusion

Narrative Middle English rhyming verse was meant to be read aloud. Late Middle English parish priests and friars addressed believers with verse homilies and saints' lives. The dialogue of mystery plays was in rhyming verse. Romances were recited to appreciative audiences. Lyrics and carols were sung to music. In texts that were meant to be recited or sung, final stop deletion was introduced as a concession to the needs of rhyme. Modification of final stops in rhymewords was adjusted to regional or colloquial conditions.

The bulk of the texts were either translated from Latin or French models or modified after such models. The language of most of the manuscripts was no longer a pure dialect because they could be several times removed from the originals. That must be one of the reasons why the Linguistic Profiles of so many of them are not analysed in *LALME*. The texts included in the data differ greatly in length, some are even incomplete. Therefore no attempt was made to count any relative frequencies. Considering the fact that this is only a pilot study with the examples picked out at random, it is not possible to present any conclusive evidence. The findings can only be suggestive.

Different types of deletion of final stops appear to have varied regionwise. The colloquial pronunciation reflected in non-standard rhymes was not entirely region-bound. An established poet like Chaucer would use contemporary prestige forms. Non-standard forms which were not prestige forms in the original poet's community must have occurred in manuscripts copied by less literate anonymous scribes, or by scribes coming from a different dialect area.

A few of the types had apparently spread all over the country. Loss of stops in final position after other stops was probably a universal phenomenon. That also applies to loss of final dentals in inflexional weak endings of French verbs in which the stem ends in a dental consonant.

Some types of final stop deletion occurred in more than one regional area. Final *d* after post-vocalic *n* in weak endings of participial adjectives and ast participles was sporadically lost in southern, eastern and western texts. Devoicing of final stops after long vowels in *d* : *t* rhymes was only found in Midland texts, both East and West.

Some types seem to have been predominantly region-bound. Devoicing of final *d* after *r*, *l*, or *n*, to occur in rhyme with final *t*, was only manifested in Western texts. Words in which final *k* was deleted after a nasalised *n* in rhyme with words ending in -*ng* were mainly found in MSS written in the West.

The contracted *k*-less forms *ta* and *ma* of the infinitives *take* and *make* occurred in texts to which the dialect reference WRY or NME was assigned by the editors of *LALME*. They could occasionally be seen in MSS written in some neighbouring county.

There are more types of loss of final plosives in manuscripts written within the boundaries of ancient Danelaw than in any of the other regions. Final *t* is dropped after other fricatives (*s*, *f*) only in MSS written in Yorkshire and the East Midlands. Final *d* was lost in the Northern present participles ending in -*and*. Words in which final *d* followed after a vowel or *r* could occur in rhyme with words ending in a dental fricative. Rhymes of this type were only found in texts written in the North and East Midlands.

Some of the types of loss of final stops in early Middle English assonating rhymes that had been legitimate in the early Middle English subperiod survived in late Middle English. Firstly, rhymes in which the rhyme-words ended in assonating clusters of nasals and final voiced stops could probably be regarded as 'good' rhymes in late Middle English after the final clusters had undergone assimilation when presented orally. Secondly, rhymes consisting of two or more words ending in voiceless final stops in assonance seem to have become acceptable if the stops were suppressed through replacement by glottal stops when the verse was recited or spoken in colloquial, i.e. casual or vulgar style.

To sum up, it appears that deletion (as well as modification) of final stops in rhyme-words occurred most frequently in regions which had earlier been subjected to Scandinavian influence, and their neighbouring counties. The central regions in this respect were Yorkshire and East Anglia. In the fourteenth and fifteenth centuries, those areas were not yet well within the reach of the growing standard language. It can only be conjectured that the rise of final stop-deletion so conclusively attested by rhymes in northerly and easterly MSS of the period must be traceable back to poets or scribes who were inheritors of ancient Scandinavian settlers in the Danelaw. In their language, the "economy of expression" must have been fairly strong, judging by the important role that assimilation has always played in the development of the Danish and Norwegian languages.

Notes

[1] The estimates marked with an asterisk were found in text editions, manuals, grammars and histories of English, or scholarly articles.

[2] Lass's map is fairly similar to the "Map of dialect boundaries" drawn by Moore -- Meech -- Whitehall in 1935, which is reproduced in *MED. Plan and bibliography* (1954: 8).

[3] *The northern homily cycle: The expanded version in MSS Harley 4196 and Cotton Tiberius E vii.*, cf. Nevanlinna (1972-84).

[4] But through this loss, a correct rhyme is achieved in (3) and (4), see also (5), (8) etc. – if the correct form had been preserved, there would be an impure rhyme.

[5] In (8) *soft*, the *t* is preserved in spelling; see also (10), (11) etc.

[6] The MS was edited by Gillis Kristensson (cf. Mirk 1974: 177-224). In line 790 the edition reads *pothe* for *bothe*. The emendation is mine.

[7] See e.g. "Maiden in the mor lay" (*IMEV* 3891.1.), a carol written down in the South in the early fourteenth century, but inserted in a late Middle English MS. The latest (expanded) edition of the text is by J. A. Burrow -- Thorlac Turville-Petre (1997: 236-237). Here, lines 18-21 read: "þe chelde water of the – / Welle was hire dryng, / Wat was hire dryng? / þe chelde water of the welle-spring." ['The cold water of the – / spring was her drink, / What was her drink? The cold water of the spring.'] According to *LALME* (1986, 4: 321), *ng* is found for *nk*, and reversely, in MSS written in the South and Midlands. Norfolk and Salop are the northernmost counties where this is seen.

[8] The contracted past participle *tane* had already appeared in early Middle English texts written further south, but not the infinitive *ta*.

[9] This religious poem in rhyming couplets entitled "Merita Misse" ['Merits of the mass'] was wrongly ascribed to Lydgate in the MS. It contains several early Middle English assonating rhymes. I found none in Lydgate's long poem "Interpretacio misse" ['Interpretation of the mass'] in 8-line stanzas rhyming ababbcbc (*IMEV* 4246.6.). The editor Henry Noble MacCracken (1911: 86-115) maintains that assonance was very rare in Lydgate, not more than six instances to 150.000 lines. The only assonating rhyme (*th* : *d* of the East Midland type) was to be seen in a spurious couplet inserted in the poem (lines 15-16): "Ne that day shall he dy soden dethe / The sacrament to se in forme of brede." ['Nor is he to die a sudden death on that day to see the sacrament in the form of bread.'] (Not included in the data.)

[10] Cf. G *Schwert* 'sword'. This rhyme is a relict from a western MS. The oldest extant MS of the text [cf. *IMEV* 220.1.] contains this rhyme.

[11] *Grid* in the MS is Eastern dialectal spelling for *grith* 'peace, security'. *Peace and grith* is a common word-pair in Middle English verse.

[12] Instead of this regional rhyme, both *IMEV* 220.3. [Lei] and *IMEV* 220.8. [Li] have a good rhyme with *erde* for *erthe*. According to *ManualME* (1972: 3, 740), the original poem was composed at the beginning of the fourteenth century, and it has been suggested that the poem is East Midland or Southeastern (excluding Kent).

[13] *Fovrthe* in the MS is introduced by a Midland scribe for Northern dialectal *ferd(e* 'fourth'. There is a recent edition of the MS, cf. Purdie (2001).

References

Burrow, John Anthony -- Thorlac Turville-Petre (eds.)
    1997   *A book of Middle English.* (2nd reprinted edition.) Oxford: Blackwell.

Dobson, Eric J.
    1968   *English pronunciation 1500-1700.* 2 vols. (2nd edition.) Oxford: Clarendon Press.

Einhorn, E.
    1974   *Old French: A concise handbook.* Cambridge: Cambridge University Press.

Gilbert, Martin (ed.)
    1985   *Atlas of British history.* Cartography by Arthur Banks. (reprinted edition.) New York: Dorset Press.

Gimson, Alfred C.
    1969   *An introduction to the pronunciation of English.* (2nd revised edition.) London: Arnold.

Gordon, E. V.
    1981   *An introduction to Old Norse.* (2nd reprinted edition.) Oxford: Clarendon Press.
    1957   Revised by A.R. Taylor.

Jespersen, Otto
    1965   *A modern English grammar:* Part I: *Sounds and spellings* (Reprinted edition.) London: Allen and Unwin.

Jordan, Richard
    1974   *Handbook of Middle English grammar: Phonology.* Translated and revised by Eugene Joseph Crook. (Janua Linguarum. Series Practica 218.) The Hague: Mouton.

Kennedy, Edward Donald -- Ronald Waldron -- J. S. Wittig (eds.)
    1988   *Medieval English studies presented to George Kane.* Suffolk: Boydell and Brewer.

Mirk, John
1974 *John Mirk's instructions for parish priests*. Gillis Kristensson (ed.). (Lund Studies in English 49.) Lund: Gleerup.

Kytö, Merja (ed.)
1995 *Manual to the diachronic part of the Helsinki corpus of English texts: Coding conventions and lists of source texts*. (3rd edition.) Helsinki: Department of English, University of Helsinki.

Lass, Roger (ed.)
1970 *Approaches to English historical linguistics: An anthology*. New York: Holt, Rinehart and Winston.

1992 "Phonology and morphology", in: *CHEL* 2, 25-155.

Luick, Karl
1964 *Historische Grammatik der englischen Sprache*. 2 vols. Posthumously edited by Friedrich Wild and Herbert Koziol. Oxford: Blackwell.

MacCracken, Henry Noble (ed.)
1963 *John Lydgate*. (Reprinted edition.) (EETS e.s. 107.) Oxford: Oxford University Press.

Milroy, James
1992a *Linguistic variation and change*. (Language in Society 19.) Oxford: Blackwell.

1992b "Middle English dialectology", in: *CHEL* 2, 156-206.

Nevanlinna, Saara (ed.)
1972-1984 *The northern homily cycle: The expanded version in MSS Harley 4196 and Cotton Tiberius E vii*. (Mémoires de la Société Néophilologique de Helsinki 38, 41, 43.) 3 vols. Helsinki: Société Néophilologique.

Penzl, Herbert
    1970   "The evidence for phonemic changes", in: Lass (ed.), 10-24.

Phillipson, Robert -- Hanne Lauridsen
    1982   *Danish learning of English obstruents.* (Anglicana et Americana 16.) Copenhagen: Department of English, University of Copenhagen.

Purdie, Rhiannon (ed.)
    2001   *Ipomadon.* (EETS o.s. 316.) Oxford: Oxford University Press.

Romaine, Suzanne
    1983   "The sociolinguistic history of *t* / *d* deletion", *Folia Historica Linguistica* 5: 221-55.

Samuels, M. L.
    1972   *Linguistic evolution with special reference to English.* (Cambridge Studies in Linguistics 5.) Cambridge: Cambridge University Press.

Seip, Didrik Arup
    1955   *Norsk språkhistorie til omkring 1370.* (2nd edition.) Oslo: Aschehoug & Co.

Skautrup, Peter
    1944   *Det danske sprogs historie.* Vol. 1. Copenhagen: Gyldendal.

Stanley, Eric G.
    1988   "Rhymes in English medieval verse: From Old English to Middle English", in: Kennedy -- Waldron -- Wittig (eds.), 19-54.

Wright, Joseph
    1905   *The English dialect grammar.* Oxford: Frowde.
    1968   Reprinted edition. Oxford: Clarendon.

Wyld, Henry Cecil
   1956   *A history of modern colloquial English.* (3rd reprinted edition.) Oxford: Oxford University Press.

Hyphens and hyper-hyphens in Middle English (corpus-based)

Manfred Markus (Innsbruck, Austria)

1. Introduction

Hyphens, and English punctuation marks in general, have been a minor, almost non-existent concern of English linguistics, whether synchronic or diachronic. Only a few, usually prescriptive rather than descriptive, studies are available at all.[1] This is not surprising in view of what McArthur's *Oxford companion to the English language*, in a substantial article on the hyphen, has to say: "The use of the hyphen to mark compound words ... and ... in words such as *to-day* and *without* ... has always been variable and unpredictable" (1992: 491).[2] In another article of the same source (s.v. 'Punctuation'), punctuation before the 17th century is generally called "haphazard and erratic, with little attention payed to syntax".

While the validity of this statement is non-disputable from a present-day point of view, one may well question whether our grammatical principles of today, and syntax in particular, are the proper tool for elucidating the rules of historical English punctuation. Moreover, most studies on hyphens in PDE have neglected derivations in favour of compounds.[3]

Two types of hyphens are usually distinguished: *link hyphens*, used within words, and *break hyphens*, used for breaking the line, i.e. for syllabification. The alleged inconsistency and "erratic" quality of the rules in PDE apply to both types alike.[4] But for lack of time and space, this paper will leave the bibliographical analysis of the break hyphens to another occasion and focus on aspects of word formation in connection with the link hyphen.

Traditional studies of Middle English word formation, such as those by Hans Sauer (cf. 1988 and 1992), have been onomasiological, starting from composition types and gleaning examples of the types from various texts without quantification. In this paper, I would like to try out a semasiological approach, taking the hyphens as used in ME manuscripts seriously and raising the question of their function.

The procedure is based on the hypothesis that the more we go back into the history of hyphens, the more will we be able to grasp the deeper reasons for what seems inconsistent. And the assumed marginal quality of hyphens as a merely allographic and negligible feature of language will turn out to be a misconception in view of the historical data that can now be retrieved from machine-readable sources such as the *OED* on CD-ROM and historical English corpora.

2. Rules for the usage of hyphens today

Link hyphens are generally used in PDE to mark two or more morphemes of compound words to be somewhat, yet not totally connected.[5] But in recent usage, there is a trend against the hyphenation of compounds, particularly in AmE. The reasons for or against hyphenation in these cases are manifold. According to McArthur, hyphenation is discouraged among other factors by:

(a) the monosyllabic structure of the elements (*birdsong*, not **bird-song*);
(b) the well-established association of a word's elements by usage, even with longer formations (*businesswoman, nationwide*);
(c) the first element of a word being a prefix that was formerly separated from the base by a hyphen, for example in the case of hiatus, as in former *co-ordinate* or *re-use*, now *coordinate, reuse*.

The use of the hyphen is, on the other hand, encouraged by:

(a) otherwise awkward collisions of letters (*breast-stroke, co-worker*);
(b) the need to mark syntactic connection in ambiguous constellations, for example in *Frénch-speaking vísitors* vs. *French spéaking vísitors*, or *twénty-odd péople* vs. *twenty ódd péople;*
(c) the need to connect the elements of combined words used attributively (*19th-century novel, Christmas-tree lights*).

McArthur also mentions the use of hyphenated derivations, such as *re-enact, re-form*, where the reason for the hyphen may be phonetic (*re-enact*), graphemic (*anti-Darwinian* vs. *antidote*) or semantic (*re-form* in its literal meaning, as opposed to *reform*). Two general thumb-rules can be articulated: AmE is less fond of using hyphens in border cases; and hyphenation very much depends on "how established and recognizable a formation is" (492).

All this may be confusingly indefinite to a learner. But the basic function of the link hyphen is what the term suggests: to link lexical elements half-way that otherwise, i.e. if spelt separately or in one word, would be subject to misinterpretation. The possible reasons for this misinterpretation are variable, but at any rate the basic motivation of language users to apply or avoid hyphens is to spell words in such a way that they appear clearer to the recipients, i.e. readers.

This pragmatic and historically conditioned motivation of hyphens is also to be found in Middle English. The hyphen marks the evolution of composition from the state of separateness to that of union.

3. Historical evidence from the *OED*

The *OED* on CD-ROM (2nd edition) is disappointingly limited in retrieving hyphens. Though a mode is available in the "Settings" menu for recognising hyphens as search characters,[6] there are different reasons in the various parts of the lexicon entries to prevent the user from identifying the hyphens. There is no way of scanning the quotation texts generally, i.e. with wildcards, and as regards the initial parts of the entries, i.e. the lemmas and the variant forms, hyphens are misleadingly used from a modern point of view and, what is worse, in a mixed mode, namely as object language, i.e. as proper parts of words, and also as metalanguage, i.e. as an abbreviative substitute of left-out syllables. For example, hyphenated *-mite* and *-mett* are given as variants of the lemma *hermit*, for the reader to complement the first syllable *her*.

However, the *OED* software does allow quotation searches of hyphens and wildcards in combination with at least one character. The query *a-**, for example, provides a results file of 3953 quotation words with initial hyphenated *a-*, as in *a-bede*, *a-brod*, etc. This search mode also allows for combinations with other parameters, for example, the date parameter. Limiting the search period to 1000-1499, the computer provides 2235 samples of hyphenated words with the prefixoid *a-*.

Whether this *a-* is really a prefix or eventually a free morpheme, can, of course, not be decided by the computer; but the question is of secondary importance in the context of this paper. In any case, separation of morphemes by hyphens was obviously quite common in the Middle English period.[7] This impression is confirmed by the test on other prefixoids, such as *be-*, *ge-/ʒe-*, *i-*, *y-* and others (cf. Table 1):

Table 1: Hyphenated prefixes 1000-1499 (*OED*)

be-	780
ge-, ȝe-/i-/y-	3798
for-	1070
to-/te-	1313
un-	124
bi-/by-	1293
(a)gain(e)-/(a)gayn(e)-	18
in-	805
of-	188
ofer-/over-	71
on-	271
thurh-/thurgh-/thorugh-/thro(u)gh-	32
under-	48
up-	116
ut-	27
with-	807

A similar list can be provided for compounds with common pronominal adverbs as determinants, such as *here-, there-,* and *where-* (Table 2) or with common words such as *man-* and *God-/Gode-/Godd-* (Table 3):

Table 2: Common ME adverbs with hyphens

her(e)-	120
ther(e)-	774
wher(e)-	65

Table 3: Common ME content words with hyphens

man-/mon-/men-	69
God-/gode-/Godd-	26

The native quality of these words or morphemes arouses the suspicion that Romance words may be less concerned by hyphenation. To check this, I have selected those Latin and French prefixes that are less subject to variation caused by assimilation[8], such as *ante-, de-, per-/par-, post-, pro-*/OF *pour-, re-,* and *trans-*/OF *tres-*. Except for *de-* (30 cases) the output varies from zero to only five occurrences (cf. Table 4).

Table 4: Hyphens after Romance suffixes

	numbers of hyphens	numbers of no hyphens
ante- ('before')	0	162
de-	30	0
per-/par-	0/4	0
post-	2	209
prae-/pre-	0/2	5144
pro- (Lat)/*pour-/pur-* (Fr)	1/3	2040
re-	5	0
trans- (Lat)/*tres-* (Fr)	0/0	456/944

How can we interpret these data? All in all, the hyphens give evidence of attempted analyses of words, and sometimes re-analyses.

In terms of etymology, native words could naturally be analysed more easily than French or Latin words. The reason for the low figures with Romance words is not that the foreign prefixes were altogether less frequent than the native ones. *Ante*, for example, is used as an initial word element in 162 *OED*-quotations during the period at issue,[9] but not even once with a hyphen. As Table 4 shows, *post, prae/pre* and *trans* have even higher figures of word-initial occurrence, with hardly any evidence of hyphenation. The reason seems to be that these classical morphemes did not cause any problems of misunderstanding. But morphographemic support was needed in the case of the Old English prefixes that lost ground in the course of Middle English or even died out, such as *be-/bi-, for-* (in the sense of German 'ver-'), *ge-/i-, æt-* and *gain-* (as in PDE *to gainsay*).

In addition to this basic distinction between native and foreign words, the minor difference between French and Latin prefixes is striking. Thus, Latin *per-* is not once marked as a prefix by a hyphen, but its French equivalent *par-* is, if only in a few cases - as in *par-avnter* (Lydgate; 4 occurrences). Likewise, Latin *prae-*, according to the *OED*, never evoked a hyphen until 1499, but a query for its French equivalent *pre-* yielded two examples: *pre-supposyd* and *pre-elect*. Finally, I could find no example of Latin *pro* plus hyphen,[10] but three cases of its French equivalent, i.e. hyphenated *pour-* or *pur-*, namely *pur-dew, pur-poynt*, and *pur-sued*.

De-, according to Table 4, seems exceptionally prone to be hyphenated. But as the *OED*, in a special article on this prefix, points out, a large number of Latin verbs formed with *de-* lived on in French as popular words. The words that can be gleaned from the list of the 30 quotations provided by the *OED* are mostly first occurrences between 1290 and the 15th century. This means that they had not fully made their way into English yet, so that the hyphen was applied to mark the morphemic structure of such words and thus their foreignness – as in *de-bonerli* (= 'de+bon+aire+ly'), *de-clar, de-cre, de-foule, de-parte, de-gres* ('flight of stairs'), *de-fend, de-deyn* ('disdain') etc.

Comparing the role of hyphens with native words and with the French borrowings, we can conclude that hyphens were used in Middle English derivations in the case of morphemes that were either about to lose their productivity or, as in the case of new borrowings from French, on the point of being adapted to English. In either case did benevolent scribes try to add to the clearness of a word's meaning.

Given this motivation, the Middle English hyphens did not have a particular prime time. Their preference rather depends on the morpheme at issue. *ge-/ȝe-*, continuing the Old English verbal prefix *ge-*, was already on the decline in the 11th and 12th centuries; accordingly, hyphens were used for "supporting" this morpheme. *i-* and *y-*, as reduced forms of *ge-*, particularly in the South, were naturally used later. The more than 1000 quotations with *y-* are mostly from the 14th, some even from the 15th century. To get a clear temporal profile for a special case, I will select one of the more frequent prefixes, namely *a-*.

The number of occurrences provided by the *OED* must, of course, be seen in relation to the total number of quotations within the same period. This relationship is expressed in percentages in the following Table (5):

Table 5: Temporal distribution of *a-* in Middle English

	number of quotations	*a-*	%
1000-99	11810	5	0.04
1100-99	5944	15	0.25
1200-99	30946	395	1.28
1300-99	95718	990	1.03
1400-99	113792	830	0.73

It is clear from this survey that the tendency to mark *a-* as a prefix by a following hyphen was most striking in the 13th century, with a massive increase before and a gradual decrease afterwards. Why should there have been more of a need in the 13th century than before or after to make the morphological structure of words clear by spelling? It stands to reason that with the increasing influx of French words in the 13th century there was an extra source of confusion about what initial *a-* could etymologically and semantically stand for.

As the 20 examples of the 11th and 12th centuries (5+15) show, the morphological situation was then still fairly clear in that there were only three options: *a-* was either the OE prefix *a-*, corresponding to Gothic *uz-* and German *er-*, with the meaning 'away from' as in *a-rearan* and *a-streccan*. Or it was the reduced preposition *on/in*, as in *a-dun, a-bed*, or otherwise the reduced prefix ȝe-, mentioned above, as in *a-mong* (< ȝe-*mang*), *a-ware* (< OE ȝe-*wær*). It is not a coincidence that all the words of this group are native words.

The picture is different in the 13th century. With the large number of French words with initial *a-*, as in the many assimilated versions of Latin *ad-* and *ab-* (*adopt, acclaim, abuse*, etc.) there was an extra need to keep them apart from the native words and to mark these as morphologically transparent. Not that all scribes of the 13th century did this, but, as the statistics above shows, more felt the inclination at that time and during the 14th century than before or after.

Given that the basic motivation for abundant hyphenation in the 13th and 14th centuries was the tendency of marking native morphemes that were prone to be misinterpreted, other causal factors that were to play a role in Modern English have to be backgrounded, as the avoidance of hiatus (*pre-eminence, pre-exist*), the marking of nonce words (*pre-telegraph*) and (implicit) contrastive usage of different prefixes (*pre-* vs. *post-Romantic*).[11] The hyphens in Middle English are simply too frequent to be generally explained by such specific causes.

The hyphen seems to have been so fashionable that some scribes obviously forgot its original function and used it hypercorrectively. In a passage of the *South English Legendary* (c1290) we read "for-to bringe A-cord and loue ... bi-twene thomas and þe king". This scribe, according to the *OED*, was the first to hyphenate the French loanword *accord*, and a quick check on *for-to* in the *OED* reveals that he was about the only one from 1000 to 1499 to hyphenate it, with the 61 quotations provided by the *OED* almost all by this very scribe.[12]

What we have, then, is statistical evidence: hyphens were first used by medieval English scribes in reaction to the imminent etymological obscuration of the language, namely with the intention of marking native prefixes. This was quite a fashion – with the result that the habit well spread, particularly later, to French loanwords (as *a-cord*), and to the free morphemes of compounds or frequent syntactic groups mutating into compounds. Such hyper-hyphens, based on sometimes idiosyncratic exaggeration, paved the way for the partial inconsistency of hyphenation in PDE, particularly in compounds. But in Middle

English, when hyphens were mostly used for prefix-marking, hyper-hyphens are exceptional cases, typical of particular works and scribes.

In the following, we will have a closer look at hyphen-buffs and hyper-hyphens, on the basis not of selective samples from the *OED*, but of a full-text data-base.

4. Evidence from the Innsbruck Prose Corpus

The first few lines in Horstmann's MS Laud edition of the *South English Legendary* look as follows (ll. 1-14):

10 Sancta Crux

ÞE holie rode **i-founde** was : ase ich eov nouþe may telle.
Costantyn þe Aumperour : muche heþene folk gan **a-quelle**,
For huy ore louerd iesu crist : to strongue deþe brouȝte,
And alle þe heþene men þat neiȝ him were : sone he dude to nouȝte.
Eleyne, þat was is moder : to Ierusalem he sende
to sechen after þe holie rode : and heo gladliche forth **i-wende**.
þo heo cam þudere, heo liet crie : ase heo hire red hadde **i-nome**,
þat alle þe giwes of þe cite : before hire scholden come.
þo þe giwes **i-somoned** were : huy hadden grete fere;
gret conseil huy nomen **þare-of** : ȝwat þe enchesoun were.
þo seide on, þat hiet Iudas : 'Ich wene þat ich wot
ȝwat Þis somunce **a-mounti** schal : ȝif þat ich ou telle mot.
Ich wene þat þe quene enqueri wole : ase heo hadde **i-þouȝt**,
Aftur þe rode þat Iesu crist : to deþe was on **i-brouȝt**.'

The text shows that the scribe uses hyphenation to a still moderate extent and for transparent purposes. Table 6 presents the output of the total first page:

Table 6: Hyphenation at the beginning of *South English legendary*

i-founde ('found')   *a-quelle* ('kill')   *Þare-of* 3x
i-wende ('gone')   *a-mounti* ('amount')   *op-on*
i-nome ('taken')   *a-knowe* ('recognise') 3x
i-somoned   *bi-tidez* ('happens')
('summoned')
i-þouȝt ('thought')
i-brouȝt ('brought')
i-saiȝ ('seen')

The scribe uses hyphens for the grammatical prefix *i-* (left column), for the derivational prefixes *a-* and *bi-* (middle column), and for compounding, as in *pare-of* and *op-on*. These findings are apt to confirm what we found in the *OED* earlier, namely that hyphens were preferably used for native morphemes, particularly the prefixes that were in the danger of getting lost.

But a more elaborate analysis of hyphens based on computer analysis unveils the less regular and therefore more interesting cases of Middle English hyphens. In line with the above information from the *OED* that 13th and 14th century scribes were particularly prone to hyphenate their words, I scanned texts of the Innsbruck Prose Corpus with the help of WordCruncher, paying special attention to 13th- and 14th-century manuscripts, and found a particular density of hyphens in the following texts (Table 7):

Table 7: 13-/14th-century texts with many hyphens

Title	date	number of words	number of hyphens	%
Ancrene riwle (Tit. MS)	1230	62,713	2206	3,5
Ayenbit of inwyt	1340	104,128	1564	1,5
Kentish sermons	c1220	3,996	165	4,1
OE homilies	c1200	42,394	192	0,5
St. Marherete (Roy)	1230	8,818	184	2,1
Vices and virtues	c1200	28,569	203	0,7
Wills	1387-1454	41,532	648	1,6

Looking at the first text, the *Ancrene Riwle* (Titus MS), in close-up, the use of hyphens is at first sight most erratic indeed. The words *again/against* are presented, apart from other spelling variation, in the following way:

Table 8: *again* hyphenated in *Ancrene riwle* (Titus MS)

1. *a-ʒain*   1
2. *aʒ-ain*   1
3. *aʒa-in*   1
4. *aʒai-nes*   1
5. *aʒain*   79

Obviously, the systematicity, if there is one, is both non-syllabic and non-morphological. But the editor (Frances Mack) makes clear in her introduction of

Ancrene Riwle (XIIf.) that the Titus MS does not have any link hyphens at all, but only end-of-line hyphens. Obviously, the lines were so economically used in the manuscript that lines and words were broken wherever necessary, irrespective of syllable or morpheme boundaries. In other words: the link hyphens in the editorial text are, in fact, break hyphens in the original manuscript.

In *Ayenbite of Inwyt*, the next example of Table 7, the general pattern for the use of hyphens is again based on the obvious intention of the scribe to mark the native morphemes, namely *a-* (*a-roos*), *all-* (*al-so*), *an-* (*an-het* 'heat up'), *be-* (*be-fore*), *bi-/by-* (*bi-leued*), *where* (*huer-of*), *i-/y-* (*i-write*), *in-* (*in-to*), *mis-* (*mis-do*), *of-* (*of-acsed*), *on-* (*on-lepi* 'single, sole'), *op-* (*op-nymynge* 'taking up'), *ouer-* (*ouer-al*), *out-* (*out-kestinge*), *to-* (*to-broke*), *uor-* (*for-*), and *with-* (*wy-oute* 'without'). There are also a few hyphenated compounds in the text (*bezide-zitteres, þi-zelue*), as can be expected. The only inconsistency is that there are two cases of hyphenated French words (*pre-ciouse*[13], *re-formeþ*) and one case of a pseudo-prefixation (*uor a-yer*, i.e. 'for a year') - such cases are examples of "hyper-hyphens", applied, perhaps thoughtlessly, by way of analogy. However, in more than 1500 samples altogether, these three exceptions are a negligible quantity.

The other inconsistency is that the hyphenated words are also spelt without hyphens, usually in the majority of cases. Thus, the adverb *again-*, i.e. the word of the title *Ayenbite*, is varied as regards the hyphen: 33 occurrences are hyphenated, 117 are not. The same ratio is provided by the word *away*: it is hyphenated in 2 cases, but non-hyphenated in 16. Such variants, as Middle English spelling variants in general, are apt to confuse modern minds. But while they are structurally inconsistent, they can be seen as didactic measures of scribes: the reader is occasionally, if not permanently and systematically, reminded of the literal composition of the old words that were still morphologically transparent.

In this didactic endeavour some scribes were prone to overdo things, occasionally motivated by lexical misanalysis to put in hyphens wrongly. Such misanalyses can also be found in the other texts of Table 7, and even more in later Middle English texts, i.e. in the 15th century, when the Old English prefixes had partly disappeared and hyphens were used, if at all, mainly for compounds.[14] Here is a small collection of hyper-hyphens, with tentative explanations of the hyphenated morphemes:

foreign or hybrid formations
   an-vie < OF *envie* (Lat *invidia*): *an-* (= AN) perhaps affected by OE *an* 'on'[15];
   an-amylyd ('enameled') (*Wills*) < OF *en+amayl*: *an-* = AN[16]
   a-resunede: *a-* < OE *a-* (former *ar-* [cf. G *er-*] + *reason-ed* (< OF)
   i-attred (OE *ge + a + try + ed*): *a-* is doubtful; *try* < OF *trier*
   ante-quam (Lat) 'before-that' (*OE homilies*)
   commissa-que
   corpus-que/corpusque
   de-faut (OF)
   overe-plus (partial trans. of OF *surplus*)
hyphenation of suffixes
   gylt-leas
   senne-leas
   nied-fulle[17]
   rihtwis-nesse/riht-wisnesse
   liht-inde (pres. part. 'lighting')
   me-warde (< OE *-weard*)
hyphenation of non-morphemic syllables (often with de- or agglutination)
   he-þen ('heathen')
   a-loone (< *all + ane*)
   a-noon ('anon') < *on + ane*)
   a-noder (*an + oder*)
   a-schappe ('escape'): < OF *es-capper* < Lat *ex + cappa*): deglutination
   a-noynted: < OF *en-oint-*
syntactic groups
   un-of-earned ~ un-ofearned: 'un + (earned of)'
   ðin-hierte ('thine-heart') (Rolle1)[18]
   warpest-me ('throw-me') (*OE homilies*)
   Þer-a-fore ('there before'): < OE *þær+on+foran*
   what-soeuer/whatso-euer/what-so-euer
   my sone-is wyf ('my son his wife')
   Thomas West-is soule
   fulfille-wyth
   a-bateile: a (art) +('battle') (context: *ther shal be a-bateile*)
   in-esspeciall
   now-of-dayes
   neuer-þe-les

Hiatus
   y-ered ('ploughed')
   de-inde ('doing')
   mou-oð ('mouth-oath')

5. Resume

The computer queries in the *OED* 2 do not allow a total wildcard search for hyphens, but only searches for hyphens after at least one character. Given this restriction, our results based on the *OED* were bound to be selective. Only the most striking prefixes were taken into consideration, and only the most common variants of these could be included in the investigations. For example, the prefix *ge-*, apart from *i-/y-* and *ȝe-* (with a yogh), also occurred in Middle English as *ȝi-*, *ȝæ*, *ȝie-*, *ȝy-*, *ie-*, *hi-*, *e-* and *a-* (*OED* y-prefix). All these variants, hyphenated or not, had to be ignored.

The tracing of hyphens in the Innsbruck Prose Corpus with the help of WordCruncher was, on the other hand, not restricted in the way of the *OED*; all the hyphens in a text could be found with one command. But then this search was limited by being work-specific.[19]

The combination of the two methods, however, provided a quantitatively sufficient basis for us to draw the following conclusions:

(1) The greatest proportion of hyphenated words in Middle English is found in the 13th and 14th centuries, amounting to more than 1 % of all word occurrences. This result seems to be connected with the confusion about word structures, caused by the influx of French loanwords in the 13th and 14th centuries.

(2) Until 1400, prefixes or prefixoids were far more affected by the trend of hyphenation than compounds. The 15th century initiated the later fashion of hyphenating compounds.

(3) Among the prefixes, both the native ones which were doomed to die and the all-purpose prefix *a-* were the best candidates for hyphenation, followed by the well-established French prefix *de-*. Other French prefixes and, above all, Latin ones remained almost untouched by hyphenation.

(4) Hyphenation in Middle English was a didactic measure of scribes to keep the structure of words, particularly of old native words, transparent. It can be seen as a reaction to the creolisation process that had had its impact on Early Middle English.

(5) The Middle English written documents give evidence of various types of a hypercorrective use of hyphens, particularly in the later Middle English period, when the original purpose of hyphens was no longer fully comprehended.

(6) Our present rather confusing system of hyphenation is a legacy of the late Middle English fashion of using hyphens in a more and more subjective and impressionistic way, particularly in compounds. In earlier Middle English, by contrast, hyphens were used with a surprising consistency.

Given the extreme spelling variation in Middle English texts, the high degree of consistency in hyphenation is apt to support the work of both readers and researchers of word formation. Seen thus, the study of Middle English hyphens is, as I hope to have shown, more than a historical linguist's trivial pursuit.

Notes

[1] A query in the *MLA* CD-ROM (last fourty-odd years) on 'hyphen' and 'English' provided no more than 25 hits. The only descriptive study on hyphens in historical English was Burchfield (1994), on line-end hyphens in the *Orrmulum* MS. – For hyphens in PDE, I consulted Partridge (1953: 134-151), Carey (1958: 80-83) and Friederich (1977: 52-57).

[2] Cf., in a similar vein, Friederich (1977: 52): "... kein Gebiet so uneinheitlich und umstritten wie das der Bindestrichsetzung".

[3] Partridge (1953: 148-150) and Friederich (1977: 57) are two of the few who have provided rules for hyphens after prefixes.

[4] From my work with the Innsbruck Corpus, it has become known to me that lines in manuscripts are often broken in the middle of a word without any marker of syllabification.

[5] In this chapter, I very much draw on McArthur (1992: 491f.), Graustein – Thiele (1987: 61-63) and Carey (1958: 80-84).

[6] The option 'hyphens' has to be unmarked in the menu 'Settings'.

[7] It can be trusted that editors of ME texts, and accordingly the *OED* editors, have used hyphens in line with the manuscripts. To make sure, I checked the authenticity of the hyphens for the seven texts of Table 7 below. Apart from *Ancrene riwle*, the editor of which explicitly states that the hyphens used are those of the manuscript, we only have indirect hints: the distinction of hyphenated and non-hyphenated forms of a word; the role

of hyphens in the glossary, and the policy of pedantically abiding by the unique manuscript in other respects.

[8] By contrast, Latin *ab, ad, cum* and other prefixes were usually assimilated.

[9] Not always, it must be admitted, as a morpheme.

[10] The one output example has 'pro-' in brackets, where the hyphen is abbreviative usage of the *OED* editors.

[11] Cf. *OED* under *pre-prefix.*.

[12] *For to* (without a hyphen) is quoted by the *OED* no less than 3632 times for the same period.

[13] < OF *precios*, Lat *pretiosus* (< *pretium* 'price') (*OED*). There is no historical reason in English to put *pre-* apart.

[14] Cf., for example, *abbey* and *alpha1*.

[15] To split *vie* from what is suggested to be a prefix does not make sense, not even in view of AN, since there is no semantic connection to *la vie*, but to Lat. *videre*.

[16] The word was first borrowed in its Central French version with *en-* (*OED*); the AN *an-* version (with and without the hyphen) first appears in 1420, i.e. some 100 years after its first occurrence (*OED*). There is no reason why AN should have been so influential in the 15th century.

[17] *-leas* and *-full* are rightly identified by the *OED* as suffixes for Middle English since they had already developed a specific suffixal meaning.

[18] The phrase is so frequent in Rolle's mystical text that he hyphenated it as if he meant to mark the single notion by using a single word.

[19] This article was written in 2001. From a present point of view (August 2006), WordCruncher should be replaced by a more modern concordance programme allowing the analysis of several texts at a time, such as WordSmith.

References

Burchfield, Robert
1994   "Line-end hyphens in the Ormulum Manuscript (MS Junius I)." Godden -- Gray -- Hoad (eds.), 182-87.

Carey, Gordon V.
1958   *Mind the stop: A brief guide to punctuation.* Harmondsworth: Penguin.

Connell, Tim
1998   "Is the end of the hyphen in sight?", *English today: The international review of the English language* 14: 2 (54): 15-20.

Falkner, Wolfgang -- Hans-Jörg Schmid (eds.)
1999   *Words, lexemes, concept: Approaches to the lexicon: Studies in Honour of Leonhard Lipka.* Tübingen: Narr.

Friederich, Wolf
1977   *Die Interpunktion im Englischen.* München: Hueber.

Godden, Malcolm -- Douglas Gray -- Terry Hoad (eds.)
1994   *From Anglo-Saxon to Early Middle English: Studies presented to E.G. Stanley.* Oxford: Clarendon.

Graustein, Gottfried -- Wolfgang Thiele
1987   *Englische Zeichensetzung.* (4th edition.) Leipzig: VEB Verlag Enzyklopädie.

Markus, Manfred
1999   "English historical lexicology in the age of electronic reproduction: Some suggestions", in: Falkner -- Schmid (eds.), 365-78.

Markus, Manfred (ed.)
1988   *Historical English: On the occasion of Karl Brunner's 100th Birthday.* Innsbruck: Institut für Anglistik.

McArthur, Tom
    1992   s.v. 'Hyphen' and 'Punctuation', in: McArthur (ed.).

McArthur, Tom (ed.)
    1992   *The Oxford companion to the English language.* Oxford: Oxford University Press.

McDermott, John
    1990   *Punctuation for now.* London: MacMillan.

Partridge, Eric
    1953   *You have a point there: A guide to punctuation and its allies.* London: Routledge & Kegan Paul.

Sauer, Hans
    1988   "Compounds and compounding in Early Middle English: Problems, patterns, productivity", in: Markus (ed.), 186-209.

    1992   *Nominalkomposita im Frühmittelenglischen: Mit Ausblicken auf die Geschichte der englischen Nominalkomposition.* Tübingen: Niemeyer.

Medieval English and German: A guide to modern similarities and dissimilarities

Horst Weinstock (Aachen, Germany)

1. Primaries

English-speaking visitors arriving at Austrian, German, or Swiss airports and railway stations can firmly trust in Otto Jespersen's logical and grammatical category of "primary words". In oral announcements and on written signboards (in competition with pictograms), primaries as substantial and substantival keywords help to satisfy present needs. Some two or three dozen English nouns (now internationalized or even globalized) draw attention to public services such as

> *arrivals buses car rental change city centre customs departures exit first aid gates hotel (left/lost) luggage minimarket passports police post office souvenirs taxi trains WC.*

Most of these predominantly Romance loanwords date back no earlier than to Middle English or Early Modern English. By the close of the first millennium, the continuity of Common Germanic had still been functioning homogeneously enough. For a long time, Anglo-Saxon missionaries to the Continent had more easily succeeded in winning the hearts and minds of their nonmonastic disciples by preferring West-Germanic vernacular speech to clerical Latin. In the *Battle of Maldon* in 991, the Anglo-Saxons needed no interpreter in order to communicate with the North-Germanic Vikings. Besides, Saxon English had not yet turned into Norman English with its Romance admixture above all among primaries.

Naturally, a "Guide to Modern Similarities and Dissimilarities" clearly asks for a presentation from documented evidence through cogent reasoning to tenable conclusions. At least for comparative and contrastive studies, both written and oral tradition can and do attest to similarities and dissimilarities.

2. Segmental description

Throughout the history of exegesis and pivotal ideas, Biblical, Classical, Medieval, Early Modern, and Modern approaches crystallized into a widely accepted canon of fundamentals. It starts with the small, simple, plain, easy, and minor units, with anything overt, obvious, literal, and partial, and it ends with the large, complicated, complex, difficult, and major, with the covert, hidden, figurative, and whole. For correct and complete description, it will be essential to combine universalistic with particularistic views.

As to the fundamentals of linguistic change and segmental description, the similiarities rest on various tempo patterns of instruction and penetration versus obsolescence and elimination respectively.

(1)	Phonographically, the stability and continuity of letters normally outlives the variation and change of sounds.
(2)	Morphologically, the surface structure depends upon contextual functions. Lexical word-composition varies more readily than syntactic inflexion does.
(3)	Lexicologically, the basic vocabulary of inherited words of all classes except nouns remains fairly stable. Yet, nouns have undergone constant change or rearrangement in the face of cultural, scientific, and technological advance and competition.
(4)	Syntactic structures resist change over long periods. Habits of word-order tend toward longevity.

3. Phonology

To start with phonology, Aristotle and Greek philosophers had already noticed the original and historical priority of sound over script. Roman thinking brought discontinuity, focusing on the documentary value of written evidence for the past, present, and future. The Roman tradition was still alive with Jacob Grimm at the time of the first edition of his grammar. It announced phonology as the chapter "Über die Buchstaben" ['On Letters'], judging living speech by the alphabet and the typographer's letter-case. Within the evolution and history of language, high frequency or ample distribution of typologically identical or similar features used to allow structurally systemic stability with slow and little change. By contrast, low frequency or rare distribution promoted fast and ample change. Thus, the quantity of sounds indirectly forms and determines their quality.

Striking similarities between English and German stem from the First or Common Germanic Consonant Shift about 500 or 400 BC. From then on, Indo-European labial, dental, and tectal plosives went on keeping their old places of articulation. With respect to the manner of their articulation however, they turned from voiced to voiceless and from plosives to fricatives. To demonstrate but one subcycle out of three on its way from West Indo-European to Common Germanic, West Indo-European voiced /b d g/ (for instance) remained stable in Latin, but shifted into Common Germanic voiceless /p t k/. Thus,

Latin se labi edere iugum

stand against East, West, and North Germanic:

Common Germanic	*slapan	*etan	*jok
Gothic (East)	slepan	itan	juk
English (West)	sleep	eat	yoke
Dutch (West)	slapen	eten	juk
(Old) Swedish (North)	(slapa)	äta	ok

North- and some West-Germanic dialects still stick to voiceless plosives. Yet among the West-Germanic languages and in contrast to Old English and Early Netherlandic, Old High German shifted the voiceless plosives /p t k/ into the initial voiceless affricates /pf ts kx/ and the medial or final fricatives /f s x/. Known by the name of the Second or Old High German Consonant Shift, a consecutive change occurred about 600 AD south of a line leading from Aachen via Düsseldorf, Kassel, Magdeburg to Frankfurt-on-the-Oder:

West Germanic	*slapan	*etan	*jok
Old High German	sla(p)fan	ezzan	jo(k)h
Modern High German	schlafen	essen	Joch
Modern English	sleep	eat	yoke

Thus, Modern English unshifted *sleep, eat, yoke* stand against Modern German shifted *schlafen, essen, Joch*. Affrication and frication, no doubt, discontinued the English/German similarity and established dissimilarity or divergence instead.

From the 11th century onwards, another consonantal dissimilarity was creeping in throughout the Hohenstaufen Realm (East Switzerland, West Austria, South Germany). The clusters /sp st/ varied in allophonic coarticulation and phonemicized by standardized dissimilarity into Modern German /ʃp ʃt/. So, English /sp/ and /st/ in *spare* and *stone* differ from German /ʃp/ and /ʃt/ in German *sparen* and *Stein*. As an exception to the rule, the cluster /sk/ ended in total assimilation and dissimilarity. In words such as *Schule* or *Schottland* versus *school* or *Scotland*, /ʃ/ even lost its partial similarity with /sk/.

In the late 12th and early 13th centuries, Middle English triggered off a vowel lengthening in open syllables under the main word-stress. It ended in a dissimilarity of a fairly wide range. In disyllabic words, Middle English went far beyond German, particularly so in configurations before affricates and fricatives.

Thus, the Middle and post-Middle English vowels in *eat, ape, open* differ from Modern German *essen, Affe, offen* in both quantity and quality.

Linguistically and phonologically, by far the greatest change happened shortly after Chaucer, namely in the 15th century. Called the Great Vowel Shift (GVS) on Otto Jespersen's suggestion, the large-scale phenomenon touched late Middle and Early Modern English much more markedly than it did historical German. Long vowels under the main stress moved upwards by one tongue position in English. As for the highest vowels /i:/ and /u:/, the impulse ended in English as well as in German diphthongization. German *Zeit* and *Haus* follow the same pattern as English *tide* and *house*. Yet otherwise and in partial contrast to German with its 'Petty Vowel Shift' only, all late Middle and Early Modern English mid-high and low vowels rose to the tongue positions above. This makes Modern English long stressed vowels sound dissimilar from their Continental equivalents:

Modern English	Modern German
see /i:/	sehen /e:/
name /ei/	Name /a:/
loose /u:/	lose /o:/

4. Varro's conception

With all its extrinsic evidence, it should not be left unsaid that the Great Vowel Shift dealt phonography a serious blow. Among other acquisitions, the Roman and post-Roman impact on grammar and on letters as its smallest segments had helped to consolidate Early Medieval writing and spelling habits. Both Old English and Old High as well as Old Low German had come to adopt the Latin alphabet. On the whole, scholastic masters of the *Trivium* propagated the pansystem of the Latin alphabet in Varro's conception of the 1st century BC. He had subdivided, subsystematized, and more or less decreed it for shorter and easier memorization in the trinomial shape of vowels (V), consonants (Cĕ), and semivowels (ĕC). The subsystems yield three observations and conclusions:

(1) Long and stressed vowels in isolation had no chance to escape being raised from their lower to their higher tongue-positions. The Great Vowel Shift raised or diphthongized the original, natural, and unsystemic sound-values of A, E, I, O, U.

(2) For some five hundred years, English writers have spelt the letter-names of full consonants or plosives with double <ee> for spoken /i:/:

Bee Cee Dee Gee Pee Tee

German spelling has held on to Classical and Scholastic simple <e> for spoken /e:/:

Be Ce De Ge Pe Te

British boys and girls internalize their /ei bi: si:/; German pupils rather stick to Latin /a: be: tse:/. Yet even German gangsters shun the FBI /ef bi: ai/ and not an */ef be: i:/. The dissimilarities testify to the existence of certain exceptions to rules rather than to laws. The phonemic subsystems may vary from language to language. German carries on Latin *Ha* and Latinized Greek *Ypsilon*. English shifted to *Aitch* from French *Ache* and Latin contiguous consonantal *(H)A*, *Ka* and to *Wy* upon the contiguity of native *U* preceding foreign *I grec* within the vocalic subsystem *A E I O U Y*.

(3) None but semivowels within their subsystemic premodification in the shape of a short prop-vowel could stand a chance to survive the Great Vowel Shift as letter-names in unaltered similarity. Both English and German speakers spell the so-called *elementum* (*eLeMeNtum*) identically to this very day:

eF eL eM eN eS eX

5. Germanic initial word-stress

With regard to prosody and suprasegmentals, both English and German share initial word-stress on the stem or root syllable. The di- or trisyllabic names of the days of the week may serve as examples of similarity:

Monday/Montag *Tuesday*/Dienstag *Wednesday*/Mittwoch *Thursday*/ Donnerstag *Friday*/Freitag *Saturday*/Samstag *Sunday*/Sonntag

Anglo-Saxon words of three or more syllables allow the same pattern of Germanic initial stress:

afternoon busybody caretaker doorkeeper everybody forefather grasshopper handwriting insider merry-go-round pickpocket runaway seafarer shortsighted sightseeing thanksgiving watertight

With the influence of Romance foreign words and components on their path to loanwords in Norman English, Germanic initial main stress attracted the Anglo-Norman final main stress. The two contrasting weight-principles changed their ranks and ends on the basis of the superior countertonic principle:

> *brevity carpenter chairperson comedy gentleman globetrotter, grandmother headquarters metrical noticeboard resident surgeon tragedy*

The results of the countertonic principle in Medieval Norman English have brought about another dissimilarity, namely the sharp contrast between Insular loanwords and Continental foreign words:

> *ágriculture*/Agrikultúr *áppetite*/Appetít *cóntinent*/Kontinént *élegy*/Elegíe *fántasy*/Phantasíe *hóspital*/Hospitál *líterature*/Literatúr *mánuscript*/Manuskrípt *médicine*/Medizín *mónument*/Monumént *quálity*/Qualität *quántity*/Quantität *sécondary*/sekundär *sýmbolism*/Symbolísmus *témperament*/Temperamént *tólerance* /Toleránz

A historical comparison of the similarities and dissimilarities between English and German yields two identifying sound-profiles:
(1)   Phonically, the sound pattern of English differs from ancient West Germanic more strikingly than its German equivalent does.
(2)   Prosodically, the dynamic pattern of word-stress in English resembles the ancient West Germanic more closely than its German equivalent does. English initial stress has never ceased to integrate the originally final stress of Romance borrowings.

Next in segmentation comes graphemic transcription. Historically, sound must have preceded script for ages. Speaking follows some natural, innate, spontaneous, and rather unreflected urge to communicate and interact. In contrast to this, writing originally needed invention and cultivation, and later on it depended on instruction, acquisition, and internalization.

6. Graphonemics

Roman minds at some stage started to hold writing in higher esteem than they did speaking: *Verba volant, scripta manent.* Indeed, words do fly and die away, while written documents live for centuries or for good. In the modern era, historical philologists have come to look back upon the same phenomenon both from identical and from different angles. Extant script can serve as the sole means to reconstruct bygone sound. In other words, the graphically living can revive the phonically dead. The optics of letters as visual communication witnesses to the acoustics of silent voices from the past. Spelling and writing, so to speak, function as unique keys to the history of language. Yet, the correlation between sound and letter needs cautious interpretation.

Much more so than speaking and hearing, writing and reading meet the expectations of a medieval *ars*. They impart a skill both teachable and learnable. The deaf and dumb excepted, all human beings could and would speak; but only a few experts or writing-masters knew how to write as well. With no more than two dozen letters as against some four or five dozen modes and places of articulation at human disposal, the uneasy task has ever consisted in proper disambiguation. A scribe or writer has had to hit the ideal or at least the canonized grapheme for the precise value or power (*potestas*) of the phoneme. Only the acoustic target would serve its proper semantic function. For lack of a one-to-one correspondence between sound and letter and in search of unattainable phonography, scribes and readers took refuge to audible thinking along or spelling aloud what they were going to write down. For this sort of activity, medieval observers coined the phrase "barking at books".

Since the introduction of the Latin alphabet to Germania, English and German have shared many similarities in the course of adopting an identical system and substance of transliteration. Both Otfrith of Weissenburg and Aelfric expressly stated a certain unevenness and some absurdities within the triad of *nomen, figura,* and *potestas* of letters.

After a period of ample variation as mirrored in allographic and idiographic writing, Late Medieval English and High German arranged and stabilized their own independent subsystems. From the 15th century onwards, Late Middle and Early Modern English scribal practice and spelling habits in the London area created a Chancery Standard. For graphonemic exemplification, Middle English vowel length can demonstrate one of the most intricate systems. Long vowels under the main stress and in closed syllables appear as digraphic duplications of the identification vowel:

<ii ee aa oo uu>

Long vowels under the main stress but in open syllables appear as digraphic combinations of identification vowel, hyphen for variant consonant, and final <-e> stemming from inflected forms:

<i-e (e-e) a-e (o-e) u-e>

The absence of digraphic combinations for the mid-low vowel values /ɛ:/ and /ɔ:/ reminds posterity of the circumstance that they correspond with the nonsystemic because nonduplicating digraphs <ea> and <oa>. Like many other languages, English has never regained its early medieval state of near-phonography. Middle English attempts at graphonemics or at least graphonetics stabilized before the initial stage of the Great Vowel Shift. Tudor and Early Modern English eventually led to completely (though still systematically) shifted long-vowel values.

By comparison and contrast, the Early Modern German Chancery Standard in the wake of Martin Luther's Reformation and Bible translation did not precede but rather followed a phase of sound-changes. Thus, the digraphs <ei> and <au> in German *Zeit* and *Haus* echo the diphthongization of high front /i:/ and high back /u:/. Besides, the late Middle High German 'Petty Vowel Shift' would not touch mid and low long vowels at all. Yet graphically, High German vowel-lengths have carried on as many as four more or less unfathomable subsystems: three for closed syllables and one for open syllables. As the German long and umlauted vowels *ä*, *ö*, *ü* had produced additional sound values and diacritic letters within the possible tongue positions and as mid-low open /ɛ:/ rendered dialectal variation or idiolectal modulation, the pansystem could work without the English oppositions of closed /e:/ and /o:/ versus open /ɛ:/ and /ɔ:/, leaving things more or less at neutral /E:/ and /O:/. Consequently, the three plus one subsystems have functioned in the following configurations:

(i) duplication of identification vowel;
(ii) simple identification vowel plus <h>;
(iii) simple identification vowel without diacritic letter <Ø>;
(iv) simple identification vowel plus heterosyllabic <-e>:

/e:/ <ee eh eØ e-e>
leer Schnee See Ehre Lehre sehr Keks stets wer geben lesen These

/a:/ <aa ah aØ a-e>
Haar Paar Saal Zahl zahm Zahn kam Rat Tal Hase Nase Phrase

/o:/ <oo oh oØ o-e>
Boot Moos Zoo hohl Kohl wohl groß Not Ton Hose Pole Rose

With all its irregularities, the graphonemic system of English as a compromise between custom and reason can pass for less complicated than the four practically haphazard subsystems of German. Even native writers of German obtain but little help from pondering on etymological origins. To the eyes of foreign readers, the four parallel subsystems must look like some chaotic "anything goes" (but not in any case).

To conclude the section on spelling in script and print, an old truism should be kept in mind: Whenever sound-changes have brought about a maximum difference between sound and script, experts will become active and try to reduce the growing discrepancies through a spelling-reform. German has for a couple of years been caught up in a very controversial spelling-reform. Meanwhile, some seventy per cent of the population are still hesitating or simply ignore the reform altogether. Advanced learners of German will best wait and see for another five years or so. Asking for orthographic help, information, or guidance will in all likelihood embarrass experts, nonexperts, and shirkers.

7. Morphology

The structural comparison continues with morphological findings. As a rule of thumb, philologists maintain that the farther two or more cognate languages date back, the more closely their morphologies will resemble each other. So, the two West-Germanic languages equally point towards time-honoured patterns. In retrospect, English and German carry at least as many dissimilarities as they show similarities. August Schleicher's "pedigree theory" cannot apply in its rigid form, as English (far more so than German) has evolved as a mixed composition of Germanic and Romance elements. Thus, English needs a corrective explanation based upon Hugo Schuchardt's "wave theory" for intersectional loans as well.

Among the English/German similarities, three phenomena deserve priority mention:
(1)   initial word-stress with the consequence of reduced final syllables;
(2)   the typological preservation of strong versus weak conjugation; and
(3)   some centripetal force to regain uniformity or similarity by analogy.

First, initial word-stress could lead to the syncopation of the middle syllable and to a reduction of vowel-timbre in the final syllable. Latin *munisterium* survives as English *minster* and German *Münster* without medial *i* and without final *u*. In other configurations, the total reduction of final vowel-timbre in English converged in /e/ and /ə/. Ultimately, ə caduc ended in zero /Ø/ with loss of the final syllable. In German, the partial reduction stopped at indistinct but syllabic /ə/. So, word-lengths often diverge by one syllable less in English.

In late Indo-European and Common Germanic, an original and regular, so-called strong conjugation indicated the past tense and past participle by means of gradation or ablaut of the stem vowel. By and by, a sporadic but spreading, a so-called weak conjugation indicated the past tense and past participle by means of a dental suffix. The ablauted examples demonstrate the strong conjugation considered as irregular now:

begin	*began*	*begun*	beginnen	begann	begonnen
drink	*drank*	*drunk*	trinken	trank	getrunken
eat	*ate*	*eaten*	essen	aß	gegessen
sing	*sang*	*sung*	singen	sang	gesungen
speak	*spoke*	*spoken*	sprechen	sprach	gesprochen
steal	*stole*	*stolen*	stehlen	stahl	gestohlen

The examples with a dental suffix demonstrate the weak conjugation considered as regular now:

end	*ended*	*ended*	enden	endete	geendet
land	*landed*	*landed*	landen	landete	gelandet
mean	*meant*	*meant*	meinen	meinte	gemeint
plant	*planted*	*planted*	pflanzen	pflanzte	gepflanzt
say	*said*	*said*	sagen	sagte	gesagt

Present-day English and German use the dental suffix as the regular and functionally active formation. Ablaut no longer occurs outside a limited but old and high-frequency stock of verbs. Moreover, English and German have followed similar trends in restoring prior verbal roots by way of analogy or system constraint. For instance, Old English and Old High German gave up grammatical change through rhotacism in

	freosan	*freas*	*fruren*	*gefroren*
	freeze	*froze*	*frozen*	
and				
	frieren	fror(en)	gefroren	

As a matter of fact, analogy seldom thrives to the full dominance of systematics. The grammatical change described by Karl Verner's Law allows exceptions such as *seethe/sodden* or *was/were*.

A survey of the dissimilarities between English and German morphology should certainly not skip two self-evident features of the surface structure, namely grammatical gender and plural formation. To English eyes and ears, it must seem rather strange that German native speakers should say:

der Kreis   die Kurve   das Dreieck

for what could more simply be:

the circle   the curve   the triangle

To Greek, Roman, and Germanic minds, gender-based niceties of the sort echo ancestral and aesthetic voices from afar. Yet for all that, educated native speakers of German should honour lapses of gender simplification as tokens justified or even superior otherness. As obedient teachers, however, native speakers should never cease to further linguistic correctness and human education by adding the proper solution in loving kindness.

Leaving aesthetic lapses and turning to the rational level of possible misunderstandings, Modern English excels in a higher degree of regularity by rule and grammaticalization. For instance, Modern German carries on the old and much more complicated system of variant forms which tolerates many idiomatic and thus tricky allomorphs. Plurals end either in vocalic -*e* or in consonantal -*n* or -*r*:

M(asculine)	Berg/Berge	Weg/Wege	Zug/Züge
F(eminine)	Dame/Damen	Katze/Katzen	Straße/Straßen
N(euter)	Buch/Bücher	Dorf/Dörfer	Haus/Häuser

Present-day English prefers graphemically uniform, but allophonic plurals in -*s* instead:

/s/	*books*	*cats*	*streets*
/z/	*ears*	*trains*	*ways*
/ɪz/	*houses*	*pages*	*villages*

In a commercialized world and a tendentiously 'pluralistic' society, careful speakers will mind the language universals and plural markers in order to avoid costly mistakes.

One of the most obvious dissimilarities of Modern English as against Modern German lies somewhere in between morphology, lexis, and syntax. For diachronic minds, Modern German numerals (cardinals as well as ordinals) from *twenty-one* to *ninety-nine* namely *ein-und-zwanzig* to *neun-und-neunzig*, cannot fail to be associated with Old, Middle and Early Modern English similarities of usage. Morphophonologically, the German compounds fall in with the Old Germanic sound pattern of initial stress. By contrast, English deviates from its normal pattern and echoes Romance final stress. Any deviation, of course, means markedness or special emphasis. Strange to say, both regular initial stress in German and irregular final stress in English suggest diverse methods of counting units. Indoor or abstract counting follows the Arabic abacus and the Romance metric system of registering from hundreds via tens to units, while outdoor or concrete tallying follows the Germanic sequence "*determinant*-and-*determinatum*". Dissimilarities and interferences of this kind do not disturb bilingual communication. For speakers of Educated English with a wide reading in historical documents, the Old Germanic word-order of "units-and-tens" as mirrored in *ein-und-zwanzig* or *neun-und-neunzig* makes Continentals appear older than their real age. "Unit-and-ten" numerals agree with the language of *Beowulf*, Chaucer, and some of the characters in Shakespeare.

To sum up the morphological findings, the loss of inflections in declension as well as in conjugation was almost total by the period of Early Modern English, whilst it has been only partial up till Present-Day German. With all consequences for globalization, the modern dissimilarities make the teaching and learning of English easier than a second-language acquisition of German. Yet unlike mere synchronics, a diachronic command of historical English can open up comparative aspects. It helps to overcome dissimilarities by finding or pointing out bygone similarities as the missing link.

8. Lexicology

Proceeding from smaller to larger units of segmentation, the survey comes to lexicology. Weighing statistics versus dynamics and constant versus variable factors, the stock and increase of lexis clearly form the most dynamic segment of all. Common origin, early evolution, and subsequent history make English and German share many inherent similarities. On the whole, a once almost pure, equal, and predominantly Germanic vocabulary in either language started to diverge over the centuries. By and by, English came to absorb an enormous number of French words compared with the modest pre-Enlightenment influx into Continental German.

With a modicum of reservation about anything too clear-cut, some seven waves of French influence can be discerned from century to century. A first wave between 1066 and 1250 brought a great many Anglo-Norman borrowings such as:

> *butler city count duke judge nephew niece parish reign servant tailor*

and the complete hierarchy of military ranks. Within two hundred years, they turned an originally homogeneous Germanic vocabulary of Saxon English into Norman English, into a heterogeneous mixture of Anglo-Saxon and Gallo-Romance. None of these early Gallicisms even entered into Middle High German.

In the same 11th and 12th centuries, a second wave of Northern French loanwords from chivalry and courtly culture described activities and instruments connected with armour, clothing, cuisine, festivals, games, hunting, jousting, society, and acquisitions such as:

> *armour bachelor blame chance dance danger dinner duty fashion feast gentle honour jest leisure manner mischief order supper table very virtue*

A striking though quantitatively less marked similarity between English and German speaks from parallel loans. Lexemes such as

> *Blamage Chance Fest Manier Tournier*

and morphemes such as English and German

> *des- dis-* / Des- Dis-   *-eer* / -ieren   *-ery* / -erei

must have expanded from the Flemish or Lower Lotharingian Court at Ghent to the Cologne area.

A third wave occurred between 1130 and 1300 in the period of the Hanseatic League. The trading route from London via Calais, Bruges, and Antwerp to Cologne furnished English and German with French loanwords such as:

> *cable*/Kabel   *dozen*/Dutzend   *fine*/fein   *place*/Platz
> *price*/Preis   *profit*/Profit   *sluice*/Schleuse

A fourth wave of Northern French influence between 1100 and 1400 may have reached Germany some decades in advance of England. In a complementary vein to the monastic canon of the *artes liberales* in Patristic and Scholastic days, the Talmud Torah academies founded and supervised by Rashi in the 11th and 12th centuries promoted a spiritual exchange along the eastern Moselle route from Troyes via Metz/Trier to Speyer/Worms/Main (SHUM) and vice versa. With the foundation and flourishing of universities in Western Europe, the southern Maas route from Paris and Reims via Liège or Stablo to Cologne spread thousands of French loanwords. In the 12th and 13th centuries, religious sources of inspiration radiated to Oxford and Cambridge. In Latinized or in vernacular shape, one dozen out of thousands of borrowings can demonstrate English and German equivalents such as:

> *cognition*/Kognition *definition*/Definition *essence*/Essenz *existence*/Existenz *figure*/Figur *hospital*/Hospital *justice*/Justiz *lesson*/Lektion *line*/Linie *medicine*/Medizin *session*/Session *study*/Studium *theology*/Theologie

A fifth wave in the 14th century concerned the knowledge of Central French among educated readers and speakers on insular as well as on Continental soil. The ideal of a medieval *poeta doctus* and his audience presupposed firm familiarity with French literary terms and standards:

> *cadence*/Kadenz *chronicle*/Chronik *comedy*/Komödie *elegy*/Elegie *epic*/Epik *epilogue*/Epilog *essay*/Essay *lyric*/Lyrik *miracle*/Mirakel *morality*/Moralität *mystery*/Mysterium *pause*/Pause *poet*/Poet *prologue*/Prolog *prose*/Prosa *style*/Stil *verse*/Vers

Even a fraction of evidence will suffice to demonstrate the similarity between English and German. And it does not militate against some dissimilarity either. Owing to its rather monolingual culture, Middle High German failed to bring forth three poetically polymath master poets comparable to Gower, Chaucer, and Langland.

A sixth wave in the late Tudor period 1570 to 1625, according to the recent state of research, appears to have formed the true summit of French influence. Other experts in lexicology, of course, argue that the impressions gathered stem from the growing number of publications in general as well as of dictionaries and handbooks in particular. In any case, the observation implies dissimilarity to German.

The seventh wave between 1650 and 1800 attained the highest degree of expansion, circularity, and internationality with English, French, and German original thinkers such as Descartes, Locke, Leibniz, Pope, Montesquieu, Chesterfield, Voltaire, Johnson, Hume, Frederick the Great, Kant, Lessing, Mendelssohn, and others. As a period of Rationalism and Enlightenment, it touched topics, ideas, and values of universal interest and trusted in the mediation of educated minds. In company with abstract nouns long familiar to Medieval and post-Medieval English ears, a sample catalogue reads:

autonomy compromise democracy equality federation fundamentals harmony humanity individual justice liberty literacy prejudice privilege progress realism society tolerance tyranny

With regard to surface structure, the Enlightenment or Authoritarian English wave was the first period to incorporate second-language acquisitions in their nonadapted forms, namely with foreign phonemes and accentuations as well as with foreign graphemes including diacritic marks and accents. In all similarity, English and German took over French foreign words from the fields of art, cuisine, fashion, life-style, and so forth with their originals unchanged:

beaux arts cliché comme il faut élan esprit genre œuvre on dit savoir-vivre tableau tête-à-tête vis-à-vis

Leaving the comparative aspect of French influence upon English and German, the section on vocabulary should not end without mentioning the direct exchange between the insular and the Continental Germanic sister languages. A wax-and-wane chart of English/German give-and-take shows rising/falling figures for the German influence on 18th- and 19th-century English. British dictionaries list Germanisms such as:

Abbildung Biedermeier Biergarten Bildungsroman Dankeschön Delikatessen Doppelgänger Ersatz Gemütlichkeit Gestalt Glockenspiel Götterdämmerung Heimweh Kindergarten Jugendstil Kulturkampf Lederhosen Rathaus Realpolitik Schadenfreude Sturm und Drang Umlaut Völkerwanderung Volkslied Weltanschauung Auf Wiedersehen Zeitgeist Zollverein

The low percentage of Anglicisms found in Johann Christoph Adelung's *Grammatisch-Kritisches Wörterbuch der Hochdeutschen Mundart* (1793–1801) suggests a more distanced attitude. Shortly before World War II, labels such as "Engländerei" or "Amerikafimmel" escalated into hostilities as harbingers of imminent war. After 1945, theory and practice went through prompt correction. Politics, the media, world trade, and the generation between eighteen and thirty have gained a mighty say in snatching new and foreign words.

Quite recently, the clipping-compound *Denglish* (obviously modelled on *Franglais*) as well as an ironical column of letters to the Editor of *DIE ZEIT* (March 2001, Number 11) under the title "Needen Sie Help?" leave no doubt about the latest vogue. Anglo-Americanisms in Modern German (including Austrian and Swiss German) tend to increase beyond what used to be customary.

Whosoever may really need help during her or his stay in Germany, should not hesitate to ask in English. Some aspects of the anglophile tendency do raise the question of quantity versus quality. Whilst English has acclimatized thousands of loanwords to the vernacular speech-habits, German carefully heeds the foreign surface-structures. Not seldom, it rather hatches them to the extent of its having been labelled "Imponiergehabe".

9. Syntax

Phonemes, graphemes, morphemes, and lexemes – all of them keep within the segmental structure of words. Only syntax transcends one single word for its arrangement with others. Indeed, sentences form units composed of all sorts of segments. In Indo-European and in Old Germanic verse, word-order continued to be comparatively variable. In the typological framework of Latin syntactic structures, the word-order "subject–object–predicate" or SOP had by and by reached dominant frequency. In the 2nd century AD, Apollonius Dyscolus shifted from the rhythmic pattern of poetic intonation to a rational basis of rhetorical syntax. To his mind, the word-order "subject–predicate–object" or acronymically SPO organizes things much more convincingly. The subject introduces the mental or logical foundation of a sentence. The predicate can (with or without an object) infer or deduce from it some partial aspect as a new message. So from around 400 AD onwards, medieval authors repeatedly and unanimously recommended an SP(O) word-order. A 10th-century Latin voice could still insist on the logical primacy of the substantival substance over the verb by formulating: "Omnis constructio ex substantia et actu fit". This overall formula holds good for any minimal nucleus.

In Merovingian and Carolingian days, the late Latin object-final word-order or the acronymic SPO developed into the regular Old French pattern. After the Anglo-Norman Conquest, the SPO order intruded from translations into early Middle English prose. From there, it gradually gained ground and entry to Middle English verse as a variant and ultimately as the dominant word-order as well. The transition from an etic choice between

SOP/SPO//PSO/POS//OSP/OPS

to the emic code

SPO

stands out as one of the rare dynamic changes in the history of English syntax with its normally stable and static structures. An interplay of morphological decay and syntactical restructuring must have initiated and completed the contact and influence of Anglo-Norman upon Saxon English. In contrast to Middle and Early Modern English, Middle High German, Early Modern High German, and even Modern High German have never ceased to hold on to flexible, idiomatically and stylistically conditioned subvariants. British, Irish, Scottish, American, Canadian, or Australian English visitors will soonest feel at home in Germany by recalling their university knowledge of Early Modern English with Shakespeare as a good guide. Tudor or Renaissance English still alternated between what was to remain Modern German usage and what was to become Modern English grammatical correctness. In a special liking for variety, diversity, and multiplicity, Tudor or Renaissance English tolerated a given spectrum of allosyntactic constructions. Aiming at neutrality, intersubjectivity, and interchangeability, Augustan or Authoritarian English preferred regularized and standardized patterns of utterance and language universals.

In Tudor or Renaissance English, affirmative sentences could either still vary considerably (as German syntactical patterns have done to the present day), or they could already have taken the way to stable and static structures similar to or identical with Modern English SPO:

I see him.   Ich sehe ihn.

In German, expanded structures with initial adverbs or modifying phrases will unleash an inverted word-order, which deviates from normal expectations and brings modern dissimilarity:

Yesterday, I saw him.   Gestern sah ich ihn.

In negative sentences, Early Modern English still allowed both alternative sequences, namely "predicate plus *not*" or "*do not* plus predicate". Authoritarian English decided in favour of *do not*. As another dissimilarity, Modern German has held on to "predicate plus *nicht*":

I do not see him.   Ich sehe ihn **nicht**.

In questions, Elizabethan speakers could either use the simple inversion of the full verb or the periphrastic inversion with *do*. In spoken German, periphrastic *tun* 'do' does occur in children's simplifying patterns of the mother-tongue. By and by, Modern English and Modern German have ended up in total dissimilarity. English marks questions by introductory *do* in front of uninverted SPO; German marks questions by inverting the full verb patterned on the acronymic formula PSO:

    Do you see him?   Siehst du ihn?

10. Synchronics via diachronics

The similarities and dissimilarities discussed in the tentative *tour d'horizon* were intended for the participants of the IAUPE Medieval Symposium in Munich on their way to the 18th IAUPE (Jubilee) Conference at Bamberg. This brief survey will (it is hoped) recall the fact that for the two Germanic sister languages a diachronic awareness can ease the cultural shock of synchronic communication, confrontation, and confusion. An academic knowledge and diachronic awareness of historical English may help as a 'simplistic' (though not quite unnatural) cure for synchronic problems. Shakespeare's Tudor or Early Modern English can be a safe guide. His similarities outweigh the present-day dissimilarities:

    I doubt it not.   Ich bezweifle es nicht.
    I saw him not.   Ich sah ihn nicht.
    I wot not.   Ich weiß nicht.

    Know you this woman?   Kennt ihr diese Frau?
    What sayst thou?   Was sagst du?
    What think you?   Was denkt ihr?

11. Farewell warning

This plea for historical English should certainly not close without a warning. At their return to the various destinations in English-speaking countries, the participants should forget in time about their Old, Middle, or Early Modern English. Otherwise, the Border Police or Customs Officer will suspect them of bringing in Medieval diseases or of not having set foot on their native soil since the days of *Beowulf*, Chaucer, or Shakespeare.[1]

Notes

[1] This article was also published in my collected writings, cf. Weinstock (2003: 253-59).

References

Baugh, Albert C. -- Thomas Cable
    2002   *A history of the English language*. 5th edition. London: Routledge.

Böker, Uwe -- Christoph Houswitschka (eds.)
    2000   *Einführung in die Anglistik und Amerikanistik*. München: Beck.

Crystal, David
    1995   *The Cambridge encyclopedia of the English language*. Cambridge: Cambridge University Press.

Görlach, Manfred
    2001   *Eighteenth-century English*. Sprachwissenschaftliche Studienbücher. Heidelberg: Winter.

Lehnert, Martin
    1990   *Altenglisches Elementarbuch*. 10. Auflage. Sammlung Göschen 2210. Berlin: de Gruyter.

Markus, Manfred
    1990   *Mittelenglisches Studienbuch*. Uni-Taschenbücher für Wissenschaft. Grosse Reihe. Tübingen: Francke.

Michael, Ian
    1970   *English grammatical categories and the tradition to 1800*. Cambridge: Cambridge University Press.

Sauer, Hans
    2000   "Sprachwissenschaft", in: Böker -- Houswitschka (eds.), 89–165.

Strang, Barbara M. H.
   1979   *A history of English*. (2nd edition.) London: Methuen.

Weinstock, Horst
   2003   *Kleine Schriften. Ausgewählte Studien zur alt-, mittel- und frühneuenglischen Sprache und Literatur.* Heidelberg: Winter.

Notes on contributors

Muhammad Abu Al-Fadl Badran, who hails from Upper Egypt, is a poet and scholar in Arabic literature with an international perspective and a comparatist outlook. He has especially strong connections with Germany, where he was a Fellow at Bonn University from 1988-1990, a Lecturer at Bochum University in 1991, and a Humboldt Fellow, once again at Bonn University, from 1994-1996. Since 1998, he has worked at the United Arab Emirates University in Al-Ain, where he was awarded the rank of Full Professor in 2005. His scholarly work covers both classical and recent Arabic writing; with regard to the latter, one of his main research interests is the appearance of the Faust motif in modern Arabic literature.

Alfred Bammesberger, born in Munich in 1938, studied English and French and Comparative Philology at the Universities of Munich and Oxford. He was a teacher in a secondary school, earned an M.A. at Yale University in 1964 and a Dr. phil. in Munich in 1965. He finished his habilitation in Freiburg in 1970. Since 1980, he has been Professor of English Linguistics at the Catholic University of Eichstätt. He is the author of many textbooks, has written a large number of learned articles, and is currently preparing an edition of Old English runic inscriptions.

Renate Bauer studied English and German at the Universities of Munich and York. She holds a PhD from the University of Munich (LMU) where she is a lecturer and teaches English linguistics, the history of the English language and medieval English literature. Her doctoral thesis *Adversus Judaeos: Juden und Judentum im Spiegel alt- und mittelenglischer Texte* was published in 2003. Articles include "Der antijüdische Diskurs im Mittelalter am Beispiel mittelenglischer Dramen und der *Prioress's Tale*"; "Opfer 'christlicher' Gewalt: Juden in Texten des englischen Mittelalters"; "'Lord Castlereagh moved ... Mr. Ponsonby objected': Parliamentary debates of the early 19th century".

Claire Fennell was awarded an MA in Romance Philology at Bologna University and a PhD in Comparative Medieval Literature at the Hebrew University of Jerusalem after she had graduated from Oxford (Italian and German). She has taught Old and Middle English at Bologna University. She has worked, first as assistant and then as director, in the Italian Cultural Institutes of Munich, Addis Ababa and Krakow. At present, she teaches Old English at Trieste University. She has edited and translated the Middle English debate poem *The owl and the nightingale* and the romance *Sir Tristrem*. Currently, she is working on an unpublished Middle English version of the so-called *Statuta angliae antiqua*. Articles include "Did the *anhaga* swim home? The case of Beowulf and the anonymous hero of Exeter Book, folios 76ᵛ-78ʳ"; "A note on *The owl and the nightingale*, lines 427-8"; "Hodain and the love potion"; "'Com natura libidinis perversitate polluitur:' *The owl and the nightingale*, lines 1377-86"; "MSS Rm and SP of Eilhart von Oberge's Tristrant, ll. 1672-3"; "A fifteenth century baker's price-list: MS Douce Charters a 1, no. 62".

Carol V. Kaske earned her PhD at the Johns Hopkins University. She is Professor of English Emerita at Cornell University, where she has taught since 1964 and continues to teach. She is the widow of Robert E. Kaske and has one child, Richard J. Kaske. She is the author of one book, *Spenser and biblical poetics*; has edited two, *Marsilio Ficino: Three books on life* (with John R. Clark, which she has also translated), and *Edmund Spenser, Faerie Queene, Book One*; published about 30 articles, mostly on Edmund Spenser, but also on medieval authors such as Dante and Chaucer. Articles include "Mount Sinai" and "Dante's mount purgatory"; "The audiences of *The Faerie Queene*"; and "Spenser's *Amoretti* and *Epithalamion*: A psalter of love."

Ian Kirby has recently retired as Professor of Medieval English Language and Literature at the University of Lausanne, Switzerland, where he taught the whole range of Old and Middle English literature and the History of the English language. Prior to this, he taught at the University of Uppsala, and was the first Professor of English at the University of Iceland. His principal publications include books and articles on Bible quotation in, and translation into, Old Norse, but he has also published articles etc. on medieval English subjects, and on Shakespeare. He was President of IAUPE in the years 1986-89 and organised the 14th conference of the Association at the University of Lausanne in August 1989. Since 1995, he has been Secretary-General and Treasurer of the Association.

Patrizia Lendinara is Full Professor of Germanic Philology at the University of Palermo and Dean of her Faculty. She has published on Old English language and literature, particularly on the literary relationships and on the linguistic interferences between the Latin and the Germanic world. She has written several essays on Old Frisian, Gothic and Medieval Latin literature. She has also published on modern English literature, specifically on Hilda Doolittle, and on the history of English language. Part of her work on glosses, both in Latin and the vernacular, dating from the Anglo-Saxon period has been republished by the Variorum in *Anglo-Saxon glosses and glossaries* (1999). Her present research work focuses on literature and iconography of the Marvels of the East in Anglo-Saxon England and its sources. She is a member of the editorial board of *Anglo-Saxon England* (Cambridge) and *NOWELE* (Odense), and she was president of the Associazione Italiana di Filologia Germanica and the International Society of Anglo-Saxonists.

Conrad Lindberg, born 2 August 1924, PhD (Stockholm) 1959, docent (ibid.) 1961-67, lecturer (Linköping) 1967-74, professor (Trondheim) 1974-89, retired (Linköping) 1989-. Publications: *MS Bodley 959. Genesis-Baruch 3.20 in the earlier version of the Wycliffite Bible* (5 vols.); *MS Christ Church 145* (continuation in 3 vols.); *The Middle English Bible (Prefatory epistle of St. Jerome, The book of Baruch, The book of Judges)*; *English Wyclif tracts* (1-3 and 4-6); *King Henry's Bible: The revised version of the Wyclif Bible* (4 vols.).

Manfred Malzahn was born in the Federal Republic of Germany in 1955. He studied English and German Literature and Linguistics at the University of Bochum from 1974, and he obtained his PhD from the University of Wuppertal in 1983, presenting a thesis on aspects of identity in the contemporary Scottish novel. After national service with the Goethe Institute, he joined the Department of German at Edinburgh University in Scotland, and then went on to teach in English Departments in Tunisia, Algeria, Malawi, and Taiwan. He is currently Professor of English Literature at the United Arab Emirates University.

Manfred Markus is Full Professor of English linguistics and medieval English literature at the University of Innsbruck. With a strong background in the studies of English and American literature, he has, for the last twenty-five years, focused his academic interests on historical English, contrastive and corpus linguistics. His publications include a bilingual edition of *Sir Gawain and the Green Knight*, a *Mittelenglisches Studienbuch*, and a large number of articles on historical English linguistics. He is general co-editor of the book series *Austrian Studies* (formerly *Wiener Beiträge zur englischen Philologie*). As a corpus linguist, he has compiled the *Innsbruck Corpus of Middle English Prose*, the *Innsbruck Letter Corpus* and a corpus of 18th- and 19th-century German schoolbooks of English (HEDGEHOGS). In his present research, he is particularly interested in historical English phraseology and idioms.

Saara Nevanlinna was professor of English Philology at the University of Helsinki, from where she retired in 1984. Her fields of interest are the history of English, Middle English, and manuscript studies. Apart from a number of articles, she has published the following books: *The northern homily cycle: The* *expanded version in MSS Harley 4196 and Cotton Tiberius E vii* (1972-84), and, together with Irma Taavitsainen, *St. Katherine of Alexandria: The late ME prose legend in Southwell MS 7* (1993).

Michiko Ogura is Professor of English at Chiba University, Japan. Her field of interest lies in medieval English, especially in Old and Middle English syntax and word study. Her publications include *The syntactic and semantic rivalry of QUOTH, SAY and TELL in medieval English* (1981), *Old English 'impersonal' verbs and expressions* (1986), *Verbs with the reflexive pronoun and constructions with SELF in Old and early Middle English* (1989), *Verbs in medieval English: Differences in verb choice in verse and prose* (1995) and *Verbs of motion in medieval English* (2002).

Saburo Oka was born in 1929. He is Professor Emeritus of English and Comparative Literature at Aoyana-Gakuin University, Tokyo. He was vice-president (1993-94) and president (1995-96) of the Japan Society for Medieval English Language and Literature. He has published a number of books, e.g. a Japanese translation of Chaucer's *Troilus and Criseyde* (2005) as vol. 4 of The Trojan Story Series; *Studies in Sôseki-Natsumé*, 3 vols.; *An introduction to comparative narratology of medieval literature; Researches in English medieval and modern literature*; a Japanese translation with notes and introduction of Wordsworth's *Prelude*.

Hans Sauer is Full Professor of English Language and Medieval English Literature at the University of Munich. He has also taught at the universities of Eichstätt, Würzburg, Dresden and Innsbruck, as well as at Brno, Columbus (Ohio State University), Lodz, Palermo, and Venice. He was president of the International Society of Anglo-Saxonists. For IAUPE, he organized the Medieval Symposium in Munich in 2001 and the Middle English Section in Vancouver in 2004. His publications include *Theodulfi Capitula in England* [Latin and Old English] (1978), *The owl and the nightingale* [Middle English and German] (1983), *Nominalkomposita im Frühmittelenglischen* (1992) as well as numerous articles, entries in handbooks and dictionaries, and reviews. He was an author and co-editor of the *Lexikon des Mittelalters* (1977-1999), and he is co-editor of *Anglia* (1996-), *Middle English Texts* (MET; 2000-), and *Texte und Untersuchungen zur Englischen Philologie* (TUEPh; 2000-).

Liliana Sikorska, professor of English literature and head of the Department of English Literature and Literary Linguistics at the School of English, Adam Mickiewicz University, Poznań, Poland, is the author of several books and numerous articles on medieval English literature, primarily on drama and medieval mystical culture. Her books include among others *In a manner of morall playe: Social ideology(s) in English moralities and moral interludes* (2002), and *An outline history of English literature.* (2nd edition, 2002). She edited *Aspects of suffering: Classical motifs in the literature of English* (2003), *Ironies of Art/Tragedies of life: Essays in Irish literature* (2004), and *A universe of (hi)story: Essays on J.M. Coetzee* (2005). Besides, she is co-editor of the series Medieval English Mirror. Liliana Sikorska was a visiting scholar at the University of Florida (Gainesville), University of California at Los Angeles, Brown University (Providence), and the American University (Washington, DC).

Michael W. Twomey is Professor of English at Ithaca College. His most recent publications are: "Editing *De proprietatibus rerum*, Book XIV, from the sources" (2005); "Reading Chaucer's Latin aloud" (2005); "The *Gawain*-poet" (2005). Currently, he is producing a reception study of medieval encyclopedias in England and is part of an international collaboration, based in Münster and Orléans, to edit the *De proprietatibus rerum* of Bartholomeus Anglicus.

Horst Weinstock studied English, French, and Philosophy at the universities of Mainz and Munich from 1949 to 1954. He continued and completed his postgraduate and doctoral studies in Munich, receiving his PhD in 1957 and assisting at Munich University for a postdoctoral period. From 1961 until the habilitation in 1970, he lectured at the University of the Saar in Saarbrücken. He has since been teaching English Historical Linguistics and Medieval Literature as Professor (Emeritus 1996-) at Aachen University of Technology. His publications include *Die Funktion elisabethanischer Sprichwörter und Pseudosprichwörter bei Shakespeare* (1957/1966), *Mittelenglisches Elementarbuch* (1968), *Die englische Literatur in Text und Darstellung*, vol. 2: *16. Jahrhundert* (1984), *Kleine Schriften* (2003), and the editorship of *English and American Studies in German* (1983-2005).

Studies in English Medieval Language and Literature

Edited by Jacek Fisiak

Vol. 1 Dieter Kastovsky / Arthur Mettinger (eds.): Language Contact in the History of English. 2nd, revised edition. 2003.

Vol. 2 Studies in English Historical Linguistics and Philology. A Festschrift for Akio Oizumi. Edited by Jacek Fisiak. 2002.

Vol. 3 Liliana Sikorska: *In a Manner Morall Playe*: Social Ideologies in English Moralities and Interludes (1350-1517). 2002.

Vol. 4 Peter J. Lucas / Angela M. Lucas (eds.): Middle English from Tongue to Text. Selected Papers from the Third International Conference on Middle English: Language and Text, held at Dublin, Ireland, 1-4 July 1999. 2002.

Vol. 5 Chaucer and the Challenges of Medievalism. Studies in Honor of H. A. Kelly. Edited by Donka Minkova and Theresa Tinkle. 2003.

Vol. 6 Hanna Rutkowska: Graphemics and Morphosyntax in the *Cely Letters* (1472-88). 2003.

Vol. 7 The *Ancrene Wisse*. A Four-Manuscript Parallel Text. Preface and Parts 1-4. Edited by Tadao Kubouchi and Keiko Ikegami with John Scahill, Shoko Ono, Harumi Tanabe, Yoshiko Ota, Ayako Kobayashi and Koichi Nakamura. 2003.

Vol. 8 Joanna Bugaj: Middle Scots Inflectional System in the South-west of Scotland. 2004.

Vol. 9 Rafal Boryslawski: The Old English Riddles and the Riddlic Elements of Old English Poetry. 2004.

Vol. 10 Nikolaus Ritt / Herbert Schendl (eds.): Rethinking Middle English. Linguistic and Literary Approaches. 2005.

Vol. 11 The *Ancrene Wisse*. A Four-Manuscript Parallel Text. Parts 5–8 with Wordlists. Edited by Tadao Kubouchi and Keiko Ikegami with John Scahill, Shoko Ono, Harumi Tanabe, Yoshiko Ota, Ayako Kobayashi, Koichi Nakamura. 2005.

Vol. 12 Text and Language in Medieval English Prose. A Festschrift for Tadao Kubouchi. Edited by Akio Oizumi, Jacek Fisiak and John Scahill. 2005.

Vol. 13 Michiko Ogura (ed.): Textual and Contextual Studies in Medieval English. Towards the Reunion of Linguistics and Philology. 2006.

Vol. 14 Keiko Hamaguchi: Non-European Women in Chaucer. A Postcolonial Study. 2006.

Vol. 15 Ursula Schaefer (ed.): The Beginnings of Standardization. Language and Culture in Fourteenth-Century England. 2006.

Vol. 16 Nikolaus Ritt / Herbert Schendl / Christiane Dalton-Puffer / Dieter Kastovsky (eds): Medieval English and its Heritage. Structure, Meaning and Mechanisms of Change. 2006.

Vol. 17 Matylda Włodarczyk: Pragmatic Aspects of Reported Speech. The Case of Early Modern English Courtroom Discourse. 2006.

Vol. 18 Hans Sauer / Renate Bauer (eds.): *Beowulf* and Beyond. 2007.

www.peterlang.de

Keiko Hamaguchi

Non-European Women in Chaucer
A Postcolonial Study

Frankfurt am Main, Berlin, Bern, Bruxelles, New York, Oxford, Wien, 2006.
IX, 194 pp.
Studies in English medieval language and literature. Edited by Jacek Fisiak.
Vol. 14
ISBN 3-631-55057-X / US-ISBN 0-8204-9875-0 · pb. € 39.–*

Since Jeffrey Jerome Cohen edited *The Postcolonial Middle Ages* in 2000, some scholars have applied postcolonial criticism to the study of the Middle Ages. However, even in postcolonial studies of Chaucer, the role of non-European women in his work has not yet been fully discussed. Using postcolonial theory, the author explores how Chaucer represents non-European women, his Others both in gender and in culture. Her examination of non-European women in his work from a non-Westerner's point of view reveals that his representation is complicated and ambivalent, showing diverse views. The ambivalence in Chaucer reflects his own complicated position as courtier, soldier, minor diplomat, controller of customs and poet, and also the fourteenth century's historical background and attitude.

Aus dem Inhalt: The Resistance of the Syrian Mother-in-law in the *Man of the Law's Tale* · Canacee's Problematic Marriage in the *Squire's Tale* · The Colonization of Dido · Domesticating Amazons in the *Knight's Tale* · Transgressing the Borderline of Gender: Zenobia in the *Monk's Tale*

Frankfurt am Main · Berlin · Bern · Bruxelles · New York · Oxford · Wien
Distribution: Verlag Peter Lang AG
Moosstr. 1, CH-2542 Pieterlen
Telefax 00 41 (0) 32 / 376 17 27

*The €-price includes German tax rate
Prices are subject to change without notice
Homepage http://www.peterlang.de